THE UNKNOWN GOD

THE UNKNOWN GOD

NEGATIVE THEOLOGY IN THE PLATONIC TRADITION: PLATO TO ERIUGENA

by Deirdre Carabine

WIPF & STOCK · Eugene, Oregon

FOR JACK AND MARY

Wipf and Stock Publishers
199 W 8th Ave, Suite 3
Eugene, OR 97401

The Unknown God
Negative Theology in the Platonic Tradition: Plato to Eriugena
By Carabine, Deirdre
Copyright©1995 by Carabine, Deirdre
ISBN 13: 978-1-62032-862-0
Publication date 1/22/2015
Previously published by Peeters Press, 1995

TABLE OF CONTENTS

II
CHRISTIAN *APOPHASIS*

CONTENTS

FOREWORD

the Tao that can be spoken is not the Tao
si comprehendis non est deus
if you meet the Buddha kill him
I pray to God to free me of God

When I was a young doctoral student pursuing what my friends thought was a very esoteric thematic for my theses (two doctoral theses formed the basis for this book), I always told people: "negative theology is in". And indeed it was. Today, it is even more "in" through its appropriation by contemporary "continental" philosophy. A Google search for the simple terms "negative theology" yields just under six million results, and includes papers and articles, books, wikis, blogs, YouTube videos, podcasts, and reviews. Back in the day, I had to work very hard to search out materials on the subject, and was almost entirely dependent on the inter-library loans service of The Queen's University of Belfast – each photocopy eagerly awaited like a Christmas toy. The plethora of works on the subject during the almost twenty years since The Unknown God was first published is astonishing.

Had I been researching negative theology today rather than in the 1980s, no doubt my work would have been richer in terms of secondary sources. Perhaps it would also have taken a different interpretative direction under the influence of perhaps Derrida on the one hand, or Jean-Luc Marion, on the other.[1] If it had, I think it would have been the latter because, quite simply, I believe Derrida's ultimate interpretations of Dionysius and Eckhart to be flawed.

So why is negative theology so very much in today? In very broad strokes, what began with Kierkegaard, Nietzsche, and Heidegger, coupled with the efforts of the "French Fathers" (the priest scholars of neoplatonism whose lives effectively spanned the twentieth century): Pierre Hadot, Edouard des Places, Jean Trouillard, Emile Bréhier, Jean Daniélou, A.-J. Festugière, Michel Tardieu – and among their English counterparts Arthur Hilary Armstrong, Henry Chadwick, and E. R. Dodds, to effectively make a mystic

---

1. To my great shame – or perhaps because of the insular nature of my homeland – I had not read Marion's *Dieu sans l'être* (1982) when I was writing this book. Neither had I read Derrida!

of Plato and his followers, resulted in a renewed interest in the Neoplatonists and negative theology.

As negative theology continues to go viral, its followers are growing. Marion, Lyotard, Kristeva, Caputo, Kearney, Vattimo, Bataille, Adorno, Turner, and Levinas, show how big negative theology is, how it has been trending, and how continental philosophy has "re-turned" to religion via negative theology through its resonance with the concepts of otherness and difference. While I am not an expert in the continental tradition, I have read enough to sense that the eclectic religiosity in contemporary philosophical musings has negated the particularity of revealed religion in that it uses negative theology to take its leave of the central meaning of Christianity. "There is something more ... but we cannot say what it is", shows our contemporary reluctance to profess anything. That is not the focus of negative theology. Sure, we should really not say anything of the ineffable, but the fact remains that the anything we do say contains a truth.

As contextualized in the religious traditions, the point of ridding ourselves of God is to be in the presence of God; this is not the aim of differance, nor is it the aim of negative theology as used by Derrida or more recently the anatheism of Richard Kearney. Such post-theistic theism (a sanitization of the sacred) packs little punch in my view.

Denys Turner sums it up this way:

> A recycling today of the classical, late antique and medieval vocabularies of the apophatic, but uprooted from their soil in a metaphysics, leaves that vocabulary suspended in a vacuum of rhetorics, a displaced, residually Christian semiotics, retaining the illusion of a force from the metaphysics it has abandoned as no longer possible – even if, for sure, half-remembered traces of what it was once able to signify preserve the illusion of life, as a wrung chicken struggles and kicks for a while after death. To that extent, at least, Derrida does us a service: if you insist in following fashion down that anti-metaphysical line from Nietzsche through Heidegger to French deconstruction, you had with better consistency concede to Derrida his atheistical conclusion.[2]

2. "Atheism, Apophaticism, and 'Differance'", in Marco M. Olivetti (ed),

Turner then asks who will finish the writhings of the dead theological chicken and restate the case for a theological metaphysics? For while it appears to be the case that God is no longer dead, but has simply been resurrected, freed from the particularity of historicity, what has really happened is that the link with kataphatic theology has been truly severed: "... an apophatic theology which has done away with its intrinsic link to kataphasis – finally resulting in a post-Christian religiosity, decorated with Christian vocabulary."[3]

However, I must admit that I enjoy reading Derrida, Kearney, and the others. Their words seduce me, they really do; but it is not consummated because there is little to grasp. The words have been stripped of their meaning and simply do not hold the burden of the new quasi-religious meanings assigned to them. However, the fine needlework done to unravel and then restitch a theolosophy that appeals to our contemporary sensibilities is as intricate as any of the great debates on the Trinity from the times of the Cappadocian Fathers. Ultimately, however, I side with Turner and others: the use of a language that has been loosed from its original moorings to create a new narrative, albeit an extremely engaging one, leaves the reader bereft of a solid foundation on which to build a way of life.

∼

Many moons ago, when I published my very first article on negative theology, I tried to argue for a distinction between negative theology and apophasis: "...negative theology ... remains on the level of intellection and negation [and does] little more than express man's (sic) inability to know the divine nature".[4] I am still more or less of the same opinion but now would substitute via negativa for apophasis. For the way of negation can also be a journey, not solely an intellectual word game that leads to futile nothingness. It is a continual struggle for balance, a "living without a why" as Meister Eckhart would put it, part of a very real knowing of God outside the realm of knowledge: mystical union, as many have put it, cannot be described. In that same article I noted: "Those to whom it is not given to make something very

Théologie négative, CEDAM, 2002, 241.

3. Lieven Boeve, "The Rediscovery of Negative Theology Today", in Marco M. Olivetti (ed), Théologie négative, 453.

4. "Apophasis East and West", Recherches de Théologie ancienne et médiévale (1988) 17.

similar to the Plotinian or Dionysian leap must keep their balance
and sanity on the edge of the unbridgeable chasm which is the
unknowable, unnameable, ineffable God". This very Zen approach
to the via negativa is not atheism, it is not the end result of the
stripping away of aphairesis, it simply is an unknowing knowing.
As this book constantly demonstrates in its systematic exegesis
of the primary texts examined, the via negativa is a path to God,
a path to a living reality that comes from the practice of rigorous
negation that leads to unity, as Plotinus says:

> Our way then takes us beyond knowing, there may be no
> wandering from unity; knowing and knowable must all
> be left aside; every object of knowledge, even the highest,
> we must pass by, for all that is Good is later than This and
> derives from This as from the sun all the light of day.[5]

Unity with the One, the Good, God, is the ultimate aim of the
kind of negative theology I describe in this book. By reversing our
way of thinking, as Plotinus would put it, we leave ourselves open
to the vision and presence of the Good. Elsewhere I suggested
that "the search for unity, conceived solely in metaphysical terms,
would do nothing more than refine the One out of all existence; but
such a refinement, understood in terms of the ascent of the soul to
unity with the One, adds another dimension of thought, one that is
not easily understood in terms of traditional textbook ontology."[6]
I believe that the negative theology of the contemporary French
deconstructionists may well have refined God out of existence, or
at the very least thrown the baby out with the bathwater! A faith-
based negative theology changes when it is not understood from
within the context of that great two-fold journey of katabasis and
anabasis, of kenosis and theosis, of God becoming human so that
human can become God.

According to the followers of the via negativa, knowledge
is an obstacle to be overcome. Knowledge casts a veil of clouded
particularity around the One. The subsequent stripping bare or
unveiling (aperikaluptos, as Dionysius describes it), paradoxically
reveals no thing, nothing, nada. It does not somehow expose a

5. Plotinus, *Ennead VI*, 9, 4, 7-11; translation by the great Stephen McK-
enna, 617.

6. D. Carabine, "A Thematic Investigation of the Neoplatonic Concepts of
Vision and Unity", Hermathena, 157 (1994) 46.

Godhead behind the God we have negated or a landscape barren of any reference points. Using negative theology as a knife to cut away idolatry is a necessary part of theology, but the cutting away does not reveal some thing: rather, it takes us some where. Cutting away the kataphatic can never reveal the "hid divinity", as Kenney put it.[7] It does not leave us exposed on the edge of the cliff eternally in confusion; no-one wants to be in that emptiness. Those with faith can let go (acceptance? non-struggle?), but we do not then fall into the Abyss or remain in the desert of nothingness; we let go to simply be in the presence of the One, the Good, God. When I think about this aspect of the unity of the soul with the divine, I am always reminded of the words of the Jesuit poet Gerard Manley Hopkins: "blue-bleak embers, ah my dear, fall, gall themselves, and gash gold vermillion". Eckhart is the great western master of the art of letting go (gelassenheit).

∼

In the context of contemporary uses of negative theology, perhaps I can sum up the main contours of what I understand to be an apophatic metaphysics (and I rely chiefly on Eriugena and Eckhart): the no-thing-ness of God becomes some thing when, through creation, God becomes other than God. Thus, God can paradoxically be known when other than God (God's energeia, in the Byzantine tradition). Creation as theophany, as the very alterity of God, enables the simultaneous knowing and unknowing of God, the simultaneous transcendence and immanence, the simultaneous procession and return. In this dialectical way of understanding the unfolding of God, the oxymorons of the mystics begin to make some kind of sense: silent music, bright darkness, unknowing knowing.

The unity that is the focus of the via negativa when taken to its limits, can be described from the personal level of a Moses ascending the clouded mountain (as in Gregory of Nyssa), or a Dionysian soul throwing itself relentlessly against the ray of the divine darkness, or as a cosmic adunatio, but always it is a unity that admits of distinction: it is not annihilation. Neither – and this is a most important point – is it the end of the otherness of God, but rather, its perpetual celebration. In my own view, the going

7. John Peter Kenney, *Mystical Monotheism: A Study in Ancient Platonic Theology*, reprint, Wipf and Stock, 2010.

out of God into otherness is more interesting than the return of all things to their source. In creation, being can say "I am not God! I am God's otherness". "God becomes when all creatures say 'God' – then God comes to be".[8] Creation is itself the affirmation that it is not God because it is some thing (other than God). In the eschatological moment of return to source, there is no silent repose for many candles make up its one light and many voices make up its one choir, as Dionysius would put it.

As the exegesis in this book tries to show: negative theology is, simply put, part of the dialectical understanding of the hiddenness of the revealed God. The follower of the negative way, which proceeds through systematic negations, culminating in negating one's negations, is not intended to "arrive in the end at an empty space neatly fenced by negative dogmas, which is not at all where they want to be."[9] Where they do want to be is in a "liberating ignorance in which faith rests on the Unknowable and is nourished by silence".[10] As Rainer Maria Rilke put it:

> But though my vigil constantly I keep
> My God is dark – like woven texture flowing.
> A hundred drinking roots, all intertwined;
> I only know that from His warmth I'm growing.
> More I know not: my roots lie hidden deep
> My branches only are swayed by the wind.
> —excerpt from *The Book of a Monk's Life*

Used as we are to trying to understand the divine nature from either the perspective of transcendence or the perspective of immanence, formulations such as unmanifest manifest, invisible visible stretch the mind in both directions simultaneously for the one cannot be understood without the other: God both is all things and is not all things. The idea that God is manifest in creation is true, but the fact that God remains transcendently unmanifest is

---

8. Meister Eckhart, *Sermon Fifty Five*, Meister Eckhart. *Sermons and Treatises*, vol. II, trans. and ed. M.O'C. Walshe, Watkins, London, 1981, 81.

9. A. H. Armstrong, "On Not Knowing Too Much About God", *Hellenic and Christian Studies*, Variorum Reprints, 1990, essay XV, 137-138. And Plotinus himself cautions us not to lose faith and fall into the sin of agnosticism (Ennead VI, 9, 4, 7-11).

10. Armstrong, op.cit., 145.

also true. And yet, neither are true when understood singly; the "problem" is resolved by coupling both truths in a dialectical formulation which reveals the tension between, and the simultaneous truth of both. The truth of the statement, "God is all things", is constantly undermined by the basic distinction between the divine essence and theophany which is a forceful reminder that, as an apophatic understanding demonstrates, a comprehensive account of reality can never be attained.

All that is said about the creative process is constantly under threat from the continuous moments of denial that something can be said about the divine nature. The noetic tension between the simultaneous knowability and unknowability of God is a constant feature of a negative ontology that cannot be explained away, indeed cannot be explained further as it is grounded in an ontological conception of how "no thing" becomes otherness and difference. Listen to Eckhart: "But if God is neither goodness nor being nor truth nor one, what then is He? He is pure nothing: He is neither this nor that. If you think of anything He might be, He is not that. So where will the soul find truth?"[11] Good question. I think the answer could well be in the journey. Who knows how to say what it is when discourse comes to a halt under the impetus of eros. But of course Eckhart has an answer to the soul who asks "what then shall I do?" "You should wholly sink away from your youness and dissolve into His Hisness, and your 'yours' and His 'His' so become so completely one 'Mine' that with Him you understand His Unbecome Isness and His nameless Nothingness".[12] Wow, what can a soul respond to that?

∽

Throughout the centuries the long shadow of Plotinus has continued to cast itself over many and captured their souls in the unseeing love of and unity with the Good. Apophasis was always working away in the shadows of mainstream philosophy and theology – for which many of its proponents were marginalized and criticised. Few, if any, escaped dark mutterings of pantheism and heresy or worse. An apophatic voice has, of necessity, to be part of the choir of the theologians. The voice of the negative theologian

---

11. *Sermon Fifty Four*, Walshe, vol II, 72.

12. *Sermon Ninety Six*, Walshe, vol. II, 333.

in this choir can be described as an alto voice: it is low, subdued, singing under the radar, so to speak, but without it, the choir can lose much of its richness. The way that voice has been shaped to sing in contemporary philosophy is, quite simply, different: it is NOT negative theology. Challenging kataphatic absolutism is a necessity lest our theology becomes idolatry; challenging apophatic nihilism is another thing altogether. Negative theology as I understand it, continues today, and our theological understanding is much the richer for it.

It is not my mandate here to make a reading list of recent works on negative theology – Google Scholar can do that much better and faster! I recommend that those interested in following through from where this volume leaves off in terms of secondary sources do precisely that, but start with the work of John D. Caputo and Denys Turner.

∾

This volume was originally published in 1995 by Peeters Press Louvain / W.B. Eerdmans. It has been out of print for many of the intervening years. David Burrell was the impetus for the re-printing with Wipf and Stock. My thanks both to David and my new publisher. My mentor in Neoplatonism, Arthur Hilary Armstrong was good to me as I struggled with this most complex of thematics. In the years before his death I received many epistles from him in a small, old-man, spidery hand – letters that I treasure today and hope to pass on to the academic community in soft copy soon. Finally, this volume is humbly dedicated to the memory of my teacher the late James Joseph McEvoy, who passed from this world much too soon.

15 August 2014

PREFACE

In the Kigezi area of south-western Uganda, there is a forest known as Bwindi Impenetrable Forest. The name intrigued me and I asked some colleagues whether it really was impenetrable. The answer I got was, "well, yes and no. It's not really totally impenetrable; access to parts of it are very difficult and some areas haven't yet been explored". I wasn't at all surprised by this kind of answer and it seems to me an appropriate enough analogy for negative theology. Friends have often remarked that it seemed a contradiction to write a book about the ineffability of God. Yet, negative theology is precisely a method of speaking about the Unspeakable, but from the realization that all we can say is inadequate.

There has been a renewal of interest in negative theology over recent years. The present volume is rather different in tone from Raoul Mortley's excellent two-volume study, *From Word to Silence* (Bonn, 1986). Mortley's approach, which is much more differentiated in terms of his initial understanding of the scope of negative theology, explores in greater detail the more linguistic concerns of the way of negation. The present volume is more 'open' to what constitutes negative theology: it is not simply a method of 'speaking' about God, but rather, a holistic approach to divine reality whereby, paradoxically, the unknown God can be known and related to.

It has often been said that negative theology is the attempt to refine God into a kind of 'philosophic absolute'. That criticism, however, would appear to be unjustified when we find that most of the writers studied in this volume do not stop their theology or their spiritual search when they realise that nothing more can be said of the divine nature. A. H. Armstrong said that Plotinus loved the One. The Pseudo-Dionysius loved the unknowable God. In the *Mystical Theology*, the purified soul becomes the blinded intellect

who throws itself relentlessly and unknowingly against the ray of
divine darkness in the search for unity with God.

The very strong Neoplatonic elements in most Christian forms
of negative theology hare perhaps contributed to the often-quoted
and unfortunate distinction made between the 'Christian God' and
the 'God of the Neoplatonists'. Anyone who has read the *Enneads*
cannot fail to see that Plotinus was not talking about an abstract
reality, a philosophic absolute. Neoplatonism itself was not simply
a philosophical system; it was also a way of life. Here we come
close to the truth of the way of negation. This book will attempt to
make clear that those Christian writers who trod the path of negation were not 'mystical atheists'. They were, rather, intimately
involved with the divine reality which is unnameable, ineffable
and unknowable. The ultimate concern of negative theology,
according to many of the writers examined in this volume, is unity
with God, a unity which is the result of the most radical purification. The destruction of one's concepts and even of oneself is not
a quietistic relaxation in the company of one's maker:

> 'You should totally sink away from your youness and dissolve into
> his hisness and your 'yours' and his 'his' should become so com-
> pletely one Mine' that with him you understand his unbecome
> Isness and his naked nothingness.' (Meister Eckhart. Sermon,
> 'Renovamini spiritu').

This book does not claim to be a comprehensive study of negative theology; I have omitted many authors which could have
found a place in such a volume. The authors I have chosen to
examine make up a series of enlarged details, which together give
a good picture of the development and use of negative theology in
the Greek and Christian traditions. I include chapter seven in Part
II on Christian *apophasis* since Philo of Alexandria was an important influence on the early Fathers of the Christian Church.

This book is not mine alone, for many people had a part to play
in its evolution. My teacher, James McEvoy (Louvain-la-Neuve),
formerly of The Queen's University of Belfast, directed my post-
graduate research from 1981 until 1988 with patience, kindness

and wisdom in a spirit of true friendship. I am indebted to him in very many ways, but most especially for having taught me to think for myself. The stylistic corrections he made to many of these chapters in their early stages have made the text much more readable. Andrew Smith of University College Dublin and John Dillon of Trinity College Dublin, have been most careful critics of my work and have saved me from many errors. My thanks are also due to Werner Beierwaltes, Ludwig-Maximilians Universität, Munich, who has always encouraged me to publish and to Carlos Steel, Katholieke Universiteit Leuven, who generously facilitated this process. Gregory Collins and Philipp Rosemann share my interest in negative theology and many of our late-night discussions are reflected in this book. My greatest debt, however, is to Arthur Hilary Armstrong, (Professor Emeritus Liverpool and Nova Scotia), who has, since 1983, kept a watchful and paternal eye on my work. His careful criticism and sometimes extensive commentary on many of these chapters as they emerged sometimes rather shakily onto the printed page, comes from a lifetime's intimacy with Neoplatonic texts. His own work on Plotinus and negative theology has contributed greatly to our understanding of both.

Chapters nine and eleven in the present volume began life as conference papers given in Dublin and subsequently published in Dublin and Leuven. I am grateful to the editors of *Philosophical Studies* and *Recherches de Théologie ancienne et médiévale* for their kind permission to use the latest revised versions of these chapters.[1]

On the financial side, I acknowledge the assistance of the Department of Education, Northern Ireland, who funded part of my post-graduate study; the Deutscher Akademischer Austaushdienst for the award of a Stipendium for a period of study in Munich, and University College Dublin, where I worked for three

[1] '*Apophasis* and Metaphysics in the *Periphyseon* of John Scottus Eriugena', *Philosophical Studies*, XXXII (1988-90), pp. 63-82.
'Negative Theology in the Thought of Saint Augustine', *Recherches de Théologie ancienne et médiévale*, LIX (1992), pp. 5-22.

years as a post-doctoral Newman Scholar. The Inter-Library Loans Departments in The Queen's University of Belfast and University College Dublin were most helpful in obtaining relevant offprints and the Computer Centres of both institutions patiently dealt with my queries and problems until I was eventually able to stand on my own feet.

Finally, the greatest debt of all is the one which can never adequately be paid. The dedication of this book, in recognition of that fact, is one attempt to thank them.

ABBREVIATIONS

The abbreviations below pertain to Chapter Seven on Philo of Alexandria. The numbers in brackets indicate the volume number in the Loeb edition of Philo's works.

Abr.	*De Abrahamo* (vi)
Aet.	*De aeternitate mundi* (ix)
Agr.	*De agricultura* (iii)
Apol.	*Apologia pro Iudaeis* (ix)
Cher.	*De cherubim* (ii)
Confus.	*De confusione linguarum* (iv)
Congr.	*De congressu quaerendae eruditionis gratia* (iv)
Decal.	*De decalogo* (vii)
Det.	*Quod deterius potiori insidiari soleat* (ii)
Deus	*Quod Deus immutabilis sit* (iii)
Ebr.	*De ebrietate* (iii)
Flacc.	*In Flaccum* (ix)
Fuga.	*De fuga et inventione* (v)
Gig.	*De gigantibus* (ii)
Jos.	*De Iosepho* (vi)
Leg. all.	*Legum allegoriae* (i)
Leg. Gaius.	*De legatione ad Gaium* (x)
Mig. Abr.	*De migratione Abrahami* (iv)
Mos.	*De vita Mosis* (vi)
Mut. nom.	*De mutatione nominum* (v)
Opif.	*De opificio mundi* (i)
Plant.	*De plantatione* (iii)
Post. Caini.	*De posteritate Caini* (ii)
Praem.	*De praemiis et poenis* (viii)
Prov.	*De providentia* (ix)
Quaest. in Exod.	*Quaestiones et solutiones in Exodum* (Suppl. ii)
Quaest. in Gen.	*Quaestiones et solutiones in Genesin* (Suppl. i)
Quis. her.	*Quis rerum divinarum heres* (iv)
Quod omn. prob.	*Quod omnis probus liber sit* (ix)
Sac.	*De sacrificiis Abelis et Caini* (ii)
Sob.	*De sobrietate* (iii)
Som.	*De somniis* (v)

Spec. leg.	*De specialibus legibus* (vii - viii)
Virt.	*De virtutibus* (viii)
Vita cont.	*De vita contemplativa* (ix)

INTRODUCTION

Apophasis proper begins in the speculative philosophy of late Platonism, in the typically Neoplatonic way of understanding the nature of the One and can be said to have reached its zenith in Greek philosophical thought in the works of Proclus. In its specifically religious development we can distinguish two distinct points in its history. The first was the fusion of Platonic and Hebraic ideas which is found in the writings of the first-century Jewish philosopher, Philo of Alexandria. It was his unique synthesis, centring as it does upon the theme of the transcendence and immanence of the divine, which was adopted and developed by the early Fathers of the Christian Church, a development which reached one high point in the radical negative theology of the Cappadocian Father, Gregory of Nyssa. The second, and perhaps more important moment, was the Neoplatonic fertilization of Christian principles effected in the works of Pseudo-Dionysius the Areopagite, although the influence of Plotinus on Gregory of Nyssa was also important. It was through Eriugena's translation of the Dionysian works in the ninth century, that the apophatic principles enshrined in the writings of the Areopagite became a formative influence upon the Christian scholasticism of the Middle Ages.

The developed forms of *apophasis* in Proclus and the Pseudo-Dionysius, Eriugena, Meister Eckhart and Nicholas of Cusa have received some scholarly attention; this study will attempt to trace the roots of the apophatic tradition, both in Greek philosophy and in early medieval Christian philosophy, for a correct understanding of the theme depends upon a proper consideration of its sources. The first part of this book will outline the pre-Plotinian emergence of the theme of the transcendence of the first principle in Plato and the Middle Platonists before moving on to a consideration of its development in Plotinus and Proclus. The second part will concentrate upon *apophasis* as it was utilized and developed in Christian philosophy, in the early Christian Fathers, Gregory of Nyssa and the Pseudo-Dionysius in the East, and Augustine and John Scottus Eriugena in the West.

According to the Pseudo-Dionysius, the 'sacred science of theology' comprises two distinct methods of speaking about God, the positive and the negative. In his περὶ μυστικῆς θεολογίας, Dionysius set down the distinctions between what he called *kataphatikē* (towards speech), and *apophatikē* (away from speech). Understood at its most basic level, the kataphatic, or affirmative, approach states that we can attain to some knowledge of God, no matter how limited, by attributing all the perfection of the created order to him as its source. This truth was accepted almost exclusively by the medieval scholastics and led to the idea that God cannot be known directly outside of the *oikonomia* in which he reveals himself. The apophatic, or negative way, on the other hand, affirms God's absolute transcendence and unknowability to such an extent that no affirmative concepts, except that of existence, may be applied to him, although among some of the later Neoplatonists and some of the more radical negative theologians of the Latin West, even *to on* is denied. According to the principles of negative theology, one cannot transfer creaturely attributes to the divine nature without diminishing the unrestricted aspect of God's transcendence. The formulations of affirmative theology can be understood as the attempt to provide mental forms through which aspects of the divine truth may be communicated to the human mind, while the negative way can be seen as a guard against equating the divine nature with its formal expression, an expression which relies upon terms accessible to the limited human reason. Both ways, then, take creation as their initial point of reference: the one states that God can be known through creation, since he created it, while the other states that God is beyond creation, and cannot be known in any way through it. According to Meister Eckhart who represents a most forceful case for negative theology, before creation, God existed supreme in himself; human nature must, therefore, seek to attain to a 'knowledge' of God which is not dependent upon divine economy, for God cannot be understood simply as creator.[1] Accordingly, this stance necessitates a transcendence of causal categories, which, if understood in terms of a radical negative ontology, renders understandable the heretical-sounding statements of Eckhart. It is only in the light of the practice of intense purification that the remark, 'I pray to God to make me free of God', can be understood.[2]

However, there is one very important aspect of *apophasis* and *kataphasis*, and that is that they can be understood on a more cosmological level. This characteristic is most clearly displayed in the writings of Plotinus, Gregory of Nyssa and, to a greater extent in the Pseudo-Dionysius and in Eriugena, all of whom understand kataphatic theology to signify the outgoing (*proodos*) from God who always remains in himself (*monē*), while apophatic theology signifies the return (*epistrophē*) of all things to their source. In the Pseudo-Dionysius, the way down from the original darkness of God to the light of creatures is a way of knowing, a continual theophany of being. The way up, on the other hand, is an ascent from the light of creatures to the darkness of God and is a process of leaving creatures behind. Beings can be seen only in light, yet in the light the darkness of God cannot be seen, for darkness is invisible in light.[3] It can, therefore, be said that a basic ontological premise lies at the heart of both the kataphatic and apophatic methods of philosophical and theological speculation. The kataphatic theologian relies upon the more typically Western assertion that God is the 'fullness of being', while the apophatic theologian asserts that God is best understood in terms of 'non-being'.

At first it would appear that these two methods of speaking about the divine nature are strictly opposed; there exists a continual tension between the two approaches, a tension which reflects

---

[1] See the vernacular sermons, *Beati pauperes spiritu* and *Nolite timere*. In this volume full references not given in the footnotes can be found in the bibliographies.

[2] *Beati pauperes spiritu*; see M. O' C. Walshe, *Meister Eckhart Sermons and Treatises*, vol. 2, p. 274.

[3] Dionysius the Areopagite, *Ep.* I (1065A).

the ontological dialectic operative between them. However, *apophasis* and *kataphasis* are not simply highly-schematized devices whereby we are enabled to speak of or not speak of the divine essence; they are perhaps best understood in terms of a dialectic which is of divine, not human origin. Perhaps it was unfortunate that the Pseudo-Dionysius proposed such a clear distinction between the two, since later readers and interpreters of the *Corpus Areopagiticum* tended to widen the gulf ever further, making it extremely difficult for negative theology to function fully as an acceptable way of approaching the metaphysical composition of divine and human reality. This apparently deep theological rift can boast not only of historical but also of geographical parameters, for it would seem that the philosopher or theologian who properly understands the negative way tends to belong mainly to the Eastern camp of philosophical and theological speculation.

In the West, there has always been a strong tendency to favour affirmative theology in the analogical method of the *via eminentiae*, leaving the continuance of the negative tradition to Eriugena, Eckhart and Nicholas of Cusa, among others. The affirmative way of 'speaking' about God, with its heavy reliance upon the credal formulae adopted by the Ecumenical Councils of the early Church, has sometimes tended to forget that while credal formulae provide a conceptual form through which a ray of truth can be communicated, they cannot contain the whole truth about God; they remain its expression in linguistic terms only. This understanding was officially reaffirmed at the Fourth Lateran Council in 1215.[4] A literal interpretation of anything said of the divine nature betrays, at least in the eyes of the negative theologian, the measure of human conceit, and that is seen as an attempt to enclose the mystery of the divine within a rigid set of concepts; or perhaps it validates in a measure the Jungian observation that the Western mind cannot function without the aid of concepts. Although it is generally accepted that the Eastern theological tra-

---

[4] See H. Denzinger, A. Schönmetzer, *Enchiridion Symbolorum* (34th ed. Rome, 1967), 806 (432).

dition has remained relatively more open to apophatic theology, the Byzantine theologian did not regard the 'attributes' of God as purely abstract concepts, something which has often been implied by the Western theologian's seemingly abstract method of theological analysis. However, the differences between Eastern and Western thought cannot be simply reduced to such a facile opposition, at the risk of distortion. I do not suggest that the Western theological tradition represents an attempt to enclose the mystery of the divine reality within 'a tidily arranged set of clear and distinct ideas',[5] and I certainly do not agree with C. Yannaras's general evaluation of Western theology as 'abstract intellectual discourse'.[6] Nevertheless, it is true that there was, and still remains, a tendency in this direction.

While it is extremely difficult to determine the reasons lying behind the almost overwhelming support given to the kataphatic way in the West, I would suggest that the link between negative theology and mysticism may have contributed to this neglect. It has often been the experience of those who have followed the negative way to its utmost limits that they pass beyond the traditional boundaries of theology, understood as an intellectual discipline, to the realm of 'mystical union'. Mysticism has always been a difficult area of study for the philosopher, and indeed for the theologian, as its advocates lay claim to a vision which cannot be subjected to the scrutiny of intellectual reasoning. For this reason the mystic, and by the same measure the radical negative theologian, has never been very popular with ecclesiastical authorities. The mystic has often been treated with extreme caution and even suspicion because of the claim to an intimate and direct knowledge of God. While I do not wish to overemphasize the mystical aspect of some forms of negative theology, or to suggest that the apophatic way and the mystical way are one and the same thing, the two can be linked, in that the final outcome of the apophatic way easily merges into the mystical

---

[5] See A. H. Armstrong's comments on this theme in, 'Plotinus's Doctrine of the Infinite', in *Plotinian and Christian Studies*, Variorum Reprints I, no. V, p. 58.
[6] 'Orthodoxy and the West', *Eastern Churches Review*, 3 (1971), p. 292.

way.[7] At the same time it is necessary to point out that neither method of theology need enter the realm of experimental knowledge; they can remain at the level of theological discourse.

However, having outlined the general nature of the methods of *apophasis* and *kataphasis*, I wish to stress the fact that both methods of philosophical and theological speculation belong together not only dialectically, but also necessarily, since they are two aspects of the one divine truth of revealed religion: God is both hidden and present, known and unknown, transcendent and immanent. Any failure to take both aspects of this simultaneous truth into account in a discussion of the divine nature could result in a distorted view. To stress only the affirmative account of theology in terms of univocal predication (as Aquinas puts it) could result in an anthropomorphic conception of God, while to stress exclusively the negative account in terms of equivocal predication could sever all connection between the human and the divine. The two ways of seeking an understanding of God must admit that neither way can exclude the other. The metaphysical supposition underlying the application of both methods of theology is most clearly demonstrated in the Plotinian assertion that the One is all things and yet not a single one of them: "All these things are the One and not the One: they are he simply because they come from him; they are not he, because it is in abiding by himself that he gives them."[8] In Christian terms, this truth is expressed in the affirmation of God as both transcendent and immanent. Therefore, theological speech, whether apophatic or kataphatic, stresses one or other side of this divine truth and is understood as an expression of human understanding of the composition of divine reality. On the verbal level

---

[7] The obvious connection between mysticism and *apophasis* is something which I do not intend to discuss in any detail in this volume; however a certain amount of caution is required lest the reader be tempted to equate intellectual purification with passing into the mystic night. This is a tendency to which R. Mortley appears to succumb in *From Word to Silence I. The Rise and Fall of Logos*, p. 125 and pp. 153-4.

[8] πάντα δὲ ταῦτα ἐκεῖνος καὶ οὐκ ἐκεῖνος· ἐκεῖνος μέν, ὅτι ἐξ ἐκεινόυ· οὐκ ἐκεῖνος δέ, ὅτι ἐκεῖνος ἐφ' ἑαυτοῦ μένων ἔδωκεν: Enn. V 2, 26-28; text and translation, A. H. Armstrong (Loeb Edition); see also Enn. V 2, 1, 1-2.

there will always be a tension underlying the intellect's understanding of the dialectic operative between the idea of transcendence and immanence; both are ultimately access to "lux inaccessibilis".[9]

While most Christian writers emphasize more strongly one or other aspect of this double truth, for the most part, they do realise the distorted image to which an exclusively affirmative or negative path could lead. This is why we find Augustine – who has generally been considered to rely chiefly upon the affirmative way of theology – continually proclaiming the two-fold truth of *secretissime* and *praesentissime*: 'tu autem eras interior intimo meo et superior summo meo'.[10] In the same way, Aquinas, that great master of the analogical method, displays his keen sense of the unknowable nature of God: 'hoc illud est ultimum cognitionis humanae de deo quod sciat se deum nescire'.[11] We can know only *that* God is, not *what* he is, or as Aquinas prefers to say, we know what God is not.[12] It is because we find the majority of Christian writers taking at least some account of negative theology, that I suggest that there exists, not simply two fundamentally distinct theologies, but rather, a variety of positions lying between the extremes of *apophasis* and *kataphasis*.[13]

At this juncture, it is important to reaffirm that the nature of theological discourse consists in *speaking* about God and, as such, remains on a secondary level, at more than one remove from reality. However, negative theology is not simply concerned with speech about the divine nature: it has also been utilized as a

---

[9] 1Tim 6:16.

[10] *Confessions* VII (11), ed. M. Skutella, rev. M. Jurgens and W. Schaub (Stuttgart, 1969); see also *Conf.* I, 4 and VI, 3.

[11] *Quaest. disp. de pot. dei*, q. 7, a. 5, *ad.* 14; see *S. Thomae Aquinatis. Opera Omnia*, vol. 3, ed. R. Busa (Holzboog, 1980).

[12] See *S. T.* 1a, 3, Prologue and 1a, qu. 2, a. 2, 2; the distinction between *that* (existence) and *what* (essence) is first found in Philo of Alexandria (see *Quod deus immutabilis sit*, 62), and is an important aspect of the negative approach to knowledge of the divine nature.

[13] A more detailed account of *apophasis* and *kataphasis* can be found in D. Carabine, '*Apophasis* East and West'.

method of approaching the unknowable, divine nature. A. H.
Armstrong makes this point very well:

> In considering the *via negativa* it is important to distinguish
> between the apophatic method of intellectual approach to God, or
> negative theology, and the experience of supreme transcendence
> ... which impels to and is undergone in the search for ... the
> Divine mystery beyond speech or thought.[14]

The kind of negative theology which is found in Plotinus, Proclus
Gregory of Nyssa and the Pseudo-Dionysius, is a negative theology which forces negation to its most radical conclusions, into a
cognitional crisis, which is resolved when the negative theologian
once again enters into the area of experimental knowledge. This
'knowledge' is achieved when the mind is brought beyond the
normal limits of human understanding to reach knowledge of the
divine which is the result of its former state of ignorance. Thus,
the logic of abstraction becomes clear, as Dionysius says: 'we take
away everything so that we may know that unknowing without its
being veiled'.[15]

The result of this radical *aphairesis* is not ignorance or negation
alone, nor an empty agnosticism, but knowledge which stems from
a personal communion with the unknowable God. This knowledge, which Plotinus refers to as a kind of 'presence', is called by
some followers of the negative way 'knowing by unknowing', or
'divine ignorance'.[16] The 'ultimate beyond' where one understands God to be above all affirmations or negations made on the
descriptive level, is, according to Nicholas of Cusa, an understanding of God as the *coincidentia oppositorum*, that to which
nothing can be placed in opposition.[17] The transcendence of affir-

---

[14] 'Apophatic-Kataphatic Tensions in Religious Thought from the Third to the
Sixth Century A. D.', p. 12; see also P. Hadot, 'Apophatisme et théologie négative'.
[15] *De myst. theol.* II, 1; translations not acknowledged in the footnotes are my
own.
[16] See *Enn.* VI 7, 35, 36-40, VI 7, 36, 15-19 and VI 9, 4, 3; see also Meister
Eckhart's vernacular sermon, *Ubi est qui natus.*
[17] See *De docta ignorantia*, chs. II and IV; see also *Periphyseon* 517B-C and
453A-B.

mation and negation in the *negatio negationis* can result in an incommunicable knowledge which is exemplified in the paradoxical statements of those who have attempted to describe that which lies beyond the scope of linguistic expression: 'ineffable word', 'superessential essence', and indeed, 'unknowing knowing'.

Faced with the assertion that God is best and most truly known through not knowing, it is not surprising to find that most Western philosophers and theologians have left this particular path alone, for it is a path that cannot always be charted according to the commonly accepted process of human reason. Precisely because the negative way is less categorical than the positive way in its understanding of the divine nature, it is more open to misinterpretation: its radical transformation of normal cognitional and ontological categories render it an approach to the divine which does not always conform to the accepted traditional ontological and epistemological categories.

The three-fold manifesto of *apophasis*, that God is ineffable, unnameable and unknowable, paradoxically necessitates that there must be some way to speak the unspeakable, to name the unnameable and ultimately, to know the unknowable, without compromising the essential transcendent characteristic of the divine nature. It was the attempt to do precisely this which has provided the philosophical and theological tradition of the Latin West with a way of speculation without which it would have undoubtedly been the poorer.

There are, however, two fundamental points I wish to make at the outset. The first is that even the use of the terms 'apophatic' and 'kataphatic' in the abstract is problematic. The descriptive use of the term 'apophatic' has not precisely the same meaning when applied to Plotinus, Proclus, Gregory of Nyssa, Dionysius or Eriugena. At a very basic level, however, I think we may understand apophatic theology to begin with the assertion that God is unknowable to the human mind and that one must proceed by means of negations, ultimately, even to the negation of the negation in order to attain to some 'positive' knowledge of him. Whether the methodology of negative theology is presented in a systematic form by a given writer is, however, another question entirely. I believe that the fundamental assertion of God's ineffability and unknowability is the foundation stone of both ways of theology; it is the manner in which these assertions are confronted or related to, which marks the differences between the two methods of theological analysis.

The second point I make here concerns the fact that there exists a number of ways in which the divine can be regarded as unknowable. These distinctions have been formulated by E. R. Dodds as follows.[18] God may be unknown because he is foreign or nameless, or because of the limitations of the human mind. He may also be regarded as unknown to those who have not enjoyed a special revelation or initiation. He may be unknown in essence, but partially known through his works; unknown in his positive character, but definable through negations, or finally, accessible only through the *unio mystica*. With this comprehensive account in mind it will be possible not only to chart the development of *apophasis* more clearly, but also to recognize the various positions adopted by the philosophers I shall be dealing with in this volume.

---

[18] See *The Elements of Theology*, pp. 311-312.

PART I

GREEK *APOPHASIS*

CHAPTER ONE

EARLY GREEK PHILOSOPHY AND PLATO

Ever since the beginnings of critical thought human beings have been asking questions about and pondering the nature of the gods:

> About the gods, I am not able to know whether they exist or do not exist, nor what they are like in form; for the factors preventing knowledge are many: the obscurity of the subject, and the shortness of human life.[1]

It was because of this simple, yet outspoken agnosticism that Protagoras (481-411 BC) was reputedly expelled from Athens. His treatise *On The Gods* was condemned by the authorities, and all copies ordered to be destroyed. Thus began a tradition which was to have a long, sometimes tortured history and which was reflected almost sixteen centuries later with the condemnation of twenty-eight statements from the writings of Meister Eckhart by Pope John XXII in the Bull *In Agro Dominico* (1329). It is, of course, obvious that the causes of their respective disgraces were not entirely similar, but the common denominator (if indeed one may be sought) was the admission that the divine is essentially unknowable to mortal nature. While the negative theology of Eckhart is much more profound than the untrammelled agnosticism or philosophical diffidence of Protagoras, nonetheless there remains, I think, a tentative link between the two, a link which I hope to demonstrate in the course of this book.

Although Protagoras was by no means fully representative of the Greek attitude towards the divine, he can be numbered among the members of a critical stream of thought which developed

---

[1] Protagoras, *On the Gods*, H. Diels, *Die Fragmente der Vorsokratiker*, vol. 2, 80 B. 4; translation, K. Freeman, *Ancilla to the Pre-Socratic Philosophers,* p. 126.

alongside the popular religious beliefs and customs accepted by the majority. Sacred history, which human beings attempted to recount in the form of myth, telling of the heroic exploits of the gods, was scrutinized and found to be wanting. It was this critical stream of thought which contributed, at least in part, to the Platonic attitude towards the divine.

The Old Gods Abandoned

While most studies of early Greek philosophy concentrate on the anthropomorphism of the gods of Homer and Hesiod, consequently attributing to the Ionian physicists the breakthrough from myth to monotheism, nevertheless, there are strong traces, especially in the works of Homer, of the notion of one most powerful god, to whom the rest of the gods are subordinate.[2] The idea of Zeus as the father of the gods is a Homeric theme which persisted in Greek thought and which is still visibly present in the *Enneads* of Plotinus. Although the old gods of the Greek pantheon became de-personalized during the centuries from Plato to Plotinus, they were not forgotten by the philosophers: the Homeric conception of the deities had a long history, and remained for many centuries the powerful symbolic core of Greek religious thought. However, it is true to say that because of their 'ungodly' behaviour the gods came to be regarded as 'beings unsuited by their very nature either to call forth or satisfy the deepest religious feelings of men'.[3] Although the old conception of the gods was not eradicated by the newer, more scientific or rational accounts of the nature of reality, as a wholly new kind of intellectual understanding of the deepest mysteries of the universe arose from the 'rational' explanations for realities, up to then attributed to the gods, the old pantheon began to lose its credibility.

A. H. Armstrong, while admitting the obvious differences between myth and the early Milesian philosophies, argues that the latter do conform 'to the great basic assumptions of Greek

[2] *Iliad* I, 544 and *Odyssey* I, 26.
[3] W. K. C. Guthrie, *The Greeks and Their Gods*, p. 255.

traditional religion and cosmology'.[4] W. Jaeger goes a step further and argues that there is no such great historical epoch as the dawning of an age of natural science.[5] It could be argued that the old gods merely became de-personalized; this position is strikingly true of the 'one, greatest god' of Xenophanes, who has more in common with the god Zeus than most histories have cared to admit. It would appear, therefore, that while we should not overstate the conquest of natural science over myth, the new explanations of natural phenomena were the force that began to upset the traditional notion of the power of the Greek pantheon. The early Greek philosophers who rebelled against a pluralistic explanation of the universe, represent an attempt to discover a single quasi-physical principle of being, capable of both unifying and sustaining the whole cosmos.

As a representative of the critical stream of thought in Greek philosophy I mention, very briefly, Xenophanes (b. c. 570 BC), for his ideas have an important bearing on the development of the concept of transcendent divinity. Xenophanes showed himself strongly opposed to the *muthoi* in his criticism of the prevalent notions of the gods accepted by popular cults. The myths, he said, are nothing but useless old tales which make the gods too much like the society they are supposed to govern, and mortals consider the gods to have been born like themselves.[6] According to Xenophanes, it is not fitting for the human mind to think of the gods in this way, rather we should conceive of: 'one god, greatest among gods and men, in no way similar to mortals either in body or in thought'.[7] Whatever the underlying reasons of Xenophanes in positing the idea of one, supreme god, he can be regarded as the first Greek thinker to have conceived of the gods as existing in a realm different from the realm of mortal nature. Xenophanes, like Protagoras, also insisted that human nature cannot know the truth about the gods: 'No man knows, or ever will know, the truth about

---

[4] *An Introduction to Ancient Philosophy*, pp. 4-5.
[5] *Paideia: Die Formung Des Griechischen Menschen*, vol. I, pp. 207-208.
[6] H. Diels, *Die Fragmente der Vorsokratiker*, vol. 1, 21 B. 1, B. 11, B. 14.
[7] Diels, 1, 21 B. 23; trans. Kirk and Raven, *The Presocratic Philosophers*, p. 169.

the gods and about everything I speak of'.⁸ This attitude of diffidence concerning knowledge of the gods is one which was to have
a long history in Greek thought and may perhaps be linked to
Plato's famous remark about knowledge of the father and maker
from the *Timaeus*. I will return to this point in my discussion
below.

The philosophical speculations of Parmenides (fl. c. 475 BC),
one time Pythagorean, politician, and the supposed pupil of Xenophanes, can be said to constitute a turning point in the history of
Greek philosophy, since his remarks on the properties of true being
have been regarded as the first example of an ontological system. I
mention Parmenides in the context of this study because his
description of true being (as opposed to the world of becoming) is
couched in negative terms, terms which would be repeated in the
Platonic dialogue named after this philosopher, and were to be
developed as an integral part of the negative theology of Plotinus.

According to Parmenides, the basic distinction to be made is
that which pertains between being and non-being: being can be
thought, non-being cannot be thought, an important observation
which was to culminate in the Plotinian assertion that the One
beyond being, cannot be thought. In the Parmenidean system it is
the process of reason which can come to a correct understanding
of the nature of being. Ἔστι is the antithesis of οὐκ ἔστι, and in
Fragment VIII, we find the following attributes applied to ἔστι:
ἀγένητον, ἄναρχον, ἀνώλεθρον, οὐδὲ διαίρετὸν, ἀτρεμές,
ἀκίνητον and ἀτέλεστον.⁹ Yet Parmenides does not sever being
completely from the realm of change, for it has a boundary and
limit, a place, and a shape. Although Parmenidean being is not yet
transcendent, it is, like the one god of Xenophanes, in most
respects, unlike anything in the domain of human nature or of the
visible *physis*.

At this point I wish to suggest that there was within the Greek
tradition, two strands of thought which contributed to the develop-

⁸ Diels, 1, 21 B. 34; trans. Kirk and Raven, p. 179.
⁹ Diels, 1, 28 B. 8.

ment of the idea of a transcendent reality. The first of these will be seen in the Platonic development of the 'negative ontology' of Parmenides, for the world of the Forms, as Plato conceived of it, was transcendent (though still finite), and totally removed from the world of becoming. The second contributing factor is characterized by the attitude of Xenophanes, in his radical criticism of the notion of the gods as portrayed in the popular religious tradition, and indeed, the diffidence expressed by a number of philosophers concerning human knowledge of the gods. Although it would be a mistake to suppose that from the time of Xenophanes on there was a heightening of critical powers concerning the nature of the gods, there was, all the same, a steady stream of thinkers who would not accept the ideas of the gods as portrayed by the ancient poets. Although Protagoras and Xenophanes took this critical position to its extreme in ancient Greece, there were others who were critical without adopting views similar to those of Protagoras.[10] This conflict between the Homeric gods of the majority, and the conception of the gods by those who rebelled against them, continued for a long time, even into the first century AD, when we see Dio Chrysostom strenuously defending the Homeric gods and their symbolic representations.[11] This critical attitude gradually became more a part of the method of the philosopher, and it is in the philosophy of Plato that we see the two strands of thought become almost inseparable: on the one hand, the critical attitude towards the traditional representations of the gods, and on the other, the development of a metaphysical system which is independent of the Olympian pantheon.

Socrates (b. c. 469 BC), was perhaps one of the most striking examples of a Greek who would not accept unconditionally the cults surrounding the gods of the old myths. He saw himself as a pilgrim who had received a divine mission from the Oracle at Delphi, and had been appointed to execute important educational tasks.[12] His

---

[10] See, for example, Epicurus, *Letter to Menoceus*, 123.
[11] *Oration* XII.
[12] *Apology* 21B-22E.

duty was a religious one, which in the end demanded his life. In spite of the evident religious observance in Socrates's life, an observance which cannot be thought of as entirely singular and completely divorced from the whole Greek tradition, he was found guilty of impiety. At his trial, the charge against him read: 'Socrates is guilty of refusing to recognize the gods recognized by the state, and of introducing other new divinities'.[13]

In this sense, Socrates can also be said to follow in the footsteps of Xenophanes, yet the accounts of Socrates given by Plato are much more complex than the simple categorization of his teaching as being either of this or that school of thought. Although I do not have the space here to give a comprehensive account of Socrates's teaching concerning the gods, there is one point which must be made. It was due chiefly to the philosophical speculations of Socrates (and Plato) that the course of Greek philosophy was turned in a more religious direction, and we see the beginnings of a tradition in Greek thought which can be said to have reached its culmination in the philosophy of Plotinus. The function of *psychē*, as the divine and rational element in human nature, became the force whereby the divine itself could be reached. It is to the philosophical speculations of Plato that I now turn my attention, for he has been regarded as the founder of negative theology. How far this claim can be substantiated will be discussed in my concluding remarks.

Plato

It is true to say that by the time of Plato the gods and heroes of the old myths had partially lost their credibility; Plato himself held that their truth had become concealed under various layers of fabrication. Accordingly, Plato's own conception of the gods is not that portrayed by Homer. Although he gives no systematic outline of his account of religious matters and of the nature of the gods, his attitude can be discerned quite clearly. The gods are, first and

---

[13] Diogenes Laertius, *Lives of the Eminent Philosophers*, II, 40; trans. R. D. Hicks, vol. 1 (Loeb edition, 1925).

foremost, unchanging; they know neither sorrow nor joy; they do not alter themselves like the old gods; they are not to be bribed by prayers and sacrifices to overlook evil and impiety, but are concerned only with the good of humanity.[14] For Plato, it would be scandalous not to believe in the gods, but we must, at the same time, be cautious in what we believe about them.[15] The gods are beings worthy of reverence and must be honoured with prayers.[16] It is immediately apparent that neither Plato nor Socrates has left religion behind in the search for philosophical wisdom; the gods are still regarded as very real beings and continue to play an important part in the affairs of everyday life.

However, it would seem that the gods have little or no ethical role; while they are to be regarded with respect, they do not appear to have any moral function regarding the 'ascent' of the soul. While the gods are good, they are not the *agathon*, and Plato never implies any such identification. The gods, who belong to the realm of the divine, are said to be 'friends of the forms', along with beauty, goodness, and wisdom.[17] Plato would undoubtedly have attended the festivals and observed the prevailing religious customs, but for him, the divine meant much more than the gods. *To theion* is a realm or state of knowing, which is attainable through *nous* guided by love; it is that region where the immortal soul dwells with the gods after death.[18] Therefore, while Plato would have regarded the gods as being of some considerable importance in the everyday affairs of life, in his philosophical system, it is the creative, transcendent ultimacy of the *agathon* which is more readily comparable to the Christian and Neoplatonic idea of God.

It can be said that Plato's 'new order of wisdom' replaces both the world view contained in the old myths and also in the philosophical speculations of the early philosophers. In simple terms,

---

[14] *Philebus* 33B, *Rep.* 380-381, 388C-E, *Laws* 885B and 907A.
[15] *Laws* 888B-C.
[16] *Rep.* 386A.
[17] *Phaedrus* 246E.
[18] *Phaedrus* 247C.

his philosophy can be described as the movement of the divine towards the divine. The realization that the soul itself is divine and able to partake of divine immortality, and is also capable of attaining to divine wisdom (that permanent, unchanging truth, the Good), establishes a moral and ethical code of behaviour, which prompts the human soul to follow the path to the Good.[19]

Therefore, one theme which loosely ties together much of Plato's thought is that of the unfolding of the origin and destiny of the soul. The ascent of the soul is portrayed as a journey upwards, a difficult journey to what is beyond.[20] The soul, which characterizes the human person, is akin to the divine and is itself immortal; unlike the body, it is simple and indestructible.[21] Its highest part is the rational element *nous*, which continually strives towards the forms. It is the soul's natural kinship with the divine, the immortal and eternal, which makes it long for that which rightfully belongs to it. The thrust of the soul towards the forms, towards the 'blessed perfection of the Good',[22] while remaining always a rational, intellectual movement, is indescribable in terms other than those of metaphor and symbol. The simile of the cave, with all its nuances of light, half-light and darkness, remains, in the final analysis, a forceful portrayal of an experience which does not readily admit of more direct verbal expression; Plato's half-playful scorn of language must always be kept in mind. [23]

The divine, then, is like a single thread running through all things, but there exists a gap between human nature and the forms, a gap between human nature and transcendent beings. Between human nature and the forms there is no intermediary, but between human nature and the gods there exists the world of demons; thus, the unity of the cosmos is complete, for there does not exist a being or beings which can be considered outside of this

---

[19] *Protagoras* 322A.
[20] *Phaedo* 67B, *Phaedrus* 247B and *Symposium* 201E.
[21] *Laws* 726ff, 892ff; *Phaedo* 105A-E; *Rep.* 490B, 611E-612A, and *Phaedrus* 245Cff.
[22] *Rep.* 526E.
[23] See *Ep.* VII, 341B-E.

ordered structure. It is important to note that the concepts con-
veyed by the terms 'finite' and 'infinite' in relation to the divine
are not present in Plato's thought; rather it is the immortal in the
mortal which strives towards the Immortal. Although Plato has
sometimes been regarded as the Father of *apophasis*, and while
there are certain unmistakable elements of this method in his writings, along with a rather distinctive mystical outlook,[24] Plato himself cannot be regarded as the founder of the negative way. However, it is true that his ideas provided the spark from which the
principles of negative theology were eventually derived. As we
shall see, very little movement is needed in order to identify the
'father' of the *Timaeus* with the 'one' of the *Parmenides*, but this
remains an identification which Plato himself did not make. As we
discuss various Platonic texts below, it is important to remember
that Plato did not identify any of the several highest realities present in his discussions with one transcendent source.

At this point I must note that Plato was precluded from reaching
a conception of absolute transcendent being in the style of Plotinus, because his overall concern with the theory of forms and his
conception of the forms as true being, forced him rather to make a
distinction between the real and the unreal. Although the forms
were regarded by Plato as transcendent because they were totally
removed from the world of becoming, nevertheless, they remain
still on the level of being, as that which is most truly real. It is, of
course, possible to read Plato with Christian or Neoplatonic eyes,
and to find a theory similar to that of the One in Plotinus, for
Plato's thought lends itself easily to this kind of interpretation, as
the Neoplatonists and early Christian Fathers experienced in their
different ways. Therefore, any responsible reading of Plato's work
must make the consistent effort to maintain an unbiased perspective, one which does not burden the texts with an overlay of later
Platonic or Christian thought. It is illegitimate to tie all the various
threads of Plato's thought together into one comprehensive sys-

---

[24] For an account of the mystical element in Plato's thought, see A.-J. Festugière,
Contemplation et vie contemplative selon Platon.

tem; if this were to be attempted, the result would resemble the Neoplatonic scheme of Plotinus. However, I must point out that the texts from Plato which I have chosen to examine are precisely those texts which Plotinus and the Neoplatonists would have regarded as the backbone of Platonic doctrine.

The *Parmenides* and The *Symposium*

The first text I wish to mention here and the one perhaps of greatest consequence for the Neoplatonists, is from the *Parmenides*. This is one of the most difficult of Platonic dialogues, and it caused controversy regarding its interpretation, even at an early stage in its history. Was it meant to be an exercise in dialectic, or was it a more serious presentation of the One, as the unknowable, transcendent ground of reality? E. R. Dodds has suggested that if it is read with the eye of faith, then we find a 'lucid exposition of the famous negative theology',[25] while A. E. Taylor has noted that it may have been 'an enjoyable philosophical jest'.[26] While I am concerned here to present Plato as Plato, I cannot attempt to resolve such a long-standing difference of opinion within the space of a few pages. Therefore, I will concentrate on that portion of the dialogue which is intrinsic to the ideas expounded by the Neoplatonists (the First Hypothesis), reserving judgement, at least for the present, on that which some scholars have regarded as the first matter of importance. The dialogue itself is structured in two parts: the first is an examination of the theory of forms, and the second involves a preliminary exercise, conducted by the aged Parmenides, as a training to enable the young Socrates to attempt a definition of the various forms.[27] It is proposed that Parmenides consider the initial hypothesis and both affirm and deny it, in the attempt to establish the truth of either the hypothesis or its negation.

---

[25] 'The *Parmenides* of Plato and The Origin of the Neoplatonic One', p. 133.
[26] *Plato. The Man and His Work*, p. 370; see R. Mortley's interpretation of the *Parmenides* in *From Word to Silence I. The Rise and Fall of Logos*, p. 128ff.
[27] *Parm.* 135C.

Plato takes as his starting point for the First Hypothesis: if there is a one, or if there is not a one (Parmenides began with 'exists' or 'exists not'). According to Plato, if there is a one, then it must be defined as absolutely one, and it is from this primary definition that the now famous negations are derived, negations which were to become inseparably associated with the One of Plotinus. These negations are as follows: if the one exists it cannot be many (137C); if it has no parts, it can have no beginning, middle or end (137D); it is without form (137D); being of such a nature it cannot be anywhere (138A); the one is neither at rest nor in motion (139B); the one cannot be other or the same to itself or to another (139E); the one cannot be like nor unlike itself or another (140B); the one cannot be equal nor unequal to itself or another (140B); the one cannot be younger or older or of the same age as anything (141A); the one has nothing to do with time, and does not exist in time (141D); the one has no share in being at all (141E); the one has no being, even as one (141E); the one has no name, there is no description, knowledge or perception of it (142A).

When we compare this passage with the idea of the One as Plotinus presents it in the *Enneads*, there can be little doubt where he found his inspiration. Yet in the last few negations, we are drawn back sharply from a Neoplatonic exegesis to the logically sound conclusion of Plato's argument: for the one does not exist, even as one. That which is unlimited in the way that Plato describes this one cannot have existence, for it cannot be real. Here we find the very forceful Platonic distinction between what is real and knowable on the one hand, and what is unreal and, therefore, unknowable, on the other. Although it would require a more detailed examination of the text in its entirety in order to show how the First Hypothesis slots into the whole configuration of hypotheses, it is clear that Plato was concerned with a linguistic analysis of logical thought. This conclusion is obvious if we proceed immediately to a reading of the Second Hypothesis, where the emphasis is on 'is' rather than on 'one', and the conclusion reached is the affirmation of the negations of the First Hypothesis. The ultimate conclusion at the end of the dialogue is a confirmation of the dialectical purpose of the whole exercise: 'It seems that, whether there is or is not a One, both that One and the Others alike are and are not, and appear and do not appear to be, all manner of things in all manner of ways, with respect to themselves and to one another'.[28]

The second text I wish to mention is Socrates's speech on love from the *Symposium*, another Platonic text which was to exert a tremendous influence on Plotinus. Keeping in mind the prisoner's escape from the darkness of the cave in the ascent to light and reason, here in the *Symposium*, Plato is simply characterizing a different aspect of the same kind of ascent. The journey of the soul from the sensible to the eternal world takes place in the *Symposium* through the force of *eros*, which is the desire for the Good. The setting of the dialogue is, as the title suggests, a meal/drinking party, after which each of the guests agrees to speak about love. The speech of Socrates, as the climax of the dialogue, recalls what he learned about love from the seer, Diotima.[29] This ascent, which requires a special initiation, is to be understood as an ascent through the various levels of the mysteries of love and are described in terms which betray Plato's interest in the mystery religions. These mysteries are normally kept secret, except for those capable of understanding without misinterpretation, and in the *Symposium* there may be some sort of initiation implied in the telling.[30]

According to Socrates, the young lover first falls in love with the physical beauty of one body, but must pass from there to a love of all physical beauty. Beauty of soul is the next stage in the initiation, and from there the lover is taught to love beauty in all arts, activities, institutions, and sciences. The last stage, which constitutes the final initiation, is the 'sudden' catching sight of the inconceivable beauty itself.[31] The eloquence of Plato's language here, and the evi-

---

[28] *Parm.* 166C; trans. H. N. Fowler, vol. VI (Loeb edition, 1953).
[29] 209Eff.
[30] It is interesting to compare this extract with *Phaedrus* 250B-C, where Plato speaks of the mysteries and the ascent of the soul in mythical terms.
[31] 210D; see also *Rep.* 509A.

dent passion he displays for his subject, is comparable to some of
the finest passages in the *Enneads*, and indeed in the *Confessions*
of Augustine. This vision is also one which is vouchsafed suddenly
(*exaiphnēs*), just as it will be in Plotinus and Dionysius. It is Plato's
language when describing the ultimate revelation of beauty that
interests us here, for he describes it in negative terms. There is no
positive verbal expression which would be adequate to describe
this inconceivable beauty and do it justice in the description.
Beauty, then, is eternal, ungenerated, imperishable; it does not vary
either in part, time, relation or place; it is unlike corporeal, intellectual or spiritual beauty.[32] In 'positive' terms, beauty is absolute,
existing alone with itself (*monoeides* – an idea which will be used
extensively by Plotinus), unique, and eternal; all other beautiful
things partake of it, yet do not cause it to change, increase or
decrease in any way. The similarity here with the negations of the
Parmenides is obvious in the method Plato uses to describe the ultimate beautiful reality. Even though Plato does use positive terms,
these are not terms which are commonly applied to the world of
mortal, changing reality. I remark that here Plato effects a shift in
emphasis from the contemplation of beauty to the practice of moral
virtue and goodness, for the word *aretē,* can be understood to mean
moral goodness or virtue. While Plato does not say here that
absolute beauty is goodness, it is clear that the attainment of goodness is a condition for the attainment of beauty and, therefore, of
immortality, which is the ultimate aim of the initiate.

The Mysterious

Apart from Plato's use of negative terms in describing the highest realities, it is his remarks concerning their mysterious nature,
and his consequent silence regarding their description, which bring
him close to the fundamental principles which will later guide
negative theology. Up to this point we have seen Plato use what

[32] 211A.

we understand to be the distinctive method of negative theology, but we have not heard him enunciate his reasons for doing so. I now examine a number of passages where Plato affirms the mysterious, almost unknowable nature of transcendent reality.

To lead us into this discussion I mention first a passage from the *Timaeus*, namely, that famous text which gave rise to the idea of the unknowability of the god of some later Platonists (notably Numenius): 'to discover the maker and father of this universe is a task indeed, and having discovered him, to declare him to all men is an impossible thing'.[33] This text requires little elaboration. It is clear that there remains a possibility that the demiurge can be known by at least some people. Before he embarks on his account of the nature of the universe, Plato excuses himself from providing a completely accurate explanation of the nature of things, for, he says, human reason is not equipped to render an exact account of matters concerning the gods and the generation of the universe.[34] There is a limit to human knowledge, due, we may infer, not so much to the transcendence of that which is to be discussed, but rather to the weakness of the human condition.[35]

In the *Cratylus* we find another reason for silence concerning the highest realities; this time it is the nature of the gods themselves and a consideration of their names which is under discussion by Socrates and Phaedrus. The dialogue is concerned chiefly with the correct process of naming things as part of the progress towards *epistēmē*, but there is a section which explores the correctness of the divine names, a thematic which was to have a long history in philosophical thought.[36] When asked about the kind of

---

[33] 28C; some excellent comments on this passage can be found in D. T. Runia, *Philo of Alexandria and the Timaeus of Plato*, pp. 111-113. It is interesting to note at this point that the early Fathers of the Christian Church used this Platonic text more frequently, in fact, than their pagan contemporaries or indeed, Plotinus.

[34] *Tim.* 29C-D.

[35] In the *Enneads* of Plotinus we see both these aspects - the transcendence of the supreme principle and our inability to know it - fused into a comprehensive negative theology.

[36] At this point I must note that the modern debate raised by this and other Platonic dialogues concerning names and language is of marginal interest only to

correctness involved in the naming of the gods, Socrates answers: 'of the gods we know nothing, neither of them nor of their names, whatever they may be, by which they call themselves' – an answer which is typical of the later negative theologian who states that mortal nature cannot know anything about the divine nature.[37] This reticence on the part of Socrates is prompted not only by the lofty nature of the gods, but also because he has no wish to appear impious. He cannot discuss the divine nature, but he adds that there is no impiety involved in discussing the names human beings have given to the gods.[38] This distinction is an important one for many reasons and it prefigures the great Plotinian theme of the naming process as necessary since pure negation does not indicate the One.[39] Following an etymological discussion of the names of the gods – names indicate their functions – Socrates shows a certain uneasiness because he may be too deeply involved in a dangerous area: 'for god's sake let us leave the gods, as I am afraid to talk about them'.[40]

This dialogue contains one of the strongest cases in favour of the unknowability of the gods in Plato, even though the *Cratylus* is rarely mentioned in this respect. Socrates's admission that he does not know anything about the nature of the gods, indicates an awareness that their nature is sacred; any attempt to discuss them would be tantamount to bringing the gods down to the mortal level. In this respect, Socrates is not so far removed from Plotinus, Proclus, Augustine, the Pseudo-Dionysius and Eriugena, all of whom will advocate silence concerning the nature of the divine.

In *Epistle* VII, written to Dion's associates and friends at Syracuse, Plato speaks of yet another area where human thoughts ought not to be committed to paper: the highest goal of

those interested in the historical development of negative theology; I direct the reader to R. Mortley, *From Word to Silence I*, for a discussion of these and other related themes.

[37] 400D; trans. H. N. Fowler, vol. VI (Loeb edition, 1926).
[38] 401A; see also *Laws* 884ff.
[39] VI 7, 38, 9-10.
[40] 407D.

philosophia.[41] There is a certain passivity of the philosopher, or
initiate, at the summit of the intellectual ascent, and what is gained
is given as the result of continuous, rigorous preparation and application. The goal of philosophy, the most serious of all subjects and
the object of truth, is attained only by those most capable and
solely through the application of *nous.* Those who have experienced it, according to Plato, will be reluctant to commit its secrets
to paper, rather, it should be kept in the head, which is, after all,
the most divine part of human nature.[42] We should no longer be in
any doubt that the goal of philosophy is in some way mysterious
and is not an easy subject to talk about. Thus far, we have
encountered three reasons why we may not either know or speak
of things pertaining to the highest realities. Firstly, the ancient
truth about the maker of the universe is a difficult subject for mortals to understand, for the human intellect is such that it cannot
hope to represent matters of real importance with complete accuracy. Secondly, human nature knows little of the gods for the same
reason, and indeed to speak of them or to inquire more deeply into
their nature would constitute impiety. Finally, the philosopher who
seeks the truth must keep secret the knowledge gained, lest it be
misinterpreted by the majority, who have not had the requisite
training to come to a true understanding of it in the appropriate
way. Effectively, it could be said that the reasons Plato gives constitute one single thesis, namely, the inadequacy of the human
capacity to understand the transcendent; he does not refer explicitly to the unknowable nature of these realities in themselves. Even
Socrates's fear of irreverence does not, I think, indicate that the
gods are unknowable so much as it expresses his reverent awe
before their powers.

The final text I wish to mention is the one which had the most
important influence on later Platonists who were concerned with
the nature of the highest reality, and in many ways this text throws
light upon the other extracts we have been examining. It is taken

---

[41] 341C-D.
[42] *Tim.* 44D.

from Book VI of the *Republic*.[43] When discussing the nature of the greatest study of all, Socrates says that the highest knowledge is to learn the idea of the *agathon*. Thus the passage from *Epistle* VII is immediately given a particular focus. Again Socrates explains that this knowledge is almost impossible and cannot be spoken about, or understood totally: 'that which every soul seeks and for its sake does all that it does with an intuition of its reality, but yet baffled and unable to understand its nature adequately, or to attain to any lasting belief about it as it can about other things'.[44]

There is a definite air of mystery surrounding the *agathon* in the build-up to an expected definition. Glaucon presses Socrates to attempt a clarification just as he had explained the other virtues, but Socrates denies the request and agrees instead to speak of what he calls the 'offspring of the good', that which almost resembles the good.[45] This refusal to confine the nature of the *agathon* in linguistic terms heightens further the sense of mystery; even the 'offspring of the good' (which focuses upon the distance from the true source of its being) is spoken of in terms of simile. Just as the sun in the visible world illuminates objects so that the eye can see them, so too the idea of the good enables the intellect to grasp intelligible objects. Socrates concludes that it is the idea of the good which is the cause both of intelligible objects (those things which are really true) and of the power within the knower to know these realities.[46] It now becomes clear that while the demiurge makes sensible objects by looking towards their unchanging counterparts in the world of forms, it is the idea of the good which is the cause of intelligible objects.

However, just as the visible object and the eye are not themselves the sun, so the *agathon* remains apart from both the intelligible object and the cognitive faculty; they are akin to the idea of the good, but are not identifiable with the good in itself. A shift

---

[43] 504Aff.
[44] 505E.
[45] 506D-E.
[46] 508E-509A.

from the original epistemological simile is startling, and Glaucon and the others are shocked when Socrates states that just as the sun provides the source of being for visible objects, so the objects of knowledge receive their essence and existence from the good. The good must, then, be other than the intelligible object; according to Socrates, it transcends all essence, it is ἐπέκεινα τῆς οὐσίας.[47] This is the fundamental Platonic text which is of such seminal importance for the early development of negative theology and for the Plotinian notion of the One beyond being. According to Plato, the good beyond being is an 'inconceivable beauty' (ἀμήχανον κάλλος), which is the source of all knowledge and truth, surpassing even these in beauty.[48] Once again we see the Platonic interchange of good and beauty (an interchange which can be found in many passages in the *Enneads*). 'In similar fashion, you are to say that the objects of knowledge, not only receive from the presence of the good their being known, but their very existence and essence is derived to them from it, though the good itself is not essence but transcends essence in dignity and surpassing power'.[49] It is thus that the *agathon* becomes cause, the fundamental creative principle which itself remains hidden and unknown; it is the source of all true being, but cannot be understood as being. Later, however, Socrates retracts this almost unbelievable statement, when he admits that the *agathon* is not totally unknowable: it is the last thing to be seen, but even then hardly at all.[50]

In this text, we encounter the frequently-used metaphor of vision and sight, which was to become integral to Plotinus's conception of unity with the One, for in the *Enneads* knowledge of the One is described as intuition or presence.[51] It is interesting to note

---

[47] 509B; non-being for Plato was not thinkable; see R. Mortley, *From Word to Silence I*, ch. VII, for an examination of the relationship between being, thought and language in Plato.
[48] 509A.
[49] 509B.
[50] 517B.
[51] See VI 7, 35, 36-40; see also *Phaedrus* 250D; *Rep.* 507C, 518C, 533D, 527D-E; *Phaedo* 65C; *Ep.* VII; *Symp.* 219A, and *Sophist* 254A.

that in the end Plato does not say that the *agathon* can be known, rather, that it can be seen or glimpsed, which implies, I think, a very subtle shift in emphasis. For Plato, the summit of the soul's journey to the most blessed part of reality is almost always conceived in terms of the metaphor of sight; it is a vision which is somehow imprinted upon the mind like an indwelling power which is not forgotten, and it enables those who have glimpsed reality to lead others in the same direction.[52] Thus, in Plato's terms, the *agathon* as the highest reality, is the transcendent source about which little can be said. Although it is better not to speak about it at all, if one must, then it is better to speak only of what proceeds from the good, its offspring. Yet, even the offspring of the good, if we can take it that Plato means form, must also be spoken of in negative terms, as one passage from the *Timaeus* demonstrates.[53]

However, lest we think we have found the key to the individual philosopher's (or the lover's) salvation and ultimate goal, we should remind ourselves that Plato's remarks on the *agathon* are made within an educational, social, and political framework. Plato's ultimate goal is not to be understood as the goal of the lone mystic, as has sometimes been said (unfairly) of Plotinus; the ascent to the good necessarily involves active participation in the social and political life of the state. Those who would attribute to Plato an intimate, self-enclosed mystical experience of the *agathon*, are forgetting the context of his remarks. The *agathon*, the supremely transcendent ethical, and indeed, ontological reality, cannot remain a solitary preserve of the chosen few in their flight to the good, yet at the same time, not many are enabled to reach it. The philosopher who has had even a fleeting glimpse of the good must descend again into the cave to guide those fellow-prisoners still in need of enlightenment; this 'descent' is undertaken as an ethical duty, a social act for the good of the *polis*. The philosopher

---

[52] *Rep.* 518C; the notion of a power dwelling in the mind may have had a direct influence on the Plotinian idea that there exists in human nature a likeness of the One, see *Enn.* III 8, 9.

[53] 51Eff.

is not permitted to remain in the region of the good (although in death the winged soul will remain in the region of light[54]). Plato is as much concerned with the well-ordered state (especially in the *Republic* and *Laws*) as with individual salvation. A well-ordered soul, one who has understood even partially the hidden nature of the good or its offspring, will contribute to a well-ordered state.[55] The ethical role of the good, while given the most elevated position in the realm of the forms, becomes the axis through which political and social life can be led to conformity with the life of philosophy. The good is not only the summit of all knowledge, it is also the ethical impetus for a well-ordered life geared towards the highest reality; the transcendence of the good is a necessity if it is conceived in terms of the *telos* towards which human life is continually moving. While freeing mortal nature from the bonds of injustice and disorder (both individual and political), it also constitutes the ultimate teleological value and sanction, by which we can live a good life.

Plato: Father of Negative Theology?

While each of the texts I have examined provides a trace of an embryonic 'negative theology', it is solely in the light of the final interpretation of the good that we can begin to reach some sort of awareness of how Plato's thought in this respect can be understood as a precursor to the *Enneads* of Plotinus.[56] Although Plato does not use negation in a systematic fashion as a means of describing and relating to a transcendent, unknowable reality, nevertheless the whole thrust of his thought was moving in that

---

[54] *Rep.* 519C-E and *Phaedrus* 256D.

[55] *Rep.* 506B.

[56] R. Mortley examines a different selection of Platonic texts as relevant to the eventual development of negative theology; of particular interest is his analysis of those instances where Plato uses the terms *apophasis* and *aphairesis*, see *From Word To Silence I*, pp. 135-137, although he notes that Plato does not use the terms in a metaphysical sense.

general direction. Therefore, while we cannot call Plato a negative theologian in the sense that we call the Pseudo-Dionysius a negative theologian, at the same time a complete overview of Plato's writings would go a long way towards convincing even the most sceptical reader that such a path towards transcendence was emerging in several different expressions in his thought.

However, a word of caution may be opportune at this point. We should not be tempted to interpret our previous remarks concerning negative terms and the unspeakable nature of the highest realities in the light of Plato's conception of the *agathon* as beyond being. The identification of the good of the *Republic* with the god and father of the *Timaeus* and beauty of the *Symposium*, constitutes a reduction of the rich diversity of Platonic thought, and is a later Platonic development. While Plato leaves but a short step towards this identification, he never makes it fully explicit. Yet the interchange of the terms 'beauty' and 'good', and indeed the reputed identification of the One with the Good in his 'Lecture on the Good' (see the next chapter), would go at least some way towards indicating that Plato's thought was heading in this general direction. The *agathon*, while undoubtedly occupying the highest and most elevated position in the intelligible world, remains at the apex of a host of other ideas. The good is cause, the power and divine force which holds all things together; it is almost unknowable, but it cannot, at least at this stage of Platonic philosophy, be identified with the 'father' or 'maker' of the *Timaeus*. This kind of unification of Plato's thought came, of course, to be typical of the Platonists who followed him, and even modern authors and commentators have found it a temptation too strong to resist.[57] There is no transcendent, unknowable God in Plato, but there is a hint of the idea of a transcendent, unknowable good.

Even in the light of the extract from the *Republic*, which stands alone in its explicit description of the good beyond being, it must

---

[57] See for example, H. A. Wolfson's comments in 'The Knowability and Describability of God in Plato and Aristotle'.

be remembered that the whole thrust of Plato's philosophy is focused upon the attainment of knowledge: true knowledge is of that 'truly-existing essence'.[58] In spite of the adverb *epekeina*, the *agathon* does remain in some way knowable. The fact that it is unknowable to the majority of human beings is due more to their deficient ability than to any intrinsic unknowability on the part of the good itself. The forms themselves cannot be unknowable since they are that which is really real, and therefore knowable. According to the core of Platonic epistemology, it is only that which is unreal which can be regarded as unknowable; the focus of human knowledge (in its act of *anamnesis*) is directed always towards the truth of unchanging reality. However, having said that, there is, I think, more than a hint that even the most capable, well-educated philosopher experiences some difficulty in the attempt to know the good, a difficulty which is not entirely due to intellectual deficiency. This is the most one can venture to say without producing a distortion of the texts in question.

On the basis of the texts where Plato uses negative terms to describe the highest reality, I think it is possible to say that the good and beauty are, each in some way, transcendent and indescribable. The final condition necessary for a fully-developed negative theology, that of the unknowability of the highest cause, is not explicit in Plato's philosophy. In spite of all his attempts to examine the true nature of reality, in the end, Plato does not state dogmatic doctrines. Neither may we.

---

[58] *Phaedrus* 247C.

CHAPTER TWO

AFTER PLATO: THE NEO-PYTHAGOREAN REVIVAL

When tracing the development of the idea of the divine transcendent One in Greek thought, especially when one is looking for the One beyond being and beyond intellect, most studies tend to make a rather large jump from Plato to Plotinus. The great Neoplatonist himself is so well known that often his predecessors are forgotten; yet without them, the mighty edifice of Plotinian philosophy would not have existed, not at least, in the way we know it. The gap of five hundred years is too large both historically and thematically to negotiate in the space of a few paragraphs. The work of John Dillon and more recently, Stephen Gersh, has done much to remedy the need for a good comprehensive survey in English of what is now commonly called Middle Platonism, and has contributed hugely towards scholarship in this field by providing a generous framework for research on particular themes.[1]

What we see during this period of almost five hundred years, from Plato's death to the birth of Plotinus, is the spontaneous appearance of diverse movements, many of them having as their fountain head Plato, not simply 'Plato the man and his works', but Plato, 'Verkünder eines Wissens vom Göttlichen'.[2] The main feature which characterizes the Middle Platonic period can be described as the rediscovery of the Plato who offered a path to *theologia*. While Middle Platonism was itself 'poised eternally

---

[1] J. Dillon, *The Middle Platonists* and S. Gersh, *Middle Platonism and Neoplatonism. The Latin Tradition*; see also H. J. Krämer, *Der Ursprung der Geistmetaphysik*.

[2] H. Dörrie, 'Der Platonismus in der Kultur und Geistesgeschichte der frühen Kaiserzeit', in *Platonica Minora* (Munich, 1976), pp. 195-196; see also Diogenes Laertius, *Lives of the Eminent Philosophers*, III, 2, where we find a reference to Plato conceived of Apollo and born of the virgin Perictione, an example of one of the many legends which reflect the special status of Plato.

between the two poles of Peripateticism and Stoicism', Plato can be said to have remained its foundational inspiration.[3] It is also a very complex period of philosophical development; at no other time do we find the appearance of such diverse groups: the birth of Christianity; the emergence of the early Christian apologists (Justin and Irenaeus) and the development of the Christian allegorical school at Alexandria (Clement and Origen); the birth of Gnosticism; the appearance of the Hermetic literature and the *Chaldean Oracles*; the revival of a more 'dogmatic' form of Platonism which was instigated by Antiochus of Ascalon; and last but not least, the revival of Pythagoreanism. All these developments came together in one huge melting pot, making it very difficult in some cases to trace any given idea to a single definite source. However, if we keep in mind the Platonic dialogues most relevant to the theme of negative theology, then it is possible to keep a fairly steady check on what was imported into Platonism from other sources, and even on what was shamelessly misinterpreted, with respect to the development of negative theology.

The Academy (347-130 BC)

Because of the historical turn of events, tracing the development of the theme of negative theology is relatively simpler than first sight would suggest, for within the Academy itself, the main thrust of its teaching moved away from 'Platonic' Platonism towards a more Stoic kind of Platonism. After the death of Speusippus, Stoicism, Epicureanism and Scepticism became the more dominant forms of philosophical development within the Academy, and Plato's theological and metaphysical writings became less important during the three hundred years following his death. Ethical problems became increasingly more predominant, especially in the teachings of Polemo, Crates, and Crantor. The chief concern of Epicurus was the problem of how to live well and be happy.

---

[3] J. Dillon, *The Middle Platonists*, p. 340.

According to his teaching, the gods were simply not concerned with the world and human affairs (unlike the Platonic gods); while they are *makarioi* and *aphthartoi*, they are not transcendent in the Platonic sense; they simply live in another sphere, are concerned with their own affairs, their own pleasure and happiness.[4] However, the speculations of Epicurus have little or no direct bearing on the theme of negative theology, for his concern in asserting the complete separation of the world of the gods and the world of mortal nature was due largely to his reaction against the Stoic doctrine of divine providence. The introduction of Scepticism into the Academy was rooted out, at least partially, by Antiochus of Ascalon (b. c. 130 BC) in the famous dispute with his teacher and head of the Academy, Philo of Larissa (fl. 110 BC). Therefore, the period of Platonic development from Xenocrates right down to Antiochus of Ascalon, has little to offer to the development of the idea of the divine transcendent One, apart from the contribution of Speusippus. The chief concern of the Academy, with human knowledge and ethical problems, reflects a primarily anthropocentric world view. It was only after Antiochus that the Academy began to take a new direction, in that it looked back to Plato's more theological themes. In doing so, it came to adopt a more theocentric world view, and this can be said to characterize the centuries that follow, for *theologia* again became the main preoccupation of the philosopher.

Although Antiochus officially 'abandoned' the Scepticism of Philo of Larissa, on the whole, he remained faithful to his Stoic inheritance:[5] he continued to promote the Stoic ideal of life lived

---

[4] See Diogenes Laertius, X, 139 and *Letter to Menoeceus*, 123-124.

[5] R. Mortley, in his portrayal of Greek thought as a movement from *logos* to *sigē*, sees Scepticism as an important link between Aristotle and the ideas of later antiquity. He argues that Scepticism was, at least in part, responsible for the breakdown of *logos* and reliance on discursive thought, and he notes that silence in late classical philosophy is a response to the sceptic's suspension of judgement, see *From Word to Silence I*, pp. 149-153 and 160-161; see also A. H. Armstrong's remarks on the relationship of Scepticism and negative theology in 'On Not Knowing Too Much About God', *Hellenic and Christian Studies*, Variorum Reprints II, n. XV, p. 133 and p. 140ff.

in accordance with nature, and many aspects of his philosophy
reflected the ethical colouring of Stoicism. Antiochus saw no real
difference between Plato and Aristotle, and he can therefore be
regarded as the founder of a tradition which came to be well established in Platonism by the second century. This kind of outlook,
which believed that Platonism could be enhanced by certain Aristotelian ideas, is exemplified by Alcinous in the second century
AD. The neo-Pythagorean revival, therefore, is the first important
development within the Platonic tradition which has any direct
bearing on the development of negative theology. It is generally
agreed that this revival was instigated primarily by Eudorus of
Alexandria, and it indicates a movement towards a fast-growing
religious consciousness within Platonism. However, it is generally
agreed that the neo-Pythagorean interpretation of Platonic ideas is
said to have had its origin in the teaching of the Old Academy,
especially that of Speusippus, therefore, it is to the latter that we
must first turn.

The Old Academy and the Pythagorization of Plato

I begin this discussion with some remarks on Plato's 'Lecture
on the Good', Pythagorean number theory, and Aristotle's account
of Plato's unwritten doctrines.

Ever since Schleiermacher's pioneering attempt to distinguish
Plato from the Platonic school, the discussion of the merits of the
case he made has continued. It does not lie within the scope of this
chapter to give more than the broad outline of this debate, which
can be stated simply as 'dialogues versus oral teaching'. Whether
Plato himself in his later years actually did teach Pythagoreanism
in the form that we are led to believe, is a question that cannot easily be answered. According to Aristotle's account,[6] Plato followed
the Pythagoreans, although he introduced some distinguishing fea-

---

[6] *Metaphysics* Bk. A, 987a-988a; see also J. A. Philip, 'Aristotle's Sources for
Pythagorean Doctrine', *Phoenix*, 17 (1963), pp. 251-265.

tures such as the concept of participation (*methexis*), instead of the usual Pythagorean term, imitation (*mimēsis*). It must be noted at this point that the *agrapha dogmata* controversy arose precisely because of the discrepancy between Plato as he presents himself in the dialogues, and Plato as he is represented by Aristotle; although it is somewhat difficult to see how Aristotle, having been in the Academy for some twenty years, could have gone wholly astray. H. Cherniss denies the truth of Aristotle's account, since to accept it would be akin to judging the ideas of a teacher through the notes of a student![7]

In brief, the system of Plato according to Aristotle is as follows.[8] The One and the Indefinite Dyad are opposed first principles. The activity of the One imposes a correct measure upon the dyad, which is limitless unless order is imposed on it. By acting thus on the dyad, the One generates the forms or numbers which are the causes of things. The first four numbers making up the decad (the *Tetractys*) can be used to explain the basic dimensions of being, and in *De anima*, Aristotle himself outlines the four-number theory in its geometric aspect, with reference to the soul and knowledge.[9] This can be set out as follows:

Point	Line	Plane	Solid
One	Dyad	Triad	Tetrad
nous	*epistēmē*	*doxa*	*aisthesis*

This illustration will be important in the discussion of Alcinous's method of *aphairesis*.

According to another account, that of Diogenes Laertius, Plato set out two universal principles, not monad and dyad, but God and matter: God is the mind and cause who created the universe in his own likeness.[10] This supreme creator is *to agathon*. The familiar identification of God with the Good, familiar at least to the later Middle Platonists, portrays an understanding of God, not in terms

---

[7] See *The Riddle of the Early Academy*, p. 31ff.
[8] *Met.* Bk. Z, 1028b, Bk. M, 1085a and Bk. N, 1090b.
[9] I, 2, 404bff.
[10] III, 69ff.

of the Pythagorean monad, but as the demiurge or creator. The identification of *to hen* with *to agathon* surprisingly does not occur until very late in the Middle Platonic period (perhaps with the exception of Plutarch), and is a characteristic of the *Enneads* rather than Middle Platonism.

Plato's famous 'Lecture on the Good', which provoked both ridicule and outrage, is also an important source for the development of our theme. According to Aristoxenus, the statement, ὅτι ἀγαθόν ἐστιν ἕν, was not well received by those present, although it seems to have been adopted by Aristotle himself in a slightly modified form.[11] This statement is, of course, preserved as the epitome of the lecture, and its particular context has been lost to us. As it stands, it suggests that the good, which in the *Republic* is 'beyond being', is the first principle of all things conceived in terms of the unity of the Pythagorean monad. Realistically, the One of the lecture cannot, without distortion, be identified with the One described in the First Hypothesis of the *Parmenides*; although it does indeed develop in this direction, that does not become fully explicit until Plotinus.

Speusippus and Xenocrates

Although more than three hundred years separate Speusippus, the successor and nephew of Plato from Eudorus of Alexandria, the instigator of the neo-Pythagorean revival, the teaching of the former has much in common with the teaching of Eudorus on the One. We know very little about the nephew of Plato who became head of the Academy in 347 BC. According to Diogenes Laertius, Speusippus adhered faithfully to Plato's teachings, leaving behind more than thirty works before his untimely death in 339.[12] It is generally believed that Speusippus developed Plato's thought

---

[11] *El. Harm.* II, 30-31; see also Alexander of Aphrodisias's account in Simplicius, *In phys.* 454, 24; see *Met.* Bk. N, 1091b.
[12] IV, 1-5.

along Pythagorean lines; Aristotle classes him among the Pythagoreans, though admittedly he does note the differences between Speusippus and the Pythagoreans.[13] Most of the surviving fragments of Speusippus are to be found in Aristotle, preserved chiefly in the *Metaphysics*. His teaching can be outlined briefly as follows. The One, as supreme cause, is separate both from the Good and from Beauty, for these are not themselves causes, but effects of the evolutionary process, that is, they belong to created nature.[14] This is borne out in a fragment preserved by Aetius: 'Speusippus [claimed] that *nous* is not the same as either the One or the Good, but is of similar nature'.[15] Here Speusippus would appear to distinguish the One both from Intellect and from the Good; while he admits that the God who governs the universe can be conceived in terms of *nous*, this cannot be said of the One.[16] This is a startling development which would seem at first glance to diverge from what may have been implicit in the dialogues of Plato and what was explicit in the 'Lecture on the Good'. According to the theory of Speusippus, that which is the cause of any given quality in other things cannot itself possess that quality in the same way.[17] If the One in its simplicity is the cause of both goodness and being in other things, it cannot itself be termed good or existent, in the sense that the One cannot be said to have being in the same sense as created beings.

The One cannot be called good, because good stands at the end of the process of evolution as its perfection and *telos*.[18] According to Aristotle's view, Speusippus did not believe that goodness was present in the first principle, relying on the theory that actuality

---

[13] *Met.* Bk. M, 1080bff and Bk. Λ, 1072b.
[14] L. Tarán argues that according to Aristotle, Speusippus posited the 'one' as principle of mathematical number only, not as a generative principle; see *Speusippus of Athens*, pp. 32-47; all references to the fragments of Speusippus refer to Tarán's edition.
[15] Fr. 58, p. 155; Stobaeus, *Ecl.* I, 1 (2, 29), see Diels, *Doxographi Graeci*, p. 303, 20.
[16] Fr. 28, 13-14, p. 140.
[17] Fr. 42a, pp. 148-9; perhaps Speusippus derived this idea from *Rep.* 509B.
[18] Fr. 42a, p. 148; *Met.* Bk. Λ, 1072bff.

has priority over potentiality, that is, developed plants are superior to seeds. Aristotle himself criticises this notion and maintains that from seeds (causes) come developed plants; this idea is strongly defended in the *Enneads* of Plotinus, where he argues that the seed is superior to the fully grown plant.[19] A. H. Armstrong has noted that for Speusippus to place the idea of the Good further down the hierarchical scale makes a 'curious break in the Platonic tradition',[20] because after Speusippus, the Good of the *Republic* stands at the beginning of the cosmic process, not simply at its end. However, it is difficult to maintain that Speusippus regards the Good as a principle in every way inferior to the One and from the brief fragments we possess, an argument could be constructed to suggest that the One is opposite to the Good. Just as the One is the *archē* of the cosmic process, the Good can be regarded as its *telos*. Some scholars would claim that this One of Speusippus, because it is not the Good, has no moral or religious significance, being simply an ontological principle. J. Dillon, for example, has suggested that Speusippus may have read Plato's Good in a primarily ethical context, as the object of all striving.[21] This could well be the case, for if Speusippus reasoned that goodness is a quality caused by something else, belonging as it does within the ethical sphere, its ontological significance as cause would be severely diminished. I have already demonstrated that Plato did understand the Good primarily in an ethical sense, for there is only one passage in the *Republic* (509B) where the Good assumes an ontological aspect. However, this passage from the *Republic* is singular in its presentation of the Good both as the cause of being and as beyond being; therefore, we cannot claim that Speusippus is totally inaccurate in his reading of Plato. He is, however, at variance with what we understand to be the meaning of the statement referred to from the 'Lecture on the Good'. According to L. Tarán, the fact that Speusippus did not 'hypostatize' universal concepts (numbers and

---

[19] *Enn.* V 3, 8, III 2, 2, III 7, 11 and V 9, 6.
[20] *The Architecture of the Intelligible Universe*, p. 18.
[21] *The Middle Platonists*, p. 12.

magnitudes exist separately as objects of thought), he could not have ascribed goodness or beauty to them in any way.[22] That Speusippus denies any ontological status to the Good does not mean that he is simply wrong in his interpretation. The fact that the One and the Good were understood so early in Platonic development to be two separate principles is not so very different from the later Middle Platonists, who portrayed the supreme divine being, both in terms of *archē* and *telos*, although these are to be understood simply as different aspects of the divine nature. One interesting point of connection between Speusippus and the Neoplatonists, is that the former's hierarchy of reality is quite similar. According to Aristotle, it consists of One, number and soul, a dim reflection of One, *nous* and soul in the *Enneads*.[23]

According to P. Merlan, one particular fragment in Iamblichus's Περὶ τῆς κοινῆς μαθηματικῆς ἐπιστήμης, chapter IV, may be regarded as a source for Speusippus independently of Aristotle.[24] In direct opposition to Aristotle's account, Iamblichus says that the One is non-being, in the sense that it is above being; similarly, the One can be regarded as not-beauty and not-good. The notion of the Speusippean One as presented by Iamblichus, bears a striking resemblance to the later Neoplatonic notion of the One. Here that I think some caution may well be required, for it is entirely possible that Iamblichus understood the One of Speusippus with Plotinian hindsight. According to Merlan, in the Iamblichan account, what Speusippus meant was that the One is removed from being, good, and beauty, precisely because it is the cause of these, not because it is somehow less than them. This is,

---

[22] *Speusippus of Athens*, pp. 41-42.

[23] Fr. 29a, 15-27; *Met.* Bk. Z, 1028b.

[24] *From Platonism to Neoplatonism*, ch. V; while a number of scholars follow Merlan's identification, some strenuously reject it. L. Tarán has reviewed scholarly opinion and concludes that the Iamblichan text cannot be used as a source for the reconstruction of Speusippus's thought, see *op. cit.* p. 86ff. R. Mortley, on the other hand, links the One of Speusippus with the One of the *Parmenides*, and makes a tentative suggestion that Speusippus is the father of negative theology because he placed the One outside of the range of discourse, see *From Word to Silence I*, p. 34.

of course a Plotinian idea, but it also appears in Celsus and in the *Corpus Hermeticum*, where God is denied the appellation *nous*, precisely because he is the cause of *nous*.[25] In this sense, when Speusippus denies the equivalence of One and *nous*, he may be regarded as a direct precursor of Plotinus, that is, if Iamblichus has read him correctly.

What we may interpret from the fragments of Speusippus is that while the One cannot be said to be *hyperousion*, not at least without some word of caution, at the same time it cannot be called either being or good. It would be reading too much into these isolated fragments to suggest that the One here is to be regarded in terms of the negative theology of later Neoplatonism. However, the possibility cannot be excluded totally and the temptation is certainly a strong one; perhaps it may be indulged in just a little, as P. Merlan does.[26] Tentatively, he compares Speusippus's notion of the non-being of the One with Schelling's idea that God is neither good nor evil. He suggests that a further step from asserting the 'One *above being*', which is at the same time, *not good*, could be that the principle of multitude (the Dyad) is not evil, and is, therefore above non-being. While this step would link Speusippus directly to the Pseudo-Dionysius, Eriugena, and Meister Eckhart, among others, it remains an academic indulgence and must be recognized as such.

Although we should not lend uncritical acceptance to Aristotle's testimony, his criticism does indeed put a question mark over the supremacy of the Speusippean One. If beauty and goodness are to be regarded in an authentically Platonic light, then they are signs of the perfection and completion of being. The fact that the One, as Aristotle objects, is inferior and incomplete because it cannot be said to possess these qualities may well be a serious consideration to bear in mind.[27] On the other hand, we must remember that Diogenes noted that Speusippus was a faithful interpreter of Plato; for

---

[25] II, 12-14; see also *Origen Contra Celsum* VII, 45.
[26] *Op. cit.* p. 117.
[27] Fr. 38; *Met.* Bk. N, 1092a.

this reason, and also since we possess no first hand testimony from Speusippus himself, we must keep an open mind on the question. One thing is certain, though: after Speusippus the One seems to have gone 'underground'; the whole period of Platonic development up to the time of Eudorus appears to have been concerned with other matters. While we cannot claim that Speusippus instigated a Pythagorean interpretation of the One in terms of the First Hypothesis of the *Parmenides*, his insistence on the idea that the One, simply as one, cannot be termed either being or good, has stronger resonances with many later thinkers, such as Plotinus, than with any of his own more immediate successors. His reasoning may have been different from that of Plotinus, but his conception of the One, which cannot be regarded as possessing any attribute, was developed by many, and Plotinus is certainly its greatest exponent in Hellenistic times.

Although Xenocrates (396-314 BC), the immediate successor of Speusippus, has little to contribute to the development of the idea of the transcendent One, I mention his main ideas here because he stands at the beginning of a long tradition, which, with very few interruptions, lasted right down to the time of Plotinus. Although Diogenes Laertius gives a long list of the works of Xenocrates, he tells us nothing of his philosophy during the twenty-five years he was head of the Academy.[28] According to Aristotle, the basic metaphysical division of Xenocrates is similar to that of Speusippus: the monad and the dyad are gods, and from these two principles proceed numbers/ideas, soul, and physical bodies.[29] The theology of Xenocrates has a slightly different perspective from that of Plato, for 'the first god', the monad, is identified with Zeus, the Father who rules the heavenly kingdom, and it is he who is called *nous*. The dyad, on the other hand, represents the female figure, the mother of the gods, ruler of the sub-heavenly kingdom, and the soul of all things.[30] The identification of the supreme God

---

[28] See IV, 2.
[29] *Met*. Bk. Z, 1028b.
[30] H. Diels, *Doxographi Graeci*, p. 304, 30.

with *nous* is one which lasted right through the Middle Platonic period, and may well have received its initial impetus from Xenocrates, who was perhaps influenced by Aristotle's self-contemplating divine Mind.[31] The demonology of Xenocrates is based on the deities of the Olympian pantheon, and the gods are used – in an almost pre-Stoic manner – to name the various divine elements in the material universe. Indeed as Aetius noted, many of Xenocrates's ideas were passed to the Stoics.[32] In Xenocrates, the supreme God is not a 'one' in the Speusippean sense, nor is this God transcendent: he is understood simply as existing within the heavenly region and in this way passed over into Stoic theology as the power immanent within the universe. Xenocrates, therefore, had much to offer the Stoics and indeed the Platonists, and it is to the former that we must attribute the change of direction within the Academy towards a more Stoic kind of Platonism.

The Neo-Pythagorean Revival

I turn now to an examination of the revival of Pythagoreanism in the first century BC, for it is here that we find the One once more, superior to the *nous* which had functioned within the Academy as supreme God for almost three centuries; indeed it was to continue to do so, after Moderatus and up to Plotinus. The exact delineation of the shape taken by the neo-Pythagorean revival is quite a complex affair, despite the many difficulties which have been resolved by modern scholars.

The main thrust of the Pythagorean revival was the claim that Plato himself was dependent on Pythagoras; it was this Platonization of Pythagoras which resulted in the rich stream of ideas which can be said to have culminated in the speculations of Numenius of Apamea, reputedly the greatest thinker of the neo-Pythagorean

---

[31] Although it is not explicit here, presumably the divine mind thinks the ideas, a notion that had become well established by the time of Xenocrates; see A. M. Rich, 'The Platonic Ideas as the Thoughts of God'.

[32] H. Diels, *op. cit.* p. 304, 30.

school. The characteristic themes of the revival of Pythagoreanism can be outlined as follows. It was a monistic system involving the belief in a transcendent God, a God above being; it was totally different from, and indeed very likely, a reaction against Stoic monism. However, most neo-Pythagoreans would not have gone so far as Speusippus in positing the absolute bare unity of the One, and for them the conclusion of the 'Lecture on the Good' represented an important idea. The goal of human nature was understood, in true Platonic fashion, to attain likeness to God; this in itself was sufficient to uphold the supremacy of the Platonic ideal over against that of the Stoics.[33]

The metaphysical system of the Pythagorean revival was deceptively simple. In most cases it involved the two principles, Monad and Dyad (although some variants simply had a One[34]). According to the oldest authority for neo-Pythagorean ideas, Alexander Polyhistor (who taught in Rome around 70 BC), the *archē*, the principle of all things, was the monad;[35] from it the indefinite dyad arose, and together they were the cause of all reality. The monad, therefore, has ontological superiority over the dyad, and appears to function twice as cause in Alexander's account: first as prime cause and then jointly with the dyad. In an account given of Brotinus, the One is identified with the Good: 'τὸ ἀγαθόν αὐτὸ τὸ ἕν ἐστι', and is superior to *nous*.[36] Syrianus later attributes theories of this kind to 'Brotinus', 'Archaenetus', and 'Philolaus', and says that Brotinus, who taught similar doctrines to those of Archytas (of the Old Pythagorean school), thought that there existed a third principle above both the monad and the dyad, one which was superior to *nous* in both power and superiority.[37] This explicit identification of the One superior to *nous* with the good of the *Republic* shows how the early neo-Pythagoreans received their initial inspiration for the elevation of the One, as supreme God, above being. It was the tran-

---

[33] *Theaetetus* 176B.

[34] See Sextus Empiricus, *Adv. phys.* II, 281-282.

[35] See Diogenes, VIII, 24-25.

[36] See H. Thesleff, *The Pythagorean Texts of the Hellenistic Period*, p. 56 and also J. Whittaker, ' 'ΕΠΕΚΕΙΝΑ ΝΟΥ ΚΑΙ ΟΥΣΙΑΣ.'

[37] Syrianus, *In met.* VI, 1.

scendence attributed to the neo-Pythagorean One which had extremely important consequences for the development of the Plotinian One. Yet, while the One of Plotinus is the supreme transcendent reality in a complex metaphysical system, the Pythagorean One, at this relatively early stage of its development, still retains a certain 'mathematical' character which Plotinus later criticizes.[38]

Eudorus and Moderatus

In the account given of Eudorus (fl. c. 25 BC), we find an interesting development of Platonic ideas in the light of the influence of Pythagoreanism. His philosophy (like that of the Stoics) is divided into three main areas of consideration: ethics, physics, and logic. The main account of the metaphysical teaching of Eudorus is preserved by Simplicius.[39] The One is the first principle of all things, the *archē*: it is the God above everything, the One, from whom comes both the monad (form) and the dyad (matter). Eudorus himself says that this is Pythagorean teaching, although the Pythagoreans themselves did not posit a third supreme principle; nor does the account given of the school by Alexander Polyhistor. According to J. Rist, Eudorus, in positing a One above the monad, must have misunderstood his Pythagorean source, but J. Whittaker disagrees, on the ground that this kind of speculation could be brought into line with the first three hypotheses of the *Parmenides*.[40] It is difficult to say with any certainty which is the correct interpretation, but it is more than probable that Eudorus misunderstood his source. Unless we can find this kind of idea in an earlier source, the discussion is bound to remain inconclusive. It is not unlikely that someone before Eudorus did in fact differentiate between the One and monad, but since we have no evidence of that, this too must remain an open question. On the other hand, Eudorus may well have been attempting to give his own interpre-

---

[38] *Enn.* VI 9, 5.
[39] *In phys.* A. 5, H. Diels, p. 181, 10-30.
[40] 'The Neoplatonic One', p. 391 and ''ΕΠΕΚΕΙΝΑ', p. 98.

tation of metaphysical reality with 'Archytas' the Old Pythagorean as his source.[41] Thus it requires only a little modification for Moderatus of Gades to present his own unique system, exemplifying an analogous feature, one which may have been a strong influence on Plotinus almost two hundred years later.

Moderatus can be dated simply to the second half of the first century AD, and his works include eleven books of Πυθαγορικαι σχολαι.[42] He too was concerned to present Plato as a Pythagorean, and he attempted to show how Pythagorean number theory was adapted by Plato in order to explicate his own metaphysical doctrines. In one particular passage, Simplicius (by whom Moderatus's teaching is preserved), refers to the account given by Porphyry in the Περι ὕλῆς.[43] Here, Moderatus argues that the interpretation of the structure of reality he gives goes back to Plato and the Pythagoreans, with the result that the *Parmenides* can now be read according to Pythagorean principles. According to Moderatus, there are three 'Ones', not simply the two of Eudorus: the One above being, the One at the level of the ideas, and the One at the level of soul. Although the first three hypotheses of the *Parmenides* are indeed the likely source for this elaboration, J. Rist has also noted the similarity with Plato's Second Letter.[44] He concludes that Moderatus was the first to have interpreted the *Parmenides* along Pythagorean lines, thus giving a substantial foreshadowing of the Neoplatonic structure of reality, although E. R. Dodds sees the two Ones of Eudorus as the immediate influence on Moderatus.[45] However, although we do not possess any evidence for a Pythagorean interpretation of the *Parmenides* before Moderatus, he himself says it has authority, although he does not name his source. We must also note that the metaphysical interpretation of the *Parmenides* was not taken up by the other Middle Platonists, who agreed generally in regarding the

---

[41] Stobaeus, *Ecl.* I, 41; see Thesleff, pp. 19-20.
[42] See C. J. De Vogel, *Greek Philosophy*, vol. 3, p. 348 (1285).
[43] *Ibid.* p. 350 (1285b).
[44] *Ep.* II, 321D-313A; interestingly, J. Rist suggests that this letter may have been a neo-Pythagorean forgery; see 'Neopythagoreanism and Plato's Second Letter'.
[45] 'The *Parmenides* of Plato', p. 140.

Parmenides as an exercise in logic. In Plotinus, however, the dependence upon the *Parmenides* is explicit, and it is quite likely that the great Neoplatonist had Moderatus in mind when formulating the various grades of reality. However, a word of caution seems opportune at this point, for such a triadic development, with its obvious implications for Plotinus, could well be an anachronistic reading of Moderatus by Porphyry. Some modern scholars argue that the genuine voice of Moderatus is to be heard here, although I can see no conclusive argument against Porphyry having put the words into the mouth of Moderatus. The possibility remains, nevertheless, that Moderatus may have been the first to suggest the ontological interpretation of the *Parmenides*, although I am inclined to suspect that the report given by Porphyry may have been drawn too close to a Plotinian interpretation. It is not unlikely that Porphyry was seeking a basis for his own theories in the Greek tradition before him, thereby adding the weight of tradition to the philosophical developments of his time.

While I am certain that both Eudorus and Moderatus contributed greatly to the Neoplatonic conception of reality and the hierarchical grades of being, their ideas remain undeveloped, although this may well be due to the fact that we possess only fragments of their writings. After Moderatus, the One conceived as above being seems to disappear with very few exceptions, and up to Plotinus it was for all intents and purposes ignored. What the neo-Pythagorean revival achieved was, above all, the final dethronement of the two principles of Stoicism, for God as the good, was understood by the neo-Pythagoreans and the Platonic philosophers after them, as a transcendent principle not associated with created being, as the negative terms employed by Alcinous, Celsus, Apuleius, and others amply demonstrate. The shackles of Scepticism were finally thrown off, and the Academy turned its attention to more theological enquiries. Although it was indeed the neo-Pythagoreans who came closest to the Neoplatonic idea of the One, their influence can be felt throughout the first and second centuries in the more 'orthodox' school of Platonic thought.

CHAPTER THREE

MIDDLE PLATONISM AND THE
CORPUS HERMETICUM

In seeking for the roots of the Plotinian idea of the One in the Platonism of the first and second centuries, we must look for a supreme principle beyond both *ousia* and *nous*. As we shall see, in general, the Middle Platonists were quite confused regarding the status of *ousia* and *nous*; with very few exceptions, God is understood on the level of *ousia* as the supreme *nous* (the second hypostasis in the Plotinian triad). The identification of the supreme reality, *to on*, with *nous* and *theos* is the most important general characteristic of second-century Platonism. Only rarely do we find *theos* referred to as *to hen*, and even then it is not regarded as *hyperousios*. The Platonic notion of the forms as true being, would have made it almost unthinkable for a Platonist before Plotinus to have posited a reality above being, for then it would have been beyond the reach of intellect. The identification of *theos* with *nous* has a dual source. On the one hand it bears traces of the Stoic doctrine of the divine all-pervading *logos*, and on the other, it contains elements of Aristotle's *nous*, as self-contemplating thought: Aristotle's conception of the Unmoved Mover became formative in this respect, especially in relation to Alcinous's conception of God. The use of many Aristotelian doctrines in the second century of the Middle Platonic period is indicative, not so much of attempts to reconcile the two and thereby patch up the old quarrel between the Academy and the Lyceum, but reflects a reading of Aristotle as a true Platonist and revered member of the Academy. Of course the primacy of Plato is always affirmed and, with the exception of a few scholars like Atticus, who were opposed to Aristotle, generally a healthy respect for the latter is maintained.

In this period of tremendous theological development, then, Plato assumes supremacy (rivalled only by Pythagoras and even then not in most quarters), and certain Platonic doctrines became more and more the basis of a way of life. Yet it must be remembered that although Plato is regarded as 'the Philosopher', the Middle Platonists were eclectic, and their systems, whether philosophical or theological, tended very much towards a syncretism which was by no means always deliberate.

Before moving on to a discussion of some second-century thinkers, I would like to mention the question of 'orientalism' which has arisen regarding various doctrines of the Neoplatonists. E. Norden's thesis, which reflected the ideas of the earliest historians of Neoplatonism, was that Neoplatonic thought had appropriated some radically oriental ideas.[1] In Norden's view, this oriental influence is exemplified by the idea of an unknowable God, a notion which he did not think to be familiar to pure Greek thought. This thesis would appear to have withstood the assaults of both A.-J. Festugière and J. Whittaker, for H.-Ch. Puech and E. R. Dodds would still have gone some way towards defending the idea that there were oriental themes present in the development of Hellenistic thought. Festugière and Whittaker, on the other hand, have argued that the diverse theological developments of the first two centuries AD, do not depend on Egyptian or other oriental sources. With reference to the theme I am tracing, the argument for an oriental influence rests largely on the Middle Platonic conception of the supreme divine being. It will become clear as this discussion progresses that the majority of the Platonists of the second century AD did not regard the supreme God as unknowable, but simply difficult to know; in this respect they were faithful to the original Platonic text from *Timaeus* 28C; although admittedly in Celsus and in Numenius, both of them professed Platonists, we do indeed come across references to God as unknowable (according to Numenius it is the demiurge who is knowable), although in the case of Numenius especially, it is

---

[1] See *Agnostos Theos*, p. 97ff.

impossible to exclude some Gnostic element or an influence of Hellenistic Judaism.

It was largely the theological development of this text from the *Timaeus* in conjunction with renewed metaphysical speculation which gave rise to the idea of an almost unknowable divinity in Greek thought before Plotinus; in this sense it is not such a great step to the unknowable One of the *Enneads*. Cicero, for example, in his paraphrase of the text in question, omitted the phrase 'to all men', thus removing the deity to even more remote, ineffable and unproclaimable heights.[2] My aim, therefore, in this chapter and in the next chapter, will be to show how the distance between Plato and Plotinus can be bridged by developments within the Greek tradition itself; that includes all that the Platonists took from Aristotle, the Stoics, and the Pythagoreans. Throughout this discussion we will also have occasion to observe the development of various metaphysical and theological triads which dimly prefigure the Plotinian triad of *hen*, *nous*, and *psychē*.[3] In the Middle Platonic period these triads were based for the most part on the most common one of all: *theos*, *nous*, and *hylē*, although admittedly we see some variations on this as each individual author develops his own schema of theological reality.

The great Neoplatonic theme of *proodos* and *epistrophē* is not present in Middle Platonic thought, not at least, in cosmic terms. God, understood as *telos*, is an important part of theological speculation, but it is not until the time of Plotinus that *telos*, understood in terms of the Platonic *homoiōsis theō*, is floated free from its ethical and psychological bindings to assume a truly cosmic dimension of meaning. The different 'ways' recommended by the Middle Platonists in order to attain to what they variously called

---

[2] *De natura deorum*, I; see also J. Whittaker, 'Plutarch, Platonism and Christianity', p. 51.

[3] A good account of the development of the Neoplatonic triad can be found in H. Dörrie, 'Zum Ursprung der Neuplatonischen Hypostasenlehre', in *Platonica Minora*, pp. 286-296; see also S. Gersh, *Middle Platonism and Neoplatonism. The Latin Tradition*, vol. I.

theos, nous, agathon, or *to on,* must also be discussed. These ways are envisaged primarily as taking effect through *nous,* since the supreme God as *nous,* cannot be totally inaccessible to the human intellect. By the time of Alcinous, we shall see these ways become systematized as the way of abstraction, the way of analogy and the way of synthesis.

However, although I am concerned here with tracing the development of the idea of the One before it appears in Plotinus, I wish to reaffirm the genius of Plotinus. In seeking the sources of his One, we do not reduce him to a sort of superior plagiarist, albeit one of immense native genius; on the contrary, we strengthen the thesis that Plotinian teaching, especially regarding the One and the related negative theology, is based on Greek rather than on oriental sources. In the attempt to dissociate the period of Middle Platonic development from supposed oriental influences, one runs the risk of distorting pre-Plotinian philosophy by reading too much into the all too few fragments we possess. Not everything which appears in Plotinus was already there before him, not even in embryonic form; we must allow his originality its due creative space.

I begin this discussion of second-century philosophical thought with a synoptic examination of some of the relevant texts in four figures of the second century: Plutarch, Apuleius, Maximus of Tyre and Celsus. While their individual philosophies do not contribute greatly to the development of the idea of a transcendent One, together they help to build up a picture of a more religious type of philosophy, which itself points towards the positing of a One, a spiritual absolute which differs from that of which it is the ground.[4] I continue with a brief look at some texts from the *Corpus Hermeticum* and conclude with a more detailed discussion of themes relevant to transcendence and negative theology in Alcinous, Basilides and Numenius in chapter four below.

---

[4] See A. H. Armstrong, *The Architecture of the Intelligible Universe,* p. 5.

Plutarch and Apuleius

Plutarch (AD 45-125) is not generally regarded as a fully 'orthodox' Platonist, and certainly not as an original thinker, being perhaps better known for his work on comparative religion; yet he is important in that he represents a small part of the foundation upon which the One of Neoplatonism was to be built. J. Dillon's book gives an excellent summary of his achievement, which is not necessary to repeat here.[5] Like Eudorus and Moderatus, Plutarch relied on the Pythagorean principles of monad and dyad as the basis for his account of reality, although he did not posit a principle above these as Eudorus had done. It is the use of these familiar Pythagorean principles, together with a strong reliance on a theologically-interpreted Plato, which provides the link between the Stoicism of the Middle Academy and the second-century Platonists. While much of Plutarch's writing is not important for the purposes of my theme, there are a few points which deserve mention.

The first of these concerns *Timaeus* 28C. In his Πλατωνικὰ ζητήματα, Plutarch asks why Plato had described God as both *pater* and *poietes*.[6] His bent towards Stoicism prompted him to suggest that this was because Plato was referring to one supreme God having two different functions (we will later see how Numenius interprets this passage from the *Timaeus* as the basis for his theory of two different gods). According to Plutarch, God may be called 'Maker' because he has created the universe, and in this capacity he is transcendent. He is given the name 'Father', because he has endowed the soul with rational life. J. Whittaker regards Plutarch's interpretation of this text as an attempt to reconcile the 'pantheism' of Stoicism with the transcendence of Platonism, and while Whittaker hesitates to confer upon Plutarch the title of originator in relation to this idea, he believes that it is

[5] *The Middle Platonists*, pp. 184-230.
[6] 1000E-1001C; for a detailed analysis of this text see J. Whittaker, 'Plutarch, Platonism and Christianity', in *Studies in Platonism and Patristic Thought*, pp. 51-52.

unlikely to have appeared before him. In any case, if it did it is no longer extant, so that Plutarch may take the credit, until otherwise proven.

In *De E apud Delphos* (which provides an account of the speech of Ammonius on the meaning of the letter 'E' at the Temple of Apollo), God is described as the only true One: ' but being must be one, just as one is being'.[7] Here we have an identification of God with both *to hen* and *to on*, an idea which had already appeared in Philo of Alexandria and which again appears in Numenius. This One, says Plutarch, is the same principle which the Pythagoreans had called Apollo (*a-polla*), because the simplicity of the name implies the denial of plurality.[8] (This etymology also occurs in Philo, Clement, Numenius, Plotinus and Porphyry.[9]) In Plutarch, the identification of God with *to on* and *to hen*, implies that Platonic reality (i.e., that which truly is), is equated with the Delphic deity,[10] and throughout this text, the deity is referred to in both masculine and neuter forms (as both personal God and impersonal principle).

Also in *De E apud Delphos*, Plutarch equates this highest principle with *to agathon* and while this is not original (it derives from the 'Lecture on the Good'), it is significant because it appears again only in Alcinous and Numenius.[11] *De E*, therefore, reflects a very Platonic interpretation of Pythagorean teaching, and it remains on the whole faithful to both Pythagoras and to Plato. There is, however, one point of interest which does not derive from either Platonic or Pythagorean teachings. Plutarch has Ammonius say that apart from the supreme God there is another God (or demon), who is concerned with the sublunary region.[12]

---

[7] *De E.* 393B; see J. Whittaker, 'Amonius on The Delphic E', in *Studies in Platonism,* p. 185.

[8] *De E.* 388F and 393B-C; see also *De Iside.* 381F and 453ff; R. Mortley has remarked that Apollo can be regarded as the patron saint of the *via negativa* because of the morphology of his name; see *From Word to Silence I*, p. 156.

[9] For the list of references see J. Whittaker's article on the 'Delphic E'.

[10] J. Whittaker, 'Plutarch, Platonism and Christianity', p. 54.

[11] See 372E.

[12] For further comment see J. Dillon, *op. cit.* p. 191.

This theme is present in Philo and the Gnostics, and indeed in some measure in Numenius. Leaving aside for the moment its possible Persian origins, in Plutarch's thought it may be regarded as a device to further emphasize the transcendent aspect of the nature of the supreme God, and it may also have been intended to keep the supreme God apart from the evil in the world. Be that as it may, it is not a very developed idea in Plutarch, and does not form an important part of his theological metaphysics.[13] I mention this text because its development in Numenius (from *Timaeus* 28C) leads to a further refinement in Platonism, one which will be addressed in the chapter on Plotinus below.

Although Plutarch posits a transcendent God, his metaphysical theory is neither detailed or convincing, and his role as a Hellenistic ecumenist is undoubtedly more notable than his role as a philosopher or theologian. The Pythagorean revival which began in the first century BC, is certainly an influence present in Plutarch's thought, but beside the greatest Middle Platonic Pythagorean, Numenius, Plutarch's transcendent theology of the one God pales into insignificance.[14] Nonetheless, Plutarch's midway position between Stoicism and Pythagorean Platonism, represents a significant step towards the development of a divine transcendent One.

Apuleius (b. c. AD 123), represents, like Alcinous, a typical Middle Platonic synthesis of Platonic, Aristotelian, and Stoic ideas; he represents Pythagoreanism only to a much lesser extent. He is perhaps most famous for his literary work, *The Golden Ass* (*Metamorphoses*), but his philosophical works include, *De deo Socratis*, *De mundo* (a translation of the pseudo-Aristotelian work of that name) and *De Platone et eius dogmate*. Apuleius was an initiate of the Mysteries of Isis, and he presents a more theological interpretation of Plato than does Alcinous. I mention briefly three interesting passages in the writings of

[13] See 392E-394C.
[14] See E. R. Dodds, 'The *Parmenides* of Plato', p. 142.

Apuleius which illustrate his particular development of theological Platonism.[15]

In Book I of *De Platone*, God is described as *incorporeus, unus, aperimetros*; he is Father and creator of all: *genitor rerumque omnium exstructor*, and he is the most perfect because he is *beatus, beatificus, optimus, nihil indigens*, and *ipse conferens cuncta*.[16] This lavish list of positive assertions points to the supreme transcendent God, as he is in himself, while the negatives which follow can be understood to refer to the human understanding of him. He who is called heavenly, is *indictus, innominabilis, aoratos* and *adamastos*. It is, says Apuleius, very difficult to discover anything about God; and even if he is discovered, it is impossible to tell of this knowledge to everyone: 'cujus naturam invenire difficile est; si inventa sit, in multos eam enuntiari non posse'.[17] This paraphrase of *Timaeus* 28C shows how far this Platonic text had become traditional school doctrine by the second century.

In a passage from the *De deo Socratis* (a treatise on demonology), Apuleius follows the format of *De Platone*, and describes God as ruler and author of all things: 'quorum parentem, qui omnium rerum dominator atque auctor est'.[18] He is in no way connected with or subjected to anything in the created world: 'solutum ab omnibus nexibus patiendi aliquid gerendive'. In himself, God does not change and he is in no way bound to the world; once again Apuleius paraphrases *Timaeus* 28C, although this time he notes that it is not possible to tell everyone in such a way that they would understand: 'non posse penuria sermonis humani, quavis oratione vel modice comprehendi'.[19]

---

[15] My attention was drawn to these texts in Apuleius by A.-J. Festugière, *Le Dieu inconnu et la gnose*, pp. 102-109; a more extensive treatment of the philosophical/theological importance of Apuleius can be found in S. Gersh, *Middle Platonism and Neoplatonism. The Latin Tradition*, vol. I, pp. 227-328. See also H. Dörrie, 'Die Frage nach dem Transzendentem im Mittleplatonismus', in *Platonica Minora*, p. 206.

[16] I, 5 (190); Festugière suggests that Apuleius may have coined the word *beatificus* himself, see *Le Dieu inconnu*, p. 107.

[17] *De Platone*, I, 5 (190-191).

[18] III (123-124).

[19] S. Gersh, *op. cit.* notes other terms used by Apuleius, see p. 270.

The third passage comes from the *Apologia*, where Apuleius outlines a list of negative attributes: although God is a paternal creator, nevertheless, he has no place (*neque loco*), no time (*neque tempore*); he is not implicated in any change (*neque vice ulla comprehensus*); he is able to be thought only by a few (*paucis cogitabilis*), and is to no one effable (*nemini effabilis*).[20] Here, then, we have a fairly complete picture of the God of Apuleius: while God is ineffable, he can be understood at least dimly, just as the Good from the *Republic* could be grasped or intuited. The transcendence of the supreme God does not pose a problem for Apuleius (it had not done for Plutarch either), for between the remote first God and the mortal realm, there exists a whole world of demons, drawn largely from the demonology of Xenocrates. (Two centuries later, Augustine will choose Apuleius to illustrate the views of the Platonists on demonology, which Augustine himself noted was related in some way to the transcendent remoteness of God.[21])

Apuleius's silence on a method by which the difficult task of attaining to any knowledge of God, may have prompted Augustine to comment on Apuleius's mention of the perception of God in terms of a light flashing in the darkness: the sage can attain to an apprehension of God, as in Plato's Seventh Letter, through a 'sudden illumination' in the darkness.[22] Whether this notion was bound up with Apuleius's association with the Mysteries is not certain.[23] I have one final remark concerning the particular use of *Timaeus* 28C in these passages from Apuleius and that concerns the notion that he was a devotee of the Mysteries of Isis. It may be that his insistence on the idea that knowledge of God is very difficult to obtain was prompted, not simply by the desire to safeguard God's transcendence, but also by the fact that the majority of

---

[20] *Apologia* 64.
[21] *De civ. Dei.* VIII, 14-22 and IX, 8-17; in choosing Apuleius, Augustine must have felt some affinity with his fellow country-man, having followed his path to Carthage and to Rome.
[22] *De Deo Soc.* III (124); *De civ. Dei.* IX, 16.
[23] See *De Platone*, II (20-22).

people are not equipped with the special powers which enable them to come to a correct understanding of God. Knowledge of God, in this instance, can be regarded as the preserve of the chosen few – the initiates. For instance, at the end of the *Apologia* passage cited (his trial speech to Aemilianus, who asks him about the nature of the God he worships) Apuleius refuses to describe the God he calls 'King': 'non respondeo tibi, Aemiliane, quem colam βασιλέα ... quid sit deus meus, taceo'.[24] While this refusal may well have been prompted by the reverence Apuleius had for the transcendent God, it can also be interpreted as a refusal to divulge any secrets to the uninitiated. This idea recurs in the negative theology of the later Neoplatonists, whereby it entered the Christian tradition through Proclus and the Pseudo-Dionysius, although in a slightly altered fashion. Whatever the original intentions of Apuleius, it can be said that he was instrumental in assuring the continued use of *Timaeus* 28C within the school of 'orthodox' Platonism, a use which continued right down to Numenius, who developed it in his own particular way.

Maximus of Tyre and Celsus

Maximus of Tyre (fl. AD 152) is another interesting figure of second-century Platonism, and although he was more a sophist than a philosopher, I have chosen to include him in this chapter as representative of a more 'popular' kind of Platonism. One Oration of his may be taken as representative of his theology, τίς θεὸς κατὰ Πλάτωνα;[25] Here Maximus extols one unique, supreme God, both King and Father and also many subordinate gods, his children, who reign jointly with him.[26] The supreme God has no image, and it is very difficult to come to any knowledge of him who is to be placed in the intelligible realm, which is much less

---

[24] *Apologia* 65.
[25] *Philosophumena*, no. XI (Dübner, XVII).
[26] XI, 5, p. 132.

easily known than the sensible realm.[27] God, then, in typical Middle Platonic fashion, is placed in the rank of those things which are most intelligible as the supreme first cause, precisely because he is that which is most stable and permanent, far removed from the world of flux and change. He is the most perfect *nous*, says Maximus, the *nous* which thinks everything together always.[28] Here we have a more solid identification of the supreme demiurge of Plato with the Aristotelian *nous*.

Again, in typically Middle Platonic fashion, Maximus says that for Plato this God is not nameable, because he is nothing sensible and cannot be reached through anything in the sensible world.[29] He is invisible to the eye, ineffable of speech, untouched by the body, and unknown to the ear. Interestingly, Maximus notes that God is not to be understood as beauty itself, but as the cause of beauty, an idea which will be developed much further by Plotinus as part of the aphairetic approach to transcendent reality.[30] God is, therefore, invisible, ineffable, intangible and unnameable. He cannot be comprehended except by that in the soul which is most beautiful, pure, intelligent, rapid, and noble.[31] This comprehension is possible because of the similarity that exists between the human intellect and God who is perfect intellect.

At XI 10, Maximus outlines the way to an understanding of the nature of God. This way, like the way advocated by Plotinus, consists in a removal of oneself from all material things perceived by the senses. Once this has been achieved, one can begin to rise towards the heavenly region, but the journey does not end there, or indeed with the celestial bodies, but continues towards that place beyond, the place of truth where peace reigns, 'ὑπερκύψαι τοῦ οὐρανοῦ'.[32] This journey from sensible things is clarified further

---

[27] XI, 6 and 8.
[28] XI, 8; see also Festugière, *Le Dieu inconnu et la gnose*, p. 113, where the similarities with Aristotle's νόησις νοήσεως are examined.
[29] XI, 9.
[30] XI, 10.
[31] XI, 9.
[32] XI, 10.

at XI 11, where Maximus says that in order to arrive at an understanding of him who has no size, nor colour, nor shape, nor anything of matter in his nature, we must put all sensible things away, in the same way that we unclothe a loved object in order to contemplate it in its very being.[33]

Here we have, in brief, an embryonic account of two of the three traditional ways to God: *aphairesis*, the way of abstraction, and the *via eminentiae*, the way from *nous* to the highest *nous*. In this Oration of Maximus, we are presented with a good example of the degree to which Platonic thought had filtered into more popular religious teaching in the second century. Maximus can be said to represent a non-philosophical stream of thought that claims both filiation and discipleship of Plato.

Celsus (fl. AD 160) is probably most famous for his anti-Christian and anti-Gnostic ideas (for him there seemed to be no distinction between the two). We know very little about him and there has been some confusion regarding another Celsus, who was an Epicurean (Origen, for example, understands his Celsus to have been an Epicurean[34]). Celsus may well have been an Alexandrian, and his philosophy, contrary to Origen's belief, was an eclectic type of Platonism. Further difficulties arise in dealing with Celsus because the text of his work, Ἀληθὴς λόγος, has to be reconstructed from Origen's famous diatribe against him, *Contra Celsum*. While we have quite a large portion of his text preserved, we must remember that it has been preserved by an unyielding opponent and one who may not have been inclined to read Celsus at all times with objectivity.

In agreement with the by now familiar Platonic teaching, Celsus believed in a transcendent God, who did not resemble created nature and who had nothing in common with it: God did not make human nature in his image.[35] God has no shape nor colour, and admits of no movement or change; Origen agrees with him on this

---

[33] XI, 11.
[34] *Contra Celsum*, I, 8.
[35] *C.C.* VI, 63 (16-17).

point. Although Celsus acknowledges that all things are derived from God, he himself derives from nothing and he does not even participate in being: 'ἀλλ ' οὐδ ' οὐσίας μετέχει ὁ θεός'.[36] This last statement is, no doubt, derived from *Republic* 509B, and Origen himself makes a direct reference to that text in the commentary which follows. Here, then, apart from that instance in Moderatus, we have the first explicit reference to Plato's famous statement that the Good is, ἐπέκεινα τῆς οὐσίας.

According to Celsus, the God who is beyond being, is ineffable; he has no name and he is not attainable by reason: 'οὐδὲ λόγῳ ἐφικτός ἐστιν ὁ θεός'.[37] In other words, the supreme God, the highest Good, who is thought of in Platonic terms as beyond being, cannot be expressed in human language, or thought, rather, following *Epistle* VII, knowledge of him comes 'suddenly' in the soul like a leaping spark.[38] This emphasis on the ineffable way of knowledge further heightens the fact that, for Celsus, knowledge of God is supra-intellectual, and indeed it must be so, for God is not analogous to anything in human experience. Origen then reports the interlocutor of Celsus as asking how human nature is to reach God and learn the way to him.[39] Origen himself voices his utter contempt for such a question; while he admits that even for the Christian, God is hard to comprehend, nonetheless, he attacks Celsus for his anti-incarnational polemic. It is obvious that Celsus thought the Christians had answered the question of knowledge of God by affirming the reality of the incarnation, and indeed this is partially true.[40]

Origen returns to the question of knowledge of God in Book VII, referring to the reliance of Celsus on *Timaeus* 28C.[41] It would seem that Celsus believed that Plato himself thought that not all

---

[36] *C.C.* VI, 64 (24).
[37] *C.C.* VI, 65 (24-25).
[38] *C.C.* VI, 4; *Ep.* VII, 341C.
[39] *C.C.* VI, 66 (9-11).
[40] I discuss the significance of the incarnation for Christian negative theology in ch. 8 below.
[41] *C.C.* VII, 42.

people could come to the knowledge of God, but the sage only (we have already seen a hint of this in Apuleius). There are three ways to God according to the sage: by synthesis, analysis, and analogy (by the time of Celsus it is fair to say that these three ways had become common school doctrine[42]). For Celsus, the way of synthesis may be equated with the *via eminentiae* and analysis with the method of abstraction or negation; the way of analogy explains itself.[43] As we have seen in Apuleius and Maximus, the traditional way progressed through *nous*; in Celsus, we find a break with tradition, for God is described as neither mind nor intelligence but the cause of their existence.[44] In order to support his argument, Celsus uses the familiar Platonic analogy from the *Republic*: just as the sun is to visible things (the cause of vision in the eye), so God is the cause of intelligible things, and he is not, therefore mind or knowledge.[45] Here Celsus comes very close to a Plotinian point of view: God is neither *ousia* nor *nous*, but beyond both. This perspective of Celsus is something quite new in Platonic thought and it is because God is neither mind nor being, that he is intelligible only by an ineffable power:

> He is neither mind nor intelligence nor knowledge, but enables the mind to think, and is the cause of the existence of intelligence and of the possibility of knowledge, and causes the existence of all intelligible things and of truth itself and of being itself, since he transcends all things and is intelligible by a certain indescribable power.[46]

Although Celsus calls this an ineffable way, it is very similar to the way outlined by Maximus, and it anticipates an idea which was to assume particular prominence in the *Enneads*. 'If you shut your eyes to the world of sense and look up with the mind, if you turn away from the flesh and raise the eyes of the soul, only so will you see God.'[47] According to Celsus, then, the supreme God

---

[42] See Alcinous, *Didaskalikos*, X, 5-6.

[43] VII, 42 (29-35).

[44] *C.C.* VII, 45.

[45] *Rep.* 508Bff.

[46] *C.C.* VII, 45 (28-32), trans. H. Chadwick, *Origen. Contra Celsum*, p. 433.

[47] *C.C.* VII, 36 and 39; trans. Chadwick, p. 423.

is both an epistemological and an ontological ground, completely different from that of which he is the ground. This is the idea we have been searching for in pre-Plotinian thought: a God who transcends both *ousia* and *nous*.

I wish to make one final comment here, and that concerns the mention of darkness by Celsus.[48] After the long list of negations mentioned above, the interlocutor complains that he is in darkness and his eyes cannot see distinctly. Celsus replies, in true Platonic fashion, that when people have been led from darkness into light they imagine that their sight has been impaired: if the knowledge of God comes suddenly, then the strong light of understanding will blind. This theme of 'divine darkness' has been associated traditionally with the *via negativa* of Christian theology and its greatest exponent is most certainly the Pseudo-Dionysius; yet we find here the hint of a Platonic negative theology which asserts that God is thought of as darkness only because his light is blinding, a theme remarkably similar to that developed by the Areopagite almost three centuries later. However, without the full text of *The True Account* we cannot but conjecture about the place and function of the theme of darkness in Celsus; it will suffice, at this point, to remark upon its importance as a link between the application of *Epistle* VII and the release from the cave. Thus, it is Plato himself who provides the foundation for an idea which was to assume tremendous importance in the development of the way of negation in the apophatic philosophical tradition. And yet, this dim hint of the idea of 'divine darkness' which so often accompanies the negative way, points to its development in the Christian philosophers Gregory of Nyssa and the Pseudo-Dionysius, rather than to Plotinus and the later Neoplatonists, who rely chiefly upon the more familiar Platonic concepts of light and vision.

In conclusion, what we have gleaned from this brief examination of some of the Platonists of the Academy, is a clear picture of a supremely transcendent God, who is incorporeal, invisible, immobile, ineffable, unnameable, and difficult to know. Celsus

---

[48] *C.C.* VI, 36.

would appear to have been singular among the Middle Platonists (discounting for the moment the Gnostics and a few scattered remarks in the *Corpus Hermeticum*), in his assertion that God cannot be understood as *ousia* or *nous*, because he is the cause of these (an idea dimly prefigured in Maximus when he says that God is not beauty but the cause of beauty). Therefore, the conception of God among the Middle Platonists we have examined so far, is not one which regards God as totally unknowable; he is, rather, difficult to know. However, we are beginning to see how short a step Plotinus would have to take in order to come to his conclusion that the One is beyond all being and knowledge.

The *Corpus Hermeticum*

The religion of Hermes Trismegistus originated in Hellenized Egypt, where the Greek God, Hermes, was identified with the Egyptian God, Thoth. Hermes Trismegistus (thrice-great Hermes, a salutation modelled on the traditional Egyptian address to Thoth) is regarded as the founder of the Hermetic doctrines. Its sources are pagan and Greek, and some treatises contain distinctive Gnostic elements.[49] Three groups of works make up the extant *Corpus* which emerged between the first and third centuries AD: the main body of writings, treatises I-XVIII; Asclepius (preserved in Latin), and extracts from the *Anthologium* of Stobaeus.

The basic metaphysical triad which emerges in the Hermetic writings is God, the cosmos and man, sometimes expressed in symbolic terms as Father, Son and Grandson.[50] Of the nature of the second and third elements of this triad the *Corpus* has much to say, but I shall restrict my comments to the nature of the first principle, God. As in the more orthodox Platonic tradition, God is understood as the supreme Father, the creator of the cosmos and human nature,

---

[49] Treatises I and VII.
[50] VIII and X, 14; this idea is also found in Numenius (*Fr.* 21) and Plotinus (*Enn.* V 5, 3, 16-24).

and he is not at all like the demiurge of the Gnostic system: 'think my son, how man is fashioned in the womb, investigate with care the skill shown in that work, and find out what craftsman it is that makes this fair and godlike image'.[51] It is the hidden God who creates all things; by making them manifest, he himself remains unmanifest and hidden.[52] His goodness is revealed in all things, so that he is both hidden and present.[53] He who is unmoved, moves in all that moves.[54] It is he who circumscribes all things, while remaining himself uncircumscribable.[55] God's presence in the universe is evident, in the eyes of the writer of the *Corpus*, as a presence both manifest and hidden: 'He is hidden, yet most manifest. He is apprehensible by thought alone, yet we can see him with our eyes'.[56] This way of preserving the 'transcendent' aspect of God's nature, and at the same time revealing him as an immanent and pervading force within the universe, bears a remarkable similarity to the ideas expressed by Eriugena in the ninth century.[57]

The divine nature of God cannot be understood in its transcendent aspect but only in its creative manifestation. Like Eriugena, the writer in the *Corpus* asserts that the divine essence is manifest only through its creative activity: God is both within and outside of all things.[58] Although the Hermetic writer does not use the terms 'transcendent' and 'immanent', their meaning is clearly to be found there. In the *Corpus*, God is unknowable unless he reveals himself, for there is nothing on earth that is like him.[59] God is described in typically Plotinian terms as 'not this' and 'not that', but as the cause of 'this and that': he is not mind or truth, but the cause of mind and truth.[60] Interestingly, the writer of one treatise in the *Corpus* asserts,

---

[51] V, 6; trans. W. Scott, *Hermetica*, vol. 1, p. 161.
[52] V, 7.
[53] V, 1.
[54] V, 5.
[55] XI, 18.
[56] V, 10.
[57] See *Periphyseon*, 678C.
[58] V, 10; see *Periphyseon*, 650D.
[59] XI, 5.
[60] II, 14.

in true Pythagorean fashion, that God's being is like the unit, for the unit, as the cause of all number, contains all number within itself.[61] Although he is in all things as their cause, God is not anything of the things of creation, for he is the Incorporeal, he who is without essence: *anousiastos*.[62] This is an important statement, for it would appear to rely on Plato's assertion in the *Republic* (509B) that the Good is beyond being. However, as A.-J Festugière has pointed out, *anousiastos* here is not quite the same as *anousios* in the Neoplatonic sense, rather it is more like *hyperousios*, because it has no definite or determined being.[63] For the Hermetic writer, God cannot be said to have being at all; still for want of a better word he does talk about his existence.[64] God escapes all predication; he is that which is unpolluted, without limit, colour or shape; he is immutable, self-understanding, the unalterable good, the incorporeal.[65]

He is, therefore, unknowable to the human intellect, intelligible only to himself. The God of the Hermetic writer, in keeping with the general trend of Middle Platonism, is unnameable; he is too great even to be called God.[66] In this way, the writer conveys the idea of the unnameability of God in a fashion that goes beyond any other Middle Platonic writer. However, God must be called by some names, and according to the *Corpus* the best of these are 'father' and 'good'.[67] In *Asclepius* we find the following statement on the namelessness of God:

> For I deem it impossible that He who is the Maker of the universe in all its greatness, the Father or Master of all things, can be named by a single name, though it be made up of so many others; I hold that He is nameless, or rather that all names are names of Him. For He is in His unity in all things; so that we must either call all things by his name, or call Him by the names of all things[68]

---

[61] IV, 12.
[62] II, 5.
[63] *Le Dieu inconnu et la gnose*, p. 71.
[64] See VI, 4.
[65] XIII, 6.
[66] V, 10.
[67] II, 15-17 and VI, 4.
[68] Non enim spero totius maiestatis effectorem omniumque rerum patrem vel dominum uno posse quamuis e multis composito nuncupari nomine, hunc vero

In keeping with his Platonic inheritance, the writer uses *Timaeus* 28C in order to stress the difficulty of the task of reaching any knowledge of God.[69] Given that this God is almost unknowable, unnameable, and above both *nous* and *ousia*, how then can the human intellect come to any knowledge of him? The way to God advocated in these Hermetic writings is based upon the Platonic notion that one must make oneself like God, for like can be known only by like.[70]

One idea in the *Corpus* which is not familiar to the philosophers of the Middle Platonic period is that God is made manifest through his creative activity. For the Middle Platonists, knowledge of God was a difficult knowledge to attain to, and in Maximus of Tyre and Celsus there was a very definite mystical element involved in the ascent to God. The Hermeticists, on the other hand, devised a much more down to earth approach: while God is unknowable in himself, he can be known through his creation. This idea is one which would be much more familiar to the Christian Fathers of the fourth century, where God is understood to be unknowable in his essence, but knowable, at least to some extent, through his energies. Ideas of this kind appear both in Philo of Alexandria and in Plotinus.

The *Corpus Hermeticum*, while it claims both Greek and Egyptian parenthood, is much more Platonic than 'oriental'; all the great themes of Middle Platonism are present there, although they are developed at times in slightly different ways. The transcendence of the supreme God is affirmed *because* he is creator of the universe; as Father, he is proclaimed to be unlike anything within the created world. Celsus is perhaps the one Platonist of the first two centuries who comes closest to the ideas expressed in the *Corpus*,

---

innominem vel potius omni nominem siquidem is sit unus et omnia, ut sit necesse aut omnia esse eius nomine aut ipsum omnium nominibus nuncupari: *Asclepius*, 20, trans. W. Scott, p. 333; see also *Asclepius*, Epilogue, 41. More detailed comments on *Asclepius* can be found in S. Gersh, *Middle Platonism and Neoplatonism The Latin Tradition*, vol. I, especially pp. 334-348.

[69] Stobaeus, *Fr.* 1.

[70] XI, 20.

especially in the assertion that God is neither *nous* nor *ousia*. In common with most followers of the negative way, the author of the *Corpus* recommends silence as the sole appropriate means of indicating the transcendent God: '... of whom no words can tell, no tongue can speak, whom silence only can declare'.[71]

---

[71] I, 31: trans. W. Scott, p. 131.

CHAPTER FOUR

SECOND-CENTURY PLATONISM: ALCINOUS, BASILIDES AND NUMENIUS

Alcinous: The First God

Alcinous was active in Smyrna between AD149 – 157, when Galen followed his lectures there. Although Alcinous does not appear to have been connected with the Academy, he can be regarded as one of the best representatives of 'orthodox' Platonism in the second century. He was largely forgotten until, in the fifteenth century, Petrus Balbus undertook to translate his writings for Nicholas of Cusa. Modern work on Alcinous was initiated in Germany by Freudenthal, and the first modern edition of his writings was produced by P. Louis in 1945.[1]

Two works of Alcinous are extant: a short discussion and classification of the Platonic dialogues, Εἰσαγωγή, and the Ἐπιτομὴ τῶν Πλατωνος δογμάτων, generally known as the Διδασκαλικὸς. It is possible that he also wrote commentaries on the *Timaeus*, *Phaedo*, and *Republic*, but these, unfortunately, are not extant. Essentially the *Didaskalikos* is a handbook of Platonism, and as such it may be regarded as an ancient Teach Yourself Plato! Therefore, when we refer to what Alcinous said in the *Didaskalikos*, it must be remembered that it represents the common version of Plato prevalent in the second century. His sources were, of course, Plato and Aristotle, but he also relied on the Stoics, Xenocrates, Antiochus of Ascalon, and Arius Didymus. Alcinous is important not only because he is a good representative of second-century Platonism, but also because he presents a very

---

[1] Freudenthal, *Der Platoniker Albinos und der falsche Alkinoos* (Berlin, 1879); P. Louis, *Epitome* (Paris, 1945).

close assimilation of Platonic and Aristotelian views. We find little trace of the anti-Aristotelianism that was prominent in Atticus, Lucius, and Nicostratus. P. Louis rejects the idea that Alcinous deliberately tried to assimilate the two; he claims instead that their concordance arose simply because Aristotle was understood to have been a Platonist. The fusion of Plato and Aristotle is especially notable in Alcinous's use of the 'self-contemplating *nous*' as the supreme God,[2] and the imposition of Aristotelian logic upon Platonic theology (Alcinous claimed to have discovered the categories in Plato[3]).

Although Alcinous took much from Aristotle, Plato remains (as he does for most of the Middle Platonists) the most powerful inspiration, and in the *Didaskalikos* we find the by now familiar reliance on those oft-quoted passages from the *Timaeus, Republic, Symposium*, and *Phaedo*. In the *Didaskalikos*, the *Timaeus* assumes the most important role of all the Platonic dialogues reflecting the second-century concern with theological questions about the creation of the world. The *Symposium* is also an important source for Alcinous as we shall see during the course of this discussion. As R. E. Witt points out, there are many Platonic doctrines which are wholly neglected by Alcinous; he suggests that this was due largely to the 'exigencies of compression'.[4] While this may well have been the case, we must also consider that Alcinous may have been exercising his right to select those Platonic passages which were important for a summary. In ignoring the status of the Good in the *Republic* and preferring the ascent to Beauty in the *Symposium*, Alcinous shows an originality which must not be overlooked. As the break down of the chapters in the *Didaskalikos* show, logic and physics are obviously his chief interest, and that might have influenced his choice of the ascent to Beauty, reflecting as that does a more logical progression of mind. The

---

[2] P. Merlan has suggested that the idea of God as cause of *nous* in Alcinous represents the fact that he was on the way towards elevating God above intelligence, but stopped short of it; see 'Albinus and Apuleius', in *The Cambridge History*, p. 66.
[3] *Didaskalikos*, VI, 10.
[4] *Albinus and the History of Middle Platonism*, p. 14.

ascent to the *agathon* is not systematically worked out by Plato, and what is more the Good is 'beyond being', a concept which, as I have shown, was not taken up by the Middle Platonists (with the exception of Celsus). The subject matter of the *Didaskalikos*, therefore, would lead us to believe that Alcinous was not drawn towards speculative theology; his description of the way to knowledge of God in chapter X lacks anything of the mystical feeling that was present both in Maximus of Tyre and in Celsus, although J. Dillon argues that Alcinous exhibits a distinctly mystical 'tendency' in chapter X.[5]

On the whole, the style of Alcinous is dry, as befits a school book, and is pervaded with logical arguments and the vocabulary of Aristotelian logic. His exposition of the nature of God in chapter X gives the impression that he regarded God as a metaphysical principle to be slotted neatly into the whole schema of reality. The plan of the *Didaskalikos* follows the traditional (in origin Stoic) division into logic, physics, and ethics. The chapters with which I will be concerned (VIII-XI), those which deal with theology, are treated by Alcinous under the customary heading of physics.

The basic metaphysical triad of Alcinous follows that of Apuleius: matter, the eternal ideas and 'God, the Father and creator of all'.[6] By the time of Alcinous the ideas have become firmly established as the thoughts of God, and he understands the idea as the eternal model of all things which exists naturally.[7] Alcinous continues at great length to give syllogistic proofs for the existence of the ideas: if God is a thinking being, then he has thoughts; if matter is unable to measure itself, then it must have an external means of measure which is not material.[8] The third principle in order of discussion is the one with which I am concerned here, and Alcinous notes at the beginning of his presentation that it was, according to Plato 'almost indescribable'.[9]

[5] *The Middle Platonists*, p. 268.
[6] See VIII, 1-3 and IX, 1.
[7] IX, 1 and 2; see A. M. Rich, 'The Platonic Ideas as the Thoughts of God'.
[8] IX, 3.
[9] X, 1.

Alcinous's initial concern is to prove the existence of the third principle, and he posits an intellectual hierarchy: beauty, intellect and soul, where God is placed at the level of beauty. At this point it would seem that Alcinous distinguishes between an actual *nous* and a potential *nous* on a cosmic level: νοῦς κατ ' ἐνέργειαν and νοῦς ἐν δυνάμει, although the remainder of his discussion does not take this distinction into account.[10] The hierarchy of Alcinous is interesting for two reasons. Firstly, the implied elevation of Beauty above Good is unusual, and we do not meet with it anywhere else in the Middle Platonists with whom I am concerned. Secondly, it explicitly places the first God in the realm of Beauty, which is above *nous*, an elevation found previously only in Celsus (although the idea had been hinted at in Maximus of Tyre), and one which we do not meet again in any explicit form until we find it in Plotinus. The hierarchy which Alcinous presents here is very similar to that of Apuleius as discussed in the previous chapter; however, the initial impact of the elevation of Beauty above *nous* is immediately lessened, as Alcinous hails ὁ πρῶτος θεός as ὁ πρῶτος νοῦς.[11] Throughout the remainder of his exposition of Platonic theology these two terms are used interchangeably. Once again, this interchange of terms reflects the confusion over the status of the first God; while he is the creator of *nous*, he himself is not placed in a capacity which would suggest that he is beyond *nous*.

The first God, himself immobile, is the cause of all movement in the celestial intelligence in the same way that the object of desire moves desire. It is clear that the Prime Mover of Aristotle has come to be identified with the supreme deity of Alcinous, and it is most likely that he did not think this identification to be in any way non-Platonic.[12] According to the *Didaskalikos*, God conceives himself always at the same time as he conceives his proper thoughts, thereby giving birth to the ideas, although Alcinous

[10] X, 2; for further discussion of the double *nous* in Alcinous, see J. H. Loenen, 'Albinus' Metaphysics' (1956), pp. 306-311, who says that this is a hierarchical order of values, not an ontological hierarchy.

[11] X, 3.

[12] See *Met.* 1072b and 1074b.

never uses the Aristotelian phrase, *noesis noeseos*. According to
A. H. Armstrong, this is the first time that the Aristotelian *nous*
was taken into Platonic theology, and certainly this is the most
explicit instance of its appearance so far.[13] Here, then, in Alcinous,
we have a Platonic theology, a hierarchy, at the head of which
stands Beauty, the most proper place for the first *nous*. This system, which reflects an almost complete fusion of Platonic and
Aristotelian ideas, belongs neither to Plato nor to Aristotle; it is
purely Middle Platonic, and as such not only represents a healthy
respect for Aristotle, but also provides a firm basis for the ontological hierarchy of Plotinus to come.

Alcinous describes the first God using a list of positive assertions which are by now familiar. He is the first eternal God, ineffable and all-perfect; he is divinity, essence, truth, proportion, and
good.[14] The terms used by Alcinous have the ring of a negative list
of attributes, but, in fact, *arretōs* is the only *alpha* privative used,
perhaps because in the second century this term had become a
common way of describing God, and had assumed an almost 'positive' character. H. A. Wolfson has suggested that 'ineffable' in
Alcinous (and indeed in Plotinus) goes back to Philo of Alexandria.[15] While it is more than likely that the use of the term 'ineffable' was somehow filtered into Platonism from Philo via the
'Alexandrian connection', it is unlikely that more than one of the
Platonists I have been discussing had read Philo directly.

In his ensuing discussion of the nature of God, Alcinous says
that he does not enumerate these terms in order to separate them,
but in order to make of them a 'single object of thought'.[16] He
gives the reasons why God may be called Good, Beauty, Truth and
Father, and in this instance we find the supremacy of the term,

---

[13] 'The Background to the Doctrine that Intelligibles are not Outside the Intellect', p. 402ff.
[14] X, 3; see Dillon, *The Middle Platonists*, p. 283, where he suggests that
οὐσίοτης (essence) and θειότης (divinity) are peculiar to Alcinous, although he
points to a passage in the *Corpus Hermeticum*, where οὐσίοτητος and θεότητός
are found (XII, 1).
[15] 'Albinus and Plotinus on Divine Attributes', p. 115.
[16] ἑνὸς νοουμένου: X, 3.

Good, emphasized in the same way as the term, Beauty. Although a cursory reading of second-century Platonic texts would give the impression that the Platonic principles, Good, Beauty, and One, are identified with the supreme *nous*, this is not the case. Here in Alcinous, we have the first explicit identification of God with the *agathon* since we found it in Plutarch.[17] Alcinous also refers to *Timaeus* 28C when he says that God may be called Father because he is the Maker of all; he orders both the celestial intelligence and the soul of the world. Interestingly, Alcinous never refers to God as demiurge; he orders the world, but he is not said to have made it. However, Alcinous does not follow the teaching of the *Timaeus* text to the letter – in fact, so few of the Middle Platonists do – for he notes that while God is ineffable, he may be comprehended by the intellect through *nous*.[18] According to the *Didaskalikos*, then, God is not unknowable, but it is difficult to reach any understanding of him. Alcinous then outlines three ways through which an idea of God may be reached; the first of these is the way of successive negations (*aphairesis*), the method which is best used to obtain a first idea of God.[19]

Only intellect can grasp that which has no genus, no image, no difference, is not subjected to any accident, is neither evil nor good, nor indifferent.[20] Furthermore, God has no qualities nor absence of any quality, he is not part of any thing, not a whole of parts, is neither identical nor different from any thing, and he neither gives nor receives movement. These last three negations are strongly reminiscent of the *Parmenides*, and it is quite likely that Alcinous had this Platonic dialogue in mind. A. H. Armstrong has argued that the *via negationis* here was inspired by the first hypothesis of the *Parmenides*, although he suggested that Alcinous may have been unconscious of his source, for he classifies the *Parmenides* as a 'logical' dialogue.[21] While it is more than

[17] See XXVII, 1, where God is called 'μέγιστον ἀγαθόν'.
[18] X, 4.
[19] X, 5.
[20] X, 4.
[21] *The Architecture of the Intelligible Universe*, p. 10ff.

likely that the *Parmenides* is the source for the negations expounded here, similar negations do of course occur in the *Symposium* and a passage in the *Timaeus* might also be taken into consideration.[22] J. Whittaker, on the other hand, disagrees with Armstrong about the unconscious source, and says that the 'logical exercise' view has been over-worked; its classification as such 'no more constitutes a denial of theological or metaphysical relevance than does the listing of the *Phaedo* or the *Symposium* under *to politikon*'.[23]

Interestingly, in this passage from chapter X, Alcinous does not refer to 'One'. If his was a deliberate use of the *Parmenides*, we must ask why he ignored the appellation *to hen*. I suggest that one answer to this question could be that the 'dogmatic' Platonists of the second century may have been rebelling against the Pythagorization of Platonism. For Alcinous in particular, the religious aspect of neo-Pythagoreanism may well have been the reason for this; the God of Alcinous is not generally understood to be a personal God but a metaphysical principle. The attempt to read Plato without Pythagorean glasses may have resulted in the rejection of *to hen* by Alcinous and others.

The method of *aphairesis*: is, as Alcinous says, a method similar to the notion of arriving at the idea of a point by moving from plane, surface and line.[24] As I have already noted, this symbolism had Pythagorean origins, and although Alcinous uses it, he does not use the word *monades* to indicate the point, but *semeion*. This change of vocabulary may also go some way towards suggesting that there was some sort of anti-Pythagorean feeling in the more orthodox Platonic school at this time. Be that as it may, in the *Didaskalikos*, we see the first explicit, and thoroughly Greek, theory of *aphairesis*: that is, in order to arrive at knowledge of God, we should proceed by means of abstraction, a method which was to become an integral part of the soul's return to the One in the *Enneads* and in some of the earlier Christian Fathers.

[22] *Tim.* 52A.
[23] ''ΕΠΕΚΕΙΝΑ ΝΟΥ ΚΑΙ ΟΥΣΙΑΣ', p. 99.
[24] X, 5

In his early work on Plotinus, A. H. Armstrong regarded the method of abstraction in Alcinous as a 'large undigested lump of negative theology ... a discordant and alien element in his system'.[25] I hesitate to agree fully with Armstrong here; why regard *aphairesis* in Alcinous as alien and accept it as an important part of the negative theology in Plotinus? While it is true that Alcinous himself gives the impression that it is slightly 'undigested', after all, he was simply condensing material for text-book purposes. It could also be said that since we do not find any mention of 'relationship' with God in the *Didaskalikos*, the negative theology as it appears there is somehow incomplete. The biggest question mark must be placed over Alcinous's exclusion of *Timaeus* 28C as the basis for his argument and method; we shall later see how he uses this passage in an altogether different context.

An interesting discussion developed some decades ago between H. A. Wolfson and J. Whittaker about the use and meaning of the term *aphairesis* in Alcinous. According to Wolfson, it is derived from Euclid.[26] Whittaker, on the other hand, supports the argument for a Pythagorean source.[27] I have already mentioned Aristotle's use of this geometric symbolism as it appears in *De anima*, and the movement outlined there, from sense perception to *nous* would, no doubt, have appealed to Alcinous. I suggest, therefore, that we need look no further than Aristotle for the source of Alcinous's use of the geometric analogy.

Wolfson also attempts to show how Alcinous used the term '*aphairesis*' as equivalent to what Aristotle meant by the term *apophasis*.[28] For Aristotle, the first term simply meant a taking

---

[25] *Architecture*, p. 23; in his preface to the recent French translation of this work, the author notes some general inadequacies of the book, (Éditions de l'Université d' Ottawa, 1984), pp. 11-15.

[26] See 'Albinus and Plotinus on Divine Attributes'.

[27] See 'Neopythagoreanism and Negative Theology'.

[28] R. Mortley has contributed more recently to this discussion of the relationship of abstraction to negation, and concludes that while abstraction may not be a form of negation, its logic is that of privation; abstraction and negation are not the same: they differ in purpose rather than technique; see *From Word to Silence I*, p. 149.

away, but in Alcinous and Plotinus, according to Wolfson, it had acquired the technical sense of 'negation in a logical proposition' (e.g. the wall is not seeing, as opposed to *steresis*, the man is blind). Whittaker again takes Wolfson to task, pointing out that *apophasis* was Aristotle's general term for negation, and he refutes Wolfson's suggestion of 'technical substratum', that is, the underlying reasons for the use of abstraction in Alcinous. 'Alcinous is concerned purely with the problem of forming a conception of God. The matter of negative statements lies outside the scope of his exposition.'[29] I suspect that Whittaker's interpretation is closer to the truth than Wolfson's, and that this reading is further strengthened by a remark Alcinous himself makes in chapter IV of the *Didaskalikos*: he outlines only the affirmative and negative methods of logical proposition, giving the examples, 'Socrates is walking', and 'Socrates is not walking'.[30] In his second example, we have an instance of what Wolfson would call an affirmative proposition with a privative predication; we may, therefore, conclude that the negations Alcinous uses concerning the supreme God are used with the purpose of abstracting from our concept of his nature anything that belongs to the realm of created nature.

R. Mortley's more recent discussion of the roles of negation and privation in Aristotle may shed some light on this complex problem.[31] According to Mortley, *aphairesis* in Aristotle has a metaphysical purpose; it is the science of removing successive layers to find the first principle, to take away in order to reach the essence ('whatness') of a thing. According to this view, Aristotle rejects *apophasis* because of its indefiniteness, for to say of something, 'it is not good', implies that everything else other than goodness may apply to the subject. It is, therefore, a pointless way to think of essence. *Steresis* deprives, while *apophasis* opens up a vast range of possibilities (except in the case of unity, for the denial of unity implies plurality).[32] In Mortley's view, *aphairesis*,

[29] 'Neopythagoreanism and Negative Theology', p. 123.
[30] VI, 1.
[31] *From Word to Silence I*, p. 137ff.
[32] *Op. cit.* p. 140.

as a method for reaching the unknown in Aristotle, made possible the later reconstruction of certain insights of Plato and was, therefore, instrumental in the development of negative theology in the Neoplatonists.

I have already noted the rather 'dry' style of argument which in Alcinous reveals his overall concern with the correctness of statements and the proper use of language. The attempt to form correct statements about God can certainly be regarded as the product of a more logical turn of mind, yet I cannot see how he alone of all the Middle Platonists (and indeed, Plotinus), was working from within a strictly Aristotelian logical perspective. I suggest that the method of *aphairesis*, as it is used by Alcinous, is a means by which the supreme God is elevated beyond the material world of genera and species. Even in the more fully-developed negative theology of the Pseudo-Dionysius, the term *aphairesis* is used in a way similar to that of Alcinous, namely, as a means of removing all creaturely attributes from the divine nature. In Alcinous, *aphairesis* can be said to remain at the level of intellect: he does not appear to aspire to any supra-intellectual knowledge of God. Thus, the way of *aphairesis*, as it is found in the *Didaskalikos*, is more like the *via remotionis* of the medieval scholastics, a rational placing of God above and beyond the world of created nature. In this instance, it does not appear to rise beyond *nous*.

The second way by which one can proceed to a knowledge of God is by the method of *analogia*, and here Alcinous uses the simile of the sun, taken from the *Republic*: just as the sun permits objects to be seen by the eye, so too the supreme God gives intelligible objects to the intellectual faculty.[33] The third way is similar to that which the Latin Scholastics would call the *via eminentiae*, and here Alcinous relies chiefly on the ascent to Beauty as that had been outlined in the *Symposium*.[34] Firstly, one contemplates beauty in the physical body, then in laws and institutions, until finally, explains Alcinous, using an almost direct quotation from

[33] X, 5.
[34] X, 6.

the *Symposium*, one reaches the vast ocean of Beauty, after which the Good can be conceived. The shift in emphasis from Beauty to Good, which has been noted as a viable interpretation of the original text, may not after all be so very far from Plato's own conception of the way to the attainment of Beauty.

At X, 7, Alcinous returns once again to a negative description of God: he has no parts, he is immobile and does not change, and he is incorporeal; for each of the negations Alcinous gives a logical argument why it must pertain. In the midst of these negations, Alcinous argues for the incorporeality of God, a concept which was to be developed further by Numenius, thereby refuting the Stoic idea of God as a body. His argument rests on the fact that God is both simple (*haplous*) and primordial (*archikos*) – two terms which would be used extensively by Plotinus. The use of the term 'simple' with regard to the nature of God, has much the same connotations as the Pythagorean use of the word, 'Apollo', for it too, means the denial of multiplicity.

The theology of Alcinous, therefore, presents a unique, creator God, who is strongly endowed with the characteristics of the Aristotelian *nous*; to a lesser extent, is it identified with the Platonic Good. While God is most certainly removed from the material world, his transcendence does not include an ontological superiority over either *nous* or *ousia*, and God is never referred to as *to hen*. This point brings me back to a discussion of the place of the 'one' in the *Didaskalikos*, a question re-opened by Knut Kleve, and one which J. Whittaker, R. E. Witt and H. J. Krämer all answer in the negative.[35] Kleve takes as his source the ἑνὸς νοουμένου to which I have already referred.[36] P. Louis translates it as 'un tout unique', and A.-J. Festugière as 'une même unité,[37] but Kleve asks whether it is not possible to translate it as *to hen*. He argues that, from a general viewpoint, the use of *agathon* and *kalon* in the predicative position preclude the need for the article,

---

[35] 'Albinus on God and the One'.
[36] X, 3.
[37] P. Louis, *Epitome*, p. 58 and Festugière, *Le Dieu Inconnu*, p. 98.

and suggests that it may be possible to treat *hen* in the same way, since the contemporaries of Alcinous would not have needed to read the article for a correct understanding. However, there are serious objections to this suggestion. Firstly, I cannot see how such a clarification would not have been required in the climate of thought of the second century; Plotinus himself always found it necessary to distinguish between *agathon* and *to agathon*, between *hen* and *to hen*, and I can see no reason why Alcinous should have thought it unnecessary. Quite simply, Alcinous could have written *to hen* if that was what he meant. Kleve also notes the identification of God with *agathon* and suggests that it is but a short step to an identification with *hen*; yet this remains an identification which neither Plato nor Alcinous made. In Alcinous this conflation is not even made implicitly, and I have already shown how he ignored all mention of the One in connection with his supposed use of the negations of the *Parmenides*. The fact is that God is continually called *nous*, and while this suggests his integral unity, it does not have the same connotation as an explicit reference to *to hen* would have. I have also noted that the statement from the 'Lecture on the Good' was ignored by the majority of the second-century Platonists. For these reasons, I do not believe that we find the One in Alcinous; we must for that await the mighty genius of Plotinus in the *Enneads*.

Alcinous presents a common Middle Platonic understanding of *telos* which involves the Platonic *homoiōsis theō*.[38] True happiness lies, not in the created world, but in the realm of the gods and immortals. The souls of true philosophers, after separation from the body, enter the society of the gods and participate in their life, in the contemplation of that truth which they had desired already in this life to know.[39] At this point Alcinous uses a very Platonic image, that of the vision of the 'eye of the soul' being a thousand times more precious than that of the body, an image which Plotinus was to make very much his own in the

---

[38] XXVIII, 1.
[39] XXVII, 3.

Enneads. It is for this reason that H. Dörrie speaks of a 'fourth way' in the *Didaskalikos*, that of the *via imitationis*, wherein God is understood as both *archē* and *telos*.[40] This discussion of *telos* comes at the beginning of Alcinous's chapters on Platonic ethics, and it is here that we find him making use of the text from *Timaeus* 28C. The 'greatest good', he says, is very difficult to discover, and if one does find God, it is not easy to make him known to everyone.[41] This knowledge may be made known only to the very small number of those who have been specially chosen. This point is important for a number of reasons. Firstly, it is striking that Alcinous replaces the words 'Father and Maker' with 'the most esteemed and sovereign good'. Secondly, he uses the word ῥάδιος instead of the usual ἀδύνατος. Thirdly, the actual placing of this quotation is unusual, because one would have expected to find it in support of his argument for the ineffable nature of God; yet here it is used to introduce a discussion on ethics. Certainly it would seem that Alcinous is following Plato here, at least in terms of attainment to the Good, yet the statement 'beyond being' is not used by him. It would seem that of all the Platonists included in this study, Alcinous comes closest to the interpretation of the Good advocated by Speusippus. Alcinous would have found it very difficult to reconcile the Platonic notion of the Good beyond being with their notion of the God who is attainable through *nous*.

In conclusion, although Alcinous presents the way of abstraction in its most systematic form in the period of Middle Platonism, the fact that *aphairesis* remains on the level of *nous*, indicates that his negative theology is more akin to the *via remotionis* of later medieval thought. The method of abstraction, so characteristic in second-century Platonism, rarely (the exception being Celsus) involves anything of that mystical knowledge so important in the thought of Plotinus. It is only in Numenius that we begin to see the mystical element emerge in any explicit form.

---

[40] 'Die Frage nach dem Tranzendenten im Mittelplatonismus', p. 224.
[41] XXVII, 1.

Basilides: The Not-Being God

In stark contrast to the philosophical developments in the Platonic school of the second century, stands the most intriguing of all Middle Platonic developments: Gnosticism, that troublesome 'ism' which emerged more or less contemporaneously with Christianity. The relationship of Basilides to the movement known as Gnosticism is problematical, and while he is included in most Gnostic anthologies he himself displays a certain reluctance to conform fully to any of the mainstream Gnostic sects. While many Gnostic writings have little particular relevance to the themes of transcendence and negative theology, the insistence to be found in some Gnostic tracts on the transcendence and unknowability of God cannot have failed to have had an impact on the theological development of Platonism in the second century.[42] The extent of that influence is, of course, very difficult to determine, at least with regard to Middle Platonism; it is somewhat less difficult to trace in some Neoplatonic writings.

Basilides is said to have lived at Alexandria during the first half of the second century.[43] We possess no more than a few scant details about his life: he taught among the Persians and he was a follower of Menander (who had been a disciple of Simon Magus). Basilides's own writings are not extant, but we have some quite lengthy accounts of his teachings from two of the early Christian Fathers, Irenaeus and Hippolytus. However, the account of Basilides given by Irenaeus in the *Adversus haereses* differs considerably from that of Hippolytus in the *Refutatio omnium haeresium*, and modern scholarship has still not resolved the vexing question of this discrepancy.[44] Whether the account in Hippolytus

---

[42] One of the most notable statements of divine transcendence in negative terms, can be found in *The Apocryphon of John*; see W. Foerster, *Gnosis. A Selection of Gnostic Texts*, vol. 1, p. 107. J. Daniélou has suggested that some negative terms used by Gnostic writers may have been borrowed from Platonic sources, see *Gospel Message and Hellenistic Culture*, p. 339.

[43] See Clement of Alexandria, *Stromata*, VII, 17.

[44] See M. Jufresa, 'Basilides. A Path to Plotinus', p. 1.

is an accurate account of the teaching of Basilides himself or that of someone else in his school, a pseudo-Basilides, is a question which cannot be answered satisfactorily in this study. I have chosen to comment on the report given by Hippolytus since it is the more interesting of the two accounts, and perhaps unique among Gnostic writings: it is an account of the genesis of the world from a completely transcendent, indeed, not-being God.

According to Basilides, there was a time when there was nothing, when not even 'nothing' was there. He indicates this nothingness as that which is not simply ineffable, for that is not absolutely ineffable, but that which is 'not even ineffable': οὐδὲ ἄρρητον.[45] Perhaps the reason why Basilides calls this nothingness 'not even ineffable', is because 'ineffable' is a name, whereas this nothingness has no name. He says that it must be understood without any names, for the conceptual reason that all names fall short of the reality they attempt to represent, even in the world itself, which is so multiform.

The use of the phrase, 'not even ineffable' in Basilides has been the topic of much discussion and speculation. It has been suggested that Basilides uses *oude* in order to contradict someone before him who had described God as ineffable,[46] perhaps Philo of Alexandria. However, the use of the word *arretōn* to describe God was a commonplace in the second century – almost an affirmative term – and, as Basilides suggests, it had acquired the status of a name. Therefore, it is not entirely clear who he was contradicting. H. A. Wolfson has suggested that Basilides, like Alcinous, interpreted the term, not as a privative proposition (*steresis*), but as a negative proposition (*apophasis*). According to this view, Basilides was so concerned with linguistic subtleties, that he could not even use the ordinary *alpha* privative. J. Whittaker, however,

---

[45] 'For that, says he, is not simply something ineffable which can be named; we call it ineffable, but it is not even ineffable'; Hippolytus, *Refutatio omnium haeresium*, VII, 20, 3; trans. W. Foerster, *Gnosis*, vol. 1, p. 64.
[46] See H. A. Wolfson, 'Negative Attributes in the Church Fathers and the Gnostic Basilides', p. 142 and J. Whittaker, 'Basilides on the Ineffability of God', pp. 367-368.

disagrees, for he believes that the question of privative and negative propositions was totally irrelevant to the theory of Basilides.[47] Whittaker suggests that the reasoning behind the use of 'not even ineffable' in Basilides was that he was trying 'to outdo his forerunners in the field of negative theology': his standpoint was not inspired by considerations of logic, but must be seen as 'a contribution to the terminology of transcendency'. Whittaker rightly, I think, points out that in the text of Basilides there is no reference to propositions, but rather to correctness of language. He also remarks that if *arrēton* had been considered as a privative proposition, there is no reason why all the other adverbs used by Basilides would not have been treated in the same way, i.e., prefixed with *oude*.[48]

If, as the text suggests, Basilides did regard *arrēton* as a name, we must ask why he thought it necessary to deny this particular name. M. Jufresa suggests that the motivation behind this denial was indicative of a typically Gnostic anti-Jewish tendency.[49] After the destruction of the Temple of Jerusalem the sacred name of God had become ineffable for the Jews, for they had lost the ritual formula for its pronunciation. This idea would seem to be plausible and it is a suggestion which is given even more weight when we read further in the account of Basilides and discover that the Great Archon of the Ogdoad is described as 'more ineffable than the ineffable', while the Archon of the Hebdomad, the demiurge and world ruler, who is almost certainly identified with the God of the Jews, is described simply as 'ineffable'.[50] Later, however, Basilides says that the Great Ruler of the Ogdoad is 'ineffable' and the Ruler of the Hebdomad, the God who had spoken to the

---

[47] R. Mortley remarks that because negation opens up a vast range of possibilities and only one notion is excluded, that God can turn out to be almost anything, as he did in the case of Basilides, see *From Word to Silence I*, p. 125; I am not convinced that Basilides was consciously operating within the context of Aristotelian negation or privation.

[48] J. Whittaker suggests that Basilides did not treat the other words in the same way because he regarded only *arreton* as a name, *op. cit.* p. 370.

[49] *op. cit.*, p. 3.

[50] Hippolytus, VII, 23, 3-5.

Jews, is 'effable'.[51] Whatever the case, the meaning is clear: above the creator God there is a superior God who is totally ineffable.

In respect of these comments, Basilides would seem to display an even greater anti-Jewish tendency than in the Valentinian Gnostic system, where there is one demiurge only, one who is usually associated with the God of the Jews. According to the anti-Jewish theory, if we begin from the bottom of the divine hierarchy, Basilides admitted the ineffability of the God of the Jews, the world-creator and ruler. However, since his system was not the Jewish system and his God not the Jewish God, he was forced to postulate at least one further God who was superior to the demiurge. This reasoning would appear to suggest that Basilides was not contradicting Philo, who had called God *arrētos*: in fact he agreed, at least in one instance, that the God of the Jews was indeed ineffable.

However, I suggest that in view of the 'reported' nature of the text, it is very difficult to determine with any certainty exactly what Basilides meant. Basilides does not use the term *arrēton* as descriptive of God. His account at this point was not yet concerned with the non-existent God, but about that *time* when nothing was – not even something ineffable – for he continues to say that there was no matter, nor substance, nothing insubstantial, nothing simple, nothing composite, nothing non-composite, and nothing imperceptible, no angel, no man, and no God.[52] Yet, it would be reasonable to assume that any reference to 'ineffable' refers to God, as it does throughout the whole Middle Platonic period, and later in the text Basilides does use the term in relation to the wise architect, the God of the heavenly region, and to the demiurge, the God of the world.[53] Yet, in the first instance, when Basilides uses the term 'ineffable', it is more than likely that he is referring to that time when not even the not-being God was.

---

[51] VII, 21, 4.
[52] VII, 21, 1.
[53] VII, 23, 5-6.

At that time, then, when there was nothing of the things that can be named or apprehended by the senses, or thought, the not-being God (which Basilides compares to Aristotle's self-thinking thought[54]), wished to create a world, without however wishing or willing to, without intelligence, without feeling, without intention, without resolve, without emotion, and without desire.[55] At this point Basilides (like Plotinus, Proclus, Dionysius, and many others) remarks on the limitations of language, for he says that while he is forced to use the word 'wished', all will, wish and resolve are excluded. The world which the not-being God wished to create was not the world we know, but a non-existent world, the seed of the world from which everything else will come.

Some scholars have suggested that the οὐκ ὤν θεὸς of Basilides might have been another device to distinguish this supremely transcendent God from the God of Exodus 3:14: ''Εγώ εἰμι ὁ ὤν'.[56] Whether this was in fact the intention of Basilides is impossible to ascertain, but again it would be in accordance with the general anti-Jewish trend of Gnosticism. With this point in mind, his use of the term 'apatheia' (passionlessness) may also have been employed to distinguish his God from the God of the Old Testament; on the other hand, it could also have been a direct Greek influence, since the Epicurean Gods, gods who did not love and care for their people, were portrayed as not having emotions.[57]

M. Jufresa has suggested that we should interpret this not-being God as part of the Pythagorean/Platonic understanding of the God who is considered *hyperousios*.[58] However, if Basilides were conscious of the Platonic, or rather Pythagorean, tradition in this respect, then we must ask why he did not simply use the prefix *hyper*. I think the reason lies in the fact that Basilides was not part of the Platonic tradition; the whole ethos of his writing is non-

[54] VII, 21, 1.
[55] VII, 21 2.
[56] J. Whittaker, ''ΕΠΕΚΕΙΝΑ', p. 100 and M. Jufresa, 'Basilides', p. 4.
[57] See Jufresa, pp. 12-13, n. 42.
[58] pp. 3-4; this is also Whittaker's proposal, see ''ΕΠΕΚΕΙΝΑ', p. 100, where he argues for the influence of *Rep.* 509B.

Platonic, and I cannot find anything in Basilides which would suggest that his not-being God should be interpreted in the same way as the supreme principle of the neo-Pythagoreans.[59] Of course these negations do have very strong Platonic connotations, for the negative way of describing God is a method common to both Gnosticism and Platonism. However, while the Platonists were concerned to distinguish between God and creation, Basilides was motivated by an additional desire, which was to strengthen Gnostic speculation on the divine nature by preserving its distinctiveness over against both Judaism and Christianity. If Basilides were relying on the Platonic tradition, then we would expect to find frequent references to Plato; yet there is only one instance where reference to Plato is made.[60] Although Basilides must have been familiar with traditional Middle Platonic theology, I suggest that he was, in fact, reacting against the ideas of the Platonists, who were probably too close to the Christians in any case! It is more than likely that the οὐκ ὤν θεός was inspired by a reaction against the Jewish God, for the words of Basilides do not belong to the vocabulary of the Platonists. Basilides's not-being God represents the antithesis of 'I am who am', and therefore may be interpreted as a forceful means of dethroning the God of the Jews.

In denying the power of thought to the transcendent God, Basilides once again stands outside the main tradition of Middle Platonic theology, for we have already seen that, in general, the Aristotelian *nous* took precedence over the beyond-being *agathon* as the supreme principle. This is one instance where Basilides is in agreement both with the author of one treatise in the *Corpus Hermeticum*,[61] and with the Platonist, Celsus, although the motivation of Basilides is quite different. His description of God as *anoetos* could suggest that Basilides was not acquainted with the thought of the Middle Platonists, but it is also likely that, to use J. Whittaker's words, that he was trying to 'outdo' them in the field of

---

[59] R. Mortley finds that the 'transcendence statements' of Basilides reflect some knowledge of the *Parmenides*, see *op. cit.* pp. 157-158.
[60] See Hippolytus, VII, 22, 8-9.
[61] II, 12-14.

negative theology. Whatever his reason for denying thought to the not-being God (at any rate a not-being God cannot think!), it is clear that Basilides is very close to a distinctly Plotinian idea.[62] Not only is this God without thought, but he is also without consciousness or perception.

On the positive side, however, this God did in some way 'wish' to create the world seed, although nothing emanated from him: everything was contained in the world seed in the same way that teeth are present in a new-born child.[63] The first thing to bubble forth from the seed of the world was the three-fold sonship. The first sonship sped upwards to the non-existent God because of his extreme loveliness and beauty; the second sonship also sped upwards, but did not reach the first, while the third had to remain in the fullness of the great seed. Thus begins the account of creation.[64] There arose the Great Ruler of the Ogdoad (the 'more than ineffable') who created the heavenly region, likewise the Ruler of the Hebdomad arose, the God of Moses ('the ineffable'), and he created the world. Each thought that he was the supreme God and knew nothing of that which was above both of them or of the existence of the third sonship in the seed. This ignorance can be called 'pre-restoration *agnōsia*'. To be brief, the process of restoration is begun through the Gospel, through which the rulers learn that they are begotten, become afraid of their ignorance and finally attain wisdom through acceptance of their positions. Through them, both the heavenly and earthly regions become illuminated, but still the third sonship remains in the seed.[65] At this point, says Basilides, creation is still groaning and in torment, waiting for further revelation, and in order to prevent anything desiring that which would be contrary to its nature, the supreme God caused a 'great ignorance' to descend upon everything.[66] This was done so that all

---

[62] See *Enn.* V 3, 11, 25-30.
[63] Hippolytus, VII, 22, 1.
[64] VII, 22, 8.
[65] VII, 25, 5 and 27, 10.
[66] VII, 27, 1-4.

things would be content with their lot rather than be in pain and sorrow by striving for that which is beyond them, 'like fish wanting to graze with sheep', for nothing can transgress its limits or it would perish.[67] This post-restoration 'ignorance', where everything must be content to remain in its own place without knowledge of all that is beyond, is truly 'blissful ignorance'. Thus, *gnosis*, in this system, is given simply to achieve the process of restoration: sonship to sonship, hylic to hylic, psychic to psychic, and spiritual to spiritual.

The idea of restoration in the Gnostic system of Basilides is very different from the idea of unity in Neoplatonism, or the notion of salvation in Christianity, wherein the soul returns to God and is united with him according to its capacity. In this Gnostic system, the highest level of union takes place on a tertiary level, within the sphere of the Great Ruler, who presumably has reverted agnostically to his original assumption that he alone is the highest God. For Basilides, restoration means unity within diversity, and each level remains separate and alone: nothing is united with the not-being God.

Although Gnosticism generally proposes a system of knowledge for the elect, in Basilides, *gnosis* would appear to be the principle of restoration on a cosmic level. In this respect, Basilides stands on the fringe of Gnostic thought – it is also notable that no other Gnostic writer had any difficulty in applying the term 'ineffable' to God. In the end, ignorance wins out over and against knowledge, in a system where salvation becomes ignorance of God. This idea is radically different from the Jewish, Platonic, and Christian systems, where knowledge (and even 'unknowing knowing') lead eventually to union with God.

The theology of the not-being God in Basilides does not provide a means whereby the human intellect can come to any knowledge of the divine, and therefore, there is nothing here which can truly

---

[67] VII, 27, 3; the Ptolomaic account of the passionate search of Sophia, the youngest of the Aeons, is obviously at the root of the idea of Basilides that it is impossible to reach the supreme divinity; see Irenaeus, *Adversus Haereses*, I, 2, 2.

be called a negative theology. The God of Basilides is unknown and transcendent, not simply because he is unlike anything in the created world, or because it is difficult to come to any knowledge of his nature, this God is unknown because he has made all things ignorant of him. The Basilidean razor of negative language has been so sharpened that it would appear to have severed the fragile thread of relationship between created nature and God. It has left the world in an indeterminate limbo of imposed cosmic ignorance. God has banished himself to the lonely isolation of the super-celestial region, leaving the world at the mercy of two deluded rulers; yet since ignorance has been imposed no one knows any better anyway. The system of Basilides is perhaps the first example of a religious atheism, for his not-being God can be no more than a metaphysical starting-point.

Although the so-called 'negative theology' of Basilides is radically different from the understanding of negative theology as it will be found in the *Enneads* of Plotinus, nonetheless, some Gnostic texts of this kind may have contributed to the development of negative theology in the later Platonists. If Basilides was teaching at Alexandria in the second century then he would have been contemporaneous with Numenius, and would have preceded Plotinus by some seventy years only. Certainly, it has to be said that the early Christian Apologists actually promulgated Gnostic teaching in their attempts to refute it as heretical, and it is likely that a less radical form of *agnōsia* penetrated Christian theology and scriptural exegesis in its formative years.[68]

Numenius and the Development of Pythagorean Platonism

Numenius (fl. c. AD 150) was born in Apamea in Northern Syria. We know very little about his life, as is the case with so many of the Middle Platonists. He may have taught at Rome, but

---

[68] See J. Daniélou, *Gospel Message and Hellenistic Culture*, p. 338.

other contacts, with Alexandria and Athens, are not certain.[69] Although he is known to us as a Pythagorean, older German opinion classed him as a Gnostic.[70] In 1934, H.-Ch. Puech was prepared to grant this thesis some credibility, but regarded him primarily as a Jew for reasons which will become clear below.[71] Numenius was a very versatile figure, being, among other things, a student of comparative religion, following the tradition of Plutarch and others. His main aim was the attempt to bring all other religious beliefs into line with Platonic philosophy.[72] It has also has been suggested that there are links between Numenius and the Chaldean Oracles and the Hermetic writings.[73] Primarily, Numenius can be regarded as a Platonist, although in his writings we witness an interpretation of both Plato and Aristotle along Pythagorean lines. His Pythagorean roots have been well-attested, and Origen is among the earliest writers to have noted his Pythagorean sympathies.[74] Once again, we possess only fragments of his works, preserved chiefly by Eusebius and Porphyry among others. The fragments form part of four main works: *On The Good*; *On the Incorruptibility of the Soul*; *On the Dissension between the Academics and Plato*;[75] and *On Numbers*.[76]

Numenius, as the last figure in this study of the Middle Platonists, brings us closest to the philosophy of Plotinus, who was to be accused of plagiarizing the teaching of Numenius.[77] Amelius of

[69] See J. Dillon, *The Middle Platonists*, p. 361ff.
[70] See E. Norden, *Agnostos Theos*, p. 72.
[71] 'Numénius d'Apamé et les théologiens orientales au second siècle', pp. 745-778.
[72] See *Fr.* 1.
[73] See J. Dillon, *op. cit.* p. 394ff and E. R. Dodds, 'Numenius and Ammonius', p. 10ff.
[74] *Contra Celsum*, I, 15 and IV, 51.
[75] A discussion of Numenius's views on the Academy can be found in D. J. O'Meara, *Pythagoras Revived*, pp. 10-13.
[76] The edition I have used is the most recent one by Des Places (Paris, 1973); for some of the more important points I also give references, in brackets, to the older Leemans edition, *Studie over den Wijsgeer Numenius van Apamea mit Uitgave der Fragmenten* (Brussels, 1937).
[77] See *Vita Plot.* 17, 1.

Apamea, a follower of Numenius and his chief promulgator, was
also a friend of Plotinus, and indeed the editor of the *Enneads* until
Porphyry displaced him; it is no doubt through this close link that
Numenius was read by Plotinus. The parallels between Numenius
and Plotinus are such that Guthrie argues that it is Numenius who
rightly deserves the title, 'Father of Neoplatonism'.[78] Whether this
is a valid point will become clearer as this discussion progresses.
With regard to Numenius, the question of oriental influences again
arises. It is certainly the case that there are in the extant fragments
some ideas which cannot easily be traced to either Plato or
Pythagoras, but it is now generally held that Numenius was a true
representative of the Greek theological perspective (although some
older scholars have had some reservations[79]).

The quest of Numenius for the Incorporeal (*to asōmaton*) as
true being, has an almost Plotinian or Augustinian flavour, as he
proceeds by asking the questions: 'is it the elements?' (it cannot
be for they were made and are, therefore, transitory); 'is it matter?' (it cannot be because matter is not stable).[80] For Numenius,
the unlimited, indefinite, unknowable aspects of matter point to a
principle which maintains it, and nothing else holds matter in existence other than the Incorporeal.[81] Although the more metaphysical fragments of Numenius concern *to on* in the Platonic sense, the
use of the term 'incorporeal', while it may have Platonic connotations, also has strong Philonic and Jewish overtones. The extent of
the influence of Philo on Numenius has of course been questioned,
but it is certain that Numenius was familiar with the basic outlines
of Jewish thought, whether at first or second hand it is not certain.
In a true Platonic sense, 'the incorporeal' is the only thing that can
endure; it is the only self-adjusted reality, and is not subject to the
tendencies of other bodies: it is not generated, not increased, and
not disturbed by motion. It has, therefore, the highest rank among
the things that are. In *Fragment 5*, Numenius uses the familiar

[78] *Numenius of Apamea*, pp. 95-98.
[79] See for example, E. R. Dodds, 'Numenius and Ammonius', p. 11.
[80] *Fr.* 3 (12L).
[81] *Fr.* 4a (13L).

Platonic negations concerning *to on*: it is timeless, motionless and permanent, eternal, firm, ever-equable, and identical. It admits of no generation, destruction, increase or decrease, and has no place or motion.[82] Numenius says that the name for this principle, 'the Incorporeal', is a name for which he has long been searching: Being, the Existent.[83] He has already given the reason why the Incorporeal should be *to on* in a truly Platonic sense; he repeats the negations concerning the 'incorporeal' for *ousia*, adding 'simple', a term that had already been used by Alcinous. The Incorporeal alone is intelligible, and Numenius quotes from *Timaeus* 27D, concluding that the Existent has nothing to do with matter, but as eternal and immutable, can be contemplated only by reason.[84] Once again, Numenius is following the traditional Platonic view in asserting that true being can be understood through *nous*, yet in the fragments we possess, true being is not the highest reality; that place is reserved for the first God.

The more theological fragments of Numenius are numbered 11-22 in the edition of Des Places, and it is to these that I now turn my attention. While I hesitate only slightly to draw parallels between the philosophical fragments just outlined and the theological fragments which follow, it would seem more than likely that the truly Existent, the Incorporeal, could also be called divinity or God. This notion has been the source of some contention, especially with regard to *Fragment* 13, where the first God is referred to as ὁ ὤν. I discuss this text below.

Numenius's theological hierarchy makes a distinction between the first God, who is simple and concentrated entirely on himself, and the God who is both second and third.[85] Even though the second and third God is in reality one, when he is associated with matter (the dyad in Pythagorean terms) he is divided and torn apart by it. This demiurge is not the ignorant creator of Basilides, but

---

[82] *Fr.* 5, 19-20.
[83] *Fr.* 6, 6-7.
[84] *Fr.* 7, 1 and 10 and 8, 5.
[85] *Fr.* 11, 11-14.

the demiurge of the *Timaeus*, although the distinction between a supreme God and a creator God is admittedly recognized as being a Gnostic idea.[86] However, Gnosticism may not be the source for this idea in Numenius, for it also appears in Philo. Now since it would appear that Numenius may have known the works of Philo of Alexandria (whether at first or second hand), it is possible that he borrowed the distinction from that Jewish source and applied it to his own theology; as I will later show, *Timaeus* 28C had no small part to play in this matter.[87]

In *Fragment* 11, the unity of the second and third Gods is slightly ambiguous, for Numenius calls the *kosmos* a God. H.-Ch. Puech has argued that the distinction between the second and third Gods is to be understood as a distinction between the transcendent and immanent aspects of the demiurge.[88] However, although Numenius gives *kosmos* the name *theos*, I do not think he intends it to be understood in the same way as the first and second principles are Gods (perhaps he was attempting to adapt the Stoic idea and account for the divine nature of the world as the creation of God, and therefore imbued with his presence). In *Fragment* 21, which is preserved in the *In Timaeum* of Proclus, it would seem that Numenius did call creation the third God, and this is explained in terms of 'father', 'son' and 'grandson' – here is one instance where Numenius appears to rely on the *Corpus Hermeticum*, or on a common source.[89]

This triad, first God (who is later called *nous*), the demiurge and the world, is purely a Platonic development, and can be found in

---

[86] See Irenaeus, *Adversus haereses*, I, 19, 2 and I, 26, 1. J. Dillon senses danger when Numenius suggests that the demiurge creates as a result of his *orexis* for matter, but here the supposed Gnostic element depends on the translation of *orexis* (see *The Middle Platonists*, p. 369). Dillon uses the word 'lust', while Des Places translates it as 'désir' (*Fragments*, p. 5), which is, I think, closer to the meaning of Numenius here. C. J. De Vogel also argues against equating the second God of Numenius with the Gnostic demiurge, pointing out that in Gnosticism the demiurge creates the world in ignorance of the ideas (*Greek Philosophy*, Vol. 3, p. 425).

[87] See Philo, *Leg. all.* iii, 207.

[88] 'Numénius d'Apamée', p. 756.

[89] *Fr.* 21, 7 (24L); see *C. H.* VIII and X, 14.

the *Timaeus*.[90] Having made this primary theological distinction, Numenius then accounts for the differences between the first and second divinities. The first God does not create; he is regarded as the Father of the demiurge. He is the King and free from all the work of creation, while the second God rules the world.[91] In *Fragment* 13, Numenius explains the relations between the first and second God in terms of the relation between the farmer and the sower. The second God, the 'legislator', plants and distributes in the soul the seeds sowed by the first God, who is called Ὁ μέν γε ὤν.[92] It is this phrase which has reminded some modern scholars of the text of Ex. 3:14. J. Whittaker, following A.-J. Festugière, thinks that Numenius did have this scriptural passage in mind, and suggests that the most obvious link would have been Philo.[93] I think it is likely that Numenius was, either consciously or unconsciously, appropriating some Jewish source, and although we do not have enough evidence to suggest the direct influence of the Exodus text itself, Philo is one most likely source of the idea in Numenius. It is quite likely that Numenius came across the designation in his researches into comparative religion. Although Numenius does not mention Philo by name, in *Fragment* 1b, he numbers the Jews among those who believe God to be incorporeal, and in *Fragment* 9, there is a reference to Moses as the man who became most able to pray to God. However, in *Fragment* 56, Numenius is reported as having called the God of the Temple in Jerusalem 'the Father of all the Gods' and while this kind of idea finds expression in the Old Testament,[94] it is certainly not a Jewish sentiment; in fact it provides the most damning evidence against the thesis that Numenius himself was a Jew. His repeated use of Platonic terms (in preference to biblical terms) shows that while he was sympathetic towards Judaism, he came down more

[90] 39E.
[91] *Fr.* 12 (21L).
[92] *Fr.* 13, 4.
[93] *Les doctrines de l'âme* (Paris, 1953), p. 44 and 'Moses Atticizing', p. 196.
[94] See *Contra Celsum*, IV, 51, where Origen says that Numenius used allegories on the Old Testament.

strongly on the side of Platonism, and *Fragment* 13 is the only place where he uses the term ὁ ὤν in favour of τὸ ὄν.

Fragment 16 is perhaps the most important passage left to us from the writings of Numenius: here he explains his theology more succinctly. He retains the same order of deity, but gives each level a different name. The first God is called *nous*; he is the Good in itself and the principle of being. This fragment is interesting in respect of the fact that Numenius says that the first God is the demiurge of being. The second God, therefore, is the principle of becoming. In *Fragment* 21, preserved by Proclus, it is reported that it is the first and second Gods who are double, not the second and third. Again in *Fragment* 22, Proclus repeats the idea of a close relationship between the first and second Gods. The first God is 'that which really is', and is related to the second God through *nous* and to the third God through discursive reasoning. It is because Numenius says that the first God is the demiurge of being that Proclus has grounds for relating the first and second Gods in the way that he does. However, I do not think that Numenius would have regarded the first God as the demiurge of the world; he looked upon him simply as the source of being. After all, to understand the first God as demiurge is not consistent with the sentiments of *Fragment* 11; perhaps 'principle' of being would have been a better word for him to have used (this would certainly hint at *Republic* 509B).

In *Fragment* 17, there is a very interesting interpretation of *Timaeus* 28C regarding the unknowability of God. Numenius interprets this text to mean that only the demiurge is knowable, while the first God, the first *nous*, beauty in itself, is entirely unknowable. It is this passage which has been cited in conjunction with the idea of the unknowable God of Gnosticism, and it is in reality the first Platonic reference to God as unknowable. It may well be the case that Numenius is thinking in Gnostic terms here, but equally he may have understood Plato to mean that there is both a creator and a Father. This is not inconceivable. He goes on to say that the *nous* which the human intellect perceives dimly is not the first God, because anterior to this *nous* is another mind, even more ancient and divine. Although this could be understood to mean that the first God is above *nous*, the fact that Numenius refers to the first God as *nous* lessens the impact of his statement; it illustrates that confusion over the status of the divine hierarchy which is characteristic of second-century Platonism. Like the deity of Alcinous, the first God of Numenius remains firmly at the level of being and *nous*;[95] it is not surprising, therefore, that Numenius does not use the passage from the *Republic* (509B), a passage which was to be much favoured by Plotinus. Following *Republic* 508E, Numenius calls the supreme God the 'idea of the Good', because the first God is the idea from which the demiurge receives his goodness. Therefore, while there is in Numenius a straining towards a transcendent principle who is beyond both being and intellect, in the fragments we possess, Numenius never quite makes this explicit.

There is one phrase from *Fragment* 19 which is interesting from a Plotinian perspective. Here, Numenius repeats the statement from the 'Lecture on the Good': 'the Good is the One'. Although the idea is not developed by Numenius in this instance, we may reasonably conjecture that while he does not use the term 'one' interchangeably with 'good', 'intellect', 'being', or 'God', this identification is nevertheless important; yet its impact is some-what dulled (at least it must have been for Plotinus), by the fact that 'one', even in its identification with 'good', remains at the level of being. It is strange that Numenius, as a Pythagorean, did not make more use of the term 'one' to describe the first God. Although he says that his own ideas are based on Plato and the Pythagoreans, I cannot find very much in the fragments we possess to link him with Eudorus and Moderatus. His theology has much more in common with Alcinous than with the theories of the early neo-Pythagoreans. However, in contrast to Alcinous and Maximus of Tyre, where we found the notion of abstraction (*aphairesis*), in the fragments of Numenius we do not find any-

---

[95] Although the first God is not a thinking intellect (*Fr.* 16); he calls on the help of the second God to think.

thing of the negative theology which is such an important part of the *Enneads*, unless we consider the negations concerning the Incorporeal in *Fragment 5*.

In *Fragment 2* Numenius points the way one should follow in order to reach the first God who is unknowable (*agnooumenos*);[96] it was this passage which must have influenced Plotinus, and it earned for Numenius himself the title of 'mystic'. It is also in this text that we find the closest suggestion of the method of *aphairesis*. There is no sensible object, nor anything material which resembles the Good or offers a possibility of attaining to it, so the way must be a way which transcends all sensible images. The image used to express this 'way' of reaching the Good shows Numenius at his most poetic, and immediately reminds the reader of many passages in the *Enneads*. Just as one who sits in an observation tower and sees, in one 'glance', a small solitary fishing boat, 'unique, isolated and abandoned', enveloped by the waves, so too can one catch a glimpse of the Good. It is through being far removed from all sensible things, that one may see the Good, like the 'alone to the alone'. The phrase, μόνῳ μόνον, was of course made famous by Plotinus;[97] it was he who, according to E. R. Dodds, gave it real significance in a metaphysical sense with the inspired addition of φυγή, escape, although Philo, a fellow Alexandrian, had used a similar phrase regarding flight to the uncreated.[98] In that lonely place where one finds the Good, says Numenius, there is neither man nor anything living, but 'an inexpressible, indefinable, immediate and divine solitude'. In that solitude, the Good reigns over all existence in a manner which is benevolent, peaceful and tender. This almost Plotinian description emphasizes the transcendent nature of the Good in a way that is more explicit than in any other fragment. Yet Numenius warns that this approach is not an easy one, and anyone who imagines that he has seen the Good while still in the midst of the sensible

---

[96] From the verb ἀγνοέω, to be ignorant of (*Fr.* 17).
[97] See *Enn.* VI 9, 1.
[98] 'Numenius and Ammonius', p. 17; see also *Quod Deus*, 160.

world must be mistaken – a familiar sentiment of later negative theology. In reality, this ascent to the Good involves, firstly, a movement away from sensible things, secondly an enthusiasm for the study of the sciences, and thirdly, a serious consideration of numbers; only then will one be able to attain to the object of the supreme science. These studies, which are undertaken as a preparation for one who would embark on the path to the Good, are to be understood in terms of a rigorous preparation of the mind, for the way to a vision of the supreme God was through practical training, and that involved, as it was to do for Plotinus, a study of mathematics and numbers.

It is thus that we are brought closer to the notion of the Plotinian One, and although in Numenius there is no systematic denial involved in the ascent, the Good is placed above the realm of the sensible and intelligible. While God is never described as 'beyond being', the way to the unknowable first God is not a way which can be understood as remaining on the level of intellect; it is more intuitive. In this regard it is but a short step to the Plotinian One, although there are many ideas in Numenius with which Plotinus would not have agreed. The ambiguity concerning the supremacy of *nous* and *agathon* reflects a conflict between Plato and Aristotle which only Plotinus would resolve in his own unique fashion. However, we must be careful not to propel Numenius forward into the Plotinian system, nor equally to move backwards in the attempt always to find some traditional Platonic basis for Plotinian ideas. Among the Middle Platonists, Numenius was undeniably a unique figure and important in his own right. Although much of that which is more fully developed in Plotinus appears, at least in embryonic form, in Numenius, I must reject K. S. Guthrie's proposal to adopt Numenius as the true Father of Neoplatonism; equally, I will not attempt to monopolize that title for Plotinus. If one wishes to foist the paternity of Neoplatonism on anyone, then both Speusippus and Eudorus must also be considered as likely candidates. Although Neoplatonism developed slowly over two of the most important centuries of Hellenistic thought, it is useful to retain the traditional distinction between Middle Platonism and

Neoplatonism; the latter can usefully be said to have begun with Plotinus. It was he who reworked and rethought many of the philosophical and theological ideas of Middle Platonism and constructed his own system, which, although it owes much to his predecessors, Numenius in particular, remains without parallel in Greek thought.

CHAPTER FIVE

PLOTINUS: THE INEFFABLE ONE

The student of Plotinus, like the student of Augustine, Aquinas or any other major thinker who has been the subject of much detailed research, faces a number of problems at the outset of his or her research. After an initial period of enthusiasm, one begins to wonder rather despondently whether it has not all been said before. A further disconcerting aspect of the study of Plotinus is that there exists a vast amount of secondary literature which appears to deal with Plotinus under every aspect and guise; although the theme of negative theology is not a well-researched one. To date, the student of Plotinian negative theology will be indebted to J. Trouillard, J. M. Rist and, more particularly, to A. H. Armstrong. I do not intend to add to the reader's burden by prefacing this chapter with a general introduction to Plotinian thought, nor with biographical information which can be found, not only in secondary sources but also, and perhaps best of all, in the account written by the earliest biographer of Plotinus, Porphyry.

As with the other authors I am dealing with in this volume, my aim with regard to Plotinus is to attempt to set down in an orderly fashion his thoughts concerning the nature of the One, and the method or ways advocated by him in order that the One can be reached. I believe that some important texts regarding the way of negation in Plotinus have not hitherto been studied in a systematic fashion, both with regard to his Middle Platonic predecessors and to his own metaphysical scheme. As the student of Plotinus knows only too well, the *Enneads* were not intended for publication as scholarly text books, and the many inconsistencies which are apparent in them do not so much reflect a clear-cut development in

Plotinus's thought, as betray his shifting emphasis and perspective as he examines the nature of the One, the Good, and Beauty.

Much has been written on the famous assertion of Plotinus that the One is not only beyond being but also beyond thought; some have concluded that in positing such an extremely remote first principle, Plotinus has destroyed his own metaphysical system by refining the One out of all existence. I do not believe that this is a valid criticism and I hope to demonstrate in the course of this discussion that the return of all things to the One, conceived either in individual or in cosmic terms, does not have to leave a causal metaphysical scheme in place behind it, since there is no longer any need for this. The idea of an 'anarchic' ontological system can, at least to some extent help to explain Plotinus's idea of unity with the One, although we must be careful not to superimpose later thought forms on the *Enneads* in such a way as to destroy or conceal Plotinus's own meaning.[1]

Jung's observation that the Western mind finds it difficult to function without the aid of concepts, is particularly relevant to the study of Plotinus, for it is not easy to shrug off an inherited understanding of a metaphysical system in order to come to an understanding of Plotinus's way of the non-concept. The mighty, unknown One of the *Enneads* is not only the Alone – that which is unrelated to all things, above being, and beyond thought – but also the Creator and Father of all; he is infinitely desirable and always present to the soul, had it but eyes to look. In other words, Plotinus, like all the great masters of the way of abstraction or negation, advocates an understanding of the One which is not solely negative, but also positive. Although negative theology in Plotinus is built upon a more positive understanding of the nature of the One, this does not mean that Plotinus was working consciously on the principle later to be advocated by Proclus and the Pseudo-Dionysius: that we must systematically affirm before we can begin to deny.

---

[1] See R. Schürmann's excellent study on Meister Eckhart's anarchic ontological system, 'The Loss of Origin in Soto Zen and in Meister Eckhart, *Thomist*, 42 (1978), pp. 281-312.

In this study of negative theology in the *Enneads*, I have attempted to keep the following phrase always in mind: 'the Good is gentle and kindly and gracious, and present to anyone when he wishes'.[2] No radical form of negative theology can exist without some positive content, otherwise it can but lead to the despair of agnosticism; Plotinus knew this. In this chapter, therefore, as a backdrop and indeed the key to a correct understanding of negative theology in Plotinian thought, I begin by outlining Plotinus's conception of the highest principle, that conception which leans towards a more kataphatic understanding of the One. In order to simplify the account of Plotinus's use of positive and negative terms in relation to the One, I have chosen to discuss those passages where he explains the names or symbolic titles, Creator, Father, King, Beauty, Good, and One – the familiar terms encountered in the writings of the Middle Platonists. These titles are distinct from the terms which are applied to the One in the manner of attributes, such as simple and unique, for Plotinus is most insistent that the One has no attributes.

Kataphasis: Beauty and Good

Like most of his Platonic predecessors, Plotinus firmly believes that the One is the first cause, the creator of all who holds all things together in the universe.[3] Following the *Timaeus*, Plotinus explains that just as the things of the heavenly world derive their being from God, so the things of this world derive their being from the gods derived from him.[4] For Plotinus, the One is conceived primarily as cause of life, mind and being, for the One is the productive power and principle of all things. God not only creates the universe, he also sustains it, because it exists only through him.[5]

---

[2] V 5, 12, 33-35; trans. A. H. Armstrong, p. 193. Unless otherwise noted, translations are from Armstrong's Loeb edition.
[3] II 1, 1, II 1, 4 and V 3, 15.
[4] II 1, 5; see *Tim.* 69C.
[5] I 6, 7; II 9, 9; II 9, 16 – 17; V 1, 7, and V 3, 11.

Thus far, it would appear that Plotinus is not saying anything different from what could have been found in any second-century manual on Platonism; yet Plotinus builds on the notion of the One's transcendence, by affirming that the cause of all things must itself be above all things that it causes.

In the metaphysical scheme of Plotinus, the Father image is a favourite one. In this respect he is not far from the thought of Numenius, in whom the related idea is also found, that *nous*, identified with the demiurge, is fathered by the One: although more often Plotinus speaks of the emanation of *nous* from the One.[6] *Nous*, as the 'son of the Good', is often identified with Zeus 'the father of the gods', 'the oldest of the gods', and 'the son of the all'.[7] When Plotinus speaks in these terms it is evident that Greek religion is not far from his thought; but when he speaks of intellect as the 'offspring of the Good', he is thinking of that passage in the *Republic* where Socrates speaks of the 'offspring of the Good'.[8]

The notion of the One as Father is, I think, a very forceful expression of the intimacy which Plotinus conceived to exist between the Father and the individual soul. His frequent use of the term *patēr* to signify the One in relation to the fallen soul is striking, and explains why Plotinus would have been read with much approval by Christians from the fourth century onwards.[9] In his treatise Against the Gnostics (II 9), Plotinus is opposed to the idea that only some people are special to God: rather, every soul is a child of that Father.[10] The One is not, therefore, simply an abstract, impersonal principle; although in the *Enneads*, 'there is a continual tension and interplay between personal and impersonal ways of thinking about God'.[11]

---

[6] V 1, 8 and VI 7, 29.

[7] III 8, 11; IV 4, 9; V 1, 11; V 8, 10-13; at V 5, 3, 16-24, Plotinus makes use of the Numenian distinction between Grandfather, Father and Son; see P. Hadot 'Oranos, Kronos and Zeus in Plotinus' Treatise Against the Gnostics', in *Neoplatonism and Early Christian Thought* (London, 1981), pp. 124-137.

[8] V 1, 6; see *Rep.* 506D-E.

[9] See for example, I 6, 8.

[10] II 9, 16, 9.

[11] See A. H. Armstrong, 'Plotinus's Doctrine of the Infinite', p. 57.

The Plotinian use of the term *basileus* is no doubt derived from the Middle Platonic use of the word as found in Apuleius, Maximus of Tyre and Numenius. However, the original inspiration for the application of this term can be traced back to Plato's Second letter.[12] Plotinus uses the image of a kingly court in procession in order to show how everything is dependent on the last and highest of things[13] (I will return to this passage in due course because it reveals a very important theme in Plotinus, namely, that there are various levels of knowledge concerning the King of all.) It would seem that Plotinus uses the word 'king' in more than simply metaphorical terms, for at one point he says that this king has 'the most just, the natural sovereignty and the true kingdom'.[14] Once again, Plotinus's use of this word would have struck a note in harmony with the Christian Fathers who later read him.

That the first principle was for Plotinus supremely beautiful is evident even from a cursory reading of the *Enneads*; his treatise On Beauty (the sixth tractate of the first *Ennead*), is perhaps the most well-known of all his writings, both in ancient times and indeed today. In his general account of the ascent towards Beauty, Plotinus follows the Platonic ascent as described in the *Symposium*: one moves from the appreciation of the nature of beautiful bodies inwards to soul and character, and from there upwards through various levels to the Good itself. It is important to note at this point that when Plotinus speaks of the One as Beauty, and indeed Good, these are not to be understood as real qualities of the first principle.[15] I have already pointed out that when Plotinus is speaking of the supreme Beauty he often refers to it as the Good, for the Good is that which is supremely beautiful. It is so beautiful that once it has been seen, the seer is 'full of wonder and delight, enduring a shock which causes no hurt, loving with true passion

---

[12] 312E; see H. Dörrie, 'Der König', in *Platonica Minora* (Munich, 1976), pp. 390-405.
[13] V 5, 3 and VI 8, 9.
[14] V 5, 3, 15-21.
[15] I 6, 6.

and piercing longing'.[16] Yet although it is the most beautiful of all things, its beauty is not the kind of beauty that is composed of a symmetry of parts, for it is *amēchanos*.[17] One further point intimately bound up with the interchange of terms used by Plotinus when speaking about the highest Beauty, is that he is not entirely clear whether the Good is Beauty or whether it lies beyond it. Although Plotinus would not deny that the Good is beautiful, there are some passages in the *Enneads* where he appears to shift his emphasis slightly to assert the supremacy of the Good over Beauty. The Good, he says, holds Beauty as a screen before it, and is itself beyond Beauty.[18] Here Plotinus identifies Beauty with *nous*; thus, to speak of the Good as Beauty is to speak, as Plotinus puts it, in 'a loose and general way'.[19]

I suspect that one reason why Plotinus is sometimes a little reluctant to place Beauty on the same level as the Good is because of the very obvious beauty which exists in the physical world: earthly beauty can sometimes be dangerous, he says, in that it can involve a falling into evil if the lover loses sight of the highest Beauty in the veneration of earthly beauty.[20] Thus, while Plotinus would be reluctant to say that the love of earthly beauty is of itself evil, he does warn against the dangers which are to be found in the ascent towards absolute Beauty. Yet it is not only earthly beauty which can distract from the One, but intelligible beauty also.[21] In *Ennead* V 5, Plotinus describes 'the First' as enthroned upon a pedestal which is *nous*, and although this Beauty is 'inconceivable' or 'uncontrived', it remains firmly on the level of Intellect. In another passage from the same *Ennead*, Plotinus asserts that the passionate love of beauty, even intellectual beauty, 'causes pain,

---

[16] I 6, 7, 15-18.
[17] I 6, 8, 2 and V 5, 3, 8; see *Symp.* 218E.
[18] I 6, 9.
[19] I 6, 9, 39-40.
[20] III 5, 1; on this theme, see A. H. Armstrong, 'The Divine Enhancement of Earthly Beauties: The Hellenic and Platonic Tradition', in *Hellenic and Christian Studies*, Variorum Reprints II, n. IV.
[21] V 5, 12 and VI 7, 22.

because one must have seen it to desire it'.[22] Love of beauty, therefore, is secondary to the more ancient and unperceived desire for the Good. Beauty itself is dead without the 'colour cast upon it from the Good',[23] for Beauty is younger than the Good (in truth, not in time), and Beauty needs the Good, whereas the Good does not need Beauty.[24] Ultimately, however, both participate in the One who is before them both;[25] this is one of the few places in the *Enneads* where Plotinus speaks of the Good as being somehow subordinate to the One, for the thesis which appears to be the backbone of the *Enneads* is that famous Platonic statement from the 'Lecture on the Good': 'the Good is the One'.

Yet, there are many passages in the *Enneads* where Plotinus speaks of the First as absolute Beauty and I think his emphasis is coloured by the context or perspective from which he is speaking. For example, when he is referring to the ultimate vision of the One, he speaks in terms of sight; and since Beauty is what is beautiful to the eye, it is, therefore, the 'content' of the vision. Plotinus does not talk about the vision of the One in the same way that he talks about the vision of the Good and the Beautiful. When he is referring to the vision of the highest Beauty, he calls it the 'Beauty above Beauty', and the 'beyond Beauty'.[26] Therefore, while Plotinus does not hesitate to speak of the One as the first Beauty, strictly speaking, Beauty belongs to the level of *nous*. In terms of a strict negative theology, which was I think a very important part of Plotinus's thought, the One or the Good must be free of everything, even Beauty itself.[27] In this sense, the One must be thought of as being beyond Beauty.

In three specific treatises in the *Enneads* Plotinus deals explicitly with the question of the nature of the Good, although his thoughts on the subject are scattered throughout his writings.[28]

---

[22] V 5, 12, 15-16.
[23] VI 7, 22, 6.
[24] V 5, 12.
[25] V 5, 12, 31.
[26] VI 7, 32, 29 and VI 7, 33, 20.
[27] V 5, 13.
[28] See I 7, VI 7 and VI 9.

While the negative terms applied to the Good are an important element in Plotinus's thought, his conception of the Good as expressed in 'positive' terms is, I think, the more prominent element in the *Enneads*. At this point I shall give only the very general outline of the ideas concerning the nature of the Good as Plotinus presents it in the *Enneads*.

In positive terms, the Good is the absolute Good; it is at the same time Beauty and beyond Beauty, and also the One.[29] The transcendent Good, as the cause of goodness, is that upon which everything depends and to which all things aspire; it is the *telos*, the end of human desire, for all things need the Good as if they realised that they could not live without it.[30] Even though the Good is conceived in terms of the dynamic out-flowing good for all things, in general terms, the Good shares with the One the most elevated position in Plotinus's ontological system and ultimately, nothing can be said about its nature. However, his use of the term 'Good' to convey some positive information about the nature of the One, remains firmly embedded in the post-Platonic tradition of philosophy. I have already mentioned the conclusion of Plato's 'Lecture on the Good' in chapter two of the present study, where I noted that after Plato, the Platonic school was hesitant to equate the Good with the One (with the exception of the neo-Pythagoreans). However, not even in Numenius, supposedly the greatest Pythagorean of his day, do we find such an explicit identification of the One and the Good as we do in Plotinus. It would appear that the six centuries between Plato and Plotinus had the effect that the stark conclusions of the *Parmenides* lost some of their original meaning and acquired a strong theological significance. There is no doubt that Plotinus read the *Parmenides* with the 'single eye of faith', as E. R. Dodds put it,[31] but the actual progression which transformed this Platonic dialogue into a theological doctrine is most difficult to trace with complete accuracy. I have attempted to

---

[29] I 4, 3; I 6, 6; I 6, 9, and II 9, 1.
[30] I 4, 4; I 6, 7; I 7, 1; I 8, 2; V 5, 1 and 12; VI 7, 25, and VI 8, 13.
[31] 'The *Parmenides* of Plato and the Origin of the Neoplatonic One', p. 133.

outline these steps in the previous chapters, but so much of the literature of the period is not extant that we remain on very shaky ground on all but the basic outline. I now turn my attention to the nature of the One in Plotinus's thought, with the reminder that by whatever name we call it, we must think of it as a single nature: it does not possess attributes such as goodness and beauty as part of its nature, for it is to be understood as absolutely one.

The One

Plotinus read the *Parmenides* very carefully and accordingly his conception of the nature of the One owes much to that source. The definition of One for Plotinus, is simply 'oneness', and those 'attributes' which portray the One simply as a one, are outlined as follows. The One is primarily simple (*haplous*), it is the 'simply one' who is at the same time the cause of all multiplicity.[32] Simplicity for Plotinus also means that the One must be understood as unmixed, single, and pure.[33] The One must be simple, because if it were composite it would be dependent on its parts; since it is before all things as their cause, it cannot be a part of any thing, therefore it is the First of all things. Plotinus often couples 'simple' and 'primal', for in the metaphysical scheme of the *Enneads*, there is something simple which exists before all things.[34] The One is the most simple; it is simpler than *nous* and simpler than the intelligible world, because it is a one whereas they are composite. For Plotinus, to speak of the One as simple is to speak the truth about it, even though to speak thus does not say anything clear or distinct about it.[35]

In positive terms, at least in respect of those terms which are not negative or prefixed with the *alpha* privative, there is a number of concepts which appear to depend upon the notion of the One as

---

[32] II 9, 1; III 8, 10; V 2, 1; V 3, 1; VI 7, 25, and VI 7, 37.
[33] See I 6, 7, 9-10.
[34] V 3, 11, V 4, 1, and V 5, 10.
[35] III 8, 9, 16-18.

simple. However, I do not wish to suggest that Plotinus was working with the intention of logically predicating certain attributes of
the One; since it seems to me rather that the term 'simple' is of the
utmost importance: all other concepts would appear to be dependent upon it.

The One must be self-sufficient (*autarkēs*) for the same reason
that it is simple; for it cannot be dependent on a number of parts,
nor is it a compound of any kind.[36] Being self-sufficient, the One
is totally without need and lacks nothing; the transcendence and
self-sufficiency of the One means that while it does not need
anything, all other things need the One.[37] Plotinus's strongest
statement regarding the self-sufficient nature of the One is
that, 'he would not have cared if it [the world] had not come
into being'.[38] This is one consequence of affirming the absolute
unity of the One. At this point, I must mention that Plotinus
experienced some difficulty in explaining how multiplicity
came from this absolute, simple unity; this, however, is not a
question which is related directly to my theme, except in so far
as multiplicity is, as Plotinus puts it, a 'one-everywhere', or
a 'one-many'.[39] This notion is related to the concept of the
presence of the One in the universe and as such plays an important part in the conversion of the soul to the One. I discuss this
theme below.

Other 'positive terms' which Plotinus uses concerning the One
include perfect (*teleios*): it is perfect because it is totally without
need; it is 'always perfect' and indeed the most perfect of all
things[40] (this was also an important idea in the *Didaskalikos* of
Alcinous, although there, God was understood as the most perfect
being). As perfect, the One is also unique in form (*monoeidēs*) or,
as Plotinus prefers to say, formless (*aneideon*), and being in such
a manner perfect and unique, unlike all other things, it is self-cre-

[36] II 9, 1; V 6, 2; V 7, 38; VI 7, 23; VI 8, 7, and VI 9, 6.
[37] I 8, 2; III 8, 11; V 3, 12, and V 5, 10.
[38] V 5, 12, 40ff; see also V 4, 1, 10-15.
[39] V 3, 15, 20-22.
[40] V 1, 6, 38.

ative, self-tending, self-related and self-defined.[41] Such a perfection, then, since there exists nothing else like it, cannot but exist on a level which is totally its own: it is alone; in fact, it is the Alone.[42] The famous expression 'μόνον καὶ ἔρημον' is ultimately derived from Plato, although it is possible that the use of this phrase by Plotinus owes more to its employment by Numenius than to Plato, by whom it is used in a totally different context.[43]

There is one other 'positive' term used very frequently by Plotinus, and this is *metron*. Interestingly, it is not a term afforded much discussion by the Middle Platonists, and by its very nature, it is a term which stands out from all the other positive terms used by Plotinus. Like Plato, Plotinus would have been totally opposed to the Protagorean dictum, 'man is the measure of all things', for the measure of things must be their cause, and for Plotinus this was, of course, the Good.[44] This activity of the Good (that is, the imposition of measure and definition) is totally opposed to the characteristics of evil, which is unmeasured because it has not been subject to the limitation of form. Measurement, as an act of the divine measure upon an object, is, therefore, a 'kind of Reason-Principle'.[45] Yet for Plotinus, the One itself is never identified with the principle of *nous*; even though the One is the measure of all things, the One itself is unmeasured, and does 'not come within the range of number'; 'for who is there to measure it?'[46]

At this stage I wish to pause for a moment to draw breath, for Plotinus has drawn a very vivid picture of the One as the creator, father, and king of the universe who is absolute Beauty and absolute Good. In this respect, Plotinus shows his reliance on the Middle Platonic school of thought, and is particularly close to the ideas of Alcinous. The other 'positive' terms used by Plotinus:

[41] VI 8, 14-17 and VI 9, 3, 43-44.
[42] V 5, 10 and VI 7, 32.
[43] *Philebus* 63B; see A. H. Armstrong's note in vol. V of the Loeb edition, p. 104.
[44] See I 8, 2, 5 and VI 8, 18, 3.
[45] VI 1, 9, 24-25.
[46] V 5, 4, 13; V 5, 11, 2-3, and VI 6, 18, 6.

simple, self-sufficient, and so on, are, upon closer examination, not capable of revealing very much about the One, except that it is not compounded, does not need anything, does not lack anything, is not like anything and is not related to anything. It is at this point that some Christian theists complain that the idea of a supreme being who has no contact with humanity is not sufficient to sustain belief and love. It would seem, therefore, that even when Plotinus is speaking about the One or the Good from what would appear to be a kataphatic viewpoint, his thought is still more inclined to a negative rather than to a positive conception. For what knowledge does the human intellect obtain when it thinks of the One in this way? Even though the One is spoken of in terms which are derived from the realm of the finite, these terms do not tell us anything about the One except that he is self-sufficient, perfect, and so on; we do not know what perfection is in relation to the One, because we know only limited, determined being. The important point here is that the words we use enable us to have some point of contact, however dim and uncertain, with the infinite.

The close relationship between Plotinian thought and Christian thought in many cases makes the whole question of the correct interpretation of Plotinus quite problematic at times. We cannot criticize Plotinus because his idea of the One is found wanting from a perspective which relies heavily upon the biblical, more kataphatic, understanding of God. Nonetheless, it is often quite difficult to scrape away the layers of a Christian theology and overlays of meaning with which we come to the reading of the *Enneads*. While it is true that the One is the primary point in the metaphysical scheme of Plotinus, I think A. H. Armstrong's comment, that Plotinus believed in the One, is something that the reader must not forget.[47] Plotinus's quest for the fatherland where the Good is, the Good who is gentle, kindly and gracious, is a quest which cannot under any terms be said to be a cold, metaphysical exercise.

---

47 'Plotinus's Doctrine of The Infinite', p. 57.

Although Plotinus speaks of the One as the Good and Beauty, there are many instances where he uses the most superlative of terms, chiefly with the prefix *hyper* or by using *epekeina*, and in these passages it can be said that Plotinus is attempting to express the absolute transcendence of the Good, which nevertheless stands in some sort of relation to human nature; this is what A. H. Armstrong has called the 'negative theology of positive transcendence'.[48] The Good is the 'best of things', the excellent; there is nothing above it, for it is the highest; there is nothing equal to it or mightier.[49] It is 'beyond what is best';[50] it is the most self-sufficient, the most simple, the most perfect, the most blessed, the most powerful;[51] it is 'truer than the truth', the cause of causes, and the king of kings.[52] It is the One beyond the two, and even 'more one than God'; it is Beauty beyond Beauty and even the Good above the Good.[53] The kind of language Plotinus uses to express the nature of the One can be regarded as one outcome of the method of the negative theology: these statements do not say what the One is, yet their means of expression gives the human intellect some sort of positive content. However this way of working (affirmation, negation, and super-affirmation) was not uppermost in Plotinus's mind, for the kind of negative theology which emerges in the *Enneads* is not thematically developed in the way that Eriugena develops his '*plus quam*' method of resolving the problem of speech about God. However, when we read the passages in the *Enneads* where Plotinus insists that the Good cannot be spoken of in any way (save in terms of what comes after him), and indeed cannot be known, it is clear that his fundamental outlook is not so very far removed from the ideas expressed by Eriugena some six hundred years later.

It is to negation in the *Enneads* that I now turn my attention. My aim is to show that there are at least two levels of the operation of

---

[48] *The Architecture of the Intelligible Universe*, p. 29ff.
[49] I 7, 1; V 5, 1; VI 7, 23; VI 7, 32; VI 7, 34; VI 8, 16, and VI 8, 17.
[50] I 8, 2.
[51] II 9, 1; V 4, 1; V 5, 2; VI 5, 11, and VI 7, 23.
[52] V 5, 3; VI 7, 34, and VI 8, 18.
[53] I 6, 9; I 8, 2; II 8, 9; VI 7, 32; VI 7, 34; VI 8, 13, and VI 9, 6.

negation with relation to the One. At this point, while I do not wish to make any clear-cut distinctions, I would suggest that there exists the negation which is necessarily entailed by the nature of the One simply as one, and there is the negation which goes beyond this in affirming the absolute unknowability of the Good and the One.

The *Parmenides*

The *via negativa* proper is not a concept which is thematically developed in the *Enneads* in the same way as it is found in Proclus or in the *Mystical Theology* of the Pseudo-Dionysius. However, Plotinus's ideas on the subject are nonetheless clear. I have already pointed out that the absolute unity of the One, as Plotinus expresses it in positive terms, can also be expressed in negative terms – for example, 'simple' means 'not compounded' in its very basic sense. It is because of the absolute unity of the One that it is not like anything in the created order; one of Plotinus's most frequently repeated phrases is that the One is not related to anything, while all things are related to it; the One is other than, or not one of the things, and, therefore, has no contrary.[54]

There is one passage in the *Enneads* where Plotinus advocates, like Proclus and the Pseudo-Dionysius, beginning from the negation of the lowest things and proceeding to the negation of the highest things.[55] There is, however, one important point to keep in mind: although the *Parmenides* was most probably an exercise in logical dialectic, by the time of Plotinus, it had become a doctrine 'indispensable to salvation'.[56] Therefore, the negation of created attributes, like shape and size is, for Plotinus an ordinary part of the idea of the One as one, but the negations of the other concepts,

---

[54] II 9, 9, 2-3; III 8, 9-10, and I 8, 6, 20-21; see W. Beierwaltes, 'Andersheit. Zur neuplatonischen Struktur einer Problemgeschichte', in *Le néoplatonisme*, pp. 365-372, and *Identität und Differenz*, pp. 24-56.

[55] VI 9, 3.

[56] E. R. Dodds, 'The *Parmenides* of Plato', p. 133.

such as knowledge or naming, have now become imbued with a deeper, more theological meaning. I would suggest that Plotinus found it necessary to negate 'attributes' such as *nous* and *ousia*, not simply in the search for an absolute unity conceived of in metaphysical terms, but also from the viewpoint of a 'lived experience' of negative theology. I begin, then, with a brief discussion of those negations which place the One outside of all created being.

The One has no size or extension; it is shapeless and has no parts.[57] To have no shape or size indicates formlessness, or as Plotinus puts it, it is 'formless form'.[58] Since it is formless, it cannot be placed in any category into which created being can be placed; therefore it has no place.[59] Neither is the One in time and neither movement nor rest can be attributed to it, but from it comes all movement and rest.[60] I have already noted that the One has no principle; it is, therefore, ungenerated, the origin that has no origin.[61] Since the One is not generated, it must be self-creative, although Plotinus explains that this self-making is not to be interpreted in a literal sense but in the sense that what the One is, it is from before eternity, for it is simultaneous with itself.[62]

However, there is a number of negations in the *Enneads* which are not explicit in the *Parmenides*, and these are: the One is unlimited (in the sense of indefinite rather than infinite), unmeasured and uncircumscribed. That the One is boundless is in the Plotinian scheme of things, a notion which is difficult to reconcile with the Platonic notion of the forms. As the cause of all things, the One must be placed outside of all limit, for it is the principle of limit for all other things; it cannot be restricted by either number or proportion. The more familiar Greek understanding of matter as *apeiron* obviously posed a problem for Plotinus, and it is an idea which demands some clarification. In the *Enneads*, matter

[57] VI 4, 1, 30-31; VI, 7, 18, 39, and VI 9, 6, 8.
[58] VI 7, 32, 9-10; VI 7 17, 39-40; VI 7, 17, 35-36, and VI 7, 33, 4.
[59] II 2, 2, 24.
[60] III 9, 7, 1-2; V 5, 10, 17, and VI 5, 11, 14.
[61] VI 8, 10, 1-2 and VI 8, 11, 8-9.
[62] VI 8, 16, 17-18.

is unlimited, but not incidentally: it is unlimited because it has not been subject to the limitation of form.[63] Plotinus then asks the obvious question: how do the two kinds of unlimitedness differ? Herein lies the crux of the whole matter. The simplest answer would be that the unlimitedness of matter in this world would be less unlimited than the unlimitedness of matter in the intelligible world, for the One is more than all things; but this cannot be the case. It is, rather, more unlimited because 'it is an image which has escaped from being and truth'.[64] Unlimitedness is more present in that which is less defined, and matter is truly unlimited of itself, whereas the One is essential unlimitedness, precisely because it cannot be limited by anything, and is, therefore, a rational formative principle.[65] In the Platonic scheme of reality, the world of the forms, as that which is really real, is being in the fullest sense, and belongs to the realm of limit, definition and knowledge. If one can know only that which belongs to the realm of the defined and limited, then, it is not surprising that in the Plotinian scheme of things the One, conceived as being outside all limit, cannot be known. It is not the case that Plotinus has turned Platonic ontology on its head, rather, he developed this Platonic notion further, for if true being is that which is limited, definable and knowable, then the Good, beyond being, beyond the world of forms, must be unlimited if it is to be the principle of limit.

The notion of the 'infinity' of the One in Plotinus is a complex notion in the context of Platonic thought, and Plotinus was the first Greek philosopher to introduce the notion into his thought, albeit very tentatively. It is understandable that when Plotinus is speaking of the One as infinite, he often displays a certain uneasiness, no doubt because the term was one normally applied to the indefiniteness of matter.[66] He is more comfortable when speaking of the

---

[63] II 4, 15; see J. Heiser, 'Plotinus and the *Apeiron* of Plato's *Parmenides*'.

[64] II 4, 15, 23-24.

[65] II 4, 14, 32.

[66] 'Indefinite' is on the *kakon* side of the Pythagorean table of opposites and engendered a prejudice which was not fully overcome until the Athenian Platonists, Syrianus and Proclus.

infinity of the One in terms of the unlimited nature of its power.[67] The other two concepts, unmeasured and uncircumscribed, are also bound up with the notion of the One's unlimitedness. Because the One is the principle of measure it cannot be measured.[68] Since nothing existed before the One, it cannot be contained in anything; neither is it confined within bounds.[69] Thus, in the *Enneads*, matter is a kind of unlimitedness, unmeasuredness and unboundedness in relation to the limiting, measuring and binding powers of the One, but the One remains above the things it limits (or brings into being), and cannot itself be understood in terms of limit or measure. Plotinus's solution to the problem of the unlimitedness of the One hinges upon his thesis that the two kinds of unlimitedness can never be regarded in the same way: the One is unlimited by excess, as the giver of limit, whereas matter is unlimited by defect because the measure of the One has not reached it.

Apophasis

Thus far, the negations I have outlined have followed naturally and logically from the affirmation of the unity and simplicity of the One and very few of these negations (with the exception of unlimitedness) would have been alien to Middle Platonic thought. There is, however, a number of negations not to be found in the common Middle Platonic understanding of the supreme principle; these are, 'not beauty', 'not good', 'not intellect', and 'not being'. While the denial of such terms must be regarded as a strengthening of the notion of the One's transcendence and simplicity, they are at the same time bound up with the idea of the One as ineffable, unnameable and unknowable. Metaphysical speculation which affirms the absolute transcendence of the One in terms such as these (not being, and not thought), leads naturally, although not of

[67] V 3, 8, 36-37; see *Rep.* 509B.
[68] VI 5, 11, 11-13.
[69] VI 4, 2, 2-3 and VI 5, 4, 14.

course mechanically, into negative theology, for one is forced to examine the human relationship with and response to such a Principle. Leaving aside for the moment the Gnostic theories of Basilides, for the Middle Platonists it would be unthinkable to deny thought or being to the supreme principle. Celsus had denied that God can be thought of in terms of intellect or being, but we have no evidence to suggest that he went further and denied self-thought to God. The not-being God of Basilides comes closest to Plotinus's thought in this respect, but I do not think that a case can be made to suggest that Plotinus was consciously appropriating a Gnostic source in denying activity, consciousness and will to the One (and Plotinus does not reject the term 'ineffable' as Basilides had done). It is only in the *Enneads* that the beyond-being Good, hinted at by Plato in the *Republic*, attains to its full stature in Greek philosophy. The negations I discuss below, including the negation of Good and unity, bring the negative theology of Plotinus very close to the ideas expressed by the Pseudo-Dionysius more than two hundred years later.

I have already noted that at times Plotinus subordinated Beauty to the Good; the most important aspect of the denial of beauty to the Good is that even the addition of beauty would deprive him of being Good, or at least diminish his goodness. The Good cannot be Beauty because he holds Beauty as a screen before him; he is the source of all beauty.[70] In *Ennead* V 5, Plotinus argues that since the Good is simply *the* Good and not *a* good, he cannot be said to possess goodness in himself, rather, he has nothing at all.[71] However, we may use the name 'Good', says Plotinus, only if we do not mean by that name 'one of the things'.[72] Although the term, 'the Good' is generally retained by Plotinus (for we must have some means of indicating it), there is at least one instance where he questions the aptitude even of this term to describe the nature of the One. Any addition of being at all, even to say 'He is good',

---

[70] I 6, 9, 41-42.
[71] V 5, 13, 1ff; see also VI 7, 38.
[72] V 3, 11, 27-28.

cannot apply to the One and Plotinus explains that he uses the word to convey identification, not as a means of predicating goodness of the One.[73] However, under the strictest rules of negation, even to say 'the Good' is not exact, but we use the term since pure negation does not indicate the One: 'we do need to add some words of encouragement to what has been said, if discourse can indicate it in any way at all'.[74] The name Good, then, asserts the identity of the Good without affirming being, but we must be careful not to think of the One as in any way related to a good: it is purely and simply the Good which exists before all things, the 'more than Good'.[75]

The ideas expressed by the Middle Platonists, especially Alcinous and Numenius, to the effect that God was to be thought of as true being, had been singularly opposed by Celsus, for whom God, as the cause of being, was beyond being. Even though Plato had hinted at the idea a transcendent Good above being in the *Republic*, his successors were, as I have already explained, hesitant to apply to the Good the phrase, 'beyond being'. True being was intelligible and was therefore equated with *nous*, that is, with the world of the forms. This position is also evident in the *Enneads*, for being is always thought of in a Platonic sense as that which can be defined and understood. The Plotinian argument for the transcendence of the Good beyond being, rests on the frequent assertion that the cause can be none of the things it causes, a perfectly reasonable development of the Platonic theory of forms as transcendent being.

It is because the One is the cause of being that it cannot be understood to possess being: it is different from all that comes after it.[76] *Nous*, as the first act of the Good and the first substance, means that being must be understood as that which is truly real and intelligible.[77] True being, as *nous*, is that which lacks nothing

[73] VI 2, 17.
[74] VI 7, 40, 2-4; see also VI 7, 38, 9-10.
[75] VI 9, 6, 40.
[76] II 6, 1, 50-51.
[77] I 8, 2, 21-22 and III 6, 6, 10-11.

and is the cause of all reality. It is this highest kind of being, which Alcinous and Numenius would have understood as God, which in the *Enneads* is placed on the level of intellect. Like the Middle Platonists, Plotinus asserts that real being, since it is to be conceived of as perfect being, ought not to be placed within the realm of physical being; it is, rather, *asōmatos*.[78] This true being does not have any 'this or that' about it, but its 'is' is the truest thing about it.[79] The beyond being is, and simply is, but yet, '... he is not even the 'is'; for he has no need whatsoever even of this'.[80]

Plotinus claims to have found his inspiration for the grades of reality in Plato, although he admits that this hierarchy was not explicit in ancient authors. The 'Beyond-Essence darkly indicated by the ancients' is not, according to Plotinus, something completely new in Greek philosophy.[81] He deduces three 'Ones' from the *Parmenides*, and by doing so remains faithful to the Greek tradition, from Parmenides on, in the identification of thought with being.[82] The first One, the beyond-being One, is excluded necessarily from the realm of being, to such an extent that the One cannot even say 'ἐγώ εἰμι'.[83] We find, then, in Plotinus, an ontology which asserts that the One is not simply absolute transcendent Being, but an understanding of the One as transcendent non-being.

Considering Plotinus's understanding of being as intellect, it is not surprising that the One should not only transcend being but also intellect. To make the Good either thinker or thought would be to identify it with being; it would then be necessary, says Plotinus, to find another principle above that.[84] Although Plotinus has no hesitation in elevating the One beyond being, he does find it necessary to offer a more persuasive argument for placing the One

---

[78] III 6, 7.
[79] III 7, 6, 15-19.
[80] VI 7, 38, 1-2.
[81] VI 8, 19, 12-14; see also V 1, 10, 1-2 and VI 1, 8, 25-26; see *Ep.* II 312Eff, *Ep.* VI 323D and *Tim.* 43Bff.
[82] See P. Merlan, *Monopsychism, Mysticism and Metaconsciousness*, pp. 30-47.
[83] VI 7, 38, 1-2; see W. Beierwaltes's pertinent remarks on this theme in *Platonismus und Idealismus*, p. 21ff.
[84] VI 7, 40.

beyond intellect. The One, as the God and cause of *nous*, must be beyond the 'supreme majesty of Intellect', for the One cannot itself be what it causes.[85] If the One is to be placed beyond intellect, then it cannot even have thought.[86] Plotinus uses two main ideas to support this most radical thesis. The first is that the One, in its self-sufficiency, does not need anything at all, even thought; the second is that if the One had any kind of thought that would compromise its simplicity, thereby making it a duality of thinker and thought.[87] This is where Plotinus shows himself to be most original. He criticizes Aristotle's conception of the first principle on the grounds that when Aristotle asserts that God knows himself, he reduces God's position to the level of intellect.[88] To think of the One as either Mind or God is, as S. MacKenna translates it, to 'think too meanly'.[89] Plotinus goes even further than denying thought to the One, for he says that the One cannot even be said to have self-thought.[90] He points out that while some philosophers have denied that God can know lesser things, they have attributed self-knowledge to him, for it is nobler.[91] In his own unique way, Plotinus describes the difference between one thing thinking another and one thing thinking itself: the latter goes further towards escaping being two.[92] Yet even this is not far enough for Plotinus, for if the One were able to know himself intellectively, he would cease to be simple and become two. This idea is a prominent feature of the negative theology of Eriugena who also argues, in a very Neoplatonic way, that only higher essences can know lower essences; since there is nothing higher than God, no one can know God's essence, not even God himself, for that would compromise his infinity.[93]

[85] V 3, 13, 1-2.
[86] III 9, 7, 4 and VI 7, 39.
[87] V 3, 11, 27-29.
[88] V 1, 9.
[89] VI 9, 6, 12; S. MacKenna, p. 619.
[90] III 8, 9, 15.
[91] VI 7, 37.
[92] V 6, 1.
[93] *Periphyseon* 589B.

Plotinus then asks how we can speak of a One who is void of self-knowledge and self-awareness, for even if the Good were to say 'I am the Good', that would be an affirmation of being which would posit a distinction between the Good and his knowledge of himself.[94] According to Plotinus, if self-intellection is the awareness of the self as something distinct, then the One cannot possess it – he must remain above duality in a 'majestic rest'.[95] Nous, noēsis and noēton are identical in the One; yet even this way of thinking the One's intellection makes a distinction and only subsequently reduces it to a unity of a kind which the One can never be. 'We also, then, must not add any of the things which are later and lesser, but say that he moves above them and is their cause, but not that he is them.'[96]

It would appear, therefore, that Plotinus has gone as far as it is possible to go in attempting to maintain the absolute unity and simplicity of the One. However, just as he had questioned the aptitude of the name 'Good', there are at least two passages in the Enneads where Plotinus hesitates to use the term 'One' or 'unity'. We call it One, he says, in order to indicate it by a designation which conveys its partlessness; the implication is that even the term One is not an adequate term and is used simply as a pointer to its unity.[97] In Ennead V 5, Plotinus suggests that the name One, which we use because we want to indicate it to ourselves in the best possible way, is perhaps only a denial of multiplicity.[98] He refers to the Pythagorean etymology of the name 'Apollo' (which had appeared in Plutarch), as the denial of all multiplicity. He says that he is now unsure whether we ought to give it a name at all; perhaps even this name should be denied, for it too may not be worthy to indicate that nature. This is one passage where Plotinus comes closest to the idea of the negation of the negation, for a denial of this name would mean 'not not-many'.[99] The hesitancy

---

[94] VI 7, 38, 11-16.
[95] VI 7, 39, 21.
[96] V 5, 13, 17-20.
[97] VI 9, 5.
[98] V 5, 6.
[99] V 5, 6, 26.

of Plotinus with regard to the denial of the term unity (indicated by his use of *tacha*) is understandable, for the ultimate negation of the One would leave us in 'sheer dread of holding to nothingness'.[100] Are we then to lose faith and think of it as nothingness, asks Plotinus? The answer is, of course, no. The search for unity, conceived solely in metaphysical terms, would do nothing more than refine the One out of all existence; but such purification, understood in terms of true negative theology, adds another dimension of thought, one which is not easily understood in terms of traditional 'text-book ontology'. I discuss this aspect of Plotinian thought below.

There is one further point which I should mention at this juncture. Plotinus notes that the unity of the One is not like the unity which is said to belong to the monad or the point.[101] Like Philo of Alexandria, he says that we use these concepts symbolically in order to indicate the simple nature of the One. Plotinus mentions the method of abstraction as outlined by Alcinous, and says that while this kind of movement to the point or monad ends in unity, it is a unity which is achieved by using the method of abstraction and which consequently ends with the smallest particle possible. It is the movement of thought from the solid, through the surface and line which attains to a unit or unity which is a reduction from something previously added to it. The One can never be conceived in such terms, for it is never a unity of parts, or even one part of something.[102] This may be a direct criticism of Alcinous's use of the geometric analogy to explain how the human intellect can arrive at an idea of God. Although Plotinus finds no fault with the method as it had been used by Alcinous – indeed it plays a major part in his own conception of the return of the soul to the Good – he does warn against thinking about the One in terms of the unity achieved by taking away something which was not simply added, but was part of the object in the first place.

[100] VI 9, 3, 4-6; S. MacKenna, p. 616.
[101] VI 9, 5, 38-46; see also VI 9, 6, 3 and VI 6, 10.
[102] VI 9, 6, 2-9.

However, I must point out that this interpretation of negative theology in the *Enneads* would suggest that Plotinus began with affirmation and then systematically proceeded to negate the concepts he had affirmed. While this kind of progression is not totally alien to Plotinian thought, Plotinus does not treat abstraction thematically, even though he notes that, 'it is not possible to say "not this" if one has not experience or conception of "this"'.[103] Nor is it true to say that, having conceived of an absolutely simple unity, Plotinus was then forced to make it somehow more accessible through affirmation. J. Rist has suggested that one of the 'problems' inherent in Plotinus's conception of the One was that he was aware that the human intellect could not be satisfied with 'negative generalities' about the One, and that this awareness led him to attribute to the One quasi-personal features, such as the notion of fatherhood.[104] I am not convinced that this is a valid way of interpreting the progression of Plotinus's thought. The addition of more 'personal' features does not make the One any more accessible to the intellect, although it does provide the imagination with something more satisfying to think about. Plotinus would reject any implication that the One can be contained within human thought, with the result that the ultimate 'way' to the One is not through thought but through non-thought, the way of intuitive 'mystical' vision. The key word in Plotinus's thinking about the One is not the addition of personal features, but on the contrary, the taking away of everything that human thought has added to the One.

Longing for The Absent

The *Enneads* contain not only an account of metaphysical reality in terms of the procession of all things from the One, but also a description of the journey of the soul back to the One. Although

---

[103] VI 7, 29, 20-21.
[104] See *Eros and Psyche*, pp. 72-73.

there would appear to be no relationship between the One and the soul – the One cannot be understood in terms normally accessible to human consciousness – it is obvious as one reads the *Enneads*, that there does exist a relationship between the two. The being of the One may be different in kind from our being and exist on a totally different level, but ultimately we came from the One and it is to the One that we will return.

According to Plotinus, our final goal is, as it is in the *Theaetetus*, to be made like the Good and that involves 'escaping' from this world.[105] Our concern is not merely to be sinless, but to be God;[106] here Plotinus is developing a very Platonic notion in a way that was unrivalled in Greek thought before him. We must become what we were before we came 'here' and we do this by looking towards the Good alone and being made like it.[107] Before we were born, says Plotinus, we existed 'there' as pure souls; we must, therefore, attempt to effect our escape from the 'disturbance' which comes of being born 'here'.[108] Our task is to become good and beautiful, like the Good itself.[109] Every soul is a child of the Father, but has forgotten him and become ignorant of itself through *tolma* and through its delight and dependence on the things of this world. The body has become a tomb, the fetters of the soul, and we experience misery in being born, precisely because our birth is the cause of our ignorance of the Good.[110] Therefore, at the bottom end of the scale, before the soul begins the ascent to the highest things, it exists in ignorance of the Good, and, as I shall explain, when it has ascended as far as it is able, it will even then experience ignorance of the Good.

The alienation the soul experiences in this world is an important theme in the *Enneads*, for it provides at least part of the impetus needed for the soul to make the ascent to the other world. Quoting

---

[105] 176B; I 2, 1, 3-4.
[106] I 2, 6.
[107] I 2, 6, 7-8.
[108] VI 9, 9, 33-38 and III 4, 6, 5-6.
[109] I 6, 6, 19-21.
[110] V 1, 1 and IV 8, 3-4.

from Homer, Plotinus exclaims, 'Let us fly to our dear country', but there is a sense of dismay in his tone as he asks how we can do this: 'but how shall we find the way?' 'What method can we devise?' 'What then is our way of escape, and how are we to find it?'[111] Plotinus's vivid expression of spiritual homesickness is, I think, not simply a matter of rhetoric, but evidence of the experience of being totally cut off from one's origin, of feeling like a stranger in an alien land. For Plotinus, the logical way to begin the ascent back to the fatherland is to strip away everything that the soul took on in its descent – to separate from oneself what has been added to the self.[112] Yet this is no easy task, for it involves a double movement in the practice of purification: the one inwards to the core of the self, and the other to what is above. The method which Plotinus advocates as the best way to effect our escape, is the way of *aphairesis*.[113]

However, the misery experienced in being bound by the body is not enough to spur the soul on to the search for higher things; it is here that Plotinus's doctrine of the One as truly desirable attains it full force.

> So we must ascend again to the good, which every soul desires. Anyone who has seen it knows what I mean when I say that it is good, and the desire for it is directed to good, and the attainment of it is for those who go up to the higher world and are converted and strip off what we put on in our descent.[114]

Considering the huge gap and the difference between the sensible and noetic worlds, how can the soul make itself like the One, if the One is not like anything within its experience? This question is not problematic for Plotinus, for in the *Enneads* we are able to grasp what the One is like because there exists something of it within. There is a likeness of it in us, a likeness which exists in us because the soul has not fully descended to the level of this world

---

[111] I 6, 8, 1ff.
[112] I 6, 7, 1ff.
[113] On the concept of *aphairesis* in Plotinus, see W. Beierwaltes, *Denken des Einen*, p. 108ff and p. 129ff.
[114] I 6, 7, 1ff.

– the soul is not completely sundered from its origin.[115] It is this likeness that we must attempt to uncover through the practice of *aphairesis*. If we do manage to uncover the likeness of the One within us, we shall be in a better position to come to some knowledge of it, for Plotinus believed in the age-old Greek maxim, like can be known only by like – a theme which is developed at length by Proclus.

Having discovered the image of the Good within and seen its presence, both in the self and in the universe, the soul becomes consumed with even more desire for the Good. Desire for the One is the key whereby the door to the ascent is opened: all things reach out to the Good and desire it. 'For all things reach out to that and long for it by necessity of nature, as if divining by instinct that they cannot exist without it'.[116] It is a fact that every soul seeks the Good; yet this desire is not simply a longing to which one comes after strenuous training and through one's own effort, for, according to Plotinus, the longing and desire for the Good is given by the Good and implanted in our souls from the very beginning.[117]

> The grasp of the beautiful and the wonder and the waking of love for it come to those who, in a way, already know it and are awake to it. But the Good, since it was there long before to arouse an innate desire, is present even to those asleep ...'.[118]

It is here that Plotinus comes closest to the theory of grace which plays so important a part in the Christian theology of salvation; yet we must not be tempted to read what Plotinus says in the light of the Christian doctrine of grace. It is a notion which is expressed very tentatively in the *Enneads*: it is not a separate supernatural action in Plotinus, but a creative constitution in being which is natural. The soul hungers for the Good without being able to tell why, but it is the light from the Good shining upon the soul which awakens its desire, its longing and its ardour.

[115] III 8, 5; III 8, 8-9; V 1, 10; VI 7, 31, and VI 9, 8.
[116] V 5, 12, 7-9.
[117] III 5, 1, 16-19.
[118] V 5, 12, 9ff.

But when a kind of warmth from thence comes upon it, it gains
strength and wakes and is truly winged; and though it is moved
with passion for that which lies close by it, yet all the same it rises
higher, to something greater which it seems to remember ... it naturally goes on upwards, lifted by the giver of its love.[119]

In fact, unless this light falls into the soul the latter remains indifferent.[120] The soul loves the Good because it has been stirred to
love it by the Good itself, and love is nothing other than the activity of desire in action. Just as lovers here mould themselves to the
image of their beloved, so too does the soul want to become like
the Good, when it begins to love the Good.[121] 'Then the soul,
receiving into itself an outflow from thence, is moved and dances
wildly and is all stung with longing and becomes love'.[122] Human
nature cannot, therefore, decide to return to the Good by its own
impetus; the light from the Good falls into the soul and awakens
desire. The Good, as *eros*, gives naturally the love needed for the
soul to return to it; there is no need for the One to love the soul,
for desire has been implanted within it from the beginning; there
is also no need for Plotinus to construct a doctrine of grace as a
supernatural gift from the One: the Good itself draws all things
back to it simply by being what it is – the source and power of all
things – as S. MacKenna's lovely translation puts it: 'surely we
need not wonder that it be of power to draw to itself, calling back
from every wandering to rest before it. From it all came and so
there is nothing mightier; all is feeble before it'.[123]

At this point I must I must note that in Plotinus's thought there is
no one way of return, but there is a number of ways, all having the
same goal but differing only in their emphasis or perspective. For
example, there is the way advocated for the philosopher, and for the
musician and the lover.[124] As in Numenius, the ascent in the

---

[119] VI 7, 22, 14ff.
[120] VI 7, 22, 12-14; see also VI 7, 33.
[121] VI 7, 31 and III 5, 4.
[122] VI 7, 22, 8-10.
[123] VI 7, 23, 2-6.
[124] I 3, 1 – 4; see *Phaedrus* 248D; see W. Beierwaltes's interpretation of this text
in *Denken des Einen*, p. 14ff.

Enneads begins for the philosopher with the study of mathematics, followed by dialectic. Dialectic involves a move from the study of the things in the sensible world to those of the intelligible world; then it must leave logical activity altogether for the contemplation of the Good alone. Relying on the *Philebus*, Plotinus makes a distinction between intelligence and wisdom (*nous* and *phronēsis*), for the latter is concerned with real being but the former with what is beyond being.[125] The philosopher must pass from the level of wisdom to the realm of *nous*, for it is only through *nous* that one is able to come to the contemplation of the One. The ascent to Beauty, described in the last tractates of *Ennead* I 6, is perhaps the most celebrated account of the ascent of the soul in Plotinus; here he relies chiefly on the ascent outlined in the *Symposium*, speaking in the most vivid and intimate terms of the ascent to a vital, life-giving principle. The ultimate vision of that which is truly beautiful, that is, the Good, is a vision which cannot be described; but for it a person would give up even kingship and despise all former loves. Whatever way Plotinus describes the ascent, the movement is always from the sensible to the intelligible, and then to that which is above *nous* through which the soul is able to 'see' the Good.

Yet, it is unclear whether or not the ascent, as Plotinus envisages it, is reserved solely for those with a philosophical training – those who know from the study of philosophy that the One exists. While it is the case that anyone can wonder about the Good through the contemplation of nature since the One is present to the universe as its cause, nature itself is only a pointer towards the Good and as such cannot tell anything about the being of the Good; it contains a trace of the Good only.[126] In the contemplation of nature one might hear it say that it too was made by the Good and is striving towards it. Just as one can look up to the stars in the night sky and think of their maker, seeking him, so it is with those who contemplate the intelligible world, for they too are led to the contemplation of its maker, the beyond-being Good.[127]

[125] I 3, 5, 7-8; see *Philebus* 58D.
[126] V 5, 10, 1-2.
[127] .III 8, 11 and II 9, 16.

At this point I return to a text mentioned earlier. It would appear
that not everyone is led to the contemplation of the highest things:
for some it is enough that they become aware of the presence of
the Good in the simplest manner. In *Ennead* V 5, Plotinus illustrates this point by using the image of a kingly court in procession: the lesser ranks precede the king, moving through the ranks
of those who are closest to the king until, finally, the king himself
is revealed.[128] However, there is one phrase here which has much
in common with an idea present in Philo of Alexandria, and that is
that some people went away before the king appeared because
they were satisfied with the vision of what preceded him. Not
everyone, then, is capable of sustaining the vision of the highest
things. I mention this text in order to illustrate that when Plotinus
is speaking of ultimate unity with *nous* or the Good, he is likely to
be thinking of the ascent in terms of the best and holiest of souls.

Aphairesis

> When you have put away all things and left only himself, do not
> try to find out what you can add, but if there is something you
> have not yet taken away from him in your mind.[129]

It is through the process of *aphairesis* that the soul is able first
to rise to the contemplation of *nous* and then to what is beyond
nous, the contemplation of the Good. In practical terms this
process involves first of all taking away everything that the soul
has taken on in its descent into the body, the removal of all that is
alien to its true nature. Secondly, it entails a rigorous intellectual
purification concerning our thinking about the Good, a purification
required because our thinking is not simple. We must take away
everything from our idea so that we will think of the Good as it is
in itself.[130] In its practical application, *aphairesis* involves the

---

[128] V 5, 3; see also VI 7, 42.
[129] VI 8, 21, 26-28.
[130] III 8, 11; V 5, 13; V 5, 4; V 3, 17; VI 7, 41; VI 8, 21; IV 3, 32; V 3, 9, and
IV 7, 10.

abandonment of multiplicity and of all human concerns.[131] In this sense, the 'way' that Plotinus advocates is other-worldly, for the most rigorous purification takes place on the level of intellect. Plotinus's understanding of purification is very definitely concerned first and foremost with moral purification, for the philosopher could not be a true lover of wisdom without being a good person; moral excellence is, therefore, an *a priori* for the purification of the intellect.[132] Having left behind all concerns with the body and human affairs, the soul is then faced with the task of making itself pure and unmixed: that is, to be made like the One in its simplicity. Plotinus (like Plato, Dionysius and Meister Eckhart), uses the image of the statue-maker chipping away at a piece of stone in order to reveal the statue cleared from all encumbrances and additions.[133] In such a way, the soul becomes free from all that has been added to its real nature and is enabled to behold the vision of the Good.

The other aspect of *aphairesis* entails the purification of one's 'Good-concepts'. We must, says Plotinus, 'take away everything', because the One is none of the things of which it is the origin.[134] We must say that it is nothing of the things of created nature; but if we cannot predicate anything of it, either being, or substance or life, how shall we think of it? The answer is, if we take away everything that we have added to the idea of the Good, we will be filled with wonder and know it by intuition as it is in itself.[135]

---

[131] For a study of Plotinian purification, see J. Trouillard, *La purification Plotinienne*. H. A. Wolfson's analysis of *aphairesis* is, I believe, too concerned with logical predication; I am not convinced that Plotinus was transferring the Aristotelian meaning of *apophasis* to *aphairesis*; see 'Alcinous and Plotinus on Divine Attributes', pp. 120-121.

[132] Plotinus's own life serves as a remarkable illustration of moral purification; Porphyry reports that he was 'mild and kind, most gentle and attractive ... he sleeplessly kept his soul pure and ever strove towards the divine which he loved with all his soul': *Life* 23, 1-8. On the moral aspect of Plotinian thought, see J. M. Rist, 'Plotinus and Moral obligation', in *The Significance of Neoplatonism*, pp. 217-233.

[133] I 6, 9.

[134] V 3, 17, 38; V 5, 13, 13, and III 8, 10, 28-29.

[135] III 8, 10, 31-32.

We work through the process of *aphairesis* by not adding anything to it which would make it deficient. The Good cannot be
'this or that': it is 'not this', 'not that', and 'not like'.[136] It is so
unlike anything in the created order that everything must be
denied, everything that is, that we think the Good to be. We
allow him his existence, *to estin*, and that alone, for he does not
possess anything of the things which come later and are lesser
than him, and that includes being; the One simply is.[137] The
thought Plotinus expresses here, that we must seek the Good outside of the things which have been created, is typical of the
forms of negative theology as expressed by Philo, Dionysius,
Eriugena and Meister Eckhart. Eckhart's distinction between
Gott and *Gottheit*, an attempt to free God from the bounds of
economy, in the exhortation for human nature to free itself from
the idea of God it has created, is here prefigured in the
Enneads.[138] Before all things came into existence the One was,
and he is the same now as he was before he brought all things
into being. Therefore, we should not add to his being anything
which comes from the realm of created existence.[139] This is one
of the most radical consequences of negative theology, for it
demands that we come to the Good through the absolute negation of all terms of reference with which we are familiar. If we
are content to let the One be, we will not even think of it as
cause, for that is to affirm something happening to us rather than
to the One.[140]

Plotinus makes a clear distinction between cause and sequents
in connection with speech about God, but he also uses the distinction in terms of human knowledge about the One: we cannot know
the One except through that which comes after it, its sequents, and
the knowledge obtained in this way is not knowledge of his nature,
but is simply knowledge that the One is the transcendent cause of

---

[136] III 8, 11, 12-13; V 5, 6, 22-23, and VI 9, 3, 51-54.
[137] III 7, 6, 17-19.
[138] See Eckhart's vernacular sermon, *Beati pauperes spiritu*.
[139] VI 5, 12, 42-43 and VI 7, 23, 9-10.
[140] VI 9, 3.

all things.[141] We say *that* he is, but we can not say *what* he is[142] –
a familiar idea in the writings of the early Christian Fathers. Yet,
in the *Enneads*, the paradox is that the Good cannot be known
truly through his sequents: he cannot be known through them in a
way that will tell us of his nature but only in so far as they tell us
what he is not. We know now what the Good is not: he is not one
of all things; but we have no knowledge of what he is. I have
already discussed how the Middle Platonists employed the terms
'ineffable' and 'unnameable', and how they could not have
thought of God as unknowable. In the last lines of the First
Hypothesis, Plato concluded that there can be no speaking about
the One; it cannot be named and there cannot be any thought
about it. Plotinus took his master at his word.

The Ineffable, Unnameable, Unknowable One

"There is neither discourse nor perception nor knowledge" because
it is impossible to predicate anything of it as present with it.[143]

The Good must be ineffable, says Plotinus, for anything we say
about it will always be taken from what is beneath it. Therefore,
the only true way of speaking about the Good is to say that it is
'beyond all things and beyond the supreme majesty of intellect'.[144]
The best we can do is point to it or makes signs about it to ourselves.[145] What are the signs that we may make about it? Plotinus's answer is that we may talk about it in terms of what comes
after it, in terms of created things; but this is, of course, not positive speaking 'for we say what it is not, but we do not say what it
is'.[146] For how can we ever hope to describe the absolutely simple,
he who is higher than speech, thought and awareness? Plotinus's

---

[141] VI 8, 11, 1-3 and III 8, 10, 32-35.
[142] V 5, 6.
[143] VI 7, 41, 37-39; see *Parm.* 142A.
[144] V 3, 13, 1-3.
[145] V 3, 13, 5-6.
[146] V 3, 14, 6-7.

insistence on the ineffable nature of the One is expressed in the most radical of terms. We must call a halt to all our questioning about the One, for questioning deals with the nature of a thing in all its aspects, such as quality, cause and essential being; but since the One cannot be said to possess these things, we cannot speak about him.

> We must go away in silence and enquire no longer, aware in our minds that there is no way out ... we must make no enquiry, grasping it, if possible, in our minds by learning that it is not right to add anything to it.[147]

The awareness that we cannot speak about God is an essential part of negative theology, and Plotinus, like Gregory of Nyssa, Proclus and Eriugena takes the idea seriously: he stubbornly refuses to commit the nature of the Good to the constraints of human language. However, this refusal to speak about the Good should not be considered as a 'retreat into an irrationality which refuses to speak clearly and plainly ... but the admission of the insufficiency of finite, temporally-bound thought.'[148] Because we cannot speak about the Good except in terms of what comes after it, and that is to say what it is not, 'we hover, as it were, about it, seeking the statement of an experience of our own, sometimes nearing this reality, sometimes baffled by the enigma in which it dwells.'[149] Strictly speaking, because there is no way of speaking about the One, there cannot be any name which is apt to describe it; but since we find ourselves compelled to name it, we can designate it to ourselves as 'unity'.[150] We can also call it 'Good' and 'One'; however, these names must not be understood as real names, but names which we have designated for that which cannot be named at all.[151]

---

[147] VI 8, 11, 1ff.

[148] W. Beierwaltes, 'Image and Counterimage? Reflections on Neoplatonic Thought with Respect to Today', in *Neoplatonism and Early Christian Thought*, p. 246.

[149] VI 9, 3, 52-54; S. MacKenna, p. 617.

[150] VI 9, 5, 31-32.

[151] VI 7, 38, 4-5; see also V 3, 12, V 5, 6 and VI 2, 17.

In asserting the ineffability and unnameability of the One, Plotinus does not stand outside the tradition of Platonic thought which he inherited, but in proposing that the One is unknowable, Plotinus is developing the last part of the First Hypothesis of the *Parmenides* in a way that was unparalleled in Greek thought before him. Although Celsus had claimed that God could not be known through intellect but rather through an 'ineffable way', we have no way of knowing how far he developed the idea of the unknowable nature of God. In the *Enneads* it is logical that there should be no thinking about the One since there can be no speech about the One. The One is so completely different from human nature, that there is nothing within the world which can be of assistance in obtaining knowledge about it. According to J. Rist, by insisting on the idea of the One beyond human knowledge, Plotinus 'opens up the possibility of avoiding the construction of a first principle in man's image'.[152] However, this is not the most pertinent aspect of the idea of unknowability – Celsus had already opened up this possibility in Platonism (and in the Platonic tradition before Plotinus, God was never conceived of as being like human nature, except perhaps through the relationship of *nous*). The most important consequence of asserting the unknowability of the One is that Plotinus is forced to examine other areas of 'knowledge' whereby we can rise beyond intellect and attain to some knowledge of the One.

Once the soul has performed the exercise of purification to the extent that it no longer has anything left of itself, but has become totally *nous*, the way of intellect has been left behind. In terms of further rational enquiry, we can seek no further; 'we can but withdraw, silent, hopeless'.[153] But we ought not to lose faith and think of the One as nothing; we should not fall into the sin of agnosticism, for we have reached the stage where we have become like the One in its simplicity. We have reversed our way of thinking; we have left ourselves open to the presence of the Good.

[152] 'The One of Plotinus and The God of Aristotle', p. 77.
[153] VI 8, 11, 1-3; S. MacKenna, p. 604.

Henosis: The Way of the Non-Concept

Before I comment on what I have called the way of the non-concept in Plotinus, I interject a timely reminder that language is not adequate to express accurately and without misconception, what Plotinus is attempting to describe: 'once more we must be patient with language; we are forced for reasons of exposition to apply to the Supreme terms which are strictly ruled out; everywhere we must read "so to speak"'.[154] If we want to grasp the 'alone', we ought not to think at all, for since it is not *nous*, there can be no thinking about it.[155] To make the One an object of knowledge is to make it many; since it is absolutely simple, we can have no thought about it.[156] Yet we cannot simply begin at the point of saying that we do not know the One, for the ascent to the highest things is effected by moving first of all to *nous* and then beyond *nous*. We contemplate the intelligible and then we move beyond it by letting the intelligible go. It is only through the contemplation of the intelligible world that the soul can rise to what is beyond it.[157]

If we are aware of the One as that which is totally simple – even self-thought would compromise this simplicity – then it is understandable that the One cannot be the object of thought. The fundamental precept that we have followed, that is, to become like the Good, involves becoming like the One, becoming simple, so the soul must also abandon its thinking, which is by nature multiple. When the soul becomes like intellect (when it thinks) it becomes united with *nous* through which we learn *that* the Good is.[158] When the soul has let go of all other things and become pure thought, it becomes like *nous* in its contemplation of the One. We cannot go any other way to the Good than through intellect, because the unknowability of the One makes it accessible only through its

---

[154] VI 8, 13, 47-50; S. MacKenna, p. 607.
[155] V 3, 13, 32-33.
[156] V 3, 14, 2-3.
[157] III 8, 11, V 5, 6 and VI 8, 7.
[158] V 3, 8, 45-48.

'offspring'; and at this point we can be said to be at a second rather than at a third remove from the One.[159]

In other words, Plotinus advocates that we must first obtain some knowledge of the Good before we can leave knowledge aside, and the three main ways to obtain knowledge of the One are through ἀναλογία, ἀφαίρεσις and through γνώσεις ἐξ αὐτοῦ.[160] Maximus of Tyre, Celsus and Alcinous had already outlined the ways of knowledge in these terms and Plotinus does not develop the theory much further than they had done. What is important for Plotinus is not the methods used to obtain a primary 'knowledge' of the One, but the ultimate letting go of all knowledge in order to know the One truly and become united with him.

> The soul or mind reaching towards the formless finds itself incompetent to grasp where nothing bounds it or to take impression where the impinging reality is diffuse; in sheer dread of holding to nothingness, it slips away, the state is painful; often it seeks relief by retreating from all this vagueness to the region of sense, there to rest as on solid ground.[161]

'In sheer dread of holding to nothingness' – this is the classic boundary which marks true negative theology from that kind of negation which is concerned solely with the intellectual negation of metaphysical concepts. The way to attain to unity with the Good, or to see the vision of the Good, is simply to let go of all other things, and that includes knowing; the way of Plotinus goes beyond knowing:

> Our way then takes us beyond knowing; there may be no wandering from unity; knowing and knowable must all be left aside; every object of knowledge, even the highest, we must pass by, for all that is good is later than This and derives from This as from the sun all the light of day.[162]

Although there is at least one passage in the *Enneads* where Plotinus does not absolutely rule out intellection of the Good, the way

---

[159] VI 9, 5 and I 1, 8.
[160] VI 7, 36, 7.
[161] VI 9, 3, 4-9; S. MacKenna, p. 616.
[162] VI 9, 4, 7-11; S. MacKenna, p. 617.

most frequently advocated is the way of the non-concept.[163] Having silenced one's intellectual faculty and conformed oneself to the simple nature of the Good, that is, having no duality left, the soul can do nothing else but must content itself with waiting. One must not chase after the Good, says Plotinus, 'but wait quietly till it appears'.[164] The experience of letting go of all things is not an easy task to accomplish, as Plotinus testifies. The experience of waiting without thought and concept is not a comfortable state to endure, and the soul often slips away, back to the realm of noetic experience. However, if one persists, the soul can wake to 'another way of seeing', which, says Plotinus, 'everyone has but few use'.[165] This awakening to another way of knowing is an awakening to the presence of the Good, which itself can neither come nor go; it has always been present (indeed without the presence of the Good the universe would not exist); it is the soul, putting on non-being, which has turned from the presence of the Good. Therefore, the Good is always present to the soul, when it puts away all otherness.[166] At the same time, although the Good is present everywhere as the giver of being, he cannot be said to be anywhere, for he is in no particular place. Thus, he is not absent to anyone save those not fit to perceive his presence. Those who do not perceive the presence of the Good are those who have not been conformed to it by their likeness to it. This perception of the presence of the Good cannot be called knowledge for the Good cannot even have knowledge of himself; it is, as Plotinus puts it, 'a presence superior to knowledge'.[167] The Good does not give knowledge of himself at the summit of the ascent, he gives something better than knowledge: 'he gives them rather to be in the same place with him and to lay hold on him, as far as they are able'.[168]

---

[163] See VI 7, 40, 32-36 and VI 7, 35, 44-45.
[164] V 5, 8, 3-5.
[165] I 6, 8, 24-27.
[166] VI 9, 8, 33-45 and VI 5, 12, 16-29.
[167] VI 9, 4, 3; see W. Beierwaltes's excellent chapter on *henosis* in *Denken des Einen*, pp. 123-154.
[168] V 6, 6, 34-36; presence is superior to the noetic order, see J. Trouillard, 'Valeur critique de la mystique Plotinienne', p. 431.

At this point I would like to suggest that in the over-passing of all knowledge Plotinus does not end by denying human reason. This kind of criticism, based as it is on the post-Cartesian emphasis on the rational autonomy of the intellect, cannot be levelled against the philosophy of Plotinus without some very persuasive argument. Plotinus was not concerned with the task of reason in the ascent to the Good, for the highest part of the mental capacity is intellect, not reason. For Plotinus, and indeed the philosophers of the medieval period, the movements or discourse of reason were what brought them to the point where the intellect could become operative on a higher level. It is evident in the *Enneads* that Plotinus does not advocate the destruction of reason; what he does advocate is a surpassing of *nous*, and that is a different capacity altogether. At the highest level of the Plotinian ascent it is through the power of intellect that one is able to see the vision of the Good, but it is through a *nous* without content, not through the abdication of reason that one is enabled to do so.

The perception of the presence of the One is described by Plotinus as a kind of simple intuition, but it is an intuition which is experienced only when the soul has become wholly one with *nous*.[169] In this way, Plotinian mysticism is, as P. Merlan suggests, a mysticism of *nous*.[170] Although this union is not by any means an ordinary, everyday experience, there is evidence in the *Enneads* to suggest that there are moments of mystical experience wherein the soul becomes totally united with the One itself. While the state of being in the presence of the Good is a gift given by the Good, nevertheless, it is a state to which the human intellect can attain under the impetus of the desire for the Good and by following the example of a wise and holy guide.

However, it can sometimes happen that the soul is lifted out of this state into an experience of absolute unity with the One. Although I would interpret this kind of experience as distinct from the experience of waiting in the presence of the Good, the distinc-

---

[169] III 8, 10, 31-32.
[170] *Monopsychism*, p. 2.

tion is not so obvious in Plotinus. In the passages where he describes such union, the emphasis is placed on the passivity of the soul, for all striving has been left behind; there is nothing more for the soul to strive for. It is the wave of *nous* that lifts the soul who has been united with it into a different realm of experience.[171] It is the use of the word 'suddenly' (*exaiphnēs*) which is important in this context, for this word expresses a vision or unity which, as A. H. Armstrong explains, is not something that one can plan for, or call up whenever one wishes.[172] Plotinus explains this kind of unity a great deal better than any paraphrase can do:

> It is there that one lets all study go; up to a point one has been led along and settled firmly in beauty and as far as this one thinks that in which one is, but is carried out of it by the surge of the wave of Intellect itself and lifted on high by a kind of swell and sees suddenly, not seeing how, but the vision fills his eyes with light and does not make him see something else by it, but the light itself is what he sees.[173]

The fact that the soul would appear to be 'lifted' is an important point to take into consideration, for it answers, at least in part, those who would criticize Plotinus's account of unity with the Good on the grounds that the soul seems able to attain to unity with the Good through its own efforts. What exactly is the content of the soul's 'seeing' at this level? This is a question which of necessity cannot be answered, for the soul is so 'oned' with the One that it no longer knows anything, not even that it is united with the One.[174] Plotinus, in true Platonic fashion, always speaks of the unity experienced at this level in terms of light and vision, although this seeing cannot be understood in terms of having a real object present before the eyes – Plotinus always insists that he is speaking metaphorically. The true end of the soul is to 'see' that light alone in itself, not through the medium of any other thing; this kind of

---

[171] VI 7, 35, 36-40.
[172] See vol. V of the Loeb edition, p. 135, n.1; further references to 'suddenly' include, V 3, 17, 28; V 5, 3, 13; V 5, 7, 23, and VI 7, 34, 13.
[173] VI 7, 36, 15-19.
[174] VI 9, 3, 11-12.

vision excludes the possibility of the soul knowing that it is united with the One, for it can no longer distinguish itself from the object of its intuition.[175] The lifting of the soul from the relative solidity of the non-concept into the light of the Good is something which defies rational analysis. Plotinus himself insists that anyone who has seen the vision will know what he is talking about.[176]

The experience of *ekstasis*, described by Plotinus in this one very striking passage, when the soul is raised outside of itself, is also described in terms of vision and light.[177] Although he says that it would be better not to speak in dualities, the light metaphor is the best way to describe that which is scarcely vision except in an unknown mode.[178] Plotinus explains the vision as a unity of seer and seen: 'for there is no longer one thing outside and another outside which is looking in, but the keen sighted has what is seen within'.[179] Thus, the object and the act of vision have become identical.[180] To become sight, that is, to become nothing but true light, is to become 'the eye which sees the great beauty'.[181] Unity, expressed in terms of vision and sight, tends always to give the impression that there must be an object of the vision, but Plotinus is emphatic that the act of vision itself is the object of the vision. Meister Eckhart likewise explains unity with God in such metaphorical terms: 'oculus in quo video deum, est ille idem oculus in quo me deus videt. Oculus meus et oculus dei est unus oculus et una visio vel videre et unum cognoscere et unum amare'.[182]

---

[175] VI 9, 3, 13.
[176] VI 9, 9, 46-47.
[177] VI 9, 11, 23; J. Trouillard notes that *haplosis* is better than *ekstasis* to describe the movement of the soul to the One, see 'Valeur critique', p. 433. A. H. Armstrong also notes that *ektsasis* is not necessarily the best word for describing mystical union in Plotinus; see his note on this passage in the Loeb edition, vol. VII.
[178] VI 9, 11, 22-23.
[179] V 8, 10, 35-36; see also V 8, 11.
[180] VI 7, 25, 14-16.
[181] I 6, 9, 24-25.
[182] 'The eye with which God sees me is the same eye with which I see God. My eye and God's eye are one eye and one vision or seeing and one knowledge and one love;' see G. Théry, 'Edition critique des pièces relatives au procès d'Eckhart contenues dans le manuscrit 33ᵇ de la bibliothèque de Soest', *Archives d'Histoire doctrinale et littéraire du Moyen-Age*, 1 (1926), p. 224 (19).

There is one very interesting and complex passage in *Ennead* V 5, where Plotinus discusses the vision of the light of the Good in terms of an optical analogy.[183] This theory explains the various parts played by the source of the light, the objects (themselves containing light) which are illuminated by the light and the eye which sees the objects. Plotinus's great light analogy is built upon the theory that sight occurs through a conjoint action of the intromission of rays of light from objects and the extramission of rays from within the eye itself. He maintains that if the eye does not look at the light falling on the objects of sight, but concentrates instead upon the medium by which it sees them (that is, upon the light itself), then it will see the light alone. Since even this idea involves an externalization of the light (for the eye is, after all, still looking at an object), Plotinus stretches his optical theory to its very limit and expresses the vision of the light in the following terms. Sometimes, the eye at night, or when closed, sees a light which is not alien or external to it: images which appear on the eyelid. This, says Plotinus, is the truest analogy for the vision of the light of the Good, for the eye no longer looks at the light present in any medium or reflected from any object, instead it looks at the light by itself – that is, the light in its own eye. In a similar way, the intellect truly sees by veiling itself from all other things; then, when it is not looking at anything else, the light itself may suddenly appear within it. At this point, Plotinus uses a phrase which was to become seminal for the negative theology of the Pseudo-Dionysius: 'for then in not seeing it sees, and sees most of all'.[184] Although Plotinus uses the word 'suddenly', the light cannot be said to have come at all; it is seen as 'not having come, but as being there before all things'.[185] The soul, having become like the One in its simplicity, actually sees the One, the source of all light, through becoming the light itself: 'seeing and the seen coincide, and the seen is like the seeing and the seeing is like the seen'.[186]

[183] V 5, 7.
[184] V 5, 7, 29-30; see *De myst. theol.* II, 1.
[185] V 5, 8.
[186] V 3, 8, 16-17.

It is, therefore, through the not-seeing of anything else that the soul can come to the vision of the Good. This is a true reversal of one's thinking, for the soul, in turning away from all other objects of knowledge and vision, must learn to see and to know in another way. This idea is the central theme of such later philosophers and theologians as were to embark upon the way of negation: only through not knowing, that is, through the unknowing of creation, can one come to knowledge of the transcendent.

The experience of being in the same place as the Good is the soul's final *telos*, but the experiences in which the soul becomes the vision of the light, are perhaps reserved for those, like Plotinus himself, most capable of sustaining the vision.[187] In the unity of the soul with the Good, the soul is restored to the state in which it was before it came from the Good. Yet the soul cannot remain for long in that experience of unity, and the reason is that while it is here on earth 'it has not escaped wholly', to the place of the Good.[188]

> There one can see both him and oneself as it is right to see: the self glorified, full of intelligible light – but rather itself pure light – weightless, floating free, having become – but rather, being – a god; set on fire then, but the fire seems to go out if one is weighed down again.[189]

But there will come a time of unbroken vision when the soul will pass over into everlasting unity with the Good. It is in this state that the soul truly finds its peace, for it has attained to that which it has always desired. Plotinus himself laments the state of those who have not attained to this unity, but says that those to whom the experience sounds strange may understand it by means of our own experience of earthly love.[190] In the meantime, until we have escaped fully from the fetters of the body, we are forced to live within the tension created by the dialectic operative on the level of

---

[187] See *Life* 23, 16-18, where Porphyry describes how Plotinus attained to union four times while he was with him.
[188] VI 9, 10, 1-2; see also VI 9, 9 and VI 4, 14.
[189] VI 9, 9, 57-60.
[190] VI 9, 4; VI 9, 9, and VI 9, 10.

the One's own manifestation of himself through his presence in the universe, and of his 'being', which is beyond being and intellect. The human experience of the One is an experience of absence and presence, for sometimes we are lifted into an experience of unity with him and 'know' him, while at other times we are bereft of his presence and do not know him.

It could be argued therefore, that in the *Enneads* dialectic operates on two levels. Firstly, from a metaphysical point of view, the One is both everywhere and nowhere; it is neither limited nor unlimited; it both is in all things and yet in no thing; it contains all but is not itself contained; it is simple and yet not simple; it is form which is formless, and unity which is partless; and, finally, it is multiple, yet above all multiplicity. In sum, all things both are and are not the One.[191] All things can be said to be the One, since it is present to them as their source; on the other hand, they are not the One, because the One cannot be the things into which its power flows.[192] On the second level of the dialectic operative in the *Enneads*, the One is both present and absent, not simply through his metaphysical manifestation of himself, but also in terms of his presence, as he is in the universe, as he is in himself: he is neither far nor near, neither here nor there.[193] In other words, he will never be fully present or near, until the soul has finally made good its escape from the body. The tension created by the dialectical understanding of the One in the *Enneads* was to become an important part of the later development of negative theology. In the Pseudo-Dionysius, God is all things and yet none of all things; he is both manifest and hidden.[194] It is, however, in the philosophy of Eriugena that the Neoplatonic dialectic, interwoven as it is with his doctrine of theophany, reaches its fullest stature.[195] Therefore, Plotinus stands at the beginning of a tradition which took the dialectic of

[191] V 5, 2 and V 3, 12.
[192] VI 4, 3.
[193] V 5, 9; VI 4, 2; VI 4, 3, and VI 9, 4.
[194] See *De div. nom.* II, 11; V, 10, and V, 11.
[195] See *Periphyseon* 620C, 658C and 678C.

Plato as it was applied in the *Parmenides* and gave it a new and transformed theological meaning in relation to the nature of the One.

How can anyone suppose that the experience of unity with the Good is nothing more than the final unity of all things with some lofty and aloof metaphysical principle? No one who has read those passages in the *Enneads* to which I have referred could suppose that Plotinus was thinking anything other than that the Good was supremely real. As W. Beierwaltes has remarked, the question about the nature of the One 'ist für Plotin alles andere als eine 'abstrakte' Frage, es ist die Lebens-Frage schlechthin'.[196]

There is one final point I wish to make before I turn to some concluding remarks; this concerns Plotinus's use of *Timaeus* 28C. In the *Enneads*, the whole notion of the ineffability of the One is derived from the conclusion of the First Hypothesis of the *Parmenides*; Plotinus makes no use of the *Timaeus* text to support the thesis that the One is unknowable. The Middle Platonists used the text quite freely, as I have shown above, because they believed that although God was not easily accessible to the human intellect, nevertheless the mind could come to some knowledge of him. The reason why Plotinus did not use the passage from the *Timaeus*, is that the Good of the *Enneads* is not simply difficult to know, he is above human knowledge altogether. The only explicit reference to *Timaeus* 28C occurs when Plotinus refers to the 'Maker of all',[197] although there is one further passage where he expresses the inability to state the Supreme.[198] Even though Plato's text had become doctrine for the Middle Platonists, in the *Enneads* it is not a fundamental text employed in the same way as Plotinus uses the seminal text from *Republic* 509B.

---

[196] 'Plotins philosophische Mystik', p. 42; see also A. H. Armstrong, 'The Escape of the One', p. 79.
[197] V 9, 5, 20.
[198] VI 9, 10, 19-21.

Conclusion

It remains for me now to attempt an evaluation of Plotinus's
negative theology both in the light of his own metaphysical system
and in the light of his Platonic and Middle Platonic sources. When
we view Plotinus in the light of his Platonic predecessors, we find
in him ideas and theories similar to theirs. Indeed, to read the
Enneads without having travelled the long, hard road from Plato
through the Middle Platonists, is bound to lead to a certain amount
of distortion. While it is true that Plotinus owes much to the ideas
of the Platonic predecessors upon which he cut his philosophic
teeth, his philosophy represents a point in Platonism which was to
be difficult to parallel.[199]

With regard to the development of negative theology in the
Enneads, it can be said that Plotinus was building upon ideas that
had already appeared in Alcinous, Numenius and others. Plotinus's distinctive originality is that he proposed the notion that neither the human intellect nor the One itself, can have any knowledge about the One. This idea would have been utterly scandalous
to the Platonists of his day – think of how Glaucon was incredu-
lous when Socrates spoke of the Good beyond being.

There are many instances in the *Enneads* when one is reminded
forcefully of ideas present in the thought of Philo of Alexandria,
but in spite of H. A. Wolfson's championship of Philo as the
source and originator of many Neoplatonic ideas, we still have no
conclusive evidence to suggest that Plotinus was consciously
appropriating the Jewish source. Although E. R. Dodds, among
others, finds it difficult to believe that Plotinus would have taken
Philo seriously, it is not totally unthinkable that Plotinus would
have been familiar with the writings of his fellow Alexandrian.[200]
I would suggest that closer examination of those passages where
Plotinus appears to be in agreement with Philo may reveal some
interesting points of connection. That, however, would be another

---

[199] See P. Merlan, *Monopsychism*, p. 142.
[200] 'The *Parmenides* of Plato', p. 142.

study. There is, of course, a number of instances where Plotinus appears to be relying on Numenius, who also had Alexandrian connections; Porphyry reports a charge of plagiarism.[201] However, even though Plotinus was influenced by the speculations of the Platonists before him, the negative theology of the *Enneads* is one which was unparalleled in Greek thought. For further development of its principles we must await the genius of Proclus.

According to A. H. Armstrong's analysis, there are in the *Enneads* three forms of negative theology: the negative theology of positive transcendence; the mathematical negative theology, and the negative theology of the infinite subject.[202] What Armstrong calls the mathematical negative theology (the One as the principle of measure, which cannot itself be measured and which transcends what it measures) looks upon the first principle 'as an unpredictable unity standing at the origin of number' which 'carries with it little depth of religious feeling.' While it can be said that Plotinus does regard the One as the source of all multiplicity, I must point out that he uses terms such as 'monad' and 'point' simply as illustrations of the simplicity of the One.[203] The method of abstraction from the solid through the surface and line to the point (as used by Alcinous) does indeed appear in the *Enneads*, but as an object of criticism rather than approbation. This method of reaching an understanding of the One is not adequate, for through it we reach a point which was formerly a number of parts; thus, this mathematical illustration does not exemplify the method of reaching the true understanding of the One. Plotinus would, I think, hesitate to adopt this particular illustration for anything but the simple method of *aphairesis*, for he would regard the point simply as an example of the simplicity of the One, and the method itself as a mathematical one. As an explanation of the negative theology of positive transcendence, Armstrong points to *Ennead* VI 8, which he calls the 'classic treatise' for this theology of tran-

---

[201] *Life* 17.
[202] *The Architecture of the Intelligible Universe*, p. 29ff.
[203] VI 9, 5, 38-46.

scendence. The One, as the first cause which is beyond being, is expressed in terms of negative theology: 'only because its reality cannot be adequately expressed in terms of the realities we know; phrases are preferred which make it clear that the transcendent reality is more than what is denied of it'.[204]

This is the true position of negative theology, for the purpose of denial, according to the Pseudo-Dionysius, is so that we may be able to affirm on the highest level possible. The 'negative theology of the infinite subject' is described by Armstrong as that moment when all limitation is denied, the frontier between subject and object breaks down, and all things are resolved into a unity – a unity which generally stops at the level of *nous*. However, the denial or overcoming of any boundary between the All and the Self is not, strictly speaking, negative theology; it may perhaps be a distinct moment within the experience of the negative theology, but it is a moment which is not the sole prerogative of the way of negation, for positive theology is not, nor can it be, excluded from such mystical union. In general terms, the truest description of the negative theology is what Armstrong called the 'negative theology of positive transcendence'; indeed there cannot be any other kind of negative theology.

Plotinus himself stood at the frontier of a developing tradition of negative theology which has not, as yet, been understood in all its radical implications. It is certain that when Plotinus speaks of the One as a supreme metaphysical principle, or as the father and king of the universe who is at the same time so simple that he cannot be thought of, except in terms of the strictest unity possible, as the Good, the desirable *telos* and ultimate resting place of the soul, he is speaking of one and the same principle. Thus, we cannot understand the *Enneads* unless we understand that the highest principle may be viewed from a number of different perspectives. However, having said that, it is clear that Plotinus was anything but consistent – although we must remember that he wrote over a period of sixteen years many different treatises, none of which was

---

[204] *Op. cit.* p. 30.

intended for scholarly publication. Neither must we forget that he was most likely of Greek background, living in Rome, surrounded by many and various religious practices; hence it is not surprising that we should find references to the old Greek deities firmly embedded in his thought. In view of this, I do not think there is any tremendous difficulty posed by the fact that the One is understood as 'father and maker', the 'One' and the 'Good'. It is not possible to understand Plotinus's negative theology without first acknowledging his conception of the One which is expressed in more positive terms; for this is, after all, the conception which is dominant in the *Enneads*.[205]

In terms of the Plotinian metaphysical system, the absolute simplicity and unity of the One, understood as the transcendent cause of all being, has serious implications with regard to negative theology. If *apophasis* is not understood in terms of the journey back to the One, negative theology can play only a subordinate role, for it would indeed postulate a cold metaphysical principle, and that alone. It is only if the One is understood as *telos* that negative theology becomes a reality.

Therefore, it would appear that the spiritual (for want of a better word) aspect of the negative theology in the *Enneads* is based upon and derives its main tenets from Plotinus's metaphysical conception of a simple, transcendent, unknowable unity. Statements to the effect that the One does not know himself, or that he is above being and intellect, do not in themselves constitute negative theology: it is only when the soul attempts to bridge the gap that has been understood to exist between the cause and effect that negative theology, correctly understood, becomes operative. However, in making the distinction between the negations used to describe the transcendence of the One and the actual experience of negation in practice (the purification of one's Good-concepts), I do not wish to suggest that Plotinus would have thought of *apophasis* in those terms. We ought not to read the *Enneads* selectively: in order to understand the negative conception of the One,

---

[205] *Ibid.* p. 44.

the *Enneads* should be read in their entirety; only then can we appreciate that Plotinus's unique mixture of apophatic and kataphatic elements constitutes the only true theology, and the one cannot exist without the other. And just as negative theology should not be regarded simply as a corrective measure against a too anthropomorphic conception of the Good, in a similar way, the kataphatic elements in Plotinus's thought should not be regarded as a means of making the inaccessible Good more accessible. In the end, even in the state of union, the One of the *Enneads* is not knowable. In this at least, Plotinus can be regarded as one of the most honest of all those who have undertaken an exposition of the theology of negation. As Armstrong says, 'Plotinus often faces the consequences of this doctrine with remorseless clarity, without any softening down or explaining away'.[206]

I am aware that the analysis of negative theology I have presented in this chapter has its limitations, for Plotinus is no easy author to understand and his thoughts are not by any means laid out in a systematic fashion. I am also aware that I have omitted many ideas which may have a bearing on the theme of negative theology in its wider implications, but the inclusion of ideas related only indirectly to negative theology would have made my task practically impossible. Negative theology in Plotinus is not the fully-thematized concept that is found in the *Mystical Theology* of the Pseudo-Dionysius, but all the basic elements found in the Areopagite's short work are already present in the *Enneads*.[207] Perhaps the only concept which became important in the negative theology of the later Neoplatonists but which is not fully explicit in the *Enneads*, is the *negatio negationis*. Plotinus's attempt to preserve the transcendence of the One and also to see the Good as the desirable end of the search of the soul, points to an intimate understanding of negative theology. If the unknowable Good is not viewed as *telos*, negative theology can at the most be regarded

---

[206] 'The Escape of the One', p. 80.

[207] Gregory of Nyssa's reliance upon certain key Plotinian texts provides an indirect link between Plotinus and the Pseudo-Dionysius, for the latter utilized many ideas of the Cappadocian Fathers; see chapter 8 below.

as a negative philosophy. To enter into negative theology, to go where we have no sure footing, demands that we exercise our intellectual capacity to its fullest extent before we can ultimately let it go. Those of us who have not been 'There' experience a certain amount of bewilderment in trying to imagine how we can find the way of the non-concept. Plotinus was one man who was not afraid to look the questions of negative theology in the face without shrinking from their consequences. This is one reason why Plotinus is a philosopher worthy of study nearly 1,700 years after his death.

CHAPTER SIX

LATER NEOPLATONIC *APOPHASIS*

The development of the theme of *apophasis*, especially in terms of the Neoplatonic interpretation of the *Parmenides* in the period between the death of Plotinus and the birth of Proclus, has, until recently, been largely uncharted in philosophical terms.[1] Although it is indeed necessary to read Proclus in the light of his predecessors, here I confine myself chiefly to some brief introductory comments on The Anonymous *Commentary on the Parmenides*, which serves as an introduction to the kind of negative theology we find developing in the late Neoplatonic period.

It is generally held that the post-Plotinian form of Platonism, under the initial inspiration of Porphyry and then Iamblichus, began to take on a more religious dimension, in that it tended more and more towards theurgy.[2] When tracing the development of any theme in the period between Plotinus and Proclus, one must be aware of the very powerful impact of religious and magical ritual which began to have a discernible effect on philosophical speculation. Whatever the reasons for an ever-deepening interest in theurgic practices, it can be said that the concept of the absolute unknowability of the One must have played some role, for it forced the philosopher (and the theologian) to explore other avenues whereby the One could be reached other than through intellect. Although it does not fall within the scope of this chapter

---

[1] See R. Mortley, *From Word to Silence II*; Mortley notes as the key figures Plutarch of Athens, Syrianus, Alexander of Aphrodisias and Dexippus, p. 85. Mortley also discusses some relevant texts of Syrianus and Dexippus in order to demonstrate the influence of Aristotle on the Neoplatonic understanding of the First Hypothesis; see p. 94ff.

[2] See A. Smith, *Porphyry's Place in the Neoplatonic Tradition*; part two gives a comprehensive account of theurgy in Porphyry, Iamblichus and Proclus.

to offer an account of the influence of theurgic practice on philosophical/theological speculation, it may be said that Porphyry's legacy to later Platonists lies not so much in his development of Plotinian principles, but rather, in his appropriation of theurgy. It would appear that he did not contribute significantly to the theme of negative theology – although Plotinus himself did not, as we shall discover, have the last word on the theme of the transcendence of the One. However, a small word of caution may be apposite at this point: in view of the fact that so little of Porphyry's output is extant, it is very difficult to be dogmatic; one should be wary of generalizations.

Although the Neoplatonic interpretation of the *Parmenides* can be said to have reached its zenith in the great *Commentary* of Proclus, he did, in fact, owe much to his immediate master Syrianus, for he elaborates and accepts his opinions with some regularity. Interestingly, the more distant Neoplatonists are never mentioned by name, although they are the focus of some sustained criticism at times: Porphyry in particular, appears to be most often the subject of Proclus's criticisms.[3]

Ever since the publication of P. Hadot's research, in which he argued that Porphyry was the author of the fragmentary *Commentary on the Parmenides*,[4] scholars have been debating the question of the supposed authorship. Generally, opinion has been divided on the subject and a whole-hearted acceptance of Hadot's argumentation for the authorship of Porphyry has not as yet become apparent.[5] The question of the authorship of this *Commentary* is not simply a historic curiosity, rather, it is of some considerable importance, chiefly because a number of themes contained in it raise the question of whether the author believed the One to be

---

[3] The J. Dillon and G. R. Morrow translation of the *Parmenides Commentary* is extremely useful in that the translators give references to themes in the pre-Proclean Neoplatonic tradition.

[4] See 'Fragments d'un commentaire de Porphyre sur le *Parménide*'; 'La métaphysique de Porphyre', and *Porphyre et Victorinus*.

[5] The debate has recently been re-opened by J. Dillon, who is more accepting of Hadot's original thesis and I am grateful to him for permission to use an unpublished article entitled, 'Porphyry's Doctrine of the One'.

above being, or whether he contradicted Plotinus on this point. The remarks made by Damascius, to the effect that Porphyry identified ὕπαρξις with τὸ ἕν (described by A. C. Lloyd as the 'telescoping of the hypostases'), have made the question of Porphyry's allegiance to Plotinus a critical point in the earlier development of post-Plotinian Platonism.[6]

The central problem revolves around the supposed identification of πατήρ or ὕπαρξις with τὸ ἕν, which would imply that the One is the first principle of the intelligible triad: τὸ ἕιναι μόνον as is stated in the *Commentary*. This interpretation would stand in direct opposition to the Plotinian concept of the One as ἐπέκεινα τοῦ εἶναι. While I cannot hope to resolve a complex question of such long standing, I find J. Rist's conjecture most plausible, namely, that Porphyry's significant divergence from Plotinian principles may well have been the result of his contact with the *Chaldean Oracles*.[7] J. Dillon, on the other hand, presents a case for an interpretation of Porphyry which is very close to the (sometimes ambiguous) position of Plotinus himself. He concludes that since Proclus may not have known the *Commentary*, his criticisms were not fully representative of Porphyry's thought.[8] Although Porphyry must have spent some considerable time in the preparation of the *Enneads* for publication, he was not by any means an uncritical disciple of Plotinus.[9] We should not, therefore, be surprised that he did not slavishly repeat the theories of his master.

The Anonymous *Commentary on the Parmenides*

The concept of the One contained in the fragments of the *Commentary* does, in fact, lay some considerable stress upon the notion

---

[6] See Damascius, *Dub. et solut.* 43; P. Hadot, *Porphyre et Victorinus*, vol. 1, p. 423 and A. C. Lloyd, 'The Later Neoplatonists', p. 288.
[7] See 'Mysticism and Transcendence in Later Neoplatonism', p. 220ff.
[8] See J. Dillon's remarks in the introduction to the translation of the *Parmenides* Commentary, pp. xxiii-xxx.
[9] See A. Smith, *op. cit.* p. xvi.

of divine transcendence.[10] One familiar Plotinian sentiment occurs many times: there is nothing before the One, who is the principle of all things. Although the author does not work out a systematic theory of divine nomenclature as Proclus was to do, he notes, in true Plotinian fashion, that we apply the name 'One' in order to signify his infinite power as principle and supreme cause.[11] Strictly speaking, however, he is anterior to the One, for from him come both the One and the Monad – a rather curious neo-Pythagorean echo from pre-Plotinian times.[12]

In fragment IV, the author applies himself to a discussion of *to me on*, and concludes that in relation to the One all other things are non-being. That is the reason why they do not have the power to come to any knowledge of him. They lack the appropriate faculty for a direct apprehension of that which has no relation to any other thing.[13] It is here that we find the author confirming that all things which come after the One are non-being, while the One is 'the only being above all things'.[14]

In fragments V and VI, the author addresses the question of God's knowledge, and asks whether such knowledge, if it can be said to exist, would introduce the notion of multiplicity to the simplicity of the divine nature. Interestingly, he concludes that the 'knowledge' which is proper to God is a knowledge which is above both knowledge and ignorance, anterior to all things known and unknown (a concept which is later developed, although in a different fashion, in the *Periphyseon* of Eriugena).[15] One point our author stresses time and time again, is that God cannot be known either by reason or through intellect, for he is above all discourse and thought.[16] One cannot even know the mode of the procession

[10] I, 4-5.
[11] I, 24ff.
[12] II, 13-14; see also X, 24-25.
[13] See also IX, 20ff; since there is nothing to compare with the One, he is μονώσεως: IV, 10 and 31.
[14] IV, 8-9.
[15] V, 10-11: ὅτι φημὶ εἶναι γνῶσιν ἔξω γνώσεω(ς) καὶ ἀγνοίας, ἀφ ' ἧς ἡ γνῶσις.
[16] X, 14-16 and IX, 24-25.

of the One into the things which have come from him.[17] Can the human intellect then come to any knowledge of the supremely transcendent unknowable principle? How can it make the return journey into union with the Father who is desired and loved?[18] The author of the *Commentary* mentions the return to unity in three fragments: II, VI and X. In fragment II (14ff), he echoes a most familiar Plotinian (and indeed Proclean) exhortation: do not add anything to the One. By being true to this principle and by turning away from all things, one can come to a 'non-comprehensive comprehension' of the One, a 'conception which conceives nothing'. In VI (21ff), the method of approach to God is described in terms which would not have been alien to the *Mystical Theology* of the Pseudo-Dionysius: one must abandon all things, even oneself, and by not thinking of anything, become separate from all things.[19]

It is perhaps in fragment X that the author comes closest to a clear (though non-systematic) exposition of the main principles of negative theology: since God is unknowable both by reason and through intellect, we must abandon all rational and intelligible pursuits: those symbols, similes and metaphors we have formed about him. This path towards unity is, then, the path of intellectual purification.[20] When we have let go of intellectual conceptualizations, our 'concept' will be without content or formulation: we must remain in ignorance about the One.

Although this brief glimpse into the *Commentary* does not do full justice to the employment of negative theology by our anonymous author, it serves to highlight the fact that from the time of Plotinus onwards, Platonism was moving towards an ever more transcendent conception of the unknowable One. It also leaves one strong and lasting impression, namely, that it is a more 'religious' form of negative theology than was to be found explicitly in the *Enneads*. The ideas we find in the *Commentary* are certainly a

[17] See X, 29ff.
[18] See II, 25ff.
[19] See *De myst. theol.* I, 1.
[20] X, 6-11.

striking mixture of Plotinian and pre-Plotinian themes, and yet in some of the extant fragments, we are drawn forward into an almost Dionysian and sometimes Eriugenian framework for negative theology.

Whatever scholars may decide regarding the metaphysical inconsistencies of terminology and thought, it remains true that the God portrayed here is supremely unknowable and the path to unity is solely through the abandonment of the intellectual concept. Although the author stresses more consistently than Plotinus had done the concept of the unknowability and transcendence of the One, there is little which could be said to contradict the Plotinian understanding of negative theology. Whether or not its author was Porphyry, must, at least for the present, remain an open question.

Proclus: The Way of The One

In the year 485, more than 200 years after the death of Plotinus, Marinus of Samaria recorded an incident in the final illness of the seventy-five year-old Proclus, who saw a serpent, the symbol of regeneration near his head.[21] A similar incident occurred in the year 270, at the death-bed of Plotinus.[22] Quite apart from the obvious implications in terms of the reincarnation of soul, this very powerful sign can perhaps be understood in a secondary sense, as symbolic of an assurance of the continuance of the master's teachings. While the teaching of Plotinus continued in the Neoplatonic schools (although he is seldom referred to by name), the teaching of Proclus was to take a very different direction, but it was continued nonetheless.

Proclus, visionary, healer, soothsayer, theologian and philosopher beloved of the gods, is perhaps the best representative of the kind of Platonism flourishing in the fifth century; he sets out a comprehensive philosophical system which was, at least to our

---

[21] *Life* 30.
[22] *Life* 2.

knowledge, unrivalled before him. Proclus saw himself as a member of a 'divine choir' who sang the mysterious truths of divine principles; this 'choir' consisted of Plotinus, Amelius, Porphyry, Iamblichus, Theodore of Asine, Plutarch and Syrianus.[23] Although Proclus is generally regarded as representative of a type of Neoplatonism different from that of Plotinus and Porphyry, the very complex interweaving of what is known as the Roman and Athenian schools, centring as it does upon the 'Alexandrian connection', makes it very difficult to say with complete certainty what is distinctive to the Roman school and what is distinctive to the Athenian school. It was, however, at Athens that later Neoplatonism flourished, and Proclus can certainly be described as its greatest principal.

In the pages to follow, I will confine my remarks to a discussion of the Proclean interpretation of the First Hypothesis of the *Parmenides*.[24] The Proclean interpretation of the first two hypotheses of the *Parmenides* differs notably both from that of Iamblichus before him and also from Damascius after him. Proclus did not think it necessary to posit an ineffable super-One above the One/Good as Iamblichus had done and as Damascius was to do.[25] For him, the first two hypotheses refer respectively to the One above being, and to Being itself; further complications were considered unnecessary.

> Parmenides abides in the transcendent One, Zeno projects the Many on the One, and Socrates turns back even these many to the Parmenidean One, since the first member in every triad is an analogue of rest, the second of procession, and the third of reversion.[26]

This brief statement encapsulates the core of Proclean metaphysics, for the typically Neoplatonic triad: *monē, proodos* and

---

[23] *Platonic Theology* I, 1, p. 7 (5-8); see also I, 1, p. 6 (16ff).

[24] The edition used is that of V. Cousin; the surviving portion of Book VII follows the Latin edition of R. Klibansky and C. Labowsky. Translations are taken from Morrow and Dillon (page numbers are given in brackets). All references are to the *Parmenides* Commentary unless otherwise noted.

[25] Iamblichus, *De myst.* VIII, 2, pp. 195-196 (Des Places), and Damascius, *Dub. et sol.* II, 8.

[26] *Parm.* I 712. 43-41 (p. 86).

epistrophē underpins the myriad hierarchical structures of Proclean thought. It also serves to focus attention upon the underlying principle in his philosophical system: the search for unity. 'Unity, then, is the most venerable thing, which perfects and preserves everything, and that is why we give this name to the concept that we have of the first principle.'[27]

To characterize the thought of Proclus as the search for unity situates the last great Platonist firmly within the tradition established by Plotinus. For Proclus, as for Plato and Plotinus, the highest goal of *philosophia* culminates ultimately in *theologia*, and it is with a genuine spirit of deep religious fervour that Proclus begins his most comprehensive discussion of the principle of unity in the *Parmenides* Commentary.

Ὦ πάντων ἐπέκεινα

O You, the Beyond all things!
How else is it fitting to sing of You?
How can words be a hymn to You?
no word can express You.
How can mind perceive You?
no mind can grasp You.
You alone are unutterable,
though all that is spoken is from You.
You alone are unknowable,
though all that is thought is from You.[28]

Thus begins the hymn to the first principle (formerly attributed to Gregory Nazianzus), a litany of negation which encapsulates the Proclean conception of the One beyond all.[29] The transcen-

---

[27] VII 56K. 1-3: Quia igitur venerabilissimum le unum, perfectivum existens et salvativum entium omnium, propter hoc utique eum qui apud nos de primo conceptum sic vocavimus; see also I 620. 29-31: 'when the One is taken away there is complete confusion and disorder among the Many' (p. 21).

[28] The complete Greek text of this hymn can be found in *PG*. 37, 507ff.

[29] The ineffable and unknowable principle above all is celebrated (ἀνυμνέται) – see *P. T.* I 10, p. 42 (1-2) and II, 11, p. 65 (5-7) – with a hymn without saying

dent terminology of the One to be found in the writings of Proclus is perhaps the most comprehensive of any other Neoplatonic
philosopher and represents the high point in the development of
apophasis in Greek thought.[30] Basing his conception of the One
upon the negations to be found in the First Hypothesis of the *Parmenides*, Proclus states time and time again, that the One is transcendent over all things.[31] In this respect, Proclus notes that the
text from *Republic* (509B) is the foundation for all that is denied
of the One in the First Hypothesis.[32] It is 'simply unity' above all
essence and plurality and 'second to nothing'.[33] Even the Second
Hypothesis is described in terms which Plotinus would have
found quite acceptable for the One itself: 'for the transcendent
One-Being is truly an august object, as ensconced in unity; it is
great, as possessing an incomprehensible power, and secret, as
remaining inexpressible and inscrutable at the summit of existence'.[34]

    The basic assertion at the heart of Proclus's conception of the
One can be stated simply enough: the One is not a particular One,
but One in the absolute sense, simply One.[35] Everything that can
be qualified is not what it is absolutely.[36] The basic rule of thumb
followed by Proclus relies upon the Plotinian guideline: with
regard to the One, additions diminish. 'For whatever you add to
the One by its addition causes oneness to vanish, since it rejects
the addition of everything that is alien to it'.[37] Therefore, the One
is not any particular thing; nor is it to be understood as the
'entirety of the Forms' or the 'summit of things', for such an

---

what he is who made heaven and earth. See W. Beierwaltes, *Proklos*, p. 353, for
a discussion of the 'hymn of negations' at *Parm.* VII 1191. 32ff.
[30] W. Beierwaltes, *Proklos*, p. 352, n. 65, lists these transcendent terms in their
various formulations: ὑπέρ, ἐξ, πρό, and ἐπέκεινα.
[31] II 763. 4.
[32] 64K.
[33] II 763. 9.
[34] I 713. 16-20; see also *P. T.* II 10, p. 63 (18-20).
[35] VI 1069. 21; see also *Enn.* V 3, 13, 1ff and III 8, 10, 22: τὸ ἁπλῶς ἕν.
[36] VI 1096. 19-21.
[37] VII 1177. 20-23 (p. 527); see also *P. T.* II 10, p. 63 (13ff) and *E. Th.* prop. 8.
See *Enn.* III 8, 11, 12-13 and VI 7, 38, 2-3.

understanding would also diminish its power.[38] In its absolute unity the One is wholly unparticipated.[39] Although the concept of the transcendent unity of the One is present throughout Proclus's writings, his most systematic discussion of it occurs in the final few pages of the *Commentary on the Parmenides*.[40]

The basic Platonic analysis of cognition as three-fold: *doxa*, *dianoia* and *nous*, are each in turn applied to the One and wanting in every respect.[41] How can that which is beyond all that exists be known either through sense perception or opinion; and how can that which has no cause be the object of scientific knowledge?[42] Neither the human, daemonic, angelic, divine (or demiurgic) orders can have either sense perception or opinion about the One. Each order has its own object of knowledge (human knowledge tends towards particulars and, according to Proclus, there is nothing venerable about it[43]). Even Intellect itself, 'the intelligible union which lies hidden and unutterable in the interior recesses of being itself',[44] falls short of knowledge of the One, for all knowledge is directed at Being, not at the One. Yet, Proclus is careful to point out that it is not simply because of the weakness of the lower orders which come after the One that they cannot know it, but because of its own super-excellent nature.[45] In fact, Proclus is so meticulous in following through the notion of the unknowability of the One, that even if we can say that it is unknowable to us, we are ignorant of whether it is knowable to itself.[46]

---

[38] See VII 1199. 13-16 and II 763. 16-17.

[39] VI 1070. 13; see also VII 36K. 10-12 and *P. T.* II 9, p. 57 (22).

[40] VII 46K. 7-9: Ab omni ergo cognitione partibili et intelligentia le unum exaltatum est et ab omni contactu. Solum autem unio nos adducit uni; et hoc quidem ut melius omni ente incognitum.

[41] See also *P. T.* I 3, p. 15 (18ff) and *E. Th.* prop. 123.

[42] VII 48K. 3-10.

[43] 50K. 9-10.

[44] 50k. 17-18 (p. 589): ... et super omnes intelligentialem unionem interius quidem entem in abdito entis, secretam entem et ineloquibilem.

[45] See 62K. 17-20.

[46] VI 1108. 25-29.

It is in the *Parmenides* Commentary that we find Proclus (unlike Plotinus, who was quite content to retain the term *patēr*[47]), denying the appellations 'maker', 'father' and 'divinity', a theme which the Pseudo-Dionysius was to take up in the *Mystical Theology*. However, just as Plotinus had granted a certain superiority to some names and terms of reference for the One (principally One and Good), while maintaining that strictly speaking, no terms are appropriate, we find Proclus making a similar point. He posits a very clear distinction between God alone, as the subject of the First Hypothesis and God the generator of the plurality of the gods.[48] The primal God is to be understood as *the* One and distinct from the other gods, even from the demiurge, the intelligent father and creator of the universe. The first God, the subject of the First Hypothesis, is 'not even a father' but is superior even to the paternal divinity.[49] For Proclus, the basic rule is always that the One can never be a particular thing, but is, for example, divinity itself, in a simple, unqualified sense:[50] 'let us call the One simply God'.[51] And yet, even though we will find Proclus arguing most persuasively for the absolute unnameability of the One, he does, like Plotinus, consent to certain terms: 'the first', 'the Good' and 'king'.[52] It is to a discussion of the naming process in Proclus's writings that I now turn my attention.

The Ineffable Nameless One

Although like all apophatic philosophers, Proclus insists that the One cannot be spoken about or named, we find him setting down the ways in which the One can be spoken. His journey through the various realms of human discourse leads him, like Augustine and

---

[47] See for example VI 9, 9, 33-38.
[48] VI 1069. 12ff.
[49] VI 1070. 22-24.
[50] VI 1109. 16.
[51] VI 1096. 36-37; see *Enn.* V 5, 13, 1ff.
[52] See VI 1097. 18-20.

others, to recommend silence as the most appropriate 'method' of celebrating the One. The path to that conclusion takes him through various formulations of human discourse in the heroic attempt to discern what speech about the One can be valid.

I begin this discussion with the general validation of human discourse concerning the One: we can speak about it because of the natural striving of the soul towards it, but we can say nothing about it in the proper sense.[53] As I will later show, desire for the One is the ultimate reason why human beings can talk about it: desire is before any understanding either inexpressible or analysable, and silent understanding is before that which is put into language.[54] This descending order: desire, silent understanding and language is strongly reminiscent of the sentiments expressed by Augustine in De trinitate: whatever we think of God is truer than what can be said, but God's own being is truer still than what can be thought.[55] Proclus works out a further order when cautioning against communicating certain ideas to those of 'slovenly hearing': not all the contents of intellect are capable of being thought, and we do not speak of all that we think; neither do we write all that we speak, and finally (an apposite word of caution here!) we do not publish all that we write:[56] 'for one should convey mystical truths mystically and not publish secret doctrines about the gods'.[57] Thus we find that at each step of the process, something cannot be carried over to the next; writing is at least at a fourth remove from the reality it seeks to express, while discourse can be thought of as existing at a third remove. The transcendent One is incomprehensible in power, secret, inexpressible and inscrutable and it can be said to 'possess' these characteristics primarily; discourse, on the other hand, possesses them only sec-

---

[53] VII 1191. 5-9.
[54] VII 54K. 23-25: et propter hoc et tacitam intelligentiam esse ante elocutionalem et desiderium ante omnem intelligentiam inexpressibilem et intelligentiam ex partibus incidentem.
[55] V, 3 (4) and VII, 4 (7).
[56] I 718. 11-26.
[57] IV 928 (p. 283).

ondarily.[58] It is for this reason that any speech about the One is to be regarded as different from speech on other subject matters: 'the discourse is lofty, and for this reason, it is great; it goes beyond the usual vein and is, therefore august; it is enigmatical and therefore secret'.[59]

According to Proclus, we cannot expect to reach a definition of that which is incomprehensible and above being, when we cannot even reach an understanding of simple, partless Forms. All definitions and names (for the One is inexpressible both by description and by name[60]) belong to the realm of the composite;[61] it is not proper, therefore, to speak of the One in terms of qualities which have their place in things which are subject to comparison.[62] Nor indeed is it permissible to apply to the One the superlative form of any epithet (highest, greatest, best, etc); those who do this demonstrate a desire to convey something more about the One than it is possible to do by way of negation.[63] The One cannot be described as something, even in the superlative sense, when it does not possess that quality at all – we cannot describe something as superlatively white for example, if it is not in any sense white.[64]

Having demonstrated how far from the One human discourse is, nevertheless, there is in Proclus's thought a continual tension between the 'loose terminology' derived from the realm of being (which Plotinus expressed by his constant use of the term *hoion*) which we are forced to use when speaking about the One, and the validity of that speech.[65] This tension can be perceived especially in

[58] I 713. 13-21.
[59] I 713. 22-24 (p. 86).
[60] VII 46K. 23.
[61] IV 939. 25-30.
[62] VII 1211. 23ff.
[63] VII 1211. 33-38; this criticism is most likely levelled at Plotinus, who often (for want of better words), speaks of the One as 'the best' and 'the highest', see I 7, 1; V 4, 1, and VI 7, 23.
[64] VII 1212. 1-4; Meister Eckhart will later take up this idea which can be traced to the *Liber de causis*, prop. 6; God cannot be described as 'better' or even 'best' when he is not good at all; see the vernacular sermon, *Renovamini spiritu mentis vestrae*.
[65] See VII 1191. 3-5 and 1200. 10-14.

his discussion of the naming process, a theme which is extremely important for an understanding of later negative theology.

In Proclus's writings there are at least three prolonged discussions of the question of the divine names.[66] In each of these passages Proclus takes the Platonic text, *Cratylus* 390Dff, as his starting point and in each instance the debate centres upon the question of the conventional or natural origin of names. In Book IV of the *Parmenides Commentary*, Proclus notes that in the conventional approach to the naming process, names are set by the multitude and have their origin in perceptible things. From these, by process of analogy, wise men then set the names for invisible realities. This understanding of the origin of names results in the conclusion that the sensible thing has the name in the primary sense, while the invisible reality has it only derivatively through the process of analogous transfer. The other approach affirms that names have a natural origin: they are set by wise men and refer primarily to an immaterial form and only secondarily to the sensible object. This understanding will argue that each name carries a likeness to the object to which it is applied (part of the final argument for the unnameability of the One). In support of this thesis Proclus invokes the Platonic notion that the term 'man', for example, can be applied correctly to the intelligible form but cannot be applied correctly to a particular man.[67] Names, then, as verbal images of objects, must refer primarily to immaterial forms: 'the names of secondary things come from beings prior to them'.[68] However, Proclus is careful to note that what has been said about names is solely that which the human mind is able to consider: there are many grades of names (divine, angelic, daemonic and human), some are utterable and some are unutterable.[69]

---

[66] *P. T.* I 29, p. 123ff; *Parm.* IV 849ff and VII 50kff. For a comprehensive discussion of the naming process in Proclus, see J. Trouillard, 'L'activité onomastique selon Proclos'.

[67] IV 850. 21ff.

[68] IV 852. 17-20.

[69] IV 853. 3-8; Proclus repeats this classification of names at VII 50k.

There is, therefore, a correct order in the establishment of names. In the first book of the *Platonic Theology*, Proclus explains that at the primary level, there exist correct and truly divine names which are established among the gods themselves.[70] At the secondary level, that of intellect, there are names which are 'likenesses' of the highest names and have daemonic status, and at the tertiary level we find names which are the products of a level of discourse and are 'appearances' of divine beings.[71]

Proclus is quite clear, however, that none of the names we can discuss applies to the One, for no name is capable of revealing the essence of the One. Even in the intelligible realm, a name does not reveal essence. When we hear, for example, the word 'circle', we do not grasp its essence – in this sense, intelligible objects imitate the inexpressible and unutterable nature of the One.[72] Since the One has no attribute whatsoever, no name can apply to it: all names are 'inferior and fall short of its transcendent super-eminence'.[73] Since every name corresponds to what is named and is 'the logical image of the object', it follows that no name is capable of revealing the nature of the One.[74] What about the name 'One' itself? Proclus, like Plotinus, asks if it is possible to speak this name properly of the One. He concludes that the name, 'One' means that it is nothing else but 'oneness'; since it does not possess unity as a characteristic, it is not a true appellation for that unity.[75] Even though the name 'One' is more suitable than all other terms and names (it is 'the most divine of names'[76]), human discourse employs it although it is unsuitable and inferior – all

[70] I 29, p. 124 (3-5).

[71] I 29, p. 124 (5-9). Proclus continues this particular discussion with an account of the power of divine names in a theurgical context; see R. Mortley's comments in *From Word to Silence II*, p. 99ff.

[72] See V 985. 15ff and VII 46K and 50K; Proclus's source here is Plato, *Ep.* VII, 342C.

[73] VII 52K. 2-3 (p. 590): Omnia enim ipso deteriora sunt et deficiunt a superem- inentia ipsius exaltata.

[74] VII 52K. 9-10.

[75] VII 1196. 23ff.

[76] VII 1200. 14ff.

names refer to what comes after it.[77] We can, however, refer to it as, for example, the 'fount of divinity', if by that we mean to indicate it both as cause and *telos*.[78] Here, Proclus makes a most important point, one which had already been noted by Plotinus: by designating the One in such expressions as 'fount of divinity', we do not say what it is in itself, but what relation it has to those things which come after it, of which it is the cause.[79]

In the final part of Book VII, Proclus returns once again to the question of the name of the One.[80] If names are natural, then the first principle has no name, not even the name 'One', for if the One had a name, it would not be One. The One, he says, is even *supra spiritum*. Here Proclus relates a remarkable piece of argumentation for the unnameability of the One based upon an analysis of the letters of its name, a thematic derived from Theodore of Asine.[81] The name 'One' cannot be reduced to a simpler name, but it can be reduced to its letters: the silent breathing, the vowel and the consonant. The analysis of the name in terms of its constituents reveals that each constituent represents something different, which would mean that the first principle would not be One. Therefore, the One has no name.

However, since we do give the One a name, the validity of calling the One 'One', can be found in the human person: the name denotes not the One itself, but the understanding of unity in ourselves, which is, of course, inferior to the One itself: 'aut non illud vocamus sic nominantes, sed eam que in nobis intelligentiam unius'.[82] It is, therefore, the projection and expression of the One in us that we call One, and that name names our conception of it, since it itself is unnameable: 'in nobis unius et velut expressionem, sic nominamus unum'.[83] Our apprehension, then, applies

---

[77] VI 1108. 38 – 1109. 2 – a sentiment derived from Plotinus, see VI 7, 28, 4-5 and VI 9, 5, 31-32.
[78] VI 1108. 29-30 and 1109. 6-9.
[79] VI 1109. 12-14; here Proclus uses Plato, *Ep.* II 312E as part of his argument.
[80] VII 50k. 26ff.
[81] VII 62K. 9ff. See J. Dillon's note, translation, p. 509, n. 112.
[82] 54K. 4-5.
[83] 54K. 13.

the name 'One' to itself as 'somehow divining (*divinatio*) the reality of what transcends itself and everything else'.[84] It is in this way that Proclus resolves the problem of naming the unnameable. All other names, except that of 'One', give knowledge of the things of which they are the concepts; this cannot be the case in respect of the One.[85] Since we must give it a name, the name 'One' is appropriate, and since the One and the Good are the same ('quod idem est le unum et le bonum'[86]) it can also be called the Good. The name 'One' is the image of the procession and the name 'Good' is the image of conversion.[87]

Speaking the Ineffable: The Way of Negation

Faced with the assertion that the One is eminently ineffable and unknowable, Proclus must addresses the question whether the One can be spoken of in any meaningful sense at all. It is for this reason that we find Proclus working out a very concise method of speaking about the One in terms of a methodological application of affirmation and negation.

It is, according to Proclus, the language of negation which is best suited to discourse concerning the One who is wholly unconnected with everything and unparticipated in, apart from everything, and supremely transcendent.[88] Human beings are forced to use the language of negation when speaking about the One precisely because the One is unparticipated, because it does not exist

---

[84] See 58K. 7-11 (p. 593): Unde ille quidem nomina rebus ut cognitis inducunt; hec autem incognitum desiderans et comprehendere non potens, ponit denominationem unius non incognito – quomodo enim? – sed sibi ipsi divinanti aliqualiter hypostasim illius et a se ipsa et ab aliis omnibus (exaltatam; quid) autem, est impotens considerare. On the One in ourselves, see W. Beierwaltes, *Proklos*, p. 367ff.

[85] See 56K. 24-25 and 58K. 7.

[86] 56K. 34.

[87] 60K. 15-16: Si igitur nomen aliquid oportet primo adducere, videtur 'le unum' et 'le bonum' ipsi convenire; see also *P. T.* II 6, p. 40 (25-27).

[88] An excellent discussion of negative dialectic in Proclus can be found in W. Beierwaltes, *Proklos*, p. 341ff.

for the sake of anything[89]; for such a reality, affirmation is understood to be wholly unsuitable: 'we should rest content with negations'.[90] Since the primal One is above being, we cannot apply attributes which are proper to secondary things. In a most Plotinian fashion, Proclus affirms that if we transfer attributes to it from created nature, we will be talking about ourselves and not about the One. All attributes, therefore, must be removed from the One.[91]

However, it must be noted from the outset that Proclus does not advocate the method of negation simply as a way of guarding against making the One multiple (additions diminish), rather, he views negation in a very positive sense, for its ultimate function is to exhibit its transcendent superiority and its power.[92] Among the questions Proclus sets himself to answer concerning the negative method of discourse are the following: are negations superior to affirmations? What are the nature of the negations used in respect of the One? I begin with a discussion of the first question, basing my remarks on the well-known passage from the *Parmenides* Commentary, Book VI.[93]

In every class of being it can be stated that assertion is superior to negation, for in this respect negation denotes the deprivation of a certain quality and assertion affirms its presence. However, closer examination of the different kinds of negation reveal that assertion is not in every case superior to negation. There are, according to Proclus, three kinds of negation: one type is superior to assertion, one is equally balanced by assertion, and one type of negation is inferior to assertion.[94] Inferior negation refers to the being which is superior to not-being (as defect), the balanced negation refers to the kind of being which has the same rank as not-being and finally, the type of negation which is superior to

[89] VI 1115. 36ff.
[90] VI 1116. 11-12.
[91] VI 1073. 26ff and 1107. 20ff.
[92] VI 1074. 4-7 and 12-15 and 1108. 20-22.
[93] 1072. 19ff.
[94] This theme is repeated at *P. T.* II 5, pp. 37-38.

assertion, is expressive of the type of Non-Being which is above being.[95] It is solely when negation is expressive of the Non-Being superior to being, that it is superior to assertion. In the case of the not-being which has the same rank as being, both negations and affirmations can truly be applied to it. In the case of the Non-Being which is above being, neither assertions nor negations properly apply.[96] However, since no statement is properly true of the Non-Being wholly unconnected with being, 'at least negation is more properly uttered of it than assertion'.[97] Assertions refer to things that are, things that are defined; negations, on the other hand, refer to what is not and have, therefore, an undefined field of reference: 'assertions slice up reality, whereas negations tend to simplify things'.[98] Negations move from distinction to unity, from 'the sliced up type of knowledge towards that type of activity which is uncircumscribable, unitary and simple'.[99]

Having established that negation is superior to assertion with regard to the One, Proclus goes to great lengths to demonstrate that the form of negation he is talking about is not a form of privation (*steresis*), for the first principle is not deprived of the things that are denied of it, in the sense that it is capable of sustaining those qualities; neither is it a form of negation which is said of something absolutely non-receptive of that assertion (the line is not white).[100] Negations are not privative, for privations can refer only to something which has the faculty to actually be a definite something. Yet, in typically dialectical fashion, Proclus reminds us that even though the first principle itself is not deprived of the qualities denied of it, these things themselves are not without communication with the One, for they are derived from it.[101]

---

[95] 1072. 32ff.
[96] 1073. 14-18.
[97] 1073. 20-21.
[98] 1074. 7-11 (p. 427).
[99] 1074. 15-21.
[100] VI 1074. 22ff; see also *P. T.* I 12; II 5 and II 10. R. Mortley discusses Proclean negation from the perspective of this thematic, see *From Word to Silence II*, p. 102ff.
[101] 1074. 33-35.

Therefore, since all things derive from the One as cause, 'it is the cause of the assertions of which we apply to it the negations'.[102] Negations are, as Proclus puts it, 'the mothers of assertions', since the One itself is the cause of all processions to which assertions apply.[103] This is the reason why the negations of the First Hypothesis are affirmed in the Second Hypothesis: the unpluralized One itself gives substance to all multiplicity; itself unnumberable, it gives substance to all number.[104] It is for this reason that, according to Proclus, Parmenides denies opposite attributes of the One: as the cause of all opposition, the One transcends all antithesis and cannot be opposed to anything.[105] With regard to the denial of rest and motion, Proclus makes the following important point. If the One is not something, then to say it is the 'most x' 'is only empty words and does not say anything about the One.[106] We cannot even use such terminology as 'whole of wholes', because the One transcends and exceeds all wholeness.[107] Here I think we find an explicit criticism of the kind of statements often made by Plotinus: 'cause of causes', 'king of kings', and so on, although Proclus does not mention Plotinus by name.[108]

As cause, then, the Non-Being of the One cannot be anything of the things of which it is the cause; 'it produces everything, but is not one of al¹ things'[109] (a sentiment which Plotinus had affirmed time and time again in the *Enneads*).

> It is better, then, as Plato did, to rest content with negations, and by means of these to exhibit the transcendent superiority of the One – that is neither intelligible nor intellectual, nor anything else of the things which are cognizable by us by means of our individual mental activities.[110]

---

[102] 1075. 19-24 (p. 428).
[103] VI 1133. 3-5 (p. 472); see also VII 1208. 22-24. J. Trouillard, *L'Un et l'âme selon Proclus*, p. 89, says that it for this reason that negative theology can be understood to construct a positive ontology.
[104] See VI 1075. 26-30.
[105] VI 1076. 32ff; see *Enn.* I 8, 6, 20-21.
[106] VII 1172. 6-26.
[107] VI 1107. 30ff.
[108] See *Enn.* VI 8, 18, 33-36 and V 5, 3, 20.
[109] VI 1075. 30-33 (p. 428).
[110] VI 1108. 19-24.

However, it is not simply the weakness of the human intellect which forces it to employ negative expressions when speaking about the One, for no lower order can know the One affirmatively. Even Intellect itself knows Non-Being by means of non-being, that is, through negations.[111] Intellect knows the One through unity, it does not know it by direct vision or intuitively.[112] Intellect and divine souls possess two kinds of knowledge: they know reality as it is, that is, affirmatively, but in relation to the One, theirs is a negative form of knowledge because of the One's superiority to being. Here Proclus uses a familiar catch-phrase of negative theology: it is not *what* the One is that they know, but *what it is not*.[113] If Intellect and divine souls know the One through negation, 'why need we condemn our soul for impotence when it strives to express its incomprehensibility through negativity?'[114]

Another point which arises for Proclus in the preliminary discussion of the negations applied to the One is their order: do negations begin from the highest, most cognate things, or from the lowest, least cognate things?[115] In chapter ten below we shall see that the Pseudo-Dionysius follows Proclus closely on this matter: in the case of assertions, we must begin from the most cognate things; while in the case of negations, we begin from the least cognate things, from the things most familiar to us (which are, after all, easier to deny).

Having established to his satisfaction the nature of negations and the method in which to apply them to the One, Proclus follows faithfully the negations of the final part of the First Hypothesis of the *Parmenides*, and argues cogently for the denial of each, which he lists in summary as follows: many, whole, shape, being in itself or in another; the genera of being: like and unlike, equal and

---

[111] VI 1080. 5-7.
[112] See the translator's note, p. 593, n. 118.
[113] VI 1080. 28-30.
[114] 1080. 31-36.
[115] VI 1088. 4ff; see also V 990. 31ff. See J. Trouillard's comments on this concept in *L'Un et l'âme*, p. 146ff. Plotinus also notes that the aphairetic process begins from the lowest and moves towards the highest, see VI 9, 3, although he does not advocate that this rule be followed in any systematic fashion.

unequal, being older than, younger than, and the same age as itself or another, participation in substance, being existence itself, being participable by existence, expressibleness and knowableness. All these things are not applicable to the One.[116] Once again, the basic rule is followed in each instance: addition must be removed since it particularizes and diminishes the One.[117]

What, then, is the ultimate function of negative discourse, and what, if anything, does it reveal about the One? I have already mentioned a number of texts where Proclus suggests that negative statements 'reveal' the transcendence of the One, but that is all they do, nothing more. They do not possess any positive cognitive content. Negative statements do not have the capacity to express anything about the One, since nothing applies to it in the proper sense: neither affirmation, nor negation; it is beyond all opposition and negation: 'sed exaltatum est propter simplicitatem ab omni oppositione et omni negatione'.[118] Proclus notes that there is a distinction between saying that something can refer to the One (*de uno*) and saying that something expresses the One (*circa unum*). Negative propositions can *refer* to the One, but they do not *express* anything about it: 'quare et dicte abnegationes non sunt circa unum, sed de uno'.[119] Negations, therefore, do not possess the capacity to reveal the nature of the One: they simply point towards its superiority. In the end, even the negations themselves must be removed from the One, as we shall see below.

Knowing the Unknowable: The Way of Unity

If, then, the One is to be understood as wholly unknowable, is there any sense at all in which the One can be known? and if so, what kind of knowledge can it be? Proclus's ultimate answer to

---

[116] VII 66k. 28-33; on this point, see the introduction to the first volume of the edition of the *Platonic Theology*, p. lxviii.
[117] VII 68K. 2-9.
[118] VII 70K. 9-10.
[119] 70K. 14-15.

this question is based upon the understanding that the whole universe is not alien from the One but is connected to it, that the soul's desire actually constitutes its likeness to the One.[120] As third in the general hierarchy of being, the soul sees the ideas one by one; intellect, on the other hand thinks all the ideas as one, while the One itself is one only and anterior to all thought.[121] The soul, therefore, possesses a kind of vision which is, by its very nature, a fragmented vision; its aim is the attainment of unified vision.

For Proclus, the unity of the universe stems from the fact that all beings are constituted in their being through their natural striving for the One. 'Thus the One is the desire of all, and all are preserved by it and are what they are through it, and in comparison with it, as with the Good, nothing else has value for anything'.[122] In fact, the desire for the One is such that 'we despise all other things in favour of the One, and never overlook the One for the sake of anything else'.[123] The terms used to express this desire in Proclus's writings are indeed strong: there exists in the soul a great anguish and inborn travail which yearns for the super-eminence of the One, a great devotion to the One and tremendous yearning for it.[124] The soul is ever striving towards the super-eminence of the One, revolving around it, seeking to embrace it, 'seeking with supreme passion to be present to it'.[125] And yet all striving falls short of the One, for the soul is denied its unapproachable object. 'Impotens autem aliqualiter comprehendere ipsius incomprehensibile aut cognoscere le incognitum, diligit secundum sui ipsius processum illius participationis indicibilem

---

[120] IV 922. 38ff.

[121] III 808. 14-24; see *Enn.* III 5, 7, where Plotinus also notes that human thinking is not simple.

[122] VII 58K. 16-17 (p. 593): sic et commune desiderium, quo salvantur omnia et sunt quod sunt et cuius gratia omnia parua alia omnibus sunt, sicut et (quod) boni. See also VII 1116. 12-15, 1199. 28ff, and *P. T.* 1 22, p. 101 (27ff).

[123] VII 1144. 25-30 (p. 500) – once again a sentiment with strong Plotinian echoes, see V 5, 12, 7-9 and VI 7, 22, 12-14.

[124] VII 42K. 26-27: Sed quia isto maius desiderant, quodcumque cognoverint, propter connaturalem ipsis inexistentem supereminentie unius; see also 44K. 32ff.

[125] VII 44K. 32ff (p. 587).

perceptionem.'[126] And yet the soul really loves the One with an inextinguishable love (*amor inextinguibilis*) even though the One is incomprehensible and can never be found.[127] It is, however, unfulfilled desire which keeps the soul striving for the One, for if the desire was fulfilled then it would no longer search.

It is because the soul's desire for the One actually constitutes its likeness to the One, that Proclus finds a way out of the impasse he appears to have reached with regard to the absolute unknowability of the One.[128] The task of the soul is not any longer the attainment of scientific knowledge (for this is absolutely ruled out) but the attainment of likeness to the One, for it is only in this way that the soul can 'know' the One. Like is, after all, known by like, a thematic which Plotinus had emphasized with particular stress.[129]

It is finally in this context that the focus and function of negation become clear: just as the name 'One' refers to our conception of the One, so too, the negations we apply refer to our conception. In this sense, negation can be understood as an instrument of intellectual purification; the purpose of undertaking the dialectic of negation is a removal of all multiplicity.

> For, if we are to approach the One by means of these negative conceptions and to emancipate ourselves from our accustomed ways of thought, we must strip off the variety of life and remove our multifarious concerns, and render the soul alone by itself, and thus expose it to the divine and to the reception of divinely inspired power, in order that having first lived in such a way as to deny the multiplicity within ourselves, we may thus ascend to the undifferentiated intuition of the One.[130]

---

[126] VII 46K. 3-5; see also 42K. 27-28 and *P. T.* I 22, p. 101 (25-27) The unfulfilled desire of the soul is a theme discussed in chapter eight below in relation to Gregory of Nyssa.

[127] VII 54K. 19-21; see also *P. T.* I 22, p. 102 (12-14): desire for the One must be inextinguishable since the unknowability of the One can never be compromised.

[128] VII 1199. 28-31.

[129] See IV 975. 36-37, VI 1081. 5, VII 48K. 16-17 and *E. Th.* prop. 32; see also *Enn.* III 8, 9, 22-23.

[130] VI 1094. 29- 1095. 2 (p. 442); the same sentiments are repeated at VII 58K. 30-34.

In order to approach the One in terms of 'intuition' the soul must first purify itself: we cannot approach the transcendent with uninitiated mouths or unwashed feet.[131] The removal of multiplicity will leave open the path for apprehension of the One. Since intellectual negation itself has been rendered impotent to attain to the One, the way left open to the soul is the way of unity, the way of intellectual intuition.

The wandering of the soul through the various realms of knowledge is explained by Proclus as a journey from sense perception up to *nous* and 'intuitive cognition', which alone is the faculty capable of divining the One.[132] The ascent of the soul from fragmented vision to unified vision, is implemented through divine inspiration or inspired impulse.[133] It is because the soul possesses an image of primal causes within that it is able to invoke the power of these entities, and specifically the power of the One within: 'how else are we to become nearer to the One, if we do not rouse up the One of the soul, which is in us as a kind of image of the One'.[134] There are obvious theurgic connotations involved in the process of 'rousing up the One in us', which, according to Proclus 'warms the soul'; it is in this way able to 'connect itself' to the One:

> ... and, as it were find mooring, taking our stand above everything intelligible within ourselves and dispensing with every other one of our activities, in order that we may consort with it alone and perform a dance around it, leaving behind all the intellections of the soul which are directed to secondary things.[135]

Proclus was, like Plotinus (and indeed also Gregory of Nyssa), aware of the dangers inherent in leaving behind the realm of intellection, for the soul might be tempted to slip unawares from its negations into the invisibility of not-being by reason of its indefi-

---

[131] V 990. 31-37; see also *P. T.* 1 2, p. 10 (11ff).
[132] See IV 939. 33-34 and V 1029. 34ff.
[133] VI 1072. 3-4 and 1071. 37ff.
[134] VI 1071. 25-29 (p. 424); see also VI 1081. 4-7 and 1094. 21-22.
[135] VI 1072. 10-15 (p. 425). Proclus depicts the voyage of the soul via negation towards unity also at *P. T.* II 11, p. 64. On the idea of the dance of the soul around the One, see III 808, VI 1072 and VII 1217.

nite imagination.[136] It is for this reason that we must be guided by divine inspiration, in order that we may understand Not-Being in the superlative sense (not the non-being which is apprehended by imagination). This concern on the part of Proclus is again raised later in Book VI:

> I see here a great fuss being stirred up by those who think that these negations lead us into the absolute non-existent or something such, since by reason of the lack of definition our imagination does not have anything definite to grasp onto, in as much as nothing is proposed to, but everything absolutely is removed from the One, and for this reason they are persuaded that one must establish some nature and characteristic for the One.[137]

Both Plotinus and Gregory of Nyssa express similar thoughts on the Non-Being of the One, and they also speak about the fear the soul experiences when letting go of all concepts in the attempt to apprehend the transcendent, a sentiment which is also evident in Proclus.[138]

The soul's approach to the One is, therefore, through unity and likeness. Since, as we saw earlier, the proper object for opinion is apprehended by opinion, and so on, it follows that the One can be known only through unity: 'it is by the One that we know the One (γινώσκομεν ... τῷ ἑνὶ τὸ ἕν), for like is known by like.[139] It is here finally that the logic of negation finds its place in the process of unification, for to say that we know the One by the One, is to say that by Non-Being we know the One, which is to say that it is via negation that we know the One.

> Let us then declare it to be Not-Being, and let us recognise it by that in us which is similar to it (for there is in us a sort of seed of that Non-Being) ... It should be clear from this ... that all knowledge of the One is through negation.[140]

---

[136] VI 1072. 6-7. The same sentiments are repeated at 1082. 11-14. See also *Anon. Comm. in Parm.*, fr. VI.

[137] VI 1105. 32- 1106. 1 (p. 451).

[138] V 1029ff and VI 1072; see *Enn.* VI 9, 3, 4-9 and Gregory, *In eccl.* 7 (413-414).

[139] See VI 1081. 7-10 and 48K. 16-17 (simili simile sit cognoscibile); it is by the ineffable that we know the ineffable: *P. T.* I 3, p. 15 (21).

[140] VI 1082. 6ff (pp. 432-433); see also 1081. 10-13.

The soul, having moved from a fragmented vision to a more unified kind of vision, having become single and alone in itself, no
longer asks what the One is and what it is not, but 'everywhere
closing her eyes, and contracting all her activity', 'content with
unity alone'.[141] It is, therefore, only unification which brings us
close to the One, and unification is knowledge of a different kind
(to be learned in a different way).[142] It is divinely inspired knowledge (ἀπομαντεύομαι), higher than scientific knowledge.[143] Proclus relies chiefly upon Plato's Seventh Letter (341C) when
explaining how this 'knowledge' comes about through illumination.[144] This illumination, however, is our own particular light
('particulare enim et ipsa lumen'); the transcendent One can be
beheld only by its own light.[145]

The *Negatio Negationis*

Knowledge of the One in ourselves is attained, therefore,
through the process of negation which leaves open the path to an
apprehension of unity. However, the negation itself does not
reveal positive knowledge of the One, rather, it 'conducts us to
what lies before the threshold of the One'.[146] The excursion
through dialectic is a preparation for the strain (*tensio*) towards the

---

[141] VII 74K. 6-9 (p. 602): supergressam autem et ibi (intellectum) factam et
impetuatam in uno ente ad ipsum unum ipsam adducere et unire, non multum
negotiantem neque querentem quid non est aut est, sed omniquaque claudentem et
omnem operationem contrahentem et contentam unione solum; see also 74K. 31,
76K. 2 and *P. T.* I 3, p. 16 (1ff). See *Enn.* I 6, 8, 24-27, where Plotinus remarks
that by closing one's eyes one can awaken to another way of seeing.
[142] VII 46K. 7-10.
[143] VII 58K. 9-11.
[144] 48K. 12-14: Recte ergo dicitur et in Epistolis, ut diximus, quod alio modo
illud discibile, ex multa attentione circa ipsum lumine in nobis accenso divino per
quod possibili nobis modo illius fit perceptio secundum divinissimum nobis ipso
participantibus.
[145] See IV 951. 18-19 and 48K. 16; Plotinus also speaks of seeing the One by its
own light; see V 3, 17.
[146] 74K. 15-18.

One, but is not itself that strain.[147] The One is above all affirmation and negation ('exaltatum est propter simplicitatem ab omni oppositione et omni negatione'[148]), therefore, the negation itself must be negated, lest we think that we have finally captured the One in any linguistic form.[149]

The *negatio negationis* ('nam per negari et ipse removit omnes abnegationes'[150]), is the logical outcome of the negation process itself, and having been negated, signifies an end to all discourse. 'It is with silence, then, that he brings to completion the study of the One.'[151] The theme of silence is important in the Proclean conception of unity and is reached only after strenuous application and intellectual effort.[152]

> There is nothing astonishing if in wanting to know the ineffable through discourse, one's discourse is led into the impossible, for all knowledge which is applied to an object of knowledge which does not apply to it, destroys itself.[153]

In Proclus, *sigē* is the logical outcome of rising beyond all affirmation and negation through the *negatio negationis*. It can be understood as a movement back through the triad: desire, silent understanding, language. R. Mortley's understanding of the *negatio negationis* purely as a linguistic act which reveals nothing about the One, stands in direct opposition to the view of W. Beierwaltes, who understands the whole process of negation as a prepa-

---

[147] 74K. 20-30.

[148] 70K. 9ff; see also *P. T.* II 10, p. 63 (22ff).

[149] 74K. 18-20: Post pertransitum autem per omnia seponere oportet et hanc tamquam valde negotiosam et coattrahentem abnegatorum conceptum, cum quibus non est illi adiacere.

[150] 76K. 6. On the negation of the negation, see W. Beierwaltes, *Proklos*, p. 361ff and Appendix IV, p. 395ff and K. Hedwig, '*Negatio negationis*'. The negation of the negation is not an explicit thematic in the *Enneads* although Plotinus comes close to it, see V 5, 6, 26.

[151] 76K. 6-7 (p. 603): Silentio autem conclusit eam que de ipso theoriam.

[152] On silence see *P. T.* II 11, p. 65 (13): καὶ ὡς πάσης σιγῆς ἀρρητότερον, and II 9, p. 58 (23-24). See also A. H. Armstrong's pertinent comments on this theme in 'The Negative Theology of *Nous*', p. 34 and W. Beierwaltes, *Proklos*, p. 366.

[153] *P. T.* II 10, p. 64 (2-5).

ration for the ultimate goal of unification.[154] The silence which is consequent upon negating all negations, points beyond itself to the One who is beyond all silence. It is the means whereby we can rise beyond all levels of discourse: if the negation of the negation is not undertaken, we 'will arrive in the end at an empty space neatly fenced by negative dogmas'.[155]

Negation, then, as a movement towards unity, is a way of getting back to the One by way of being One: 'convertit ad unum rursum per unum ens'.[156] If the negations themselves are not removed, we run the risk of making the One many.[157] Discourse must come to a halt if we are not to involve the One in multiplicity.[158] Even negations can distract the soul and obstruct its pure vision: the soul must not any longer be attempting to attain something, for even the strain (*tensio*) – which is not the dialectical method – must be abandoned. After this, words are no longer necessary, for nothing more can be said. The ultimate move beyond the level of dialectic must be undertaken if one is not to continue negating one's negations *ad infinitum*. The spoken word has attained as much as it could; for the remainder, it must be contemplated in silence.

Plotinus and Proclus

Although my remarks have been confined to that aspect of Proclus's thought which is concerned with the nature of the One and negation, it would be quite illegitimate not to make the point that negative dialectic is simply one aspect of the Proclean system. *Apophasis* pertains more appropriately to discourse about the One,

---

[154] See R. Mortley, *From Word to Silence II*, p. 116ff and W. Beierwaltes, *Proklos*, p. 361ff.
[155] A. H. Armstrong, 'On Not Knowing Too Much About God', in *Hellenic and Christian Studies*, no. XV, pp. 137-138.
[156] VII 34K. 9-10.
[157] 74K. 18-20.
[158] VII 1196. 37-40. See also *P. T.* I 3, p. 16 (19ff).

whereas everything which comes after the One can be spoken of in kataphatic terms. It is in the commentary on the Second Hypothesis of the *Parmenides* that *kataphasis* comes into its own: here we find the qualities denied of the One affirmed of Being. It is, therefore, necessary to understand *apophasis* and *kataphasis* in Proclus's thought as complementary. Once again, at the risk of overworking the analogy, I have reproduced a very specific detail of the Proclean system which can ultimately find its place only in the full picture. In concentrating almost exclusively upon the apophatic elements in Proclus's thought, I have been forced to set aside many themes and aspects of his work which could elaborate his understanding of *apophasis* in the broader sense. A reading of Proclus in terms of his understanding of negation does run the risk of portraying a very hard-headed Proclus: we should not separate Proclus the philosopher from Proclus the theurgist and lover of Athena.[159] The concept of theurgy in Proclus is extremely important, both in terms of that aspect of negative theology which is concerned with divine nomenclature, and also in terms of the achievement of unity with the ineffable, unknowable One. The focus of theurgy finds its place in the fact that the One **is** unknowable, for at least some level of the divine can be attained to through ritual theurgic practice.

In these brief concluding remarks I would like to make some comments on Proclean *apophasis* from within the framework of the Plotinian approach to negative theology. The most important development in the fifth-century understanding of the apophatic method is characterized by the notable shift from the employment of the term *aphairesis* to *apophasis*, from abstraction to negation. The Plotinian understanding of the workings of *aphairesis* had not constituted a methodology, for it is not a systematically developed thematic in the *Enneads*. The brief exhortation, *aphele panta*, is not applied to the One in a strictly logical fashion, although all the

---

[159] On the religious aspect of Proclus's thought, see A.-J. Festugière, 'Proclus et la réligion traditionelle'. On theurgy, see especially the account given by J. Trouillard in *L'Un et l'âme selon Proclus*.

negations of the First Hypothesis of the *Parmenides* are indeed constitutive of the Plotinian conception of the One. In Proclus, the function of the process of *aphairesis* is given definite shape through the systematization of apophatic discourse. His exactitude in developing the precise context for the employment of negation represents the final and definitive validation of apophatic discourse. Proclus leaves nothing to chance in his careful exegesis of the negations of the First Hypothesis and in so doing, earns for *apophasis* a respectable place on the philosophic agenda. The tension evident in the *Enneads* concerning the inappropriate nature of terms derived from secondary things, had resulted in a validation of '*epekeina*-discourse' as appropriate for the One.[160] Although Plotinus himself struggled relentlessly with language – as exemplified by his frequent use of the term *hoion* – he often used terms which for Proclus are ruled out absolutely. In this sense, we can understand the Proclean framework for the employment and methodology of *apophasis* as giving a much more precise context for the rules of discourse concerning the One. Proclus always displays an exemplary ruthlessness in following the rules he lays down. For example, with regard to the question of the One's intellection of itself, Plotinus was prepared to defend his thesis that the One cannot know itself at the risk of compromising its own simplicity and unity. For Proclus, however, we must remain ignorant on the question of the One's intellection of itself, precisely because we cannot know anything at all about it.

Although it is true to say that the Proclean understanding of the One does owe much to the first great Neoplatonist, it is also true to say that Proclus's development of the methodology of negation pushes the One further and further from the reach of mortal nature. Even the term 'One' does not refer to the One itself, but to our conception of it. In the *Enneads* Plotinus had often spoken about the presence of the One which surpasses understanding;[161] according to Proclus, our apprehension of the One is simply an appre-

---

[160] V 3, 13, 1ff.
[161] VI 9, 4, 3.

hension of our conception of it, although there is a number of passages, especially in the *Platonic Theology*, where he describes the ascent of the soul in much more intimate terms, terms which are strongly reminiscent of the *Enneads*.[162] However, while it is true to say that Proclus does not, in general portray the One as the gentle, kindly and gracious Good as Plotinus had done in the *Enneads*,[163] the feebleness experienced by the soul before the mighty Plotinian One is present in Proclus's writings. For this reason, I do not think it true to say that while Plotinus was a mystic, Proclus knew only a theory of mysticism.[164]

Of course there are many themes in the writings of Proclus which do not appear in Plotinus, themes which developed in post-Plotinian Platonism under the influence of a number of different sources. With regard to negative theology, the great theme of divine names is one such example, a theme which was to be taken up by the Pseudo-Dionysius with much enthusiasm. Interestingly, the *negatio negationis* mentioned in the final pages of the *Parmenides* Commentary, another theme which is not fully explicit in the *Enneads*, was not developed by Dionysius, although the transcendent is understood to be above both affirmation and negation. This idea makes its re-appearance in philosophical discussion in the thirteenth century in the writings of Meister Eckhart.[165]

The influence of Proclus, especially with regard to negative theology, can be felt especially in the adaptation to be found in the writings of the Pseudo-Dionysius, to which I turn my attention in chapter ten below. It is there that we find a broadening out of the field of philosophical discourse about the transcendent into affirmative, symbolic, negative and mystical theologies. We also find Dionysius developing a most Plotinian theme with regard to the culmination of the negation process, that we know the One through not knowing; according to Proclus, we know the One

---

[162] See for example, II 11.
[163] See V 5, 12, 33-35.
[164] See J. M. Rist, 'Mysticism and Transcendence in Later Neoplatonism', p. 220.
[165] See W. Beierwaltes on Proclean and Eckhartian *negatio negationis* in *Proklos*, Appendix IV.

through Not-Being, that is, through negation, a subtle, yet important distinction. Although it is chiefly through the Pseudo-Dionysius that we find Proclus 'conquering Europe',[166] we also find Proclus exerting an influence upon later thought through the *Liber de causis*, the ninth-century Arabic compilation from the *Elements of Theology*, made available in Latin by Gerard of Cremona in the twelfth century.[167] It is thus, that the symbol of reincarnation seen at the death-bed of the last great Neoplatonist of Hellenistic times, can be understood truly to signify regeneration.

---

[166] See the introduction to E. R. Dodds, *The Elements of Theology*, p. xxviii.

[167] The *Liber de causis* was used extensively by Meister Eckhart. The *Elements* was translated by William of Moerbeke in 1286. For more detailed discussion of the influence of Proclus, see *Proclus et son influence*, eds. G. Boss and G. Seel (Zurich, 1987); R. Klibansky, *The Continuity of the Platonic Tradition During the Middle Ages* (2nd. ed. London, 1939), and 'Plato's *Parmenides* in the Middle Ages and Renaissance', *Medieval and Renaissance Studies*, 1 (1941-43), pp. 281-335; E. N. Tigerstedt, *The Decline and Fall of the Neoplatonic Interpretation of Plato* (Helsinki, 1974); W. Beierwaltes, ed. *Platonismus in der Philosophie des Mittelalters* (Darmstadt, 1969), and 'Hegel und Proklos', in *Hermeneutik und Dialectik*, Festschrift for H. G. Gadamer (Tübingen, 1970), pp. 243-272.

PART II

CHRISTIAN *APOPHASIS*

CHAPTER SEVEN

PHILO OF ALEXANDRIA:
THE ESCAPE TO THE UNCREATED

It is generally agreed that Philo of Alexandria's influence was not apparent in the hellenistic Greek tradition; for this reason, I have chosen to discuss Philo at this point in order to preserve the requisite degree of thematic order. Philo's philosophical speculations are closely related to the Greek Apologists, the Alexandrian and the Cappadocian Fathers, and he can be said to provide one of the links between Greek philosophy and the Christian tradition.[1] The hellenized Jewish philosophy of Philo, the product of the Alexandrian ecumenical megalopolis, gave birth to the formative theological and philosophical creations of the Alexandrian Fathers of the Church.[2] Although the early Christian Fathers nurtured a great respect for Philo, the modern scholar has sometimes tended to dismiss him merely as an eclectic Platonist, most probably because he has no discernible influence on the hellenistic tradition.[3] The Platonism and Judaism of Philo's time, although differing from a philosophical and theological point of view, were not so far apart that a cohesive synthesis was impossible – Christianity in its infancy was, of course, much closer to the parent religion. Philo achieved a mighty synthesis between the two. Whether his 'system' effected more distortion on one side than on the other is a question which will be addressed below.

---

[1] For this reason the reader will find bibliographical material for Philo grouped with works on the early Christian Fathers.

[2] See J. Daniélou, *Philon d'Alexandrie*, 1ff; D. T. Runia, sees Alexandria itself as a point of connection between Athens and Jerusalem, see *Philo of Alexandria*, p. 4.

[3] See J. Edgar Bruns, '*Philo Christianus*. The Debris of a Legend', pp. 141-145.

Whether or not we agree with H. A. Wolfson's evaluation of medieval philosophy as the history of the philosophy of Philo,[4] the fact that many of the themes most evident in the philosophical development of the Middle Ages can also be found in Philo's writings, points to the fact that he is a figure worthy of study. In this chapter, I will confine my remarks solely to those themes which I have been pursuing in the preceding chapters, namely, Philo's idea of God and his use of negative terms. Some other important ideas will find their way into my discussion: Philo's unique blend of Judaism with Platonism and Stoicism;[5] the neo-Pythagorean influence on Philo's thought; how we can talk about God and eventually find a way to resolve the dialectic which presents God as both known and unknown.[6] In view of the voluminous nature of the Philonic *corpus*, this study cannot be a complete picture of Philo. Like the frequent detail reproductions of the hand of God pointing towards Adam in Michaelangelo's Sistine ceiling, this chapter (while it cannot be compared adequately to such a masterpiece) is but a detail which must be understood as having a place in the complete context of the Philonic *corpus*. The multi-faceted nature of Philo's writings is amply demonstrated in his wide-ranging appeal to philosophers, theologians, historians, classicists, exegetes and scriptural scholars. The wide diversity of scholarly opinion regarding his writings is testimony enough to the basic difficulty of interpretation.[7] The modern scholar, when faced with a writer such as Philo, encounters many difficulties in the attempt to separate out the different strands in

---

[4] *Philo. Foundations of Religious Philosophy in Judaism, Christianity and Islam*, vol. II, p. 459.

[5] On the Stoic element in the Philonic *corpus* see D. T. Runia, *Philo of Alexandria*, pp. 480-485; for a more detailed account of Stoic theories in the treatise *Quod Deus* see J. M. Rist, 'The Use of Stoic Terminology in Philo's *Quod Deus Immutabilis Sit* 33-50', in *Platonism and Its Christian Heritage*, Variorum Reprints (London, 1985), n. III.

[6] D. T. Runia describes the idea of God in Philo's writings as the 'coping stone' of his thought; see *op. cit.* p. 433.

[7] A reappraisal of early and more recent scholarly opinion can be found in D. T. Runia, *op. cit.* pp. 7-31.

his thought, for Philo's mind, although labyrinthine, was like a butterfly.[8]

Philo's Inheritance

Most scholars are agreed that Philo was born of a wealthy family in Alexandria around 25-20 BC and died after AD 40. Further information about his life is quite scant although we do know that he was part of the delegation sent to Caligula to protest over the decree that the Emperor's image should be venerated in the Temple of Jerusalem. Philo's education was undoubtedly comprehensive. In the treatise *De congressu quaerendae eruditionis gratia*, he shows his acquaintance with the traditional schooling in grammar, music, geometry, rhetoric and dialectic – the 'handmaidens of philosophy'.[9] For Philo, philosophy itself, as the servant of wisdom in its search for the knowledge of things human and divine in their causes, is the study of the Bible.[10] His main philosophical reading was Pythagoras, Plato, Aristotle, and the Stoics; Plato, however, was his chief mentor, and the dialogues which Philo frequented most were *Timaeus*, *Republic*, *Symposium*, and *Phaedrus*. Philo would also have received a traditional Jewish education; the framework against which his philosophical ideas were developed was the Septuagint, that distinctive product of his own Alexandrian milieu.

Philo himself does not stand at the summit of a long philosophical tradition in Alexandria; in point of fact, philosophy was a relative newcomer to the curriculum of Alexandrian schooling, for the

---

[8] E. R. Dodds used a less-flattering illustration when he compared Philo's mind to a magpie, see 'The *Parmenides* of Plato and the Origins of the Neoplatonic One', *Classical Quarterly*, 22 (1928), p. 142.

[9] *Congr.* 74ff, see also 15-18; all references, quotations and translations are taken from the easily-accessible Loeb edition, where the reader will find a revised version of the critical edition of L. Cohn and P. Wendland, and an adequate English translation.

[10] *Congr.* 79 and *Gen.* iii, 43.

scholarship which had flourished before Philo's time in the Museum had been turned largely in a literary direction.[11] The Ptolemaic dynasty, while it uprooted to a certain extent the indigenous religious cults of the Egyptians, allowed freedom of religious expression, and cults such as that of Serapis were encouraged to develop in a syncretistic way. Alexander himself had decreed that both religions – the Egyptian and that of the Greeks – be allowed to flourish; this decree laid the foundations for a religious eclecticism which can be said to have reached one of its high points in Philo.[12]

The whole period from the conquest of Alexander to the second century BC, was, as P. M. Fraser has remarked, one of 'philosophical inactivity'.[13] I have already noted the contribution of Eudorus to the revival of Pythagoreanism at Alexandria,[14] and that of Antiochus of Ascalon, the 'father' of the movement which instigated the return to a more 'dogmatic' form of Platonism. It is known that he was in Alexandria before he returned to Greece to take over the Academy, around 80 BC. His influence on Alexandrian philosophy is not well documented, but it has been suggested that, through Eudorus and Arius Didymus, his teachings were transmitted to Philo. Since there is no evidence to suggest that Philo received his education elsewhere, we may conclude with plausibility that there was a flourishing Platonic library in Alexandria during the first century BC. There is also little documented evidence of Jewish philosophical activity at Alexandria before Philo; the translation of the Torah into Greek during the third century B.C. had been the impetus for the Jewish scholarly tradition, but few figures of any importance emerged. However, even in spite of his scholarship, it is a fact that the Jewish community at Alexandria did not acclaim Philo as one of their most scholarly minds.[15] E. R. Goodenough

---

[11] My remarks here are indebted to P. M. Fraser, *Ptolemaic Alexandria*.
[12] *ibid.* p. 285.
[13] *ibid.* p. 484.
[14] H. Thesleff, *The Pythagorean Texts of The Hellenistic Period* (Abo, 1965), suggests South Italy as the locus for the revival, pp. 47-50 and 78-96.
[15] E. Bréhier and E. R. Goodenough have suggested in some measure that certain Gnostic theories have elements in common with Philonic ideas.

takes the view that Philo represents a 'considerable minority of his Jewish associates in the Greek world, if not a majority', but the fact that Philo was not accepted by the Jewish scholarly community suggests that he was part of a small minority.[16]

Philo himself aimed, not at an overall theological or philosophical system, but rather, at the unfolding of a comprehensive religious outlook which would not be foreign to a philosophical framework, and he often stresses the notion (later taken up by the Alexandrian Fathers), that Plato, through the agency of Pythagoras, learned his wisdom from Moses.[17] This theme, along with many other Philonic ideas, figures largely in early Christian scriptural exegesis, betraying the inescapable fact that Philo was an important formative influence on the early Christian theological and philosophical tradition.

In Philonic scholarship, it is important that we do not draw a too distinct line of demarcation between his philosophical and biblical sources: these cannot in him be separated without sacrificing some of the richness of his thought. Modern scholars have sometimes portrayed the underlying thematic in Philo's thought as the reconciliation of the more abstract Greek concepts regarding the divine nature with the God of the Old Testament.[18] Whether the idea of an 'abstract impersonal principle' versus a loving God was indeed a problem for Philo is a question that I do not believe troubled him. When Philo read Plato, he saw, not a metaphysical absolute, but the Good, the *telos* and end of all human yearning; he did not find a naked, unadorned entity which he was then compelled to dress up in biblical garments.

In relation to his use of the Old Testament, it is interesting to note that scholars claim that he knew no Hebrew (although H. A. Wolfson contested this[19]). The fact that Philo was dependent upon

---

[16] *By Light, Light*, ch. 1.

[17] *Leg.* i, 108 and *Her.* 214.

[18] See for example, E. Bréhier, *Les idées philosophiques*, pp. 69-70; for a less dogmatic view see E. R. Goodenough, *An Introduction to Philo of Alexandria*, pp. 86-87.

[19] *Philo*, vol. 1, pp. 88-89; see also S. Sandmel, *Philo of Alexandria*, ch. 9.

the Septuagint reflects his character: he was a thoroughly hellenized Jew, but a Jew nonetheless, in that his primary allegiance was to Moses, not to Plato. Although he uses a Platonic framework for his exegesis, the law of Moses was, for Philo, the law of nature; as D. T. Runia points out, Philo does not 'read Plato into' his biblical exegesis, for him, Plato was already contained *in* the law of Moses.[20] That Philo is regarded both as a Jewish exegete and as a Platonic philosopher is, in part, due to the inconsistencies in his thought, which can offend Jew and Platonist, exegete and philosopher alike.

In general, we find very little of the age-old tension between Jew and Greek in Philo's theological works, and nothing of the kind of apolegetic to be found in Josephus. In the end, the question concerning Philo's loyalty is a difficult one; the relation of Jewish thought to Hellenic thought leads to complications today, complications of which Philo was, I think, blissfully unaware. For him, in the last analysis, Moses came first and last; Plato had simply learned his wisdom in Egypt.

Apart from the perceived tension between the God of the Old Testament and the 'God of Plato', there is, in Philo's thought, that other tension between apophatic and kataphatic impulses, one which can be found in Plotinus, Proclus, the Pseudo-Dionysius, Eriugena and others. This dialectical tension, viewed in theological terms, has traditionally been regarded as the problem of reconciling the two aspects of God's nature, the transcendent and the immanent. To begin by asserting that Philo's idea of God is radically negative only to ask subsequently how the human intellect can know God, is to succumb to the temptation to read Philo in the light of the systematization effected by the Pseudo-Dionysius. Philo himself did not attempt to deny or affirm in any systematic way. The mixture of apophatic and kataphatic elements in his thought is, on the one hand, fully representative of the Middle Platonic confusion regarding the correct interpretation of Plato, and, on the other, a reflection of the scriptural presentation of God as

---

[20] *Philo of Alexandria*, pp. 519 and 535-536.

both transcendent and immanent. In order to introduce the reader to Philo's religious background, I begin by outlining, very briefly, the main texts in the Old Testament which were responsible, alongside their Platonic counterparts, for the employment and development of *apophasis* in the religious tradition.

Generally Philo's writings are classified as follows: non-biblical or historical writings; the exposition of the Law; the allegory of the Law; and the Questions and Answers on Genesis and Exodus (preserved chiefly in Armenian). The bulk of his works are concerned more with biblical exegesis than with philosophical doctrine, and his method of exegesis was that of allegory, the method devised by the Stoics commenting on Homer.[21]

Deus Absconditus: **The Old Testament**

Truly, thou art a God who hidest thyself
(Isaiah 45:15)

The God who revealed himself as a historical figure in the Old Testament (the God of Abraham, Isaac and Jacob) was a different God from the divinities of other nations; for the God of Israel, who created human beings in his own image and likeness, bore no resemblance to the theriomorphic gods of Egypt. Unlike the gods of other nations, he was the single source of creation, and the creative sexual myths of ancient cultures became located firmly at the human level. The God of Israel was one, unique, transcendent God who had no need of any consort: 'I am the first and I am the last; besides me there is no God'.[22] It was the mixture of apophatic and kataphatic elements contained in God's revelation of himself which later became the scriptural foundation for the application of

---

[21] For Philo there were two meanings of Scripture, the literal meaning (ῥητή or φανερά) and the underlying meaning (ὑπόνοια); see J. Daniélou, *Philon*, pp. 102-117 and J. Dillon, *The Middle Platonists*, p. 142. On the role of exegesis and philosophy, see D. T. Runia, *op. cit.* p. 535ff.

[22] Is. 44:16; see also Deut. 32:39, Is. 45:14 and 43:10-12; all scriptural quotations are taken from the Revised Standard Version.

the affirmative and negative theologies in Philo and in the Christian Fathers.

One of the strongest apophatic elements in the Old Testament can be found in the prohibition of images, the second commandment of the decalogue: God's own affirmation of his supreme, transcendent nature.[23] The ancient religious divinities of other nations had always been visible and could be seen in temples and holy places in the form of statues in which they were rendered present and tangible, for temples were the dwellings of the gods. The God of Israel, as unique, would allow no such representations of himself; he was not a God who could be controlled and manipulated by graven images or magic rites. He was great above all gods, and no other god was like him in any way.[24] Therefore, he could not allow his chosen people to indulge in the worship of other gods; we find the books of the prophets filled with warnings against those who were tempted to worship false deities. (According to archaeologists, God's commandment against images seems to have been observed, at least in this period, for they have found no representations of him.) Not only was Abraham's God different from other gods, he was incomparable to any living creature: 'God is not as a man',[25] God's thoughts and ways are not human ways.[26] These are two of the primary texts used to support negative theology in the Philonic *corpus*.

It is in the Book of Job (one of the Wisdom literature texts, dating from the post-exilic period) that we find the most powerful assertion of the distance existing between mortal nature and the one, supreme, immortal God. Human nature is but clay, and does not profit God in any way; God is so powerful, so unlike the frail nature of created being, that no mortal can see him and live. It is also in the Book of Job – which A. H. Armstrong has called 'that great protest against a too facile theodicy'[27] – that we find rare

[23] Ex. 4:6, 20:23; Deut. 4:15, 5:8-10, and Lev. 26:1.
[24] 2 Chron. 2-5; Ex. 18:11; Ps. 115:3-8; Sir. 36:5, and Deut. 33:26.
[25] Num. 23:19; this idea was to become a formative principle in Philo's understanding of the transcendence of God, see *Deus*, 52ff.
[26] Is. 55:8-9.
[27] A. H. Armstrong and R. A. Markus, *Christian Faith and Greek Philosophy*, p. 3.

biblical admissions of our intellectual inability to know the God who is so great or to know the way to wisdom.[28] The one powerful attribute which affirms the transcendence of this hidden God and his unlikeness to created nature, is his holiness. The Hebrew word has the meaning of 'other' or 'separate', and can be said to constitute the essence of divinity.[29] It is used mostly by God himself, as he continually affirms his relationship with his people. Over and over again in the books of the prophets, God proclaims his lofty nature and sets himself apart from finite being.[30] There is none holy like God. 'Who is like thee, O Lord, among the gods? Who is like thee majestic in holiness?'[31] Holiness, then, creates distance between the transcendent nature of God and the sinful, finite nature of his people, an untraversable, infinite distance which sets God apart and preserves his own unique nature and identity. As R. Otto pointed out, this 'wholly other' quality inspires the reactions of fear and awe in the face of the *tremendum* that is the transcendent God.[32] Moses hides his face; Jacob trembles; Isaiah is overcome; and Job is terrified in the presence of the most high God, whom neither heaven nor earth can contain.[33] The image of God as king also creates distance between him and his people, since it affirms not only his majesty, but it also evokes the responses of reverence and respect from his loyal subjects.[34]

An apophatic attitude was at the heart of God's own revelation of himself in the Old Testament, for always his encounters with his people were conducted in a mysterious way. In the vision of Isaiah, the throne upon which God sat is described and all that surrounds the throne is spoken of in great detail, but God himself is not described.[35] Elijah experiences God as a small, still voice

---

[28] Job 36:26, 11:7-8, 28:12-28.
[29] See J. McKenzie's entry under 'Holy', in *Dictionary of the Bible*.
[30] Is. 1:4, 5:19, 12:6, 19:17, 43:14, 47:4.
[31] 1Sam. 2:2, Hos. 11:9 and Ex. 15:11.
[32] This is the central theme of *The Idea of the Holy* (Oxford, 1950).
[33] Ex. 3:16; Gen. 28:17; Is. 6:3, and Job 23:15.
[34] Ps. 24:7-10 and Is. 6:5.
[35] Is. 6:1-5; see also Rev. 4:2-3 and Ezek. 1:26-28.

without substance,[36] and Moses and the people at Mount Horeb hear the voice of Yahweh from the fire, without seeing his form.[37]

Primarily, then, this God is a *deus absconditus*, a hidden God who conceals and at the same time reveals himself under external forms, the great theophanies of fire and cloud. In the Old Testament, darkness is usually associated with chaos and disorder and the first creative act of God is the scattering of darkness, through the creation of light. The symbolic association of darkness with privation and chaos does not immediately render it an appropriate symbol for God, yet darkness is used in this way, firstly by God himself, who appropriates it as the means of his own revelation, and secondly when the writer wishes to stress the hidden, transcendent nature of God. Examples of this symbol are found especially in the Psalms: 'cloud and thick darkness are round about him'; 'He made darkness his covering around him, his canopy thick clouds dark with water'.[38]

No discussion of the hidden nature of God in the Old Testament would be complete without mention of Moses, the man who is described as having known God 'face to face'.[39] Moses's personal encounter with God was later to become a prototype for the description of negative theology in Philo, Gregory of Nyssa and the Pseudo-Dionysius. The first encounter of Moses with God (who concealed himself under the fire of the burning bush), resulted in a mission from the God whose 'name' was revealed as 'I am who I am'. Asking the name of God was important to Moses, since in other religious cults power came through knowledge of the sacred name. The exegesis of this text has long been the subject of a complex, unfinished debate; it is generally accepted that the Hebrew name of God, the *tetragrammaton* (YHWH), derives from *hawah*, the verb to be. God's enigmatic answer to Moses's question later became the foundation stone for

[36] 1Kings 19:12-13.
[37] Deut. 4:12.
[38] Ps. 97:2, 18:11; see also Job 22:14, 1Kings 8:12 and 2Mac. 2:8.
[39] Ex. 33:11 and Deut. 32:10.

one aspect of negative theology: his existence can be known, but his essence can not.[40]

In the journey from the promised land, God stays with Moses and his people to guide and protect them, as a pillar of cloud by day and a pillar of fire by night.[41] In this way, God reveals his presence while at the same time he conceals his nature. The theophany on Mount Horeb also takes place under the form of smoke and fire, and only Moses is purified enough to enter into the cloud and meet with God; the same experience is recorded a little later, when Moses, Aaron, Abihu, and the seventy leaders, again go to meet God on the mountain.[42] While the others 'see' God, they speak only of what is beneath his feet; again it falls to Moses to enter the cloud alone, this time for forty days and forty nights. The Tent of the Meeting, where Moses goes to have conference with God throughout the journey, is guarded at the entrance by a pillar of cloud. The famous incident when Moses asks to see the glory of God, is also in keeping with previous revelations: God fears for the safety of Moses and allows him to see only his back.[43] Moses hides while the glory of the Lord passes, but even so, the contact with God's glory is so powerful that Moses's face shone. Thus, even the experience of God's intimate friend is an experience of divine hiddenness. Although God's presence is strongly perceived by his chosen people, he never reveals his true nature to them; he remains *deus absconditus*.

It should now be apparent that an apophatic attitude is at the heart of God's self-revelation in the Old Testament. The lofty separateness he conveys to his people pertains only to his being, not it can be said, to his 'personality'. While his being is unknown and transcendent, his personality bridges the distance between him and his chosen people as he reveals himself actively in the shaping of

[40] This idea later became an important part of the doctrine of the Orthodox Church, see K. T. Ware, 'God Hidden and Revealed: The Apophatic Way and the Essence-Energies Distinction', *Eastern Churches Review*, 7 (1975), pp. 125-136.
[41] Ex. 13:21 and Neh. 9:12.
[42] Ex. 19:16ff and 24:9-18.
[43] Ex. 33:18-20.

their history. Not only is God the one, unique, transcendent, holy God, but he is also the immanent God who affirms his personally given covenant with Israel. He is the Shepherd who cares for his flock; the merciful helper who redeems and saves; the Bridegroom who loves his people with the covenant and pledge of everlasting love, and the tender loving Father of his children.[44]

Although God reveals himself in a mysterious, hidden fashion, the presentation of him in the Old Testament is predominantly anthropomorphic, and expressed in more kataphatic terms. The popular Hebrew idea of God as a living person endowed with the whole range of quasi-human emotions and attributes, can be said to have derived, at least in part, from the initial creative act of God making human nature in his own image. Therefore, we find the basic apophatic element in God's fundamental act of self-revelation tempered by the more positive account of his insertion into the affairs of humanity, as the personal shaper of their history. This is the constant, double truth which is the essence of revealed religion. It is the central paradox, and a seeming contradiction which asserts that the hidden God is at the same time revealed; he is both transcendent and immanent, absent and present.

The Living God: Plato and The Old Testament

For Philo, 'God' does not simply mean the God of the Old Testament endowed with all the anthropomorphic characteristics attributed to him there, for he is also God endowed with the highest Platonic epithets. We find Philo describing God as holy, everlasting and benevolent, almost in the same breath as he will describe him as the self-sufficient architect of the universe. The most important of the 'positive' attributes of God is that he is totally and uniquely one. While this concept betrays a Platonic and Pythagorean influence, Philo's insistent emphasis on it is also

[44] Ps. 23; Mic. 4:6-7; 7:14; Is. 54:5-8; Hos. 2:14-20; Deut. 1:30-33, and Baruch 4:23.

firmly based on his reading of the Septuagint: 'Hear, O Israel: the Lord our God is one Lord'; 'I am the first and the last; besides me there is no God'.[45] Philo followed the teaching of the Torah, and his emphasis on the unity and uniqueness of God can be regarded as a reaction against polytheism, especially the Chaldean belief that 'the first God' is the universe itself.[46] In the tradition of Xenophanes, Philo also disparages the impious doctrines of Epicurus and the 'atheism' of the Egyptians: ignorance of the One, says Philo, produces many fictitious gods; in foolish souls polytheism creates atheism.[47] For Philo, God is one, alone and unique and there is nothing like him.[48] Thus, while Philo's primary inspiration came from Scripture, we find him broadening its boundaries into the philosophical. The one God is, in the terms of the First Hypothesis of the *Parmenides*, pure and unmixed, while human nature is composite and mixed;[49] God's essence is simple and lucid, fixed and unchanged;[50] he is whole and incorruptible.[51] God, says Philo, in his isolation, is a unity.[52] The Plotinian reverberations here are obvious; they are even more striking when we find Philo remark: 'it is good that the Alone should be alone'.[53] This unity is the uncreated, the imperishable and the eternal.[54]

In Philo, then, we find a striking mixture of biblical and Platonic terms, and nowhere is this more apparent than in the several interchangeable terms he uses for the unity of God: τὸ ὄν, μόνος, τὸ ἕν and ὁ ὤν; these terms must be examined. Although there is some ambiguity as to whether Philo actually equates God with the Pythagorean monad, he often uses the latter as a symbol for the unity of God: the one and the monad are the only standards for

---

[45] Deut. 6:4 and Is. 44:6.
[46] *Mig.* 180-181.
[47] *Mig.* 2, *Ebr.* 45 and 110 and *Confus.* 144.
[48] *Leg.* ii, 1, *Her.* 183 and *Opif.* 23 and 172.
[49] *Exod.* ii, 37 and 68 and *Leg.* ii, 2.
[50] *Exod.* ii, 33 and 37.
[51] *Leg.* i, 44 and 51.
[52] *Her.* 183.
[53] *Leg.* ii, 1.
[54] *Jos.* 265.

determining the category to which God belongs, but he himself is prior to all number.[55] The unity is simply a form of his likeness, and it is so because it is unmixed.[56] Like Alcinous, Philo uses the Pythagorean equation of the monad with the point and the dyad with the line.[57] Philo's Pythagorean traits are too evident to be doubted, but I suspect that his Jewishness prevented him from intending anything more than the employment of the monad as an illustration of the unity of God.[58] Although the Pythagorean element was an important aspect of his thought, his use of the Platonic *to on* and the biblical *ho ōn* is much more frequent.[59] Philo's ability to interchange these terms points to his reliance on his two main sources: Plato (especially the *Parmenides*), and the Septuagint, notably Exodus 3:14. Philo remarks that Moses himself used Exodus 3:14 in order to assert that others have being in appearance only, while God is 'he who really is', the truly existent One who alone possesses pure being.[60] However, God is not simply a unity, isolated and unchanging; he is also eternal, holy, omnipotent, self-sufficient, munificent, and perfect.[61] There is nothing in the intelligible world more perfect than God, for he is all-perfect.[62] He is also good, kind and a lover of humanity; one phrase which recurs time and time again is *makarios kai eudaimon*.[63]

Apart from these attributes, God is also the good creator, provider and saviour of all that exists: 'for God is good, he is the maker and begetter of the universe and his providence is over what he has begotten; he is a saviour and benefactor.'[64] God's

---

[55] *Her.* 187; *Gen.* ii, 12; *Spec.* ii, 176, iii, 180, and *Leg.* ii, 3.

[56] *Deus* 82-83; *Exod.* ii, 37; *Praem.* 40, and *Gen.* iv, 110.

[57] *Exod.* ii, 93 and *Decal.* 24-25.

[58] Clement of Alexandria thought Philo was a Pythagorean, see *Strom.* I, 15 and II, 19; Philo himself refers to a book *On Numbers* (not extant), see *Gen.* iv, 110.

[59] See *Abr.* 80 and *Mos.* ii, 100.

[60] *Deus* 4, *Confus.* 139 and *Post.* 15-16 and 167.

[61] *Opif.* 170; *Plant.* 89; *Jos.* 265; *Sac.* 101; *Deus* 56ff; *Decal.* 81; *Mut.* 27 and 46; *Gen.* iv, 188; *Abr.* 137, and *Spec.* i, 294, 308 and 318.

[62] *Aet.* 1 and *Cher.* 86.

[63] *Spec.* i, 209 and iv, 48, *Deus* 26 and 108 and *Post.* 21.

[64] *Spec.* i, 209.

goodness in caring for the world he created is indicative of his own eternal and perfect, universal goodness, since his goodness was the motive for the creation of the world.[65] God is, therefore, good, but he is also the Good.[66] Here we have a concrete identification of the God of the Old Testament with the highest ethical and metaphysical principle of Platonic theology. God is *poietēs* and *patēr* (*Timaeus* 28C) – a phrase which D. T. Runia notes appears forty-one times in the Philonic *corpus*[67] – he is the architect and craftsman of the universe, its guide, charioteer, pilot and steward.[68] Another title which can be derived from both Platonic and biblical sources is *basileus*; God is the first and sole king of the universe.[69]

This short analysis of Philo's description of God in 'positive' terms is by no means exhaustive. It should now be evident that Philo's God is as much (if not more), the God of Plato than the God of the Old Testament. His emphasis on the Platonic attributes of God does much to temper the sometimes anthropomorphic characteristics of God portrayed by the writers of the Old Testament, and it lays more stress on what God is himself than upon how he acts in the salvific history of his people. It is no wonder that Philo was not popular among the Jews, for they must have asked themselves what had become of the God who was Abraham's friend, the God who spoke to Moses in the thick cloud of Mount Horeb and guided his people safely through the desert. Still less would the Jews have been enamoured of the Philonic idea that God is unknowable. This reflection brings us to the apophatic element in Philo's thought, an element which must be understood against the backdrop of the outline I have just given of God as the good creator, the Father who cares for his people.

[65] *Deus* 73 and 108, *Spec.* i, 209 and *Gen.* i, 55.
[66] *Spec.* ii, 53.
[67] *Tim.* 28C; See D. T. Runia *op. cit.*, p. 108; examples can be found in *Gen.* ii, 34, *Abr.* 9 and 58, *Gaius* 115 and *Decal.* 51.
[68] *Opif.* 8, *Ebr.* 30, *Mut.* 30 and *Deus* 30.
[69] *Post.* 101, *Mos.* i, 62 and *Mut.* 22.

The Transcendent God

Philo would have found himself drawn to the notion of God's transcendence by his reading of both his main sources of inspiration, although a kataphatic outlook was more familiar to the writers of the Old Testament. While the negations familiar to the Platonic school of the second century AD, are anticipated by Philo, he, unlike those later Platonists, was able to support his exegesis with scriptural texts.

There is one text which, I believe, lies at the foundation of Philo's apophatic theology and this is, 'God is not as a man'.[70] His frequent use of this text expresses his strongly anti-anthropomorphic conception of God. This key phrase is, according to Philo, a worthy epitome of God's nature, and is one of the two ideas used by Moses to explain the foundation upon which the whole of the law is built. A second text, taken from Deuteronomy: 'Like a man, God will train his son',[71] illustrates the more paternal and personal aspect of God's nature. The first, says Philo, belongs to the realm of those more akin to God, those who dissociate him from every aspect of created being; the second is for those more feeble of mind who cannot converse with God without thinking of him as possessing de finite human characteristics.[72] While Philo condemns the literal interpretation of the numerous passages in the Old Testament which represent God as a being endowed with human characteristics, like Gregory of Nyssa and Eriugena after him, he does make a concession to those not capable of understanding the divine nature in any other way. It is because statements which portray God in anthropomorphic terms are to be found on the lips of Moses, 'the theologian', that Philo accepts them. Thus, while it is not true to say that God has hands and feet and possesses human characteristics and emotions (these passages must be understood figuratively[73]), we may regard these texts as important for instruc-

[70] Numbers 23:19; see also Hos. 11:9 and Ex. 15:11.
[71] Deut. 8:5.
[72] See *Som.* i, 236, *Deus* 63-64 and *Gen.* ii, 54.
[73] *Confus.* 139.

tion, for we cannot frame our conception of the uncreated from within our own experience.[74] Ultimately, God cannot be understood in terms of the human species, for he does not belong to any class; he is a genus unto himself.[75]

The negations which follow upon and which are bound up with the scriptural assertion of unlikeness, include almost every predicate that cannot be attributed to human nature. These include, self-sufficiency (even though God created the world, he has no need of anything contained in it), uncompounded and simple, incorporeal, incorruptible, unchangeable, invisible, and uncreated.[76] In other words, God is everything that created nature is not. These negations, with their obvious Platonic reverberations, amply demonstrate how far Philo goes beyond scriptural texts in order to preserve the immateriality of God's nature. However, these more philosophical negations are not used by Philo simply as a corrective against a too anthropomorphic conception of God, because although they set God apart from man and the material universe, they are also indicative of what God is in himself. According to R. Mortley, Philo does not use abstraction as a means of gaining knowledge of the transcendent, rather he uses the *alpha* privative in order to remove anthropomorphic concepts from the divine nature.[77]

In his absolute unlikeness to anything in the created world God is the transcendent source of all being;[78] He is beyond the world, and beyond all time and place.[79] At one point, Philo argues to the idea of God's transcendence from his exegesis of Exodus 17:6, and he places the following words in the mouth of God: '(I seem) the object of demonstration and comprehension, yet I transcend created things, preceding all demonstration or presentation to the

---

[74] *Confus.* 98 and *Som.* i, 234.
[75] *Leg.* i, 51.
[76] *Leg.* i, 44 and 51; *Deus* 22, 26ff, 56ff, 57 and 160; *Mut.* 3, 9 and 54-55; *Som.* i, 73 and 249; *Confus.* 98 and 138; *Abr.* 74; *Spec.* i, 20; *Decal.* 60; *Sac.* 101, and *Congr.* 134.
[77] See *From Word To Silence I*, p. 154-155.
[78] *Decal.* 52 and *Mig.* 192.
[79] *Exod.* ii, 40, *Post.* 7 and 14 and *Som.* i, 184.

mind.'[80] However, Philo's metaphysical interpretation of this passage is, I believe, a little strained in view of the context of the Exodus text.

There are numerous other passages where Philo asserts the transcendence of God, but there is one particular instance which is extremely important, a passage which I believe to be influenced by *Republic* 509B. I have already noted that the Middle Platonists were rather cautious in their use of this Platonic text (with the exception of Celsus who asserted that God was above *ousia* and *nous*); Philo displays no such hesitation, for he says that God is beyond the material world, not in thought alone, but in essential being also: 'He has gone forth beyond its confines not in thought alone, as man does, but in essential being also, as befits God'.[81] Sentiments of this kind are not found in Platonism again until they appear in Celsus and Plotinus, although we have no evidence to suggest that Celsus had read Philo. Philo, like Celsus and Plotinus after him, had read his Plato very carefully, and he would have found the text of *Republic* 509B very close to the biblical concept of divine transcendence. I also believe that Philo would not have experienced the same difficulty as the Platonists in asserting God's transcendence over being and intellect, for unlike the Platonic God, the God of the Old Testament had already revealed himself to his people, and they knew him through his insertion into their own history.

That God has no name is a thesis which Philo considers to be based on scriptural texts. The most important of these is Exodus 3:14, which, according to Philo means: ' My nature is to be, not to be spoken'.[82] He also makes use of two further related texts: Exodus 6:3, where God tells Moses that he did not make his name known to Abraham, Isaac or Jacob, and a second text based on an interpretation of the second commandment, which forbids taking

---

[80] *Confus.* 138.
[81] *Mig.* 192; I must note at this point that D. T. Runia is of the opinion that Philo did not make use of *Rep.* 509B, see *Philo of Alexandria*, p. 435.
[82] *Mut.* 12, *Som.* i, 67, 230 and *Abr.* 51.

God's name in vain.[83] Yet even the name, 'I am', which human beings are forbidden to use, is not God's hidden name but the name of one aspect of his potencies, for God no proper name: he is *akatonomastos*.[84] If God has no name, why then do scriptural texts give him many names? This is a question which Philo set himself to answer, and I will outline only the main points here. Firstly, God can be named by created nature, but only through the 'licence of language', a licence which is God-given.[85] God allows the use of the names 'I am', and 'the God of Abraham, Isaac and Jacob', for these are his eternal names; and he allows this because of human feebleness in needing a name in order to relate to him.[86] However, even the name 'I am', is not to be understood as God's proper name but as a substitute name. The name 'He That Is' can be given to God because his existence is the one thing that can be understood.[87]

The fact that Philo interprets Exodus 3:14 as meaning, 'my nature is to be, not to be spoken', brings me to the term, *arrētos*, which H. A. Wolfson has claimed entered into the vocabulary of the Middle Platonists through Philo. God's name, says Philo, is ineffable, and not only his name, but his very being also.[88] Philo moves easily from the scriptural thesis that God's name is sacred, ineffable and not to be spoken, to say that the existent himself is unspeakable. This idea involves more than the affirmation of the term, 'ineffable', for Philo later demonstrates that the unknowable aspect of God's nature is based on ineffability.

There is, however, a distinction to be made between the words Philo uses to express the unspeakable nature of God. For instance, he uses οὐ ῥητός, ἄρρητος, or the verb λέγω with the negative.[89]

[83] See *Mut.* 13, 14, *Mos.* i, 75 and *Decal.* 82ff.
[84] *Her.* 170.
[85] *Som.* i, 230 and *Mos.* i, 76; on the related theme of *katachresis*, see D. T. Runia, *op. cit.* p. 438.
[86] See *Abr.* 51 and *Mut.* 12.
[87] *Som.* i, 231; Philo shows some inconsistency on this issue for at *Abr.* 121, he says that ὁ ὤν is God's proper name.
[88] *Her.* 170 and *Som.* i, 67.
[89] See *Mut.* 15 and *Som.* i, 230.

Thus, the concept of ineffability, the unsayable nature of God, cannot easily be separated from the notion of his unnameability. For Philo, 'ineffable' was not an assumption, as Wolfson has suggested, nor was it the starting point for the theory of negative attributes.[90] I suggest that 'ineffable', based as it is upon scriptural texts, follows closely upon the concept 'unnameable' and indeed, at times, cannot be separated from it. Although 'ineffable' is not a term which is found in Greek thought before Philo, we cannot suggest that he was responsible for its entry into the vocabulary of the Middle Platonists.

In the treatise *De mutatione nominum*, Philo says that if God, as τὸ ὄν, is οὐ ῥητός, then he must also be inconceivable and incomprehensible.[91] Philo does not feel the need to argue for the conclusiveness of this inference, for that which cannot be spoken obviously cannot be known. However, earlier in the same treatise he had stated that it should come as no surprise to the human intellect that it cannot comprehend God, when it cannot even understand itself.[92] While this statement could suggest that Philo's argument for the incomprehensibility of the divine nature is derived from his anthropology, I suggest that it could be regarded simply as a device to strengthen further his postulate, although ultimately he bases his thesis on Scripture. In an admittedly rather liberal interpretation of Exodus 33:18-23 (the incident when Moses asks God to show him his glory), Philo has God say that no creature is capable of understanding the divine nature: for it is not within the power of the human intellect to understand God's *ousia*.[93] Philo concludes that, beyond the fact that God is, he is utterly inapprehensible; the most that created nature can attain is a realization that God is beyond reach.[94] To understand the name 'I am' is to

---

[90] 'Negative Attributes in the Church Fathers and the Gnostic Basilides', in *Studies in the History of Philosophy and Religion*, vol. 1, p. 131.

[91] *Mut.* 15; see also *Som.* i, 65-67, where Philo uses Gen. 22:3ff to support the claim that God is transcendent.

[92] *Mut.* 10; see also *Spec.* i, 263; this theme is developed at length by Gregory of Nyssa, Augustine and Eriugena.

[93] *Spec.* i, 44.

[94] *Post.* 15 and 169; see also *Confus.* 138; *Deus* 62; *Det.* 89; *Her.* 229, and *Leg.* iii, 206.

understand this, and to pursue the matter further is foolishness, for not even Moses did this.[95] Therefore, according to Philo, God is unknowable not simply in himself but also because mortal nature does not have the capacity to understand him. The fact that God is unknowable has a corollary, in that God alone possesses knowledge of himself: 'He alone shall affirm anything regarding himself since He alone has unerringly exact knowledge of His own nature.'[96]

If the primary inspiration for the idea of God as inapprehensible is based on Moses's experience of God on Mount Sinai, there is at the same time another source which could have added weight to the biblical idea: *Timaeus* 28C. In *De specialibus legibus* I, we find the following paraphrase: 'Doubtless hard to unriddle and hard to apprehend is the Father and Ruler of all'.[97] While it is in fact only rarely that Philo uses the term *duskataléptos*, its employment does show that he relied upon the Platonic text and that he interpreted it correctly (unlike Numenius).[98]

The Search For the Transcendent

Do thou, yourself, O sacred Guide, be our prompter and preside over our steps and never tire of anointing our eyes, until conducting us to the hidden light of hallowed words you display to us the fast-locked loveliness invisible to the uninitiate.[99]

According to Philo, human nature is made in the image of God, and Moses is the prototype for all in their search for him.[100] Since the human intellect is incapable of coming to a knowledge of God

---

[95] *Praem.* 39 and *Spec.* i, 263.
[96] *Leg.* iii, 206 and *Praem.* 40.
[97] *Spec.* i, 32; see also *Post.* 13 and *Fuga.* 164.
[98] See *Spec.* i, 26 and *Mig.* 195.
[99] *Som.* i, 164; compare this passage with *De myst. theol.* I, 1 of the Pseudo-Dionysius.
[100] *Som.* i, 74; *Mos.* ii, 65; *Spec.* i, 81 and iii, 207, *Leg.* iii, 100ff; *Post.* 14; *Fuga.* 164-165; *Exod.* ii, 29, and *Her.* 69ff.

by its own efforts, any knowledge obtained is to be regarded as a gift given by God in his self-revelation. 'For the mind of man would never have ventured to soar so high as to grasp the nature of God, had not God drawn it up to himself, so far as it was possible that the mind of man be drawn up'.[101] Even though the one sought is elusive, the very quest itself produces happiness, a Philonic idea which was to assume tremendous importance in the writings of the Cappadocian Father, Gregory of Nyssa.[102]

Like all good Platonists, Philo advocates a turning away from the things of creation, even though the intricate ordering of the universe eventually leads to a realization that it is the work of God.[103] Here Philo's inspiration is Plato's *Theaetetus*: the one who embarks upon the way of purification will be able to reach some level of knowledge of God.[104] We are but sojourners in the body, strangers in a foreign land, and our overall quest in life is to obtain knowledge of God so that we can return to him.[105] Having turned away from the things of creation, the human intellect must then begin the arduous task of knowing itself because without self-knowledge it cannot proceed further.[106] In his exegesis of Exodus 33:12-23, Philo discusses this idea in relation to Moses, and throughout his writings he insists that those who are ignorant of themselves will also be ignorant of God.[107] Knowledge of self opens the 'eye of the soul', the true faculty of sight.[108]

Having established that in order to clear the way for knowledge of God the 'inner eye' must be opened, Philo suggests that God

---

[101] *Leg.* i, 38; see also *Post.* 16 and *Praem.* 39.
[102] *Spec.* i, 36; see Gregory's *Commentary on the Canticle*, sermon 12.
[103] *Praem.* 41-43; see also *Leg.* iii, 99 and *Gen.* ii, 34.
[104] *Plant.* 64, *Sac.* 101 and *Fuga.* 63; *Theaet.* 176B.
[105] *Som.* i, 265: 'For so shall you be able to return to your father's house, and be quit of that long distress which besets you in a foreign land;' see also *Confus.* 78.
[106] *Som.* i, 58, *Mig.* 138, 219 and *Spec.* i, 263-265; Abraham is the exemplar of a man who knew himself fully, in that he knew that man does not truly belong to created being; see *Som.* i, 60.
[107] *Leg.* i, 91 and *Spec.* i, 41ff.
[108] This very Platonic image is frequently repeated in Philo, see *Mig.* 39, 48, 57ff; *Confus.* 100; *Gen.* iv, 138, and *Her.* 16, 89.

can be known through the mind alone, but that mind must be utterly purified:

> There is a mind more perfect and thoroughly cleansed, which has undergone initiation into the great mysteries, a mind which gains its knowledge of the first cause not from created things, as one may learn the substance from the shadow, but lifting its eyes above and beyond creation obtains a clear vision of the uncreated One, so as from it to apprehend both himself and his shadow.[109]

In one of Philo's most poetic passages, and one which is highly evocative of many Plotinian texts, Philo describes how the mind must proceed in order to obtain knowledge of God. Images such as the mind straining forth and stretching higher and higher in self-forgetfulness only finally to fall back are strongly reminiscent of Plotinus's and Augustine's descriptions of similar experiences.

> When the mind is mastered by the love of the divine, when it strains its powers to reach the inmost shrine, when it puts forth every effort and ardour on its forward march, under the divine impelling force it forgets all else, forgets itself, and fixes its thoughts and memories on Him alone whose attendant and servant it is, to whom it dedicates not a palpable offering, but incense, the incense of consecrated virtues. But when the inspiration is stayed, and the strong yearning abates, it hastens back from the divine and becomes a man and meets the human interests which lay waiting in the vestibule ready to seize upon it, should it but show its face for a moment from within.[110]

However, even though Philo has suggested that the mind can attain to God in some measure, there is a number of passages where he states that God cannot be known, not even by the highest faculty of mind, an ambiguity which is typical of Philo's apophatic/kataphatic approach.[111] The gulf between created being and God is such that we cannot understand God even with the

---

[109] *Leg.* iii, 100, Philo is speaking of the mind of Moses here; see also *Spec.* i, 46 (Ex. 12:23).
[110] *Som.* ii, 232-233.
[111] *Gaius* 6, *Deus* 62 and *Post.* 19.

purest of understanding, for no human mind would be capable of sustaining the vision of God.[112]

This inconsistency in asserting that God both can and cannot be known through the power of *nous* is representative of the tension Philo must have experienced when he read Plato. On the one hand, Plato had said that the Father is difficult to know, and on the other, that the Good is beyond being (and, therefore, beyond intellect); Philo had reason to be confused. Are these two positions to be regarded as contradictory? They are not in fact contradictory, if we can read them in the light of Philo's distinction between the essence and the powers of God: while God's essence remains hidden from the human mind, his powers reveal his existence. Therefore, the mind can know *that* God is, even though it cannot know *what* God is. Both statements, then, are true. This distinction, between *hyparxis* and *ousia*, and all that it entails, is an important one, for it was adapted and developed by the early Christian Fathers.

According to Philo, the only knowledge that the human intellect can obtain of God is knowledge that he is, knowledge of his existence, for knowledge of God's *ousia* is impossible. Even Abraham sought not to attain to a clear vision of God's essence, but knowledge of his existence and providence.[113] However, even though we cannot know God's essence, Philo suggests that we must continue in the attempt to seek it out, since the quest itself is happiness, although it is sufficient to know what comes after God, that is, his powers. The end of the quest, then, according to Philo, is to know that God cannot be known.[114]

The fact that Moses was allowed to see God's back only but not his face, is the scriptural evidence used by Philo as the basis for his distinction between the essence and the powers of God.[115] Everything that follows after God (literally what is behind him) belongs

[112] *Post.* 20, *Mut.* 15 and *Fuga.* 165.
[113] *Virt.* 215 and *Praem.* 44.
[114] *Post.* 15-16; see also *Fuga.* 165 and *Spec.* i, 36.
[115] *Fuga.* 164-165; see Ex. 33:23.

to the realm of his powers, and it is precisely these powers which make his existence known.[116] However, essence and powers cannot be separated in God, except conceptually, for the extension of God's powers throughout the universe is God himself.[117] (In Philo's system, these divine powers are divided primarily into two: the creative and the kingly powers: God and Lord. He is called *theos* because he created the world, and he is called *kyrios* because he rules over it.[118]) It is in such a way that Philo preserves the essential transcendence of God, while at the same time allowing for contact with him; for the various levels of the hierarchy of powers correspond to the human capacity to know God. In *De Abrahamo*, Philo describes three classes of people: those most perfect who strive towards *to on*, the next best striving towards *theos,* and the last to *kyrios*.[119] However, Philo generally advocates that we should not in the first place attempt to reach *to on* itself but the *logos* of God.[120] Yet, although Philo divides the powers of God in this way, he insists that any division, be it three-fold or six-fold is, in reality, one God.[121]

The *logos*, is the power closest to *to on*, and it is also endowed with negative attributes (much in the same way that Plotinus attributes some negative characteristics to *nous*). *Logos* has no name of which we can speak;[122] the divine Word, as the highest of

---

[116] *Post.* 169 and *Exod.* ii, 67; on the Aristotelian influence on the relationship between *ousia* and *dynamis* see D. T. Runia, *op. cit.* p. 434.

[117] *Post.* 14 and *Sac.* 67-68.

[118] *Exod.* ii, 62; these are names which God himself has given to human nature: see *Mut.* 18-24 and *Plant.* 85-89; on the division of the powers of God see *Abr.* 121; *Exod.* ii, 62; *Gen.* i, 57, ii, 51 and iv, 87; *Her.* 166; *Gaius* 6; *Decal.* 176; *Confus.* 137, and *Sac.* 59. There are various developments of this scheme in Philo's writings, for example, in the treatise *De fuga*, he expands the basic distinction into a more complex hierarchy: *logos*, creative power, royal power, legislative powers, and prohibitive powers; the *logos* is the leader of the powers, and the first three (*logos, theos* and *kyrios*) are powers far removed from created nature, while the last three are those powers closest to created nature: *Fuga.* 95-99 and 103-104; see also *Exod.* ii, 68 and *Cher.* 27.

[119] *Abr.* 124; see also *Confus.* 97 and 146 and *Mig.* 46.

[120] *Fuga.* 97-99 and *Mut.* 19ff.

[121] *Abr.* 131.

[122] *Mut.* 15.

all potencies, is also invisible because he is the image of God and enjoys intimacy with him.[123] In his exegesis of Genesis 9:6 (in the image of God he created man), Philo remarks that nothing mortal can be made in God's image, rather it is made after the image of the *logos*.[124] At this point Philo calls *to on* the pre- *logos* God, and *logos* the second God, an idea which is very close to the later Middle Platonic understanding of *Timaeus* 28C, especially that of Numenius (although it may also have close links with a Gnostic idea). The distinction also appears in Plotinus, yet it is not common in Philo, and this is the only place, as far as I know, where it occurs.[125]

It is the *logos*, then, which along with the other powers, makes God's existence known. Although the powers themselves, in their essence, are beyond understanding, they do present a sort of impression on the mind, and this effect is their work in creation.[126] God, who has no relation to the world, projects his powers into creation, and it is these powers which are perceived as being in relation to created nature.[127] Philo's insistence on the fact that God has no need of anything in creation means that he cannot postulate a direct relationship between finite and infinite. The potencies of God which make his existence known, may be conceived as being distinct from God, but this distinction is due primarily to our innate feebleness, for Philo asserts that God is essentially one, even though human weakness has likened him to a triad.[128]

Although God's existence is revealed through his potencies, God must be understood as transcending them. Why then do the potencies, as part of God, not reveal his *ousia*? In Philo there is no

---

[123] *Fuga*. 101: 'The divine word, who is high above all these, has not been visibly portrayed, being like to no one of the objects of sense. No, he is himself the image of God, the chief of all beings intellectually perceived, placed nearest, with no intervening distance to the alone truly existent one.'

[124] *Gen.* ii, 67; see also *Her.* 231.

[125] See *Som.* i, 228-230 where Philo calls *to on* the name, *ho theos,* and *logos* the name, *theos.*

[126] *Sac.* 59 and *Spec.* i, 47.

[127] *Mut.* 27-28 and *Gen.* i, 54.

[128] *Spec.* i, 209, *Abr.* 121-123 and *Gen.* iv, 8.

completely satisfactory answer to this question. In the treatise *De sacrificiis*, Philo says, in a rather Eriugenian way, that God completely transcends his potencies, in that he is visible both apart from them and through them.[129] I think we can interpret this idea in the following way. The powers of God are simply that aspect of God which is concerned with creation, because God, who is self-sufficient prior to the creation of the world, did not change afterwards. In other words, God as he is concerned with creation, as maker and ruler, is not the full revelation of God. Even though his powers manifest his presence in the world, he himself transcends the world, and apart from his powers cannot be understood except as pure being, that which the finite intellect cannot understand.[130]

Philo's Dialectic: A Tension Resolved

Ultimately, the way in which Philo resolves the paradoxes issuing from his idea of God as both manifest and hidden, is through what I will call his *kpeitton*-theory, although this is not a fully worked-out method comparable to the way that Eriugena developed his idea of God as *plus quam bonitas* and *plus quam deitas*.[131] However, before I outline the basic texts in the Philonic *corpus* where he proclaims God as 'better than good', and so on, I wish to give a few examples of his dialectic at work.

The most repeated phrase in Philo's writings is that God contains all things, yet is not himself contained; he is the uncontained container.[132] It would appear that Philo derived this notion ulti-

---

[129] *Sac.* 60; see also *Exod.* ii, 68.

[130] See *Confus.* 137 and *Deus.* 109; I do not think it would distort Philo's thought to explain this idea simply in terms of Eckhart's distinction between God as he is in himself (*Gottheit*) and God as he is with creatures (*Gott*), see the vernacular sermons, *Beati pauperes spiritu* and *Nolite timere*.

[131] There are many Philonic themes which find an echo in the *Periphyseon*: the powers of God as *occulti manifestatio*, the *Verbum* as cosmic mediator, the powers as the vehicle for God's self-manifestation and the notion that the human intellect cannot know either God or itself.

[132] See *Mig.* 182 and 192; *Post.* 6-17; *Som.* i, 63-64, and *Sob.* 63; see D. T. Runia's comments on the Stoic connotations of this idea, *op. cit.* p. 434.

mately from Scripture: in his analysis of Genesis 3:9 (where God asks Adam, 'where art thou?'), Philo concludes that while created beings are in a place, God is not.[133] However, *topos*, as one of the Aristotelian categories, belongs primarily to created nature, and since God cannot be said to possess any created attribute, he has no place in this world, even though he fills it with himself through his powers.[134] God is the uncircumscribed measure of all things;[135] he is many-named and of no name, for in himself he is nameless, whereas his potencies have many names.[136] He is both close and far away, everywhere and nowhere.[137] It is in this way that Philo 'resolves' the difficulty inherent in the conception of God as both transcendent and immanent. This is indeed a new concept in the history of ideas, a concept which A.-J. Festugière has described as a reconciliation of the God of the *Timaeus* and the God of the *Symposium*, *Republic*, and *Parmenides*.[138]

There is yet another passage in Philo's writings which is most striking from a dialectical point of view, and this concerns the relations of the numbers within the decad: some numbers beget without being begotten, some are begotten without begetting, some beget and are begotten and one neither begets nor is begotten.[139] Although it is difficult to slot this idea neatly into the wealth of ideas in Philo's scheme itself, it is important to remark that the same idea recurs in Eriugena, in the four-fold division of *natura* used in the *Periphyseon*: '*creat et non creatur, creatur et creat, creatur et non creat* and *nec creat nec creatur*'.[140] Scholars are generally agreed that in the *Periphyseon* the first three divisions of nature were derived from Augustine, and only the last from Pythagorean number theory; but the similarity with the Philonic text is such that we must take account of the possibility

[133] *Leg.* iii, 51.
[134] *Leg.* i, 44; see also *Post.* 14 and *Fuga* 75.
[135] *Sac.* 59.
[136] *Som.* ii, 254.
[137] *Post.* 20 and *Confus.* 136.
[138] *Le Dieu cosmique*, pp. 284-285.
[139] *Opif.* 99-100.
[140] 441B.

that Eriugena derived his entire scheme from this kind of Pythagoreanism, whether found in Philo or not.[141] I have already shown that Philo speaks of God using both positive and negative terms. Although he would never go so far as to negate the superlative terms used to describe God like 'good', 'beauty', or 'one' (as Plotinus, Proclus and the Pseudo-Dionysius will eventually do), there are some passages where God is described as being 'better than', or 'beyond', good, beauty, virtue, and even 'God'. In the treatise, *De opificio mundi*, Philo remarks that God transcends virtue, knowledge, the good itself, and the beautiful itself;[142] he is also beyond blessedness and happiness and anything more excellent than these.[143] Although he is called the uncreated, the first, good, beauty, blessedness and happiness, God is better than any of these perfections: 'better than the good, more excellent than the excellent, more blessed than blessedness, more happy than happiness itself, and any perfection there may be greater than these'.[144] God is also more lucid and even more simple than the number one;[145] he is 'better than good, more venerable than the monad, purer than the unit'.[146]

Therefore, it would appear that Philo regards even the most superlative terms as inadequate to describe God, for he is always more than the meaning we understand by them. Although Philo does not work out a theory of language similar to the '*plus quam*' theory in the *Periphyseon*, his tentative attempts to reserve for God alone the most transcendent terms in human language, is an idea which is not particularly evident in the Middle Platonists – in fact, the idea that Philo's God, the God of Abraham, Isaac and

---

[141] See I.-P. Sheldon-Williams, 'Johannes Scottus Eriugena', in *The Cambridge History of Later Greek and Early Medieval Philosophy*, ed. A. H. Armstrong (Cambridge, 1967), pp. 521-523, for references to the sources of Eriugena's distinction.

[142] *Opif.* 8.

[143] *Gen.* ii, 54.

[144] *Gaius* 5.

[145] *Exod.* ii, 37 and 68; Plotinus will echo these sentiments, see V 5, 11; V 5, 4, and VI 9, 5.

[146] *Praem.* 40.

Jacob, transcends both the Platonic Good and the Pythagorean
Monad would not have made him at all popular with pagan Platonists. At this point I must conclude that Philo cannot be said to
have influenced the Middle Platonic idea of God as inconceivable,
for among the Platonists who came after him it is only in the neo-
Pythagorean, Numenius, that the idea of God as incomprehensible
occurs: for the others he is simply hard to know, as in the
Timaeus. Even so, in the Philonic *corpus* we find no developed
theory of the unknowability of God. Granted, it would have been
but a short step for him to take, but his Jewish faith would have
made it an almost unthinkable one.

It is precisely because Philo was not in the business of working
out a negative theory of knowledge of God, that we cannot subject
him to the kind of close critical scrutiny which comes from the
vantage point of having read Dionysius or Eriugena.[147] Any modern scholar who would subject the largely unformed ideas in Philo
to a scrutiny which is born of a modern 'rationalistic' approach,
has failed to evaluate correctly Philo's place in the history of
ideas. Even if Philo was indulging in 'flights of negative theology', we must understand that he was attempting to portray *to on*
as the living God of Abraham and Moses, superior to the Platonic
Good and One.[148] In the end, Philo's use of 'super-affirmation',
was not a linguistic or theological device to reclothe the divinity
he had divested of all material attributes, it was simply a use of
language which attempted to express the absolute transcendence
of the living God.

It must also be repeated that one cannot read a fully-developed
negative theology into Philo's works, nor can one read him correctly from the perspective of Plotinus. To say, as H. Chadwick has
done, that the *via negativa* leaves Philo with a ground of being that
has no other function to perform, is a gross misreading of Philo's

---

[147] These are questions which D. Baër addresses in 'L'incomprehensibilité de
Dieu et théologie négative chez Philon d'Alexandrie', p. 43ff.
[148] See J. Dillon, *The Middle Platonists*, p. 156; C. Bigg was of the opinion that
Philo transformed God into the 'eternal negation of dialectics', *The Christian Platonists of Alexandria*, p. 33.

work taken in its entirety, for God not only creates, he cares for and guides his creation.[149] Chadwick has also suggested that Philo must assert more than God's existence 'if he is to take his bible seriously'. However, I have shown that Philo's God is not simply a prefiguration of the Plotinian One but also a development of the Platonic demiurge of the *Timaeus*.[150] Philo himself never worked out a systematic method of affirmation and negation; his theology was a mixture of the two, a mixture which was typical of the Middle Platonic school itself. Although we find in Philo the main principles which were to become standard Platonic theology right up to the time of Plotinus, his own 'negative theology', like that of the early Christian Fathers, is firmly based on scriptural texts.

Although Philo's influence can be felt in the 'negative theology' of the early Christian Fathers (Eusebius, for example, assures his readers of Philo's Christian allegiance[151]), he is rarely mentioned by name. Philo's history in Jewish thought is less than substantial, for he was not studied seriously until the tenth century (by Saadya), whereupon his influence passed into Spanish Jewry and thence to Moses Maimonides, from whom Meister Eckhart took many philosophical and theological ideas.

Although it is almost impossible to state with any certainty that Plotinus had read Philo, the idea cannot be dismissed without serious consideration. There is a number of themes present in the *Enneads* which do not appear in the Middle Platonists but which are strong Philonic ideas. It is not altogether unthinkable that Plotinus was acquainted with certain Philonic ideas, either at first or second hand. While I do not press the point, I suggest that the 'Alexandrian connection' may have been more substantial than most modern scholars would care to admit.

---

[149] 'Philo and the Beginnings of Christian Thought', p. 149; see also J. Drummond, *Philo Judaeus*, vol. 2, p. 23, who says that Philo sometimes denies and then reclothes the divinity because he realized that a God known only to exist cannot be loved.

[150] A very comprehensive account of the Platonic *Timaeus* and Philo's thought can be found in D. T. Runia's excellent study, *Philo of Alexandria*.

[151] *Hist. eccl.* II, iv, 2.

CHAPTER EIGHT

CHRISTIAN *APOPHASIS* AND GREGORY OF NYSSA

Although the notion of the unknowability of the divine essence comes to prominence in Christian theology in the fourth-century Cappadocian Fathers, Gregory of Nyssa and Gregory Nazianzus, negative terms, in support of an embryonic negative theology, were frequently used by the Christian philosophers and theologians of the second and third centuries. The second-century Christian Fathers of Alexandria, Clement and Origen, borrowed from contemporary Middle Platonism the notion of the ineffability and unnameability of God, although even before the second century in the Christian tradition, we find traces of a negative definition of God.[1] Another source of Platonic ideas to find its way into the philosophical speculations of the early Fathers was, of course, derived from the application of Platonic principles to Jewish thought in the writings of Philo of Alexandria, and it was largely Philo's exegesis of Old Testament texts which provided the second-century Fathers with a basis for asserting the ineffable and unnameable nature of God.[2]

In general, the question of the 'Platonism of the Fathers' has been the subject of much scholarly scrutiny, for it is generally accepted that the early Fathers found themselves attracted to Platonism when searching for a framework for their theological speculations. As Augustine was to note later, 'there are none who come nearer to us than the Platonists'.[3] Tertullian's famous ques-

---

[1] See D. W. Palmer, 'Atheism, Apologetic, and Negative Theology in the Greek Apologists of the Second Century'.

[2] See for example, E. R. Goodenough, *The Theology of Justin Martyr*, where the author demonstrates the reliance of Justin upon the Philonic *corpus*.

[3] *De civ. Dei*. VIII, 5.

tion, 'what has Athens to do with Jerusalem?' is in effect answered by Numenius, whom we find expressing the commonly held notion that Plato learned his wisdom from Moses through Pythagoras: 'what is Plato but Moses speaking Attic?'[4] In this chapter, I propose to outline very briefly the nature of the employment of negative terms in the writings of Justin Martyr and Clement of Alexandria, as representative of the kind of philosophical speculation of the earlier Christian Fathers, before turning my attention to an in-depth exposition of the focus of negative theology in Gregory of Nyssa, undoubtedly its greatest exponent among the early Christian philosophers. I choose Gregory as illustrative of the Cappadocian development of negative theology because, as the most philosophical of the three Cappadocians, he employed its principles in a most thorough and radical fashion. Gregory's work is also important in that it provides a direct link to the Dionysian employment of negative theology.[5]

The New Testament

With regard to the development of the theme of negative theology, the earlier Christian Fathers had indeed found an ally in Platonic philosophy, for the direction taken by Middle Platonism with regard to a developing negative theology was not alien to the early Christian Fathers, and an apophatic/kataphatic mixture is characteristic of the philosophical/theological speculation of the pre-Cappadocian Fathers.[6] However, the early Christian Fathers were not

---

[4] Tertullian, *De praescr. haer.* 7; Numenius, *Fr.* 8: τί γάρ ἐστι Πλάτων ἢ Μωυσῆς ἀττικίζων; E. des Places, *Numénius. Fragments* (Paris, 1973).

[5] The kind of negative theology to be found in John Chrysostom, for example, is less interesting, for it does little more than repeat the ideas of Gregory and Basil. It is interesting to note how Chrysostom, like Clement of Alexandria, sets negative theology within a Pauline framework; it is more scriptural but much less speculative than that of Gregory of Nyssa.

[6] One of the most interesting of the Platonic texts used extensively by the Christian Fathers is *Timaeus* 28C: the Father and Maker of all is difficult to know, but knowledge is not impossible, for God is not conceived as existing beyond either *nous* or *ousia*.

simply appropriating a Philonic or Platonic thematic as part of their philosophical and theological speculations. Even though a kataphatic outlook is predominant in the texts of the New Testament, an apophatic attitude can also be found there, although it would seem that the central apophatic thrust of the revelation of God in the Old Testament fades into the background in the light of the reality of the incarnation which replaces the great symbols of cloud and fire. Darkness once again assumes a privative and pejorative sense, and symbolizes sin, hell, evil, death, damnation, and ignorance, and light becomes a focal point in its symbolization of good, salvation, happiness, and knowledge.[7]

Christ appears as the image of the invisible God,[8] and reveals his hidden nature with the message of universal salvation. He promotes a closer relationship between humanity and God with the firm establishment of the idea that we are all of us God's children. God is no longer the God of fire and cloud, but God the Father of Christ, the light of the world. And yet, in spite of the predominantly kataphatic presentation of God in the New Testament, his essential nature still remains unknown: 'No one has ever seen the Father except the Son'; no one knows him except the Son; no one has ever heard his voice or seen his form.[9] It was these negative elements in the New Testament, which, when considered alongside the assertion that we shall see God 'face to face', provided the point of departure for the controversy concerning the Beatific Vision in the thirteenth century.[10]

Through the incarnation, the Son has become the way to cross the distance between the world and the Father, and becomes the culmination of God's most supreme manifestation. Yet, this is the very area where Christian negative theology experiences the most

---

[7] John 1:4-5 and 1John 1:5-10.
[8] Col. 1:15.
[9] John 1:18, 6:46; 1John 4:12; 1Tim. 6:16; 1Cor. 2:9; Matt. 11:27; Lk. 10:22; John 5:27, and Phil. 2:9.
[10] 1Cor. 13:12 and 1John 3:2; see H.-F. Dondaine, 'L'Objet et le *medium* de la vision béatifique chez les théologiens du XIIIe siècle', *Recherches de Théologie ancienne et médiévale*, 19 (1952), pp. 50-130.

difficulty. As we read the works of Gregory of Nyssa, the Pseudo-Dionysius, Eriugena, Meister Eckhart and others, we are sometimes left with the rather vague impression that they have been speaking about the God of the Old Testament: the *deus absconditus* of the pillar of cloud and the burning bush. The Christian negative theologian who asserts that God cannot be known, is at the same time forced to take account of the central truth of the New Testament. How the early Christian philosophers resolved this question will be addressed below.

Early Christian Negative Theology

The early Christian Apologists, arguing from a monotheistic position, inaugurated the use of negative terms in order to assert the transcendence, unity and difference of the Christian God in relation to the pagan gods.[11] God was uncreated, unchangeable, invisible, incorruptible, eternal and had no form, sex or limit. The kind of negative theology (which is more than simple anti-anthropomorphism) to be found in the early Christian writers was much less specific than that of the fourth-century Fathers precisely because the former used negative terms solely as a means of establishing the unity of God; they were not concerned with a theory of negative attributes.[12] It was also less specific, and indeed much less complicated, because God was not deemed to be beyond intellect and being: he was difficult to know, not unknowable.

It is in the writings of Justin Martyr (b. c. AD 100-110) that we find a Christian philosopher for the first time establishing the validity of using negative terms to support the idea of divine transcendence. Justin's doctrine of God, which reveals Philonic and Middle Platonic influences, consolidates the established tradition in Christian writings of attempting to unite Plato and

---

[11] See E. F. Osborn, *The Beginning of Christian Philosophy*, p. 31, and D. W. Palmer, 'Atheism, Apologetic and Negative Theology in the Greek Apologists of the Second Century', p. 251.

[12] See D. W. Palmer, *op. cit.* p. 243.

Moses.[13] One of the most important concepts in Justin's thought is that God is ungenerate (*agennētos*) a notion which was to remain an integral part of theological and philosophical speculation for some generations to come.[14] Ungeneracy for Justin, implies namelessness, for the naming process involves an ontologically prior namer.[15] Since God is unnameable, he is also ineffable: 'for no one is permitted to utter the name of the ineffable God, and if anyone ventures to affirm that his name can be pronounced, such a person is hopelessly mad'.[16] The Christian philosopher who affirms the namelessness of God must address the apparent contradiction of the many names given to God in Scripture, and Justin, continuing the tradition of Philo of Alexandria does just that. The names 'Father', 'Maker', 'Creator' and 'Lord' are not to be understood as real names, they are terms of address derived from God's activities, expressions for that which can barely be defined.[17] Thus, we find Justin arguing for two of the three key concepts of negative theology: nameless and ineffable. For Justin, God was not considered to be unknowable, a concept which would be developed only in the fourth century of Christian thought, although there are intimations in Clement of Alexandria. One extremely important aspect of the kind of negative theology to be found in the Fathers of the second century, is that the notion of the transcendence of God is always related to the incarnation: the Son of God is the means whereby the Father is revealed.[18] Therefore,

---

[13] I give a very short outline of Justin's theology here; for more detailed discussion see E. R. Goodenough, *The Theology of Justin Martyr*, pp. 123-128, who stresses the Philonic background of Justin, and L. W. Barnard, *Justin Martyr. His Life and thought*, pp. 75-84, who sees Justin as more Middle Platonic than Philonic.

[14] There are numerous references to *agennētos* in Justin's writings, see for example, I *Apology* 14, 25, 49 and II *Apol.* 6 and 12. Goodenough notes the difference between ἀγέννητος which Justin uses and ἀγένητος, the philosophical term meaning no beginning, see p. 128ff.

[15] II *Apol.* 6.

[16] I *Apol.* 61; translation from T. B. Falls, *Saint Justin Martyr*, p. 100; see also I *Apol.* 63 and II, 10 and 12.

[17] II *Apol.* 6.

[18] I *Apol.* 63.

we do not find the early Christian writers explicitly affirm the unknowability of the Father; for them, transcendence only makes sense in the light of the incarnation.

While Justin Martyr was the first Christian philosopher to assert the transcendence of God in negative terms, his use of such terms was the means whereby the Christian God was differentiated from the pagan gods (by the fourth century it is not any longer the difference between the Christian God and other gods that is argued for through the use of negative terms, but the identity of God's own nature itself). Justin's journey through the various schools of philosophy, especially the Platonic school, ensured that his concept of God was a concept which stressed divine transcendence and yet Justin cannot be accused of simply applying Platonic terms to the Christian deity. There has been a tendency among some modern commentators to see a dualism in Justin's thought between the biblical, more personal concept of God and the 'Platonic', or Hellenistic Judaic idea of God.[19] I do not believe that Justin himself would have been aware of two contradictory ideas of God, primarily because he and the early Christian Fathers, were able to find scriptural texts which supported their claims of divine ineffability and unnameability. Christian negative theology, even in its earliest years, did not attempt by means of negations to make God into the 'philosophic Absolute'. Divine transcendence cannot be divorced from divine immanence, or from the reality of the incarnation, for the invisible Father is revealed through the visible Son. However, the kind of negative theology used by Justin Martyr does little more than stress divine transcendence (there is no *via negativa* in the sense of a method of negation or abstraction) and yet it is important in that it was part of the foundation for the development of negative theology among the Fathers of the fourth century.

[19] E. R. Goodenough remarks that Justin's God was more personal, and 'meant far more than the catch-words of the Absolute which he had carried over from Hellenistic Judaism', p. 137, and L. W. Barnard also sees a tension between two conceptions of deity in Justin's writings: the biblical and the Platonic, see *op. cit.* p. 82.

Clement of Alexandria's understanding of the use of negative terms as descriptive of the divine nature is not very far removed from that of Justin Martyr, although Clement's presentation is a little more systematic than Justin's. There are, I believe, three important concepts in Clement's writings which have a bearing on the utilization of negative theology by Gregory of Nyssa, namely, that we can know what God is not (not what he is), the use of the concept of abstraction and his mention of the dark cloud of Sinai, wherein God is invisible and ineffable. Here I examine only the most relevant passages from Book V of the *Stromata*.[20]

In general terms, Clement of Alexandria's underlying aim would appear to be the reconciliation of Pythagoras and Plato with Moses, but it can also be said with regard to negative theology, that he is attempting to reconcile Plato and St Paul. We find his expression of negative theology set firmly within a Pauline framework, a tradition which was to be continued by John Chrysostom. Having argued most persuasively that the highest truth, the wisdom of God, is perceived by the mind alone (it cannot be apprehended by the science of demonstration[21]), Clement paraphrases an important passage from Plato's Seventh Letter in order to demonstrate that God's wisdom is veiled in symbol and mystery: 'for the God of the universe, who is above all speech, all conception, all thought, can never be committed to writing, being inexpressible even by his own power'.[22] For Clement, then, God is essentially ineffable, and time and time again he stresses this point.

Clement's importance for the development of negative theology by later Christian thinkers is due to the fact that he does not simply repeat the negations to be found in Justin and the other second-

---

[20] For more detailed discussion see S. R. C. Lilla, *Clement of Alexandria*, p. 212ff; J. Hochstaffl, *Negative Theologie*, pp. 82-105, and R. Mortley, *From Word to Silence II*, pp. 36-41.

[21] *Strom.* V, 12.

[22] *Strom.* V, 10; trans. A. Cleveland Coxe, *Fathers of the Second Century*, p. 460; see *Ep.* VII 341C-D.

century writers; he goes much further.[23] God has no attributes: those mentioned in the Old Testament texts, are to be understood solely in an allegorical sense.[24] Like Justin, Clement stresses the notion of God's ungeneracy; he needs nothing, is always equal, immortal and ageless.[25] The Final Cause is above space and time; he has no name or conception; he is inexpressible, uncircumscribable and invisible.[26] God has no genus, species, difference, individual nor number; he is ineffable and one (neither having parts or being divisible); he is infinite (without dimension and limit); he has no form and no name.[27] Clement also follows Justin in his discussion of the names given to God: One, Good, Mind, Absolute Being, Father, God, Creator, Lord: these names are used as points of reference only. No single name can circumscribe God, rather, all names, taken together indicate the power of God. Clement also couples the ideas of ungeneracy and naming, and argues that since there is nothing prior to the unbegotten, he cannot be named, for begotten things are things which are named.[28]

It is important to note that although Clement comes very close to the idea that God is essentially unknowable, he never makes this concept actually explicit. For the most part he appears to follow *Timaeus* 28C: the Father is difficult to know.[29] He does mention the altar to the Unknown God (Acts 17:22-23), but says that the Unknown can be known both through divine grace and through the *Logos*.[30] Another idea which is derived from the *Timaeus* text is that the knowledge of God cannot be divulged to the multitude and Clement uses two very interesting scriptural texts to consolidate his argument. The first of these is Ex. 20:21:

---

[23] H. Chadwick has remarked that Clement goes as far as it is possible to go towards the apotheosis of the *alpha* privative, see 'Philo and the Beginning of Christian Thought', p. 179.
[24] V, 11.
[25] V, 11.
[26] V, 11.
[27] V, 12.
[28] *ibid.*
[29] V, 11.
[30] V, 12.

Moses enters into the cloud alone leaving the multitude behind; the second text Clement uses is Paul's description of the ineffable visions he experienced on being rapt into the third heaven (2Cor. 12: 2-4).[31] The mention of the dark cloud, although brief, is a significant one, for it is an idea which will be developed at length by Gregory of Nyssa and the Pseudo-Dionysius. According to Clement, the cloud represents the fact that God is invisible and ineffable, although for him, darkness refers to the unbelief and ignorance of the multitude.

My final point concerns the method of abstraction (*aphairesis*) as it is outlined by Clement in Book V of the *Stromata*. There would appear to be three stages on the path to wisdom: illumination, which is achieved through instruction;[32] purification, which is attained through confession, and finally, contemplation, which is achieved through analysis.[33] It is the final 'way' which is of interest here, for Clement advocates a methodology of abstraction in much the same way as Alcinous does. The abstraction from a body of all its physical properties: depth, breadth and length, will culminate in the single point which has only position; taking away position results in the conception of absolute unity. Having used a typically Middle Platonic analogy, Clement then moulds abstraction into a Christian context: he explains that to be cast into 'the greatness of Christ' and 'the immensity of holiness', the soul will reach somehow a conception of God, although the knowledge will be knowledge of what God is not, not knowledge of what he is. Although, the exact relationship of the method of abstraction to the casting of oneself into the greatness of Christ is not clear at this point, it is the employment of abstraction leading to 'negative knowledge', which has earned for Clement the status of being called the first Christian negative theologian.[34] Even though he

---

[31] V, 12.

[32] V, 10.

[33] V, 11.

[34] I find R. Mortley's interpretation of the various levels of unity operative in Clement's exposition of abstraction a little strained in view of the rather incohate description given by Clement, see *From Word to Silence II*, pp. 42-43.

does not devote much attention to the subject, it remains true that Clement is closer to the later, more 'Plotinian' form of negative theology than any other Christian writer of his time.[35]

While it can be argued that Clement's negative theology is closely related to the negative theology of the Middle Platonists, it is his use of texts from the New Testament, the framework for his expression of divine transcendence, which puts negative theology firmly on the Christian agenda.[36] The later Fathers have now an expression of negative theology within the Christian tradition itself upon which to draw. However, even for all Clement's use of the *alpha* privative and his stress upon the transcendence of the divine nature, the predominant notion in his writings is that the God who is above conception as difficult to know, can be known both through grace and, more importantly through the *Logos*.

The pre-Cappadocian forms of negative theology, therefore, are close to the negative theology of Middle Platonism, in that God is not generally understood to be beyond *nous* and *ousia*. The more 'Neoplatonic' form of negative theology which affirms that God is beyond intellect and being will create a number of problems for the Christian philosopher intent upon a more thorough application of the principles of *apophasis*.[37] Firstly, the apophatic claim that God is beyond *ousia*, immediately confronts the great Christian metaphysic based on an exegesis of Exodus 3:14 ('*Ego sum qui sum*').[38] Secondly, the apophatic assertion that God is unknowable must be reconciled with the biblical assertion that human nature is made in the image and likeness of God. An apophatic anthropology, which can follow from an apophatic theology, immediately contradicts the Socratic dictum, 'Know thyself', a notion utilized by many

---

[35] See S. R. C. Lilla, *Clement of Alexandria*, p. 214ff, where he shows the correspondances between Clement and the Middle Platonists (Alcinous, Apuleius, Celsus, Maximus, Plutarch and the *Corpus Hermeticum*).

[36] For example, he uses John 1:18 and Matthew 11:27.

[37] For a more detailed analysis of the problems involved in Christian negative theology, see D. Carabine, 'Gregory of Nyssa on the Incomprehensibility of God'.

[38] See A. H. Armstrong's comments on this theme in 'The Escape of the One', in *Plotinian and Christian Studies*, Variorum Reprints I, no. XXIII p. 77.

Christian philosophers, including Augustine, who employs it as the focal point of his own understanding of conversion towards God: '*redite ad cor*'.[39] Finally, the most serious question for the Christian Father concerns the fact that Christian revelation itself would appear to limit the scope of negative theology, for in the redemptive act, the incarnation of the Son focuses upon showing the way to the Father. The follower of the apophatic way who claims that God is unknowable, will have to answer some fairly serious questions concerning the revelation of the Father through the Son. Does the incarnation render God knowable to the human intellect? If God is unknowable, not only because of the weakness of the human intellect, but also because God's *ousia* is supremely transcendent in itself, then how does the negative theologian claim to have any knowledge of God at all? Surely knowledge of the unknowable is a contradiction? In the light of these apparent objections (which are by no means exhaustive), to the Christian adoption of a fully-fledged negative theology, we can appreciate immediately that the application of *apophasis* to Christian thought in terms which go beyond a simple corrective against a too anthropomorphic conception of God, is fraught with serious difficulties. Indeed, it would appear that an apophatic position is untenable, at least in its more radical forms, from within the Christian perspective. This observation is perhaps borne out by the fact that those Western philosophers who have had recourse to the negative way in varying degrees – notably Eriugena, and Eckhart – have been accused of promoting ideas which are not always compatible with Christian teaching. The fact that Dionysius himself escaped the condemnations which would undoubtedly have been levelled at him was one of the finest, and indeed fortunate, deceptions in the history of medieval thought. That the Cappadocian Father, Gregory of Nyssa, was able to propose a most radical form of negative theology from within the Christian perspective will be the subject of my discussion below.

---

[39] Conf. X, 6; see the article by T. Tomasic for an excellent discussion of this theme, 'Negative Theology and Subjectivity'.

Eunomius and the Cappadocians

The speculations of the Cappadocian Father, Gregory of
Nyssa, cannot be divorced from the very complex theological
background of the fourth century. Therefore, in order to set the
scene for an exposition of Gregory's employment of *apophasis*,
I must outline briefly the controversial heresies known as Arianism and Eunomianism, two of the deviant 'isms' prevalent in the
third and fourth centuries. Arius (known as a Porphyrian and
excommunicated in 321 as the ultimate heresiarch), in what is
known as the *Thalia*, stressed the ineffable, ungenerate nature of
the Father and asserted that the Son, as generate, is foreign to the
Father in essence and, therefore, cannot know the Father.[40] What
is interesting to note here is that Arius himself bases his conclusions upon the fundamental assertion of the absolute ontological
transcendence of the Father.[41] If the Father, the *agennētos archē*,
formed (that is, made) the Son *ex nihilo*, then the Son had a
beginning in time and is, therefore, distinct from the Father in
essence. The main issue for Arius appears to have been the Son's
co-eternity with the Father, for the impartation of *ousia* would
imply divisibility in the Father.[42] However, the official position
adopted by the First Council of Nicea in 325,[43] was not a complete victory over the Arian heresy, for a neo-Arian position,
spear-headed by Eunomius (d. c. 394), asserted that the human
intellect can know the *ousia* of the Father through an under-

---

[40] See J. Stevenson, ed. *A New Eusebius*, pp. 350-351. Traces of subordinationism
of this kind, however, were not limited to those who were excommunicated, for
ante-Nicene theology, especially in Justin and Origen, tended to make a rather
gnostic distinction between Father and Son.

[41] On Arian and Eunomian negative theology, see R. Mortley, *From Word to
Silence II*, pp. 128-159; Mortley develops his speculations in terms of the Neoplatonic interpretation of *steresis*, *apophasis* and *aphairesis*.

[42] See J. N. D. Kelly, *Early Christian Doctrine*, p. 226ff.

[43] The profession of faith from the 318 Fathers reads: Credimus ... in unum
dominum Iesum Christum filium dei, natum de patre, hoc est de substantia patris
... natum non factum, unius substantiae cum patre, quod Graeci dicunt *homou-
sion*; see *Decrees of the Ecumenical Councils*, vol. 1, ed. N. P. Tanner (George-
town University Press, 1990).

standing of the term 'ungenerate'; God's *ousia* is his *agennēsia*, his fundamental characteristic. It is this later heretical movement which is of interest to the student watching the development of negative theology in the fourth century, for we see two forms of negative theology vying for superiority. According to R. Mortley's reconstruction of Eunomius's position, one basic point is of the utmost importance. For Eunomius, some names bring out the essence of a thing, they are κατὰ φύσιν, and not conventional.[44] The term, 'ungenerate' can be understood as such a name, that is, in terms of negation (not privation), for it denotes God's very essence. Gregory's position is, as we shall see, very different.

Why then did the Cappadocian Fathers take issue with Eunomius when both parties appear to be arguing for the transcendence of God? In terms of the doctrinal issues at stake, the Cappadocians saw Eunomius err on two very important points. Firstly, the old Arian issue of the subordination of the Son compromised the unity of the trinity from a monotheist point of view. Secondly, the idea that the *ousia* of the Father can be characterized and known through the term '*agennētos*' was unthinkable for the Cappadocians in the light of their emerging distinction between the unknowable *ousia* of God and the knowable *energeiai*. It is, therefore, the stance of Eunomius which forces Gregory to insist so strongly upon the idea of the absolute transcendence and unknowability of the trinity. Indeed, so strong is his desire to refute Eunomius that he sometimes manoeuvres himself into positions from which he is forced to argue very skilfully in order to extricate himself.[45]

---

[44] *op. cit.* pp. 147-148; see also p. 134 where Mortley develops the idea that Eunomius sees the naming process in terms of the Philonic concept of the ontological priority of the namer.

[45] In the discussion to follow I rely chiefly on the following works: *Contra Eunomium* (*Contra Eun.*); the *Commentaries on the Beatitudes* (Sermon 6), *Ecclesiastes* (Sermon 7), *Canticle* (Sermons 2, 3, 5, 6, 11), and the *Life of Moses* (*Vita*); unless otherwise noted, references are to the Leiden edition of W. Jaeger.

The Transcendent God of Gregory of Nyssa

The question of a Plotinian influence on the fourth-century Christian Fathers of Cappadocia is one which is extremely difficult to answer conclusively. It is generally accepted in scholarly circles that it was a form of pre-Plotinian Platonism which is more prominent in the writings of the fourth-century Fathers. However, there are strong, Plotinian ideas in the writings of Gregory of Nyssa, which would indicate a Plotinian or post-Plotinian form of Platonism. J. Daniélou and P. Courcelle, among others, have made tentative explorations into the question of a Plotinian or later Neoplatonic influence on Gregory of Nyssa, although a lack of concrete evidence makes the case in its favour extremely difficult to develop with any degree of certainty.[46] Gregory's own intellectual background displays a strong reliance on Origen (although much-transformed), Athanasius, Gregory of Nazianzus, and his brother, Basil the Great, all of whom were influenced by Platonism in varying degrees. The question of a Plotinian influence on Gregory's thought is compounded by the fact that he seldom acknowledges any source other than Scripture and Basil. My own view, especially with regard to the strong apophatic element in Gregory's writings, is that he had some acquaintance with the writings of Plotinus. Even if Gregory had not read the *Enneads* himself, there is the possibility that he was influenced by Plotinian thought through Basil.[47] Had he read *Ennead* VI 9, as J. Rist suggests Basil had done, then we could conclude that the very strong *apophasis* to be found in that treatise did have some influence on Gregory's thought. The similarities between the Plotinian form of negative

---

[46] J. Daniélou has noted the influence of Ammonius Sakkas in the fourth century, see 'Grégoire de Nysse et le néo-Platonisme de l'école d'Athènes', and P. Courcelle has argued that Gregory had, most likely, read Porphyry's *Life of Plotinus* as an introduction to the *Enneads*, see 'Grégoire de Nysse Lecteur de Porphyre'.

[47] Basil's *Hexäemeron* Homilies were indebted to Plotinus, see J. Quasten, *Patrology*, vol. iii, p. 217. J. M. Rist has reviewed scholarly opinion on the question of a Plotinian influence on Basil and concluded that it was minimal, probably only V 1 and VI 9, see 'Basil's "Neoplatonism": its Background and Nature', in *Platonism and its Christian Heritage*, n. XII.

theology and that which we find in Gregory of Nyssa's writings, is a theme which I keep in mind during the course of this discussion. The ultimate question is whether Gregory's negative theology is simply a development of the form of negative theology found in Middle Platonic and earlier Christian writings, or whether it displays any Plotinian characteristics. I will return to this discussion below. For the moment, I note the very strong thematic links between Plotinus and Gregory: God is unknowable, unnameable and ineffable; we can know *that* God is but not *what* he is: we can affirm his existence but not his essence; through *aphairesis* the soul, which had become separated from the Good, is able to become like God and become once again what it was before the fall into the body. Gregory's recurrent use of Plotinian themes and terms are, perhaps, the strongest evidence that he had read at least some portions of the *Enneads*.

The early Fathers of the Church (who had found the idea also in Philo of Alexandria), experienced little difficulty in applying the Platonic term, *ho on* to God in the light of their exegesis of Exodus 3:14. It was Philo's pioneering interpretation of ἐγώ εἰμι ὁ ὤν, which gave the early Fathers their inspiration, an inspiration that was to continue in patristic circles for five centuries.[48] Like his Christian predecessors, Gregory of Nyssa shows no hesitation in developing the Platonic theme. His understanding of God's being as ὁ ὄντως ὤν, reveals that God alone possesses the fullness of being, while all other things exist through participation only.

> For even if the understanding looks upon any other existing things, reason observes in absolutely none of them the self-sufficiency by which they could exist without participation in true Being. On the other hand, that which is always the same, neither increasing nor diminishing, immutable to all change ... standing in need of nothing else, alone desirable, participated in by all but not lessened in their participation – this is truly real being.[49]

---

[48] See *De Abrah.* 80; *Mos.* ii, 100; *Quod Deus* 4; *Confus.* 139; *Post.* 15-16 and 167.

[49] *Vita* II, p. 40 (17-25), *Opera* VII, i, ed. H. Musurillo (1964); trans. A. J. Malherbe and E. Ferguson, *Gregory of Nyssa: The Life of Moses*, p. 60; see also *Contra Eun.* III, vi, 186-187 (this book is printed in Migne as VIII).

One of Gregory's most frequent analyses of reality is built upon the Platonic distinction between the intelligible and the sensible: between that which is unbounded and undetermined and that which is bounded and limited, and yet he goes beyond the Platonic distinction in placing considerable emphasis on the very obvious differences which exist between created *ousia* and uncreated *ousia*.[50] This transformation of the Platonic notion is one which immediately looks forward to the Eriugenian division of *natura* in the *Periphyseon*.

Having established that God alone is true being, it would appear that Gregory cannot assent to the Plotinian idea that God is beyond *ousia*, or indeed, is non-being. According to the Middle Platonic understanding of divine reality, the supreme principle could not have been understood to exist above the level of the forms since that would have made the deity unintelligible: true being was understood to exist at the level of intellect, that is, the world of the forms. However, in Gregory's thought it is the Neoplatonic development of this idea which is found: if the One is elevated above the level of being, that is, the forms, it must be beyond the level of *nous*. It is important to note that Gregory does not deny *ousia* of God in the way that Plotinus had at times denied being of the One. Even though Gregory argues for the incomprehensibility of God, nevertheless, God is still conceived of as being, even though that being is absolutely transcendent. In the *Enneads*, Plotinus quite often denied that the One can be thought of in terms of being for he has no need of it;[51] for Gregory, God is always understood as the cause of being who is above all being.[52]

In his treatise *Against Eunomius*, Gregory argues to the idea of an unknowable God beyond the level of intellect in terms which will be familiar to readers of the *Periphyseon*. He begins with the assertion that the human intellect cannot know the essential substance of any entity and his reasoning is as follows. If we take from

---

[50] ... εἰς τὸ κτιστὸν καὶ ἄκτιστον: *Contra Eun.* I, 295, p. 113 (26), *Opera* I, ed. W. Jaeger (1960).

[51] *Enn.* VI 7, 38.

[52] *In eccl.* 7, 413 (1-4).

a body, colour, shape, weight, position, and so on, there remains nothing for us to perceive, for we do not know the essence of a thing without the 'accidents' which make it accessible to our senses.[53] Therefore, if the lower creation, which we can see, remains unknowable to us in its hidden *ousia*, how much more is transcendent *ousia* unknowable to our intellect?[54] Even if we exhaust, as far as it is possible for us to do so, the nature of the supramundane world, we will know only that all things are the works of God and not God himself, nor will we know their essences. Let Eunomius tell us, then, challenges Gregory, what human nature is, or what a geometric point without magnitude is (a familiar analogy used by Alcinous), when we do not know what sky is or even the nature of a tiny ant, although we can see both.[55] It should be evident that Eunomius cannot assert that he knows God's *ousia* through the appellation 'ungenerate'. It is, I believe, with Eunomius in mind that Gregory declares time and time again that God's essential *ousia* cannot be known by the human intellect:

> Now the divine nature as it is in itself, according to its essence, transcends every act of comprehensive knowledge, and it cannot be approached or attained by our speculation. Men have never discovered a faculty to comprehend the incomprehensible; nor have we ever been able to devise an intellectual technique for grasping the inconceivable.[56]

However, the reasoning used to argue for the unknowability of all created essences is not solely the means by which Gregory argues to the unknowability of the divine essence; divine unknowability depends primarily upon divine infinity.[57] The human intellect, which operates always on a dimensional level,

---

[53] *Contra Eun.* II, 259-260 (Migne XIIb).

[54] *Contra Eun.* III, vi, 250.

[55] *Contra Eun.* III, vi, 262; see also III, viii, 238-239 (Migne X).

[56] *In beat.* 6, 1268B (*PG.* 44); trans. J. Daniélou and H. Musurillo, *From Glory to Glory*, p. 98; here Gregory uses Rom. 11:33 in support of his argument.

[57] D. Duclow sees the concept of infinity in Gregory as the grounding principle of the *via negativa*, see 'Gregory of Nyssa and Nicholas of Cusa: Infinity, Anthropology and the *Via Negativa*'.

cannot even begin to understand a nature which has no dimension or limitation; hence the intellect cannot understand eternity.[58] Gregory's principle, then, for affirming the essential unknowableness of the divine *ousia* is God's eternity, more specifically, his infinity, a concept which Plotinus had used principally in connection with the power of the One.[59] As Plato had argued that the human intellect cannot truly know changeable things, thereby channelling finite intellectual efforts upon the intelligible world of the forms, Gregory, like Plotinus, uses the Platonic definition of being in order to channel finite intellectual efforts upon that which is infinite, something which the Middle Platonists would not have done; the notion of *apeiron* was extremely difficult for the Platonists before Plotinus (even Plotinus himself shows some hesitation in using the term of the One). Gregory explicates his notion of divine infinity – which is closer to the Plotinian notion than to the later Christian development of the concept – in the context of his long-standing and sometimes extremely bitter dispute with Eunomius. According to Gregory, infinity means that which escapes all limitation of knowledge and naming. The bounds of a creature are necessarily finitude and limitation; it cannot, therefore, exceed the bounds of its nature to attain to a knowledge of that which is simple, pure, unique, immutable, unalterable, ever abiding in the same way, never going outside itself, good without limit, having no boundary to its perfection, having no contrary; in short, it cannot comprehend the uncreated, eternal nature.[60] Although Gregory does not use negative theology in any systematic fashion as a process of orderly affirmation and negation, the familiar negations which had been applied to the divine nature by Philo, the earlier Christian Fathers and indeed, also by Plotinus, are present in his thought: God is without shape, form, colour or proportion; he is

---

[58] *In eccl.* 7, 412-413.
[59] See for example, *Enn.* V 5, 10.
[60] *In cant.* 5, 158. R. Mortley appears to have some difficulty with Gregory's equation of all negative terms with the eternity of God, see *op. cit.* p. 178 however, eternity is not something which is predicated of God's essence, it means that God is 'not finite'.

free from passion, has no contrary or boundary and is not subject to the limitations of space and time. Since nothing else can be attributed to this nature, it cannot be perceived by the senses or the intellect; therefore, it is unknowable.

It is his initial reliance on the Platonic understanding of that which is truly real and its Plotinian development, which forces Gregory to admit to the insuperable gap which he conceived to exist between the finite and the infinite. 'Wide indeed is the interval in all else that divides the human from the divine; experience cannot point here below to anything at all resembling in amount what we may guess and imagine there.'[61] Yet, in his desire to refute the erroneous claims of Eunomius, Gregory stretches the focus of human knowledge further and further towards the unattainable infinite. Time and time again, we find him expressing the idea of divine unknowability and ineffability in the strongest possible terms:

> ... incapable of being grasped by any term, or any idea, or any other conception, remaining beyond the reach not only of the human but of the angelic and of all supramundane being, unthinkable, unutterable, above all expression in words ...[62]

Like Eriugena after him, Gregory is of the opinion that the human intellect is not alone in its state of ignorance, for the angelic intelligences are also denied knowledge of the essence of God.

In Book III of his treatise *Against Eunomius*, Gregory appears to realise the extent of his refusal to admit created intellects to knowledge of the divine essence, for he stops to ask: do we then worship what we do not know (John 4:22)? His answer to the question (which would not appeal to those who criticize the Plotinian understanding of the One from a Christian point of view) is that we worship the loftiness of his glory, we know it by the fact that we cannot comprehend it. In short, we know that we do not know.[63] This

---

[61] *Contra Eun.* I, 620, p. 205 (2-6); trans. W. Moore and H. A. Wilson, eds. *Gregory of Nyssa*, I, 39, p. 93.

[62] *Contra Eun.* I, 683, p. 222 (18-24); trans. W. Moore, I, 42, p. 99 (adapted).

[63] *Contra Eun.* III, i, 40 (Migne III); see John 4:22.

reply, echoes a more Plotinian than Middle Platonic form of Platonism, and is intimately bound up with the experiential aspect of apophatic theology, a theme I discuss below. Yet, is the knowledge of the loftiness of God's glory enough to sustain worship and faith? Do we not know something about God through the Sacred Texts? Gregory is of the opinion that we do not, for Scripture does not provide any knowledge of God's *ousia*.[64] So how, then, can we come to the knowledge of the unknowable God?

Knowing the Image of The Unknowable God

Can the finite intellect know God? Gregory's reply – following in the footsteps of Philo and Plotinus – is that we can know *that* God is, not *what* he is. Like all the great masters of the apophatic approach, we find Gregory arguing to this position from creation itself, which he interprets as God's operation in the world. We can know God 'by the process of inference through the wisdom that is reflected in the universe'.[65] However, the knowledge that we obtain in this fashion is simply knowledge of God's wisdom, not knowledge of his *ousia*. In the same way, when we look at creation, we form an idea of God's goodness, not an idea of his essence. In this way, Gregory saves himself from the accusation of a radical negativity: all the things of creation point to the operation of divine activity and show forth God's presence and his existence. It is in this context that we find Gregory employing the distinction formulated by Basil in order to explain the immanent, knowable aspect of God's nature: 'for being by nature invisible, he becomes visible only in his operations, and only when he is contemplated in the things that are external to him.'[66]

Even so, the knowledge gained through the contemplation of creation is simply the knowledge that God exists, not what he is:

---

[64] See *Contra Eun.* II, 257-258.
[65] *In beat.* 6, 1268C; trans. *From Glory to Glory*, p. 99.
[66] *In beat.* 6, 1269A; trans. *From Glory to Glory*, p. 100.

'we know nothing else of God but this one thing, that he is (for to this point the words 'I am he that is')'.[67] Although this idea appears frequently in the *Enneads*, Gregory would also have found it in the earlier Fathers and in Philo who appears to have been its innovator.[68] Gregory's distinction between the *ousia* of God and his *energeiai* – a distinction which will be developed further by Gregory Palamas (b. c. 1296) in his dispute with the anti-hesychast, Barlaam, and become standard Orthodox teaching at the Council of Constantinople in 1351 – is again an idea for which the Cappadocian Father appears to find support in Scripture.[69] Great intellects, he says, never speak of God but of his works, of that which comes after him. It is from this principle that Gregory develops his argument for affirming that we *can*, after all, speak of the ineffable God. However, he is quick to note that we cannot simply move from a knowledge of God's operations to infer the nature of their cause. We are reminded of Augustine's famous search through the realms of created nature in his quest for God, when Gregory asserts that effects point to the existence of their cause, not to its nature.[70] But what of human nature itself – can it bring us any closer to the knowledge of the unknowable God? Gregory has the following to say:

> You alone are made in the image of that nature which surpasses all understanding; you alone are a similitude of eternal beauty, the imprint of the true divinity, a receptacle of happiness, an image of the true Light, and if you look up to Him, you will become what He is, imitating Him who shines within you, whose glory is reflected in your purity.[71]

---

[67] *Contra Eun.* III, vi, 8, p. 188 (12-14), *Opera* II, ed. W. Jaeger (1960); trans. W. Moore, VIII, 1, p. 201; see also III, vi, 186-187.

[68] See *Virt.* 25 and *Praem.* 44.

[69] *Contra Eun.* III, v, 183-184 (Migne VII); see Ps. 105:2 and Ps. 144:4. For further discussion, see V. Lossky, *Essai sur la théologie mystique de l'Eglise d'Orient*, p. 65ff.

[70] *Conf.* X, 6.

[71] *In cant.* 2, 68 (4-10), *Opera* VI, ed. H. Langerbeck (1960); trans. *From Glory to Glory*, p. 162 (adapted).

It is a fact that any Christian thinker who is serious in the affirmation of God's unknowability must give serious consideration to the scriptural assertion that human nature is made in the image and likeness of God. Gregory has already denied that the cause can be known through the effect, and that the human intellect can come to the knowledge of the *ousia* of any thing. In order to be consistent, Gregory must also deny that human nature can come to a knowledge of its own *ousia*. However, in his *Commentary on the Canticle*, Sermon 2,[72] we find him arguing that if created nature does not know itself, it can never explain the things that are beyond it.[73] But having denied that the human mind can attain to a knowledge of the essences of things, can it obtain knowledge of itself? Gregory is consistent:

> ... we pass our lives in ignorance of much, being ignorant first of all of ourselves as men, and then of all things besides. For who is there who has arrived at a comprehension of his own soul?[74]

Gregory's chief reason for asserting that the finite intellect cannot know itself is precisely the fact that it has been created in God's image. In the treatise, *De hominis opificio*, he defines an image as that which does not fail in any of the attributes which are perceived in the archetype; since God's chief characteristic is unknowability, the human mind must also be unknowable to itself.[75] At this point we might be justified in asking whether Gregory's conclusion is an example of a tight spot into which he has backed himself in his desire to refute Eunomius, and yet I think it is not, for Gregory's working out of a solution to this problem is most Plotinian. It depends upon his concept of the original creation of human nature, who once had a share in the nature of the Good, 'fashioned in the most exact likeness in the image of its prototype', but through free-will, it became separated from the

---

[72] *In cant.* 2, 63; see *From Glory to Glory*, p. 160.
[73] *In eccl.* 7, 415-416.
[74] *Contra Eun.* II, 106, pp. 257-258 (28-2); trans. W. Moore, *Answer to Eunomius' Second Book,* p. 261. This idea had already appeared in Philo of Alexandria; see *Mut.* 10 and *Spec.* i, 263.
[75] *De hom. opif.* XI, 3 and 4.

Good. Therefore, before the Fall, human nature existed as an exact likeness of the Good; its present task is the restoration of that image to its original purity.

Gregory, like Plotinus, often laments the separation from the Good and his expression of spiritual homesickness is evocative of many passages in the *Enneads*: we cannot, he exclaims, ever express the great catastrophe involved in losing the Good.[76] When we can remove from our nature all that has been added, all that is foreign and corruptible (the 'garment of skins'), we will be able to relocate our original nature and become what we were in the beginning when we were created.[77] Therefore, it is the Plotinian notion of the search for our original nature that becomes the focal point of Gregory's attention in his quest for an understanding of the nature of God. The process of purification, of ἀφαίρεσις, becomes the key to his solution to the problem of knowledge of God, and it is employed in much the same way as it had been in the *Enneads*.

The question we must ask is whether one will come to any knowledge of God's essence when the process of restoration is complete. Here again we find Gregory pursuing a radical *apophasis*, for he holds to his original principle that God's *ousia* cannot be known, even by the restored soul, a theme which will later play a prominent role in Eriugena's understanding of the process of restoration. What happens in the act of *aphairesis* is that by removing from one's nature what is not natural, one becomes like God, that is, one draws closer to the Beautiful and receives the characteristics of the Good.[78] Yet because God can never be seen in himself, his image is 'seen' in the 'mirror of the soul': when the purified soul becomes as a mirror through which an image of the Son is impressed upon it it is in this fashion able to comprehend the inaccessible. Gregory has recourse to the very Platonic image

---

[76] On 'the loss of the Good', see *De virginitate*, X, 288-291.

[77] *Ibid.* XII, 297-302; see also *Vita* II, 40; interestingly Gregory does not adhere to the distinction traditional among the Alexandrian fathers between εἰκών (supernatural) and ὁμοίωσις (natural).

[78] *In cant.* 2, 68 and 3, 90.

of the light of the sun blinding the eye when looked at directly, but
when viewed through a mirror, the eye is able to gaze without
much distortion.[79]

> There is in you human beings, a desire to contemplate the true
> good. But when you hear that the Divine Majesty is exalted above
> the heavens, that Its glory is inexpressible, Its beauty ineffable, and
> Its nature inaccessible, do not despair of ever beholding what you
> desire. It is indeed within your reach; you have within yourselves
> the standard by which to apprehend the divine.[80]

In this way Gregory focuses our attention upon the perfection of
an image which we will never achieve fully, for even as the most
perfect image, the soul cannot know the divine essence as it is in
itself.[81] Therefore, self-knowledge, for Gregory, would appear to
depend upon a rigorous practice of *aphairesis,* much as it had
done for Plotinus, for the divinity can be 'seen' only in the purified soul.[82] However, this concept is slightly confusing for the soul
cannot know its own essence. What it does know is simply itself
as an image of the divine. It is in this way that Gregory 'solves'
the problem of the knowledge of God. The human person is itself
an image of uncreated beauty.

Incarnation and Negative Theology

We appear to have reached an impasse, for it is not simply the
huge gap that is conceived to exist between the finite and the
infinite which prevents the human intellect from attaining to a
knowledge of God's essence, but also the fact that its operation is
rendered invalid when it is confronted with the basic metaphysi-

---

[79] *In cant.* 3; the 'mirror' image is also found in Athanasius, see A. Louth, *The
Origins of the Christian Mystical Tradition,* p. 79.
[80] *In beat.* 6, 1270C; trans. H. Graef, *Saint Gregory of Nyssa: The Lord's Prayer.
The Beatitudes,* p. 148.
[81] *In cant.* 3, 90.
[82] See A. H. Armstrong's comments on this theme in 'The Apprehension of
Divinity in the Self and Cosmos in Plotinus', in *Plotinian and Christian Studies,*
no. XVIII.

cal constitution of reality. Yet we do not find Gregory resorting to what is sometimes referred to as a kind of 'mystical atheism', for he says, like Plotinus, that we should not give up hope on 'the plea that he is too lofty and ineffable'.[83] Yet wherein does this hope lie? For the Christian philosopher we would suppose that the reality of the incarnation could be the ultimate release from the impossible position of affirming God's absolute unknowableness.

It is in this respect that we would expect to find that Gregory's idea of God will reveal itself to be different from the Plotinian idea of the One, but here again, the reader might be surprised at Gregory's radical conclusions. In his heroic refutation of the Eunomian heresy (where we find a very clear exposition of Cappadocian trinitarian theology), we cannot but be struck by Gregory's angry and sometimes violent reaction to the Eunomian claims. That itself brings into question the radical nature of Gregory's position – he was, after all deposed from his See in 376 by Arian opponents. The basic question concerning revelation for the follower of the negative way must be: what does the incarnation tell us about the nature of God? Once again, Gregory asserts that it tells us nothing of God's essence, it simply manifests his goodness. His understanding of the incarnation as atonement has indeed a cosmic ring to it, much as it will have in the writings of Pseudo-Dionysius and Eriugena.[84] Gregory's understanding is that the incarnation makes possible our restoration to our original image. The mediation of the Son effects the ultimate restoration from death to life for humanity as a whole:

> In the suffering of his human nature the Godhead ... (joined) the elements which had been thus parted, so as to give to all human nature a beginning and an example which it should follow of the resurrection from the dead.[85]

---

[83] *De virg.* X, 291; see *From Glory to Glory*, p. 106.
[84] See J. Daniélou, *From Glory to Glory*, introduction, pp. 16-17.
[85] *Refutatio Confessionis Eunomii*, 179, p. 387 (17-22), *Opera* ii; trans. W. Moore, II, 13, p. 127 (Migne *Contra Eun.* II) (adapted).

However, it is in Gregory's ruminations on the mysteries of trinitarian theology that we find him affirming Basil's teaching that all the qualities predicated of the Father must also, of necessity, be predicated of the Son and the Spirit.[86] The consequences of this idea are immediately clear: if the Father's primary characteristic is unknowability, then the same must be true of the Son and the Spirit. In Gregory's eyes the purpose of the incarnation was not in order that the human intellect should thereafter be able to attain to the knowledge of God's essence: he uses key texts from the New Testament to support the view that it will come to the knowledge of itself as the image of God. For although the Son had said, 'I am the way', Gregory still maintains that '... the ways also that lead to the knowledge of him are even until now untrodden and impassable'.[87] From this point of view, it would seem that Gregory's christology is subordinate to his trinitarian theology, although this is not surprising in the light of the theological tumult of the fourth century. I would suggest that it is Gregory's underlying apophatic attitude which leads him to a position whereby his stress upon the relativity and unknowability of the three hypostases results in some loss of their economic characteristics.[88] While this is far from being unorthodox, nevertheless, Gregory sometimes sacrifices certain concepts which he might not have done had Eunomius not claimed to be able to characterize the essence of the Father.

The Unnameable God

One further question I would like to raise concerning the incarnation is whether the Son's manifestation makes it possible to

[86] See R. Mortley's comments, *op. cit.* pp. 160-165, on Pseudo-Basil's argument for the unity of the trinity in terms of incomprehensibility.
[87] *Contra Eun,* III, i, 107, pp. 39-40 (28ff); trans. W. Moore, III, 5, p. 147; see also Gregory's comments *In beat.* 6, where he examines the text, 'Blessed are the clean of heart for they shall see God' – although the Word appears to promise something which Gregory regards as impossible, Gregory's interpretation is that man can 'see' God through his operations and also in himself as the image of God.
[88] See V. Lossky, '*Apophasis* and Trinitarian Theology', *In the Image and Likeness of God,* pp. 13-29.

speak about the divine nature. The theme of speaking about God is a favourite of Gregory's and he returns to it again and again; indeed his comments prefigure the great Dionysian treatise on the subject. Like all followers of the apophatic way, Gregory finds it natural to assert the ineffable and unnameable nature of the divine essence (his favourite scriptural text is Phil. 2:9), and he would have been familiar with the Philonic, Middle Platonic and earlier Christian comments on this subject.[89] Once again we find him arguing to the unnameability of the divine essence from the perspective of the Eunomians who asserted that they could understand the Father's nature through the term 'ungenerate'. The basic premise upon which the idea of the unnameability of God depends is, of course, the dogmatic assertion that God's eternal nature is unknowable, for we cannot name that which we do not know. Yet, God is given many names in the Sacred Texts and it is there that Gregory begins his discussion.

Not all names in Scripture have a uniform signification (some are applicable only to the Son). Some names signify God's unspeakable glory and his divine majesty, and others contain declarations of the operations of God in creation: names like 'Lord', 'Shepherd', 'Bread'.[90] However, even the names which signify God more fully are 'man-made' names, conventional names, and we find Gregory suggesting an immediate rejection of the outward signification of these names and terms in favour of a more divine interpretation.[91] Typically down to earth with his examples and illustrations, Gregory remarks that although some men give their horses the names of men, we do not think of the horse as a man, and when Saul changes his name to Paul, we do not think that Saul has changed (at least not in a physical sense).[92] The naming process which came into force in time, cannot be applied to God who exists outside of time, and, therefore, outside all form of lim-

---

[89] See for example, Philo's treatise *Som.* i, 230; *Contra Eun.* I, 217-225, III, i, 3-9 and 46-51; *In cant.* 2, 61 and 6, 181-182, and *In eccl.* 7, 411-416.

[90] *Refutatio*, 365.

[91] *Contra Eun.* III, i, 46-51, III, v, 178-184, and III, vi, 197.

[92] *Contra Eun.* III, v, 170 and 178-180.

itation; it must, then, always be used in a metaphorical fashion. No name or term can indicate fully the incomprehensible essence of God.[93]

Like all negative theologians, Gregory asserts that although some names and terms must be allowed of God – indeed we are permitted to name the divine because of the variety of his dealings with us[94] – these pertain solely to his operation; of his essence we must not speak: '... anyone who attempts to portray that ineffable Light in language is truly a liar – not because of any abhorrence of the truth, but merely because of the infirmity of his explanation'.[95] According to Gregory, the attempt to express the divine essence in words is a conscious offence to God.[96] This rather harsh judgement forcefully expresses Gregory's basic scepticism regarding the inadequacy of all language. He argues that since we are forced to use human words about God, we must be aware that these words surpass their normal meaning when applied to the divine essence. It is, he says, the gulf between the created and the uncreated which is the 'real measure of the separation of meanings'.[97] In rejecting the 'univocal' predication of any term, Gregory appears to assent to a kind of 'equivocal' method of predication (to use Thomistic terms). The question we must now ask is, can we make a complete separation of meaning? Gregory explains as follows: we can speak of an earthly house and a heavenly mansion, but the 'sameness', the univocal sense, is solely external; these words have a human sound but possess a divine meaning. 'So in almost all the other terms there is a similarity of names between things human and things divine, revealing nevertheless underneath this sameness a wide difference of meanings.'[98]

---

[93] See *Contra Eun.* II, 257 and III, vi, 197.

[94] *Refutatio*, 365 and *Contra Eun.* III, viii, 242.

[95] *De virg.* X, p. 290 (11-14); trans. *From Glory to Glory*, p. 105; see also *In eccl.* 7, 411-412.

[96] *In eccl.* 7, 410-411.

[97] *Contra Eun.* I, 620, p. 205 (8-10); trans. W. Moore, I, 39, p. 93.

[98] *Contra Eun.* I, 622, 205 (19-22); trans. W. Moore, I, 39, p. 93; see also III, i, 46-47.

The radical severance of any connective cognitive content in terms of the divine essence once again displays the ferocity of Gregory's reaction to the claims of Eunomius. No names can refer to the essence of God; they can, however, refer, although inadequately, to the operation of God and his dealings with human nature.[99] It is with Eunomius in mind that Gregory insists frequently that the name 'Father', is not an absolute term: it does not refer to God's essence, rather, it denotes relationship.[100] What all terms used of God actually mean for Gregory is that through them one can come to an understanding of what God is not. His argument is as follows: we use terms that are positive in meaning in order to convey the idea of qualities in God (He is just), but we also use negative terms in order to convey qualities that are not in God (He is not unjust). Therefore, what we mean by terms such as, passionless and impassible, is that God is not any of these things. Finally, what we mean by the term 'ungenerate', is that God is 'not generate'; it does not refer to what he is, but to what he is not. Negative terms which are applied to the divine nature give no positive account of God's essence.[101] Names, therefore, for Gregory are used of God because the 'nameless' has allowed himself to be named; they do not represent his essence, but signify his operations.

In short, all expressions which are used of the divine nature are inadequate and should be understood in the sense that they are simply a guide to the comprehension of what remains hidden. Words are inadequate expressions of inadequate ideas: '... for as the hollow of one's hand is to the whole deep, so is all the power of language in comparison with that Nature which is unspeakable and unnameable'.[102] No term can be applied literally to God.

> But if it were in any way possible by some other means to lay bare the movements of thought, abandoning the formal instrumentality of words, we should converse with one another more lucidly and

---

[99] *Contra Eun.* III, v, 183-184 and II, 268.
[100] See especially *Contra Eun.* I, 181ff.
[101] See *Contra Eun.* II, 266-267.
[102] *Contra Eun.* III, v, 55, p. 180 (10-12); trans. W. Moore, VII, 4, p. 198.

clearly revealing by the mere action of thought the essential nature of the things which are under consideration.[103]

Perhaps Gregory is tired of the animosity between himself and Eunomius, for here we have a hint that it is the means of expression which separates the two warring parties. What we do when we speak about God is described by Gregory in a most Plotinian fashion: we move around the object of our search and announce it as best we can.[104] In the end, silence is recommended as the best course of action (Proclus, the Pseudo-Dionysius and Eriugena will come to the same conclusion).

> Thus in speaking of God, when there is a question of his essence, then is *the time to keep silence*. When, however, it is a question of his operation, a knowledge of which can come down even to us, that is *the time to speak* of his omnipotence by telling of his works and explaining his deeds, and to use words in this respect.[105]

The Way of Unknowing

I have already mentioned the many thematic connections between Plotinus and Gregory of Nyssa; as a further demonstration of the similarities between the two authors, I point to the following extracts, one from the *Commentary on Ecclesiastes*, Sermon 7 and the second from *Ennead* VI 9.

> Imagine a sheer, steep crag ... below, extending into eternity; on top there is this ridge which looks over a projecting rim into a bottomless chasm. Now imagine what a person would probably experience if he put his foot on the edge of this ridge which overlooks the chasm and found no solid footing nor anything to hold on to. This is what I think the soul experiences when it goes beyond its footing in material things, in its quest for that which has no dimension and which exists from all eternity. For here there is nothing it

---

[103] *Contra Eun.* II, 392, pp. 340-341 (28-4); trans. W. Moore, *Answer*, p. 289; see also *Contra Eun.* III, vi, 197.

[104] *Contra Eun.* II, 393-394.

[105] *In eccl.* 7, p. 415 (17-22), *Opera* V, ed. J. McDonough and P. Alexander (1962); trans. *From Glory to Glory*, p. 129.

can take hold of, neither place nor time, neither measure nor anything else; it does not allow our minds to approach. And thus the soul, slipping at every point from that which cannot be grasped, becomes dizzy and perplexed and returns once again to what is connatural to it, content now to know merely this about the Transcendent, that it is completely different from the nature of the things that the soul knows.[106]

The soul or mind reaching towards the formless finds itself incompetent to grasp where nothing bounds it or to take impression where the impinging reality is diffuse; in sheer dread of holding to nothingness, it slips away. The state is painful; often it seeks relief by retreating from all this vagueness to the region of sense, there to rest as on solid ground.[107]

The thematic similarity of these two texts not only represents part of the case for a Plotinian influence on Gregory, but is also a clear exposition of a form of negative theology which is not simply content with making negative statements about the divine nature. Although the soul has slipped back to what it knows, it now knows that knowing God consists in not knowing God; as Plotinus says, our way takes us beyond knowing.[108]

Gregory, unlike Plotinus, who can be called 'a mystic of light', explains the ascent of the soul as the continual practice of *aphairesis,* as a journey from light, through cloud, to darkness. For this ascent he uses Moses as the prototype (as Philo of Alexandria had done), and relies heavily on the search of the bride for her beloved in the Canticle.[109] He describes the three stages of the journey of the soul as a movement from light, which is the knowledge of created effects, through cloud, which involves the removal of foreign matter so that God can be known in the 'mirror of the soul', and finally to the darkness of union with God, whereby the transcendent is 'known' through not knowing. It is the final stage of the journey which is of most interest to the negative theologian. Both J. Daniélou and V. Lossky have noted that Gregory uses the

---

[106] *In eccl.* 7, 413-414 (5-13, 1-9); trans. *From Glory to Glory*, p. 127-128.
[107] VI 9, 3 (4-9); trans. S. MacKenna, *Plotinus. The Enneads*, p. 616.
[108] VI 9, 4 (3-4): κατὰ παρουσίαν ἐπιστήμης κρείττονα.
[109] *Vita* II, 86-87, *In cant.* 10, 311-314, and 11, 315 and 322.

symbol of darkness in two senses, the one objective and the other subjective: it denotes both the incapacity of the intellect to comprehend God and God's unknowable nature in itself.[110] However, Gregory's portrayal of the spiritual darkness in which the soul finds itself in its attempt to know God, is a darkness which does not have a negative meaning. It is, rather, a 'luminous darkness', for the soul has entered into the place where God himself is, the 'secret chamber of divine knowledge'.[111] Yet, the knowledge obtained in this darkness is simply the knowledge that God cannot be known. It is in the *Life of Moses* that Gregory develops this idea most fully: 'this is the true knowledge of what is sought; this is the seeing that consists in not seeing, because that which is sought transcends all knowledge, being separated on all sides by incomprehensibility as by a kind of darkness'.[112] Gregory's expression of unity, of being in the same place with God, as an experience of divine presence, is another concept which is found in the *Enneads*: Plotinus describes the final experience of unity in terms of presence, not in terms of knowledge.[113] For Gregory, the presence of God is experienced, his essence is never seen.

This kind of experience of God, which is usually associated with the *Mystical Theology* of Pseudo-Dionysius, is representative of a seeing and a knowing which can no longer be said to conform to the normal operations of the dimensional cognitive faculty: the 'vision' of God is ἀπερικάλυπτος: a vision which no longer operates through the 'veil' of existing things.[114] The bride in the

---

[110] See V. Lossky, 'Darkness and Light in the Knowledge of God', *In The Image and Likeness of God*, p. 32, and J. Daniélou, *Platonisme et théologie mystique*: Daniélou structures this volume according to Gregory's conception of the ascent from light, through cloud to darkness; see especially pp. 209-210 on the two-fold meaning of the theme of darkness. See also A. Louth, *The Origins of the Christian Mystical Tradition*, pp. 80-97.

[111] *In cant.* 11, 323, *From Glory to Glory*, p. 247; see also *Vita* II, 86-87 and *In cant.* 6, 181-182.

[112] *Vita* II, p. 87 (6-9); trans. A. J. Malherbe and E. Ferguson, 164, p. 95. In Philo of Alexandria we find that the end of the search for God consists in knowing that he cannot be known, see *Post.* 15-16, *Fuga* 165 and *Spec.* i, 36.

[113] VI 6, 6; VI 7, 34; VI 9, 4, and VI 9, 7 and 8.

[114] See *De myst. theol.* I, 3 and *In cant.* 12, 369-370.

Canticle has her veil taken away by the keepers of the city so that she knows that what she seeks can be understood only in the very inability to comprehend the divine essence.[115] 'But I am suddenly introduced into the realm of the invisible, surrounded by the divine darkness, searching for him who is hidden in the dark cloud'.[116] The process of *aphairesis*, then, applies not only to the moral realm but also to the intellectual realm, for Gregory notes that intelligible attributes are a hindrance to those seeking 'knowledge' of God; all things that can be contemplated by reason or sense are left behind in the search for the incomprehensible.[117] The purification of one's God-concepts, according to Gregory, begins in Plotinian terms with the injunction: *aphele panta*.[118] At this point it would seem that Gregory is suggesting that this 'knowledge' of God is not any longer dependent upon divine economy, and for this reason the 'knowledge' obtained has no perceptible cognitive content. This is indeed the radical conclusion of negative theology when taken to its limits: something 'positive' is discernible in the experience and yet nothing further can be said of it since words pertain only to divine operation in the world.

It is precisely because the foot has slipped over the edge of the cliff that it cannot be spoken of – there are few who have stepped from a great height in such a way and are able to tell of the experience! Yet, for Gregory the end of the quest is not rest in 'luminous darkness', for God's infinity can never be circumscribed, even by the resurrected soul: there is always something more to find, something more to spur the soul on in its unending search.[119]

> The First Good is in its nature infinite, and so it follows of necessity that the participation in the enjoyment of it will be infinite also, for more is always being grasped, and yet something beyond that which has been grasped will always be discovered, and this

---

[115] *In cant.* 6.
[116] *Ibid.* See *From Glory to Glory*, p. 201.
[117] *In cant.* 6.
[118] V 3, 17.
[119] Further comments on Gregory's understanding of *epectasis* can be found in J. Daniélou, *Platonisme*, pp. 309-333.

search will never overtake its Object, because its fund is as inexhaustible as the growth of that which participates in it is ceaseless.[120]

Accordingly, the soul does not reach a state of 'rest', a state of perfection, for ultimately, the 'vision' of God consists in never being satisfied in the desire to see him.[121] Therefore, although the soul is able to grasp something of the divine nature, Gregory is careful to protect always the inviolate, unknowable nature of the divine essence: since God is infinite, the quest must also be infinite - the bride will discover more and more of the incomprehensible through all eternity. In the end, although the darkness in which God hides is a 'luminous darkness', it is unknowable and inaccessible to the created intellect; it remains always 'inaccessible light'.[122] The light/dark imagery used by Gregory as descriptive of the ultimate state of the resurrected soul, is wholly scriptural in origin and it is precisely his use of scriptural texts which marks the differences between Gregory's understanding of the state of union and the understanding of Plotinus. Philo had commented on the journey of Moses up the dark mountain of the *deus absconditus* and it is this form of exegesis that Gregory appropriates and develops. In contrast, we take note of the fact that the Plotinian and Proclean expressions of unity with the supreme are always described in terms of light and vision.

What we have found, in our examination of Gregory's negative theological approach is a very forceful expression of divine transcendence and the constant proclamation of infinity over and against finitude. His is a vivid portrayal of the uncomfortable experience of the gap which exists between the human and the divine, the created and the uncreated. Gregory's constant reminder to the created, finite intellect is that it can never attain to a com-

---

[120] *Contra Eun.* I, 291, p. 112 (15-20); trans. W. Moore, I, 22, p. 62; see also *In cant.* 6, 179-181 and 11, 320-321.
[121] *Vita* II, 239; see also Philo's *Spec.* i, 36.
[122] The theme of 'inaccessible light' (1Tim. 6:16) is the subject of *Contra Eun.* III, x (Migne XII).

plete knowledge of its creator. Yet, it is precisely finitude which
constitutes the quest for the infinite God as a return to the divine
nature. Gregory relentlessly thrusts human nature forward into the
realm of infinity wherein we are constantly forced to reaffirm our
own finitude. At the same time, we are always being reconstituted
in our finitude, becoming more and more a better image of the
infinite itself.

It should be clear that Gregory does not use the principles of
negation in any systematic fashion as Eriugena was to do in the
Periphyseon; his is a more Plotinian, more *aphairetic* form of negative theology. The fact that Gregory does not use the *via negativa*
in the 'sense of a way or a technique to be systematically pur-
sued',[123] does not mean that his is not a truly apophatic theology.
Even though a systematic form of negation is not evident in his
writings (we do not find him advocating negation and super-affirmation, or the negation of the negation), nevertheless, the negative
theology to be found there is indeed radical, for the distinction
between *energeiai* and *ousia* makes it possible for Gregory to
develop the Philonic notion that even the restored soul will never
experience fully the *ousia* of the God who is absolutely and eternally ineffable, unnameable and unknowable. It was, I believe, this
Cappadocian understanding of never 'seeing' or experiencing fully
the essence of God, which was adopted and developed by the
Pseudo-Dionysius whereby it influenced Eriugena. In this sense,
Gregory's negative theology is much more thorough than that of
Eunomius who declared knowledge of God's essence and thereby
compromised the principle of divine unknowability.

I return now to the question I raised at the beginning of this discussion: is Gregory's utilization of the principles of *apophasis* a
development of the Philonic themes developed by the earlier
Fathers through the mediation of Middle Platonism, or is it a more

---

[123] See R. Mortley, *op. cit.* pp. 177-178 and 191; Mortley's criterion for determining the *via negativa* appears to be quite Neoplatonic and indeed technical in
character: 'there is no recognition of the unveiling power of the negative' (p.
189). According to Mortley, Gregory's use of negation is, therefore, tantamount to
saying nothing.

Plotinian form of negative theology? I must admit that this question cannot be answered satisfactorily, or conclusively. Even though the Plotinian themes so obviously present in Gregory's work make a strong case in favour of a Plotinian influence, there is little in Gregory that could not have been developed from his reading of Philo of Alexandria, the earlier Christian Fathers, the Middle Platonists and his fellow Cappadocians. Although it is true that Gregory's employment of the principles of negative theology is closer to the Plotinian understanding than any other expression of negative theology in the fourth century, yet in one sense, it goes much further, for it is developed as theological reflection upon the central message of the New Testament. The difficulties which Gregory was forced to resolve were not a central issue for Plotinus. Whatever his guiding force in the development of a radical negative theology, it seems most likely that it was Gregory's understanding of *apophasis* which was to be adopted, at least in part, by the Pseudo-Dionysius one century later. Although the Areopagite is credited with the transformation of Proclean *apophasis*, I believe that the Cappadocian influence on his thought was extremely important, especially in the *De mystica theologia*.

The chief characteristic of Gregory's inventiveness in the realm of negative theology is that he is able to push the finite further and further away from its own limitations without compromising the fundamental notion that God is, and will always remain, unknowable. Had the heretic Eunomius not had the audacity to claim a knowledge of God's essence and had Gregory not been forced to defend divine unknowability from every possible angle and vantage point, then we would have been unable to appreciate that even a radical form of negative theology can retain a prominent position within a formative source of the philosophical and theological tradition of Eastern Christianity.

CHAPTER NINE

SAINT AUGUSTINE: A NEGATIVE THEOLOGY?

Saint Augustine's recollection of his boyhood reluctance to learn Greek, 'driven with threats and savage punishments', left him with a certain distaste for it which evidently stayed with him throughout his life.[1] The simple statement he makes in the *Confessions* leads the reader to wonder what direction his thought might have taken if he had read the *Enneads* of Plotinus in the Greek original, and not simply the selective translation of Marius Victorinus, especially with regard to the more apophatic elements in Plotinian thought. Nevertheless, Augustine presents an interesting case for the probings of the student of *apophasis,* not simply because he represents one of the most formative influences upon the philosophical and theological speculations of Western thought but also because he was developing his own speculative thought at a point when *apophasis* had not as yet made its definitive entry into Christian theology, which it was to do through the writings of the Pseudo-Dionysius. Although by 386-390 Augustine was closely acquainted with the Neoplatonism of Plotinus and Porphyry, both at first hand and through the varying influences of Ambrose, Marius Victorinus and Simplicianus,[2] his own writings do not immediately confront the reader with an explicitly developed negative theology. Despite that, the predominantly kataphatic thrust of Augustine's thought conceals a strongly and fundamentally apophatic thrust, one which, I believe, is at the foundation of

---

[1] *Conf.* I, 13.
[2] For an update on the various arguments concerning which books of the Platonists Augustine had read, see P. F. Beatrice, *'Quosdam Platonicorum Libros.* The Platonic Reading of Augustine in Milan', *Vigiliae Christianae,* 43 (1989), pp. 248-281.

his whole philosophical/theological speculation. Thus, even though we do not normally regard Augustine as an exponent of the negative way, the main principles of *apophasis* should be thought of as a formative influence upon his thought. I hope to demonstrate that in Augustine's case, the notions of ineffability and unknowability are crucial to the development of his thought.

However, it should be clear from the outset that Augustine does not employ the methodology of negation as a systematic process of abstraction or denial; in any case, the systematic use of negation did not become explicit in theological discourse until Proclus: even in Augustine's Eastern contemporary, Gregory of Nyssa, in whose writings we have found a most radical form of *apophasis*, the principles of negation are not systematized. Having said that, there is a number of passages in Augustine's writings in which he comes close to an explicit use of negation as a way of approaching divine reality. What distinguishes Augustine (and other more predominantly 'kataphatic' thinkers) from Proclus, Gregory of Nyssa, Pseudo-Dionysius and Eriugena, among others, is his response to the primary assertion of the ineffability and unknowability of God. Where the apophatic theologian will have recourse to the *via negativa* as a means of approaching transcendent reality, Augustine chooses another way, the *via amoris*. I will discuss the main direction of this path below.

There are, I believe, two fundamental ideas in the thought of Augustine which together determine his attitude towards divine reality. The first of these is his Platonically-based understanding of God as the fullness of being. His reliance on the Exodus text (3:14) is evident throughout his writings, and has, in general, been the main reason for counting him among the Platonists rather than the Neoplatonists (although I will later point to some texts where Augustine declares that God's 'I am' is beyond human understanding, a position Meister Eckhart will adopt almost one thousand years later). Augustine's reliance on the Exodus text obviously precludes him from propounding an apophatic ontology, for it demonstrates his refusal to subordinate being to One, ontology to henology; it does not, on the other hand entitle us to conclude that his understanding of the 'I am' of the Old Testament text is precisely conflated with the Platonic understanding of Being.[3] The second theme in Augustine's thought which determines his more kataphatic outlook is perhaps the most fundamental characteristic of his thought and is based upon his understanding of the role of faith, hope and love. Augustine was a man whose life was motivated by the hope of fulfilment in eternity: the night of this world, wherein one is guided by love and faith in the unseen God (2 Cor. 5: 6-7) will be turned into day when faith will be rewarded by knowledge – the vision of God 'face to face' (1 Cor. 13:12). Leaving aside the problems generated by Augustine's use of this Pauline text in later philosophical speculation, it is, I believe, demonstrative of his fundamental belief that in this present life the human intellect does not know God directly as he is in himself, but rather through his works (Rom. 1:20). These three Pauline texts, which could be regarded conjointly as a framework for the understanding of Augustinian theology, are elaborated by him in a fashion which is very close to the basic principles of negative theology. For Augustine, knowledge of God as he is in himself is impossible. In this world, knowledge of God is a secondary knowledge which is derived from an understanding God's works. This idea is very close to the Cappadocian thematic that while God's essence is unknowable, his energies are indeed in some sense knowable. What then are the main arguments for claiming that apophatic principles exist at the heart of Augustine's thought?[4]

---

[3] Although V. Lossky amply demonstrates the Augustinian thematic that God's being is unknowable to the human mind, he speaks only of the 'modest elements' of negative theology present in Augustine's thought; Lossky's guiding principle here is that the God of *apophasis* is the God above being; see 'Les éléments de "Théologie négative" dans la pensée de saint Augustin'.

[4] John Heiser, 'Saint Augustine and Negative Theology', claims that there are six passages in Augustine's writings where he gives more than a passing attention to negative theology; the point I make throughout this chapter is that an apophatic attitude is in reality the foundation stone of Augustine's thought.

Problems of Language: The Ineffable God

Augustine, like all followers of the negative way, frequently laments the inadequacy of language to express the ineffable, divine nature: whatever we can say of God is not worthy of him;[5] whatever we have the power of saying about God is from beneath him.[6] Indeed, we find Augustine emphasizing the ineffability of God in much the same manner and to the same extent that Plotinus had stressed the ineffability of the One. In one remarkable passage in *De doctrina christiana*, Augustine confronts head on the problem of divine ineffability:

> Have we spoken or announced anything worthy of God? Rather I feel that I have done nothing but wish to speak: if I have spoken, I have not said what I wished to say. Whence do I know this, it would not be said. And for this reason God should not be said to be ineffable, for when this is said something is said. And a contradiction in terms is created, since if that is ineffable which cannot be spoken, then that is not ineffable which can be called ineffable. This contradiction is to be passed over in silence rather than resolved verbally. For God, although nothing worthy may be spoken of him, has accepted the tribute of the human voice and wished us to take joy in praising him with our words.[7]

In this passage Augustine raises the problem of divine ineffability in much the same fashion as Eriugena was to do four centuries

---

[5] *Conf.* I, 4; see also *De lib. arb.* III, 13, *In ps.* 99 (5-6) and *In Ioh. evang.* XIII, 5; I wish to acknowledge the assistance of M. Paul Tombeur (Cetedoc) of the Université Catholique de Louvain for assistance in tracing the references to the term 'ineffable' in the Augustinian *corpus*.

[6] *In Epist. Ioh.* IV, 6.

[7] Diximusne aliquid et sonuimus aliquid dignum deo? Immo uero nihil me aliud quam dicere voluisse sentio; si autem dixi, non hoc est quod dicere uolui. Hoc unde scio, nisi quia deus ineffabilis est? quod autem a me dictum est, si ineffabile esset, dictum non esset. Ac per hoc ne ineffabilis quidem dicendus est deus, quia et hoc cum dicitur, aliquid dicitur et fit nescio qua pugna uerborum, quoniam si illud est ineffabile, quod dici non potest, non est ineffabile, quod uel ineffabile dici potest. Quae pugna uerborum silentio cauenda potius quam uoce pacanda est. Et tamen deus, cum de illo nihil digne dici possit, admisit humanae uocis obsequium, et uerbis nostris in laude sua gaudere nos uoluit: I, 6; *C. C.* vol. XXXII, *Opera*, part IV, 1, ed. J. Martin (Turnhout, 1962); trans. D. W. Robertson, *On Christian Doctrine*, p. 11.

later. Both writers recommend silence as a resolution of the 'problem', (as indeed do most followers of the negative way), although Eriugena adopts what he considers to be the only valid alternative to silence, namely, the two methods of theology: the apophatic and the kataphatic.[8] However, the fact that Augustine recommends silence is not indicative of a decision to 'overlook the problem', but is rather, an indication of his very precise understanding of the problem in hand.[9] The last line of the text quoted is, I think, the key to an understanding of Augustine's thought: the ineffable nature of God should indeed be left unspoken; and yet like all followers of the negative way, Augustine notes that human nature must have some words to speak the unspeakable. This is the apparently contradictory observation that is found at the heart of all negative theology.[10] Augustine's continual use of the term 'ineffable' is a constant reminder that while nothing worthy can be said of the divine nature, nevertheless, words are a necessary pointer in the right direction. The relationship of this passage to the extended discussion of semiotics in Book II of this work is problematic, for there Augustine focuses his attention upon the meaning attached to linguistic signs as the most important of all semiotic systems. He argues the point that meaning is conventional, not natural (or, as the later Neoplatonists would say, *kata physin*). Having endorsed a positive view of language, it would appear that the linguistic class of signs cannot function properly in relation to transcendent reality.

Although the passage in *De doctrina christiana* states the contradiction involved in speaking that which is essentially unspeakable, it is in *De trinitate* that the full force of Augustine's scepticism regarding the adequacy of language comes to the fore. Time and time again, he reminds the reader that he is attempting to express in a most inadequate fashion something which almost

---

[8] *Periphyseon*, 458A and 456A.

[9] R. Mortley, *From Word to Silence II*, pp. 219-220, suggests that Augustine does not understand how silence works: 'his rhetorical soul was not quite capable of the great leap into silence of the Greek metaphysicians'.

[10] Augustine expresses the same sentiment in *De trin.* VIII, 2 (3).

completely defies linguistic confines. His reticence when expound-
ing trinitarian theology can be seen on almost every page of that
work: 'for the nature itself, or the substance, or the essence, or by
whatever other name the thing itself that God is, whatever it is,
should be called, cannot be seen corporeally.'[11] Even at the end of
his great theological excursion into the ineffable realms of trinitarian exegesis, Augustine again admits the poverty of his thought
and the attempt to express that thought.

> I have said nothing worthy of the ineffability of that highest trinity
> among all these many things I have already said, but confess rather
> that its sublime knowledge has been too great for me, and that I am
> unable to reach it.[12]

Although we do not find Augustine working out a systematic
means of speaking about the transcendent God in the way that
later Christian writers influenced by Neoplatonism were to do,
there is a number of passages in his writings where Augustine
comments on the 'attributes' of God as they are presented in scriptural texts, just as the Pseudo-Dionysius after him was to do. References to God's emotions and feelings are, says Augustine, borrowed from moral discourses on human affections;[13] the qualities
we affirm of the divine nature are not present in God in the same
fashion as they are present in created nature. Even if we know that
God is good and that he made all things good, we still do not know
what kind of good God is.[14] One further interesting observation
made by Augustine is that although we use many words of God
(good, great, blessed and so on), all these things are not different
qualities in the divine nature, because of course his knowledge is

---

[11] *De trin.* II, 18 (35); all translations of *De trinitate* are from S. McKenna, *The Trinity*, p. 92; see also *De trin.* V, 9 (10) and *De civ. Dei.* X, 23.

[12] Verum inter haec quae multa iam dixi et nihil illius summae trinitatis ineffabil-
itate dignum me dixisse audeo profiteri, sed confiteri potius mirificatam scientiam
eius ex me inualuisse nec potuisse me ad illam: *De trin.* XV, 27 (50); *C. C.* vol.
La, ed. W. J. Mountain, *Opera*, part XVI, 2 (Turnhout, 1968); trans. S. McKenna,
p. 521.

[13] *In ps.* 118 (50).

[14] *In ps.* 134 (3-4).

his wisdom and his wisdom is his essence, due to the simplicity of the divine nature.[15] Even the revelations of God in Exodus are not to be understood as revelations of the substance of God, but only as revelations of his presence: the visible form of the invisible God who showed himself in the Old Testament cannot be identical with God as God is in himself.[16]

In fact, to say anything at all about God is not to say anything properly but by means of similitudes, using metaphorical speech.[17] In one illuminating passage from his *Commentary on the Gospel of John*, Augustine makes the following point: God cannot be understood in literal terms as 'bread', 'fountain', 'light', and so on, but in some sense he can be said to be these visible, separate things; all things can be said of him because he is all things (bread to the hungry, water to the thirsty and light to those in darkness); although in the strictest sense nothing can be said worthily of his ineffable majesty.[18] Although Augustine does not emphasize the negative attributes of the divine nature in the same manner as Dionysius and Eriugena were to do, nevertheless, we find abundant references to the transcendence of God couched in negative terms: God is unchangeable and has no human attributes; he cannot be thought of in terms of time or place; he cannot be numbered nor measured; he is uncontained, immutable and has no contrary.

Problems of Thought: The Unknowable God

For Augustine, the inadequacy of language always points back from itself to the thought which is seeking expression, and the

---

[15] See *De trin.* VI, 7 (8), VII, 5 (10) and XV, 13 (22).

[16] *De civ. Dei.* X, 13.

[17] *De trin.* V, 8 (9).

[18] *In Ioh. evang.* XIII, 5; J. Heiser (*op. cit.* p. 176) points to four passages in Augustine's writings where he deals with the way the 'attributes' of God are spoken of in Scripture; the most important of these texts is *Contra Adimantum* III, 11, where Augustine says that sometimes Scripture uses words of God which are regarded as pointing to defects in man in order to show that no words at all, even the most exalted terms, are worthy of God, a theme which is developed by Gregory of Nyssa and the Pseudo-Dionysius.

thought points back in its turn to the reality which is thought. Insofar as language cannot express the thought, in that same measure the reality of the divine nature cannot worthily be thought. The uttered sound is not the same as the thought which it attempts to make audible;[19] therefore, speech about God is, in fact, at a third remove from the reality it seeks to express: 'What I cannot utter, do you reflect on; and when you have reflected, it will not be enough. What no man's tongue utters, does any man's thought utter?'[20]

In a formula which Augustine repeats (and Eriugena will adopt), whatever we think of God is truer than what can be said, but God's own being is truer still than what can be thought.[21] Although Augustine's statements of the ineffability of the divine nature are a forceful reminder of the inadequacy of language, his observation that thought cannot worthily think the reality is a constant proclamation of the distance between the thinker and God.[22] It is in this spirit that Augustine begins his theological treatise on the Trinity:

> From now on I begin to speak of subjects which are altogether above the powers of any man, or at least of myself, to express in words as they are conceived in the mind; even our thinking itself, when we reflect on God the trinity, is conscious of the distance between itself and him of whom it is thinking; it is unable to comprehend him as he is.[23]

[19] *De civ. Dei.* X, 13.

[20] Quod sonare non possum, tu cogita; et cum cogitaueris, parum est. Quod cogitatio nullius explicat, lingua alicuius explicat?: *In ps.* 95 (4); *C. C.* vol. 39, ed. D. E. Dekkers and J. Fraipont, *Opera*, part X, 2 (Turnhout, 1956); trans. p. 471. The translations from the *Enarrationes in psalmos* have been adapted from A. Cleveland Coxe, *Expositions on the Book of Psalms*, which follows the Hebrew numeration for the Psalms; I am following the LXX numeration.

[21] Quamobrem ut iam etiam de his quae nec dicuntur ut cogitantur nec cogitantur ut sunt respondere incipiamus fidei nostrae aduersariis: *De trin.* V, 3 (4) and VII, 4 (7).

[22] *De trin.* V, 1 (1).

[23] Hinc iam exordiens ea dicere quae dici ut cogitantur uel ab homine aliquo uel certe a nobis non omni modo possunt, quamuis et ipsa nostra cogitatio cum de deo trinitate cogitamus longe se illi de quo cogitat imparem sentiat neque ut est eum capiat: *De trin.* V, 1 (1); *Opera*, part XVI, 1 (Turnhout, 1968); trans. S. McKenna, p. 175; see also *Sermon* 384 (1).

The idea of the unknowability of the divine nature is not one which is immediately associated with the thought of Augustine; yet it is, I believe, an idea which lies at the very heart of his theological speculation, for Augustine frequently proclaims that God transcends our intellectual ability: not only are we unable to comprehend God as he is,[24] neither can we comprehend the powers of God.[25] Although Augustine does not respond to the principle of divine unknowability by working out a systematic means of approaching the incomprehensible God in terms of *aphairesis*, his insistence upon the idea of unknowability is couched in terms which could well be found in the writings of some of the more obviously apophatic theologians. Even though Augustine is normally regarded as a philosopher of 'being', there is a number of passages in the Augustinian *corpus* in which he says that it is precisely because God is understood as the fullness of being that he is unknowable: the eternity and immutability of God cannot be known by a finite and mutable mind. 'Behold this great I Am! What is man's being to this? ... Who can understand that To Be?'[26] It is interesting to note at this point that although Augustine understands God's being as absolutely transcendent being, he does not adopt the more explicitly Plotinian thinking of Victorinus, where God is understood as μη ὄν because he is πρόον.[27]

---

[24] *In ps.* 49 (18), 98 (3), 134 (2, 3, 4); *De trin.* II, 18 (34) and *De civ. Dei.* X, 12.

[25] See *In ps.* 146 (9-11). It is interesting to note that Augustine, like Gregory of Nyssa, frequently couples the assertion of God's unknowability with the proclamation that the human intellect cannot know itself: Nam quo intellectu homo deum capit qui ipsum intellectum suum quo eum uult capere nondum capit? *De trin.* V, 1 (2); see also XV, 7 (13), *In ps.* 39 (21) and 99 (5); this sentiment is also found in Gregory of Nyssa; see *De hom. opif.* XI, 2.

[26] Magnum ecce Est, magnum Est! Ad hoc homo quid est? Ad illud tam magnum Est, homo quid est, quidquid est? Quis apprehendat illud esse? *In ps.* 101, ii (10); trans. p. 502; see also 121 (5) and *In Epist. Ioh.* IV, 5; in *Parisian Questions* I, Eckhart's notion of the ineffability and unknowability of God depends upon his assertion that God is *esse absolutum*, the fullness of being which is no particular being (*ens*); see also the vernacular sermon, *Quasi stella matutina*.

[27] *Letter to Candidus* II, 13; see also É. Gilson's remarks in *History of Philosophy in the Middle Ages*, pp. 68-70 and V. Lossky's comments, *op. cit.* pp. 579-580.

Not Knowing God: The *Via Remotionis*

I have already noted that there exists a number of passages in Augustine's writings which bear remarkable similarity with the aphairetic method of negative theology, passages in which he would appear to make explicit use of the *via remotionis* in order to arrive at a more correct understanding of the divine nature. One of the great themes of Christian negative theology is that God is better known by knowing what he is not, and Augustine makes use of this idea in at least four important passages. I mention first two related passages from *De trinitate*; the first of these texts is one which could well have come from the *Enneads*. Augustine lauds the goodness of creation and then says: 'but why should I add still more? This good and that good; take away this and that, and see the good itself if you can'.[28]

> If it were possible to put aside those goods which are good by a participation in the good, and to see the good itself in which they are good by participation – for when you hear of this or that good, you also understand the good itself at the same time – if, therefore, I repeat, you could put these goods aside and perceive the good in itself, you would see God.[29]

This is, I believe, the closest Augustine comes to an expression of the aphairetic method of Plotinus, although he does not elaborate the point. However, that method is, I think, given expression in Augustine's description of what he and Monica experienced in the garden at Ostia: to silence the tumult of the flesh and the images of earth, sea, air and the heavens, whereby through silencing all the works of God, including the self, one would be able to 'hear' the voice of God himself.[30]

---

[28] *De trin.* VIII, 3 (4); see also *Enn.* V 5, 6; V 5, 13, and V 6, 6.
[29] *De trin.* VIII, 3 (5); trans. p. 249.
[30] *Conf.* IX, 10.

In the second text taken from *De trinitate*, Augustine commends his readers to think of God, in so far as we are able to think of him, as follows:

> as good without quality, as great without quantity, as the creator who lacks nothing, who rules but from no position, and who contains all things without an external form, as being whole everywhere without limitation of space, as eternal without time, as making mutable things without any change in himself, and as a being without passion. Whoever so thinks of God, even though he does not yet discover all that can be known about him, nevertheless, by his pious frame of mind avoids, as far as possible, the danger of thinking anything about him which he is not.[31]

In this passage, which is one of the most developed dialectical passages of its kind in Augustine's writings, we find him confronting his reader with a most forceful denial of the applicability of the ten Aristotelian categories to God. Although Augustine denies that the categories can be applied to the divine nature, nevertheless, the reader is left with a positive thought: God is good, even though we do not know what good without quality means. This is precisely the nature of dialectical thought when applied to God in terms of negative and positive theology, and it reflects the dialectical nature of the truth of revelation itself. This kind of juxtaposition, which was to be utilized more extensively by Eriugena, is not immediately characteristic of Augustine's thought in general, although we do find numerous isolated instances of it throughout his writings: God is the uncreated creator, the unmeasured measure and the unformed form; he is everywhere and nowhere, unmoved and yet active, the uncontained container and the unnumberable number; he is hidden and revealed, both knowable and unknowable, most hidden yet most present. In one memorable dialectical passage in the *Confessions* Augustine demon-

---

[31] sine qualitate bonum, sine quantitate magnum, sine indigentia creatorem, sine situ praesentem, sine habitu omnia continentem, *sine loco ubique totum*, sine tempore sempiternum, sine ulla sui mutatione mutabilia facientem nihilque patientem. Quisquis deum ita cogitat etsi nondum potest omni modo inuenire quid sit, pie tamen cauet quantum potest aliquid de illo sentire quod non sit: *De trin.* V, 1 (2); trans. S, McKenna, p. 176; see also *Conf.* X, 6.

strates most persuasively that nothing in God is according to the human means of perceiving it.[32]

I come now to the discussion of a number of texts in the Augustinian *corpus* where we find him giving expression to the notion that God is better known by knowing what he is not. The first text is perhaps the most frequently-quoted text in favour of Augustine's adoption of the principles of negative theology and it is taken from his early and programmatic work, *De ordine*. If we do not know what nothing or unformed matter is, what the informed and lifeless is, what a body or what is lifeless in the body; what is place, what is time; what is in place or in time; what is motion or stable motion; what is eternity, what it is to be neither in place nor nowhere, what it is to be beyond time and always, what it is to be nowhere and nowhere not to be, and never to be and never not to be; and if one is ignorant of these matters and yet wishes to investigate and dispute: '... quisquis ergo ista nesciens, non dico de summo illo deo, qui scitur melius nesciendo, sed de anima ipsa sua quaerere ac disputare uoluerit, tantum errabit quantum errari plurimum potest'.[33]

The juxtaposition of the concept of place and what it is to be neither in place nor nowhere, and between the concepts of time and eternity, can, I believe, only with difficulty be applied to a dialectical understanding of the roles of positive and negative theology. The phrase of most interest here (God is better known by not knowing) has an almost Shakespearian quality of aside, and, unfortunately, Augustine does not elaborate upon it. However, there are three further texts where Augustine does elaborate much more pre-

---

[32] See *Conf.* I, 4 and XIII, 37.

[33] II, 16 (44); *C. C.* XXIX, *Opera*, part II, 2, ed. W. M. Green (Turnhout, 1970); see also II, 18 (47); R. Mortley's view is that we do not know what Augustine means by this statement and that it bears no relation to the more developed negative thinking of the Neoplatonists, see *From Word to Silence II*, p. 217. In the three passages to which I refer next, it should be clear what Augustine means: God is not one of the created realities we can see and understand. In this sense his negative thought does indeed bear a relation to the negative thought of the Neoplatonists; I direct the reader to Lossky's excellent comments on this passage, *op. cit.* pp. 576-577.

cisely on the 'not knowing' of the divine nature. The first of these is taken from his Commentary on Psalm 85. 'Deus ineffabilis est; facilius dicimus quid non sit, quam quid sit:' think of the earth or the sea: these are not God; think of all the things which are on the earth or in the sea; whatever shines in the heavens, the heavens itself: none of these things are God – not even the angels, virtues, powers, archangels, thrones, seats, principalities. 'Et quid est? Hoc solum potui dicere, quid non sit.'[34] The inner movement of the mind suggested here by Augustine, as well as in the two texts to follow, is, as always, *ab inferioribus ad superiora*, a movement, characteristic of his thought: from earth and sea to sky and finally to the heavens, God is nothing that the mind can comprehend.

In the second text I wish to mention, which is taken from his *Commentary on the Gospel of John*, Augustine notes that it is not a small matter to know what God is not; and although he does not suggest the way of unknowing as a systematic means of approaching the transcendence of the divine nature, the main focus of his thought is nonetheless clear. 'Nuncsi non potestis comprehendere quid sit deus, uel hoc comprehendite quid non sit deus; multum profeceritis, si non aliud quam est, de deo senseritis. Nondum potes peruenire ad quid sit, perueni ad quid non sit.' The text continues: God is not a body, or the earth, or the heaven, or the moon, or sun or stars – nor any of these corporeal things, nor even heavenly things. If we pass beyond all mutable spirit, beyond all spirit that now knows, now knows not ... 'ut si non uales comprehendere deus quid sit, parum non tibi putes esse scire quid non sit.'[35]

The third text is once again taken from *De trinitate*: 'Non enim paruae notitiae pars est cum de profundo isto in illam summitatem respiramus si antequam scire possimus quid sit deus, possumus iam scire quid non sit.' For God is neither earth nor heaven, nor any such thing that we can see in heaven, nor any thing as we do not see, that is perhaps in the heaven.[36]

---

[34] *In ps.* 85 (12); see also *Ep.* 120, 3 (13).
[35] *In Ioh. evang.* 23, 9-10.
[36] *De trin.* VIII, 2 (3).

These professions of ignorance in Augustine's writings bring him
very close to the *Enneads* of Plotinus, and indeed form the basis for
the argument that Augustine was influenced by the negative theology present in the Neoplatonic works he had read.[37] However, in
exposing these so-called 'elements' of negative theology in Augustine's thought, we raise a number of questions which must, at least
in some measure, be answered. It is not enough simply to bring
these passages to the fore and through them assert that Augustine
belongs, at least to some extent, to the apophatic tradition of theology. How, then, are we to evaluate this presence of negative theology in the thought of Augustine, and how does it fit into the overall, more 'kataphatic' thrust of his thought? In other words, how
does Augustine react to the fundamental assertion of the ineffable
and unknowable nature of the transcendent God?

Knowledge of God: The *Via Amoris*

Faced with the basic assertion that God, as he is in himself, cannot be known by the human mind, the negative theologian, such as
Dionysius or Eriugena, will advocate the adoption of the *via negativa* as the sole appropriate means of approaching the transcendent God. Not so Augustine; what he suggests, although once
again not in any systematic fashion, is what I think we may call
the *via amoris*.

> And he was exalted above the fullness of knowledge, that no man
> should come to him but by love: for 'love is the fulfilling of the
> law'. And soon he showed to his lovers that he is incomprehensi-
> ble, lest they should suppose that he is comprehended by corporeal
> imaginations.[38]

[37] I direct the reader to Lossky's remarks on the notion of *docta ignorantia* in
Augustine's thought, see pp. 576-578.
[38] Et exaltatus est super plenitudinem scientiae, ut nemo ad eum perueniret, nisi
per caritatem ... et cito se incomprehensibilem esse demonstrauit dilectoribus
suis, ne illum corporeis imaginationibus comprehendi arbitrarentur: *In ps.* 17 (11);
trans. A. Cleveland Coxe, p. 51.

It would appear that the way of love is based upon the assertion that God can be known (for we cannot love that which we do not know) – but he is known and loved through his works; God is not known as he is in himself. 'How far can we speak of his goodness? Who can conceive in his heart, or apprehend how good the Lord is? Let us however return to ourselves, and in us recognise him, and praise the maker in his works, because we are not fit to contemplate him himself.'[39]

It is in this sense that Augustine is very close to the guiding principles of the apophatic way as that is advocated by Gregory of Nyssa (and, indeed, also by Eriugena), in asserting that God can be known to the human mind through his works only. 'Let him return to his works ... that he may become sweet through the works of his which we can comprehend.'[40] Even though the substance of God remains hidden, the creator can indeed be known through creation itself – because divine wisdom has left its imprint upon all things.[41] The world itself, in its beauty, 'bears a kind of silent testimony to the fact of its creation, and proclaims that its maker could have been none other than God, the ineffably and invisibly great, the ineffably and invisibly beautiful'.[42]

Augustine does of course admit that even the works of God cannot be known fully; but in so far as they can be known, they show forth his presence and his beauty, for the manner of creation itself is as incomprehensible as its maker is incomprehensible.[43]

---

[39] Ineffabili dulcedine teneor, cum audio: *Bonus Dominus*; consideratisque omnibus et collustratis quae forinsecus uideo, quoniam ex ipso sunt omnia, etiam cum mihi haec placent, ad illum redeo a quo sunt, ut intellegam *quoniam bonus est Dominus*. Rursum, cum ad illum, quantum possum, ingressus fuero, interiorem mihi et superiorem, inuenio; quia sic bonus est Dominus, ut istis non indigeat quo sit bonus: *In ps.* 134 (4); trans. pp. 624-625; see also *Conf.* XIII, 32.

[40] *In ps.* 134 (6), trans. p. 625; see also 144 (9) and (11) and 148 (10).

[41] *De lib. arb.* II, 16.

[42] *De civ. Dei.* XI, 4; trans. H. Bettenson, *City of God*, p. 432; see also *Conf.* IX, 10.

[43] *De civ. Dei.* X, 12; see also *In ps.* 134 (7) and 144 (9) and *De civ. Dei.* XXII, 24.

'You look up to the heavens and are amazed: you consider the whole earth and tremble; when can you contain in your thoughts the vastness of the sea? ... how great are all these, how beautiful, how fair, how amazing! Behold, he who made all these is your God.'[44]

In this sense, Augustine's is a creation-centered theology, for creation always points silently beyond itself to the unknowable God, and it is here that the Pauline text, the invisible things of God are known through the visible creation (Rom. 1:20), assumes a fundamental role for the understanding of the place of negative theology in Augustine's thought.[45] God signifies himself in created things in order to reveal his presence and himself in them, 'but without appearing in that substance itself by which he is, and which is wholly unchangeable and more inwardly and more mysteriously sublime than all the spirits which he created.'[46]

At this point, however, I must mention that Augustine's is not solely a creation-centered theology, but also a Christo-centric theology, for the centrality of the Christian message is also of paramount importance for an understanding of the place assigned to negative theology in his thought. Firstly, and indeed primarily for Augustine, the reality of the incarnation makes the hidden God manifest to human eyes: 'The unknown one is no longer unknown; for he is known by us, our Lord Jesus Christ.'[47] God's being is too much to understand: 'Remember what he who you cannot comprehend, became for you'.[48]

The *via amoris*, for Augustine, is essentially the way of faith in the unseen God; it cannot be identified with the methodology of the *via negativa*. It is a way of living without the knowledge of God as he is in himself, but at the same time living with the

---

[44] Suspicis caelum, et exhorrescis; cogitas iniuersam terram, et contremiscis; maris magnitudinem quando cogitatione occupas? ... omnia ista, quam magna, quam praeclara, quam pulchra, quam stupenda! Ecce qui fecit haec omnia, Deus tuus est: *In ps.* 145 (12); trans. p. 663.

[45] *In ps.* 148 (10), *De trin.* VI, 10 (12), XV, 2 (2) and *De civ. Dei.* VIII, 6.

[46] *De trin.* III, 4 (10); trans. p. 105; see also XV, 2 (3).

[47] *In ps.* 98 (9); trans. p. 486; see also 137 (7).

[48] *In ps.* 121 (5); trans. p. 594.

knowledge that God, the creator of all things, became incarnate; for in this world, we walk by faith, not by sight (2Cor. 5:7).[49] And yet since faith has in some sense already 'found' God, hope seeks to find him even more.[50] For Augustine, this sentiment is expressed most forcefully in the scriptural text, 'seek his face ever more':

> Why, then, does he so seek if he comprehends that what he seeks is incomprehensible, unless because he knows that he must not cease as long as he is making progress in the search itself of incomprehensible things, and is becoming better and better by seeking so great a good which is sought in order to be found and is found in order to be sought?[51]

The 'way' advocated by Augustine is expressed clearly in his development of the notion that God is best sought within: *ab exterioribus ad interiora*, that he is recognized in his image when that image has been re-made according to its likeness with God, a theme developed at length by Gregory of Nyssa. Augustine's frequent references to remodelling and perfecting the image of God often have a very Plotinian feel, for the soul is admonished to withdraw what has been added to itself, so that the image of God may be seen more clearly within.[52] God cannot be seen as he is in himself, but he can be seen through love in his image. In this sense, Augustine's admonition, *redite ad cor*, becomes the key to an understanding of his resolution to the 'problem' of knowledge of God.[53] Augustine's

---

[49] *In ps.* 17 (12), 120 (3), 149 (3), *De trin.* VIII, 4 (6) and *In Epist. Ioh.* IV, 8.

[50] 'That discovery should not terminate that seeking, by which love is testified, but with increase of love the seeking of the discovered one should increase': *In ps.* 104 (3); trans. p. 521.

[51] Cur ergo sic quarerit si incomprehensibile comprehendit esse quod quaerit nisi quia cessandum non est quamdiu in ipsa incomprehensibilium rerum inquisitione proficitur, et melior meliorque fit quarens tam magnum bonum quod et inueniendum quaeritur et quaerendum inuenitur? *De trin.* XV, 2 (2); trans. S. McKenna, p. 452; see also *In Ioh. evang.* LXIII, 1 and *In Epist. Ioh.* IV, 6; once again, we find Augustine expressing an idea which is developed at length by Gregory of Nyssa; see *Contra Eun.* I, 219 and *Vita Mos.* I, 5 and II, 219.

[52] See *De trin.* X, 8 (11) and X, 10 (13); see also *In ps.* 94 (2) and *In Ioh. evang.* XXIII, 10; *Enn.* III 8, 9; VI 7, 31, and VI 9, 8.

[53] *In Ioh. evang.* XVIII, 9-10.

'way', *ab exterioribus ad interiora, ab inferioribus ad superiora*, carries with it the sense of the method of negation. His journey is portrayed in terms of a movement away from creation into the self and upwards towards the transcendent God.

Reappraisal

What then are we to make of Augustine's 'negative theology'? Are we to understand him primarily as a follower of the kataphatic way, or are we to re-evaluate his position and place him in the apophatic tradition of the Latin West? Keeping in mind that all theology is in some measure apophatic, it would appear that Augustine's position affirms this statement. Moreover, the degree of negative theology found in Augustine's thought is certainly not minimal, nor is it simply a trace of the Neoplatonic writers he had read. While it is true that Augustine does not develop an explicit and systematic method of affirmation and negation as the Pseudo-Dionysius will do, that does not mean that the principles of negative theology can be simply relegated to the background of his thought. R. Mortley's appraisal of the 'traces' of negative theology in Augustine's thought, as appearances of the language of the Neoplatonists, where any negation found is simply a preparation for affirmation, is an unwarranted reduction of the rich apophatic principles found in Augustine's writings.[54] No Christian philosopher or theologian ends theology in absolute negation, for negation is undertaken, as Meister Eckhart says, in order to affirm in the truest sense possible.[55]

Augustine was closer to the negative theology of Plotinus than to the kind of negative theology developed by the Athenian Neoplatonists; therefore it is illegitimate to attempt an evaluation of his negative theology in the light of an ultimate and systematic *negatio negationis*. It remains true that Augustine was first and

---

[54] *From Word to Silence II*, pp. 217-218.
[55] *Quasi stella matutina*.

last a man who accepted, lived and preached the reality of the Christian message, and for him, that message was expressed in the dialectical truth of revelation itself: God is most hidden and yet most revealed.[56] Augustine was not simply being selective in emphasizing the immanence of God over against his transcendence; his Christo-centric theology is precisely the most important indication of how Augustine attempted to guide his flock to the vision of the unseen, unknowable God. No Christian philosopher who embraces the apophatic way in all its radicalness can afford to neglect the consequences for negative theology of the reality of the incarnation, and yet in Western theology, this has sometimes been the case. In this sense, Augustine saves himself from certain difficulties which were to trouble some later thinkers. In conclusion, it may be said that Augustine's use of negative theology, although by no means systematic, achieves a certain balance in theological method, one which is not found again in the Western tradition until Aquinas's re-evaluation of the role of negative theology in the thirteenth century.

> What is promised to us? 'We shall be like him, for we shall see him as he is.' The tongue has done what it could, has sounded the words: let the rest be thought by the heart.[57]

---

[56] Tu autem eras interior intimo meo et superior summo meo: *Conf.* VII, 11.

[57] *In Epist. Ioh.* IV, 6.

CHAPTER TEN

THE PSEUDO-DIONYSIUS: BEYOND THEOLOGY

The authority of one known as 'Blessed Dionysius the Areopagite' was appealed to for the first time (erroneously, as it turns out, in support of the Monophysite position) at a theological assembly in Constantinople, in the year 532.[1] Thus began the public life of the *Corpus Areopagiticum*, an inauspicious enough beginning, but one which was to have enormous repercussions in both Eastern and Western Christian scholarship throughout the Middle Ages and indeed right down to the present day. Although the authenticity of the *Corpus* was questioned most courageously by Peter Abelard in the eleventh century and later by Nicholas of Cusa and the Italian Humanist, Lorenzo Valla (among others), it was only the astute detective work of J. Stiglmayr and H. Koch at the turn of this century which established (independently) that the works were not of first-century provenance.[2] The assumed identity of St Paul's Athenian convert was not arbitrarily, but rather well chosen, for it heralds the meeting of Athens and Rome at the altar to the Unknown God. However, it was a most auspicious deception on the Areopagite's part, for without the authority of sub-apostolic status, his works would undoubtedly not have exerted

---

[1] An excellent study of the Christian heritage of Dionysius can be found in A. Louth, *Denys the Areopagite*, ch. 1.

[2] H. Koch, 'Der pseudo-epigraphische Character der dionysischen Schriften', *Theologische Quartalschrift*, 77 (1895), pp. 353-421 and J. Stiglmayr, 'Der Neuplatoniker Proclus als Vorlage des sog. Dionysius Areopagita in der Lehre vom Übel', *Historisches Jahrbuch*, 16 (1895), pp. 253-273, and 721-748. John of Scythopolis, the earliest scholiast of the *Corpus Areopagiticum*, was the first to have doubts about its authorship; see H.-D. Saffrey, 'New Objective links between the Pseudo-Dionysius and Proclus', pp. 66-67.

the enormous influence they did upon the philosophical and theological development of Christian thought, most especially in their role as a vehicle for the consolidation and diffusion of the principles of *apophasis*. Although the debris of the various legends surrounding Dionysius have finally been swept away, the identity of the Areopagite remains still shrouded in mystery.[3] However, it is evident, from the Proclean, or Athenian form of Neoplatonism his work displays, that he was writing, most likely in Syria, at the turn of the fifth and sixth centuries.[4]

Although the influence of Dionysius was far reaching and his writings commanded a wide readership, he is not an easy author to read. Quite apart from the subject matter of the works, his language and means of expression makes understanding a difficult task; the *Corpus Areopagiticum* is unlike anything else in early Christian literature. The complexity of the Areopagite's thought is such that many times he is forced to coin new words – as indeed were his commentators in the Latin tradition – in his attempt to steer language further and further towards its limits.[5] The fact that scholars from John of Scythopolis in the East, and Eriugena in the West, right down to the present day have been attempting to elucidate his thought, is ample proof of the complexity of these early texts. However, even for all the secondary literature that exists on almost every conceivable aspect of Dionysian thought, there still remains a certain underlying ambiguity which is focused upon his own peculiar fusion of Christian and Neoplatonic principles, one which involves even the modern reader in a battle for objectivity.

---

[3] R. F. Hathaway has reviewed scholarly speculation on the identity of this most elusive writer, see *Hierarchy and the Definition of Order in the Letters of Pseudo-Dionysius*, pp. 31-35.

[4] Apart from the later Neoplatonic influence, Dionysius himself, although extremely careful to protect his assumed identity, makes a number of slips: he mentions Ignatius (*D. N.* IV, 12, 709B) and Clement (*D. N.* V, 9, 824D). All translations of the Dionysian works are from C. Luibheid and P. Rorem, *Pseudo-Dionysius. The Complete Works*.

[5] Dionysius himself claims to be elucidating the more 'condensed and singular mental gymnastics' in the writings of his master, Hierotheus, see *D. N.* III, 2 (681B), p. 69.

One reading of Dionysius sees in the *Corpus Areopagiticum* a continuation of the patristic tradition, and concludes that he presents a truly Christian theology;[6] while another reading stresses his Neoplatonic inheritance and concludes that Dionysian theology is not Christian theology.[7] Although such eminent scholars as V. Lossky and J. Vanneste (to name but two) give careful and illuminating accounts of the Dionysian system, they are each guilty of emphasizing only one aspect of the Areopagite's thought. The student of Dionysius has every right to be confused regarding what appears to be the central underlying issue: Christian or Neoplatonist?

Although the Proclean and later Neoplatonic influence on Dionysius was obviously important, indeed his expression of negative theology owes much to that source, his patristic inheritance has often been relegated to a place of less significance. The blame for this can be said to be the author's own. Although he was a Christian writer who must have been well-schooled in earlier patristic literature, Dionysius never mentions any source by name (with the exception of his master, Hierotheus), confining himself to scriptural authority at the risk, of course, of compromising his assumed identity. Therefore, while it is extremely difficult to say with absolute certainty that Dionysius had read the earlier Fathers of the Greek Church, it is possible to establish strong thematic links in the *Corpus Areopagiticum* where the author appears to depend largely on his Christian predecessors in the patristic tradition.[8] Since much has been written on the Dionysian dependence upon Proclus and the later Neoplatonists in terms of *apophasis*, my underlying aim

[6] See for example, R. Roques, V. Lossky and A. Louth.

[7] J. Vanneste, R. F. Hathaway and J. Meyendorff.

[8] H.-Ch. Puech's study of the employment of darkness and cloud in Dionysius suggests that between the scriptural concept and the Dionysian interpretation, there stood an intermediary who inspired him, namely, Gregory of Nyssa; Puech concludes that this particular aspect of Dionysian thought firmly situates the *Mystical Theology* 'dans la perspective continue de la tradition patristique', see 'La ténèbre mystique chez le Pseudo-Denys l'Aréopagite et dans la tradition patristique', p. 53; see also V. Lossky, *The Vision of God*, p. 100ff.

during the course of the discussion to follow will be to probe the
Areopagiticum for traces of earlier patristic sources.

Divinity Veiled and Unveiled

The Areopagite's understanding of the divine nature is well
known, popularized by the anonymous English work of the four-
teenth century, *The Cloud of Unknowing*. In terms of the development of negative theology, the Dionysian works contain the apotheosis of negation, for God's essential quality is transcendence.[9]
Throughout the *Divine Names* and the *Mystical Theology*, Dionysius heaps negation upon negation, as the first few chapters of the
Divine Names demonstrate: the divine nature is invisible, incomprehensible, inscrutable, unsearchable and infinite; there is no perception of it, no image, opinion, name or expression for it, no contact with it.[10] It is neither word, power, mind, life nor essence, but
is separate from every condition: movement, life, image, opinion,
name, word, thought, conception, essence, position, stability and
boundary.[11] The great hymn of negations in *Mystical Theology* IV
and V is the finest, and indeed most radical statement of divine
transcendence in Greek Christian thought.

However, Dionysius does not attribute to God, or negate of the
divine essence, any concept which cannot be found in either the
Christian or Neoplatonic traditions before him, with the exception
of the distinctions within the trinity and the trinity itself. His originality comes from the hard-won alliance of the Neoplatonic
method of 'super'-affirmation with the Christian notion of divine
transcendence, and it gives Christian negative theology a new
twist. Never before had any Christian writer found it necessary to
stress so comprehensively the utterly unknowable and transcendent nature of God. Why then did Dionysius go to such great

[9] See *Ep.* I (1065A).
[10] *D. N.* I, 2 (588C) and I, 5 (593A).
[11] See *D. N.* I, 5 (593C).

lengths in his attempts to place the unity of the divine essence beyond the limits of thought and speech? How does such a radical expression of transcendence find its place within Christian theology? In other words, how can God be known?[12]

The central aspect of Christianity, of revealed religion, is that the transcendent God is known, first and foremost as the immanent cause of all creation which is eternally moving back to its likeness in him. 'It is the life of the living, the being of beings, it is the source and cause of all life and of all being, for out of its goodness it commands all things to be and it keeps them in being'.[13] God is not entirely uncommunicable and unnameable, for as the divine ray works outwards to multiplicity, he reveals himself in order that all things may be drawn upwards to himself.[14] God is known, therefore, from the orderly arrangement of all things which are, in a sense, projected out of him; this order – in Dionysian terms, hierarchy – possesses certain semblances of the divine. God is known in all things as cause, and yet is distinct from all things as transcendent, a familiar Neoplatonic statement about the One.[15] The tension between transcendence and causality (as the foundation for divine immanence) is the axis upon which the Dionysian system revolves, and as such, can be said to reflect the central dialectic at the heart of theism.[16] Causality, as the principle of divine economy, establishes both the relationship and the distance between the created and the uncreated.

One very important aspect of the Dionysian system, indeed the central thesis at the heart of his theology and one which links him directly to the Cappadocian Fathers, is that God is knowable through his works (*energeiai*) or distinctions (*diakriseis*), but he

[12] Dionysius himself asks and answers this question; see *D. N.* VII, 3 (869C).

[13] *D. N* I, 3 (589C); trans. p. 51.

[14] *D. N.* I, 2 (588D) and *C. H.* I, 2 (121B).

[15] *D. N.* VII, 3 (872A).

[16] J. Vanneste sees the apparent opposition between transcendence and causality in the Dionysian works as a reflection of a Neoplatonic schema; see *Le mystère de Dieu*, pp. 130-131.

is unknowable in his essence (*ousia*) or unity (*henōsis*). This crucial distinction is the foundation for the function and constitution
of the two theologies: since God is all things in all things, he can
be spoken about, and since he is no thing among things, he cannot be spoken about.[17] 'We therefore approach that which is
beyond all as far as our capacities allow us and we pass by way
of the denial of all things and by way of the cause of all things.'[18]
Every attribute, therefore, can be predicated of him, and every
attribute must also be denied.[19] The dialectic at work in the juxtaposition of essence and energies (or powers) is explained by
Dionysius using a typically Neoplatonic metaphor: the bright
rays which stream out from one luminous source can be seen and
apprehended; just as the source itself cannot be seen, God can be
apprehended only in the 'rays', the manifestations which proceed
from him.[20] Knowledge of God, therefore, is limited in that it is
knowledge which is derived from God's powers or manifestations; it is not knowledge of his essence. One can know only that
God is above all things, that he is transcendent; one cannot know
what God is in his *ousia* or *henosis*. Dionysius makes it very
clear that the methods of theological investigation, the affirmative and the negative, refer only to what is next to the divine
unity, to the providence of God which is made known to human
nature, not to that unity in itself.[21] Dionysius, like Augustine,
uses the Pauline text, the visible creation makes known the invisible things of God, to suggest that it is by way of creation (the
orderly arrangement of all things) that one can be led back to the
maker.[22]

He is all things since he is the cause of all, and yet he is superior since he is above everything: he is every shape and struc-

[17] *D. N.* VII, 3 (872A).
[18] *D. N.* VII, 3 (869D-872A); trans. p. 108.
[19] *D. N.* V, 8 (824B).
[20] *Ep.* I (1065A) and *D. N.* I, 4 and I, 2.
[21] *M. Th.* V (1048B) and *D. N.* V, 2 (816C).
[22] Rom. 1:20; see *Ep.* IX, 2 (1108B). See also *Ep.* X (1117A): ἀληθῶς ἐμφανεῖς
εἰκονες εἰσι τὰ ὅρατα τῶν ἀοράτων.

ture, yet at the same time, he is formless and beautyless.[23] If God is both manifest and hidden, the cause of all yet beyond all, in all things yet not in anything, surely this must indicate some form of duality in the divine nature. According to Dionysius, God's nature is the ultimate paradox of unity in distinction: even though the light of the sun is one, it can be understood in distinction for it renews, nourishes, protects and perfects all things.[24] The powers of God which can be apprehended, are 'part' of God in so far as they partake of his nature and make him manifest, yet they are not God, since they are not his essence; they are distinctions adapted by the divine in order that human nature may be raised up to him.[25] The visible things of creation, which proceed from the divine ideas, are signs of the invisible, and in their similarity to God they are traces of the divine.[26] To praise the divine, we must turn to creation, for visible things make known the invisible.[27]

However, any knowledge which can be gained of the divine nature through the study of created things must be secondary knowledge which is adapted to human nature; it is not knowledge of God as he is in himself.[28] It would appear, therefore, that secondary knowledge is the only option open to the human intellect. Can there be any other 'knowledge' of this supremely transcendent and unknowable God? This is precisely the question Dionysius addresses in the *Mystical Theology*, and I return to this point below.

---

[23] *D. N.* V, 8 (824B).

[24] *ibid.*; God remains one in plurality and unified in procession, see *D. N.* II, 11 (649B).

[25] Dionysius explains the powers of God in terms of the radii of a circle which meet in the centre, and all numbers which pre-exist in the monad; see *D. N.* V, 6 (820D-821A).

[26] *C. H.* I, 2 (121B-C) and *D. N.* IX, 6 (913D-916A).

[27] *D. N.* VII, 3 (869C-D) and I, 5 (593D).

[28] *C. H.* II, 1 (137B) and I, 2 (121B-C).

Affirmative and Symbolic Theologies

Theology according to the Areopagite is the 'science of God',
or the word of God;[29] it is also a tool for the examination of
what Scripture says about the divine nature. Since theology is
the word of God, the truth about the divine essence must be confined to what has been revealed in the Oracles, the sacred texts;
one must be lifted up through the manifold forms given in Scripture to the divine simplicity itself.[30] A correct investigation of
Scripture, which is a form of divine manifestation, becomes the
means of the ascent to divine unity; the journey of *logos*
descending must be retraced upwards.[31] The theology of Dionysius is, therefore, scripturally based. The sometimes blatant
Neoplatonic principles to be found in his reading of the sacred
texts is explained by our author in *Epistle* VII where he recon-
ciles his two sources: philosophy is concerned with the knowledge of beings, and with the same wisdom and knowledge which
St Paul sought.[32]

Theology is also the means of differentiating the divine unity,
for it refers to the manifested being of God, that is, the divine processions, which come to us wrapped in sacred veils: 'so that what
is hidden may be brought out into the open and multiplied, what is
unique and undivided may be divided up, and multiple shapes and
forms be given to what has neither shape nor form'.[33] Beyond the
veiled representations of God, his mystery remains simple and

---

[29] *D. N.* II, 1 (637A); for a fuller discussion of theology in the Dionysian *corpus*,
see R. Roques, 'Notes sur la notion de *theologia* chez le Pseudo-Denys
l'Aréopagite', p. 204, and P. Rorem, *Biblical and Liturgical Symbols in the
Pseudo-Dionysian Synthesis*, ch. 2.

[30] *D. N.* I, 1 (588A), *C. H.* II, 1 (137A) and I, 2 (588C). Dionysius uses the word
logia rather than *graphē*.

[31] *D. N.* I, 1 (588A), VII, 4 (872C) and *M. Th.* III (1033B-C).

[32] VII, 2 (1080B) and II, 2 (640A); trans. p. 60: 'if ... someone is entirely at log-
gerheads with scripture, he will be far removed also from what is my philosophy'.

[33] *Ep.* IX, 1 (105B-C); trans. p. 283; see also *D. N.* II, 4 (640Dff), II, 5 (641Dff),
II, 11 (649A-C) and V, 1 (816B).

unveiled;[34] therefore, we must look beyond the image to the hidden beauty within.[35] The task of Dionysian theology, therefore, can be described as a journey towards unveiled mystery.

It is well known that Dionysius advocates the employment of two main branches of theology in his search for truth: the kataphatic and the apophatic. A wider interpretation of the two theologies broadens into four: affirmative, symbolic, negative and mystical, although Dionysius himself does not make this distinction formally.[36] These 'theologies', however, should not be viewed as separate sciences, rather, they are to be understood together as the expression of one continuous movement back to the transcendent source of all being. Kataphatic theology, which can be said to culminate in symbolic theology, is concerned with the manifestation of God and how he can be named through his effects. Apophatic theology, which uses affirmations as a springboard from which to proceed to negation, culminates in mystical theology and is concerned with the nature of God as he is in himself, apart from his effects. However, Dionysius always makes it quite clear that whatever theology can say about God, it does not speak of transcendent unity itself, but about the providence of God which is made known to human nature.[37] His theological method pivots upon the repeated and central question: how we can say something about God when he is above that something?[38]

It is the aim of the treatise on the *Divine Names* to investigate how we can use the names of special importance which have been given to the nameless in the Oracles. The rationale behind the employment of affirmations can be understood as *logos* descend-

[34] *M. Th.* I, 1 (997A). On the concept of veiling in Dionysius, see F. O'Rourke, *Pseudo-Dionysius and the Metaphysics of Aquinas,* pp. 9-10.

[35] *M. Th.* II (1025B).

[36] I. P. Sheldon-Williams interprets affirmative theology as the science of God as efficient cause (cause can be named from effect), symbolic theology as the science of God as final cause and mystical (negative) theology as the science of God as *monē*; see 'The Pseudo-Dionysius', p. 460.

[37] *D. N.* V, 2 (816C).

[38] *D. N.* I, 5 (593A-B).

ing of which there can be many words, but these words must be
interpreted correctly lest anyone be led to an improper idea of the
transcendent. This treatise places Dionysius firmly within the
Christian patristic tradition from Justin and Clement, up to
Eunomius and Gregory of Nyssa, although interest in the question
of names is also, as we have seen, a Neoplatonic thematic –
employed chiefly in the context of theurgy in Iamblichus and Proclus.[39] However, the treatise of Dionysius remains the most exact-
ing and comprehensive of all discussions on this theme in the early
medieval Christian tradition.

The *Divine Names* is a detailed exposition of the different
names and titles of God: intelligible names, such as Good, Beautiful, Light, Love, Being, Life, Knowledge, Intellect, Word, Wisdom, Power, Justice, Salvation, Redemption, Righteousness,
Omnipotent, Eternity, Time, Place, Faith, Truth, Perfect and One;
sensible names: sun, cloud, stars, fire, water, wind, dew, stone and
rock, and biblical names: 'All Powerful', 'Ancient of Days',
'Peace', 'Holy of Holies', 'King of Kings', 'Lord of Lords' and
'God of Gods'.[40] Dionysius follows the Cappadocian Fathers in
making a distinction between different types of divine names:
those used for the whole deity (unified or common names), those
denoting cause, and finally, distinctive or differentiated names.[41]
He insists, however, that all names must be ascribed to the divinity in its entirety, even though they pertain solely to the manifestation of God.[42] Names must be understood as symbolic titles for
they are what we say of God, not what God is in himself; this will
become the fundamental reason for their ultimate denial. Dionysius quotes the angel's rebuke to Manoah from the Book of Judges

---

[39] R. Mortley address the Neoplatonic background of the naming process in his
chapter on Dionysius in *From Word to Silence II*; on the Syriac inheritance of
Dionysius on this point see A. Louth, *op. cit.* p. 79ff.

[40] Dionysius also considers the application of some philosophical terms: small,
great, same, different, equal, unequal, similar, dissimilar – a very definite Neoplatonic theme based ultimately on *Parmenides* 137Cff.

[41] *D. N.* II, 3 (640B) and II, 11 (652A).

[42] *D. N.* II, 1 (637C) and II, 11 (652A).

in support of his claim that the human intellect cannot know the name of him who is celebrated both with no name and with every name.[43] The Areopagite explains that names are given in order to reveal God to finite intelligence: so that we may be drawn upwards and transcend their literal interpretation.[44] We must, he insists, resist the temptation to measure the divine by human standards. For instance, to call the transcendent God, 'life', 'being', 'light' or 'word', points to the fact that the mind lays hold of God as 'life-bearing', 'cause of being', and so on.[45] Therefore, for Dionysius, affirmative theology is imperfect since it proceeds by the way of analogy, and yet it is an important starting point, for it constitutes the rapport between the human and the divine.[46]

The highest level of affirmative theology for Dionysius, is trinity: the three-fold distinction within the unutterable unity of the divine essence. Yet even trinity is a title which must ultimately be understood as falling short of the unknowable Godhead – an idea which can still cause tremors of shock in some theological circles. For Dionysius, God is the unknown oneness beyond the source of all unity.[47] It is for this reason that Dionysius also denies the title 'One', for God is One beyond the One. The reasons for the denial of both 'three' and 'one' (trinity and unity) are to be laid at the door of his fascination with the later Neoplatonists. In their desire to protect totally the unknowability of the One, they pushed language and conceptualization to their furthest limits. If Dionysius was to deny One, then he would also be forced to deny Three.[48] In sweeping aside the bounds of trinitarian theology in this way, Dionysius is not denying the triune nature of God, but attempting to find the three beyond the three. According to V. Lossky, Dionysius succeeds in freeing the trinity from the bounds of economy, to

---

[43] Judges 13:17-18; see *D. N.* I, 6 (596A).

[44] *D. N.* VII, 1 (865C-D) and XIII, 3 (980D).

[45] *D. N.* II, 7 (645A).

[46] On Dionysian analogy, see V. Lossky, 'La notion des "analogies" chez Pseudo-Denys l'Aréopagite'.

[47] *D. N.* II, 4 (641A) and XIII, 3 (981A).

[48] *D. N.* XIII, 3 (981A).

become the 'unitrinity' of Christian transcendence: 'if the God of the philosophers is not the living God, the God of the theologians is only such by halves, as long as this last step has not been taken'.[49] Ultimately, the names 'trinity' and 'unity' are simply names for that which is above every name (Phil. 2:9) and in the final chapter of the *Divine Names* Dionysius presents the most forceful expression of divine ineffability in Christian thought.[50]

Symbolic theology is concerned with the ascent of the mind from the realm of the sensible to the level of the intelligible concept and it is focused upon the manifestation of God in Scripture.[51] In the *Mystical Theology*, Dionysius tells us that the (supposed) treatise, *Symbolic Theology*, is concerned with the interpretation of the anthropomorphic images and attributes said of God in the Oracles, which can sometimes appear absurd or shocking, things which are transferred from the sensible to the divine realm: God's places, parts, organs, anger, grief, sickness, sleeping and awakening.[52] Scripture often uses images and pictures derived from the lowest of things: God can be described as a perfume, a corner-stone and even as a lowly worm.[53] 'All this is revealed in the sacred pictures of the Scriptures so that he might lift us in spirit up through the perceptual to the conceptual, from sacred shapes and symbols to the simple peaks of the hierarchies of heaven.'[54] The importance of the symbol is its intelligible content and that is why the process of metonymy must be reversed: 'all this is to enable the one capable of seeing the beauty hidden within these images to find that they are truly mysterious, appropriate to God and filled with a great theological light'.[55] For example, Dionysius explains that 'drunkenness' in God is nothing else but the ecstatic overflowing of his love

---

[49] *In the Image and Likeness of God*, p. 28.
[50] XIII, 3.
[51] Symbols bear the mark of the divine as manifest images of the unspeakable, *Ep.* IX, 2 (1008C).
[52] *M. Th.* III (1033A-B), *Ep.* IX (1104B) and *D. N.* I, 8 (597A-B).
[53] *C. H.* II, 5 (144D-145A).
[54] *C. H.* I, 3 (124A); trans. p. 147.
[55] *Ibid.*

and goodness to all creatures.[56] Symbolic theology, therefore, discards the sensible clothing of the symbol in order to unveil and apprehend its significant intelligible content. 'We must make the holy journey to the heart of the sacred symbols'.[57] This Dionysian thematic can be illustrated in a liturgical sense as a movement behind the iconostasis to the hidden mysteries beyond it. In the same way, Scripture is understood to be a veiling of the divine which must be transcended.[58] It is in this sense that symbolic theology can be regarded both as the culmination of affirmative theology and the beginning of negative theology.[59]

One most important idea in the Dionysian explanation of the function of the symbol is that unlike-symbolism is more appropriate to God than like-symbolism: like-symbolism, being no less defective than unlike-symbolism, can end up as an idol in place of the transcendent divine itself.[60] The fact that unlike-symbolism is more easily negated (the 'sheer crassness of the signs is a goad'[61]), makes it a good starting point for the whole process of negation. At this point, and indeed at many others, Dionysius cautions that the inner secrets veiled by symbol are not to be revealed to the unholy, the uninitiated, for it is precisely the function of symbol to protect the inexpressible and invisible from the many.[62] It is only the genuine lover of holiness who is led to leave aside the protective covering of the symbol and enter into the simplicity of the divine nature; knowledge is not for everyone.[63]

---

[56] *Ep.* IX, 4 (1112B-C).

[57] *Ep.* IX, 2 (1108C); trans. p. 284. According to Sheldon-Williams if this process is not undertaken, the methodical science of God will end in adolatry; see 'The Pseudo-Dionysius', pp. 463 and 467.

[58] See *E. H.* III, 2 (428C), *C. H.* I, 2 (121B-C) and *Ep.* IX, 1 (1108A-B); on the liturgical aspect of the symbol in Dionysius, see P. Rorem's excellent study.

[59] See R. Roques, 'Symbolisme et théologie négative chez le Pseudo-Denys', p. 105.

[60] *C. H.* II, 2 (140C).

[61] *C. H.* II, 3 (141B); trans. p. 150; P. Rorem notes: 'The lowest point of the divine procession into dissimilarity reveals most forcefully that its essential purpose is to provoke a movement in the opposite direction'; *op. cit.* p. 96.

[62] *C. H.* II, 2 (140B), *M. Th.* I, 2 (1000A), and *E. H.* I, 1 (372A).

[63] *Ep.* IX, 1 (1105D) and *D. N.* I, 8 (597B-C).

Negative Theology

At the point where the mind has divested itself of symbolic protection in its search after the unity of the divine, comes the moment when it begins the ascent through negation. Since God cannot be comprehended through intellect, only the ultimate destruction of all conceptual limitations will free the reality of the Godhead from its association with human forms of thought. The role of negation in Dionysius is first and foremost a corrective measure against any anthropomorphic and even intellectual representations, and, therefore, is to be preferred to the method of affirmations.[64] The panegyric of negations in *Mystical Theology* IV and V denies the validity of all concepts, beginning with the lowest and moving successively towards the highest. Even the highest names and titles are denied in this most radical act of negation: wisdom, one, divinity, good; even spirit, paternity and sonship, the distinctive names of the trinity are denied, for God is totally beyond the linguistic realm.[65]

Yet, Dionysian negation is not simply a denial at the verbal or intellectual levels, for the negative concept pushes conceptualization to its utmost limit of affirmation, a limit which once again finds expression, although in more cumbersome terms.

> When we talk of God as being without mind and without perception, this is to be taken in the sense of what he has in superabundance and not as a defect. Hence we attribute absence of reason to him because he is above reason ... and we posit intangible and invisible darkness of that light which is unapproachable because it so far exceeds the visible light.[66]

Negative terms are used in a contrary sense to deprivation in order to indicate that God is above all affirmation and negation.[67] In

---

[64] *C. H.* II, 3 (140Dff) and *D. N.* XIII, 3 (981B). On the priority of negation, see J. W. Douglas, 'The Negative Theology of Dionysius the Areopagite', and F. O'Rourke, *op. cit.* pp. 16-21.

[65] According to R. Mortley, *op. cit.* p. 230, this is an act of reductionism on the trinity.

[66] *D. N.* VII, 2 (869A); trans. p. 107.

[67] *D. N.* VII, 1 (865B).

moving beyond the limits of affirmative and negative theology, we must understand God to be super-good, more than good, the super-excellent goodness, the super-divine divinity (ὑπὲρ τὸ εἶναι θεότης[68]), the super-real real and the oneness beyond the source of oneness.[69] He is the more than ineffable and more than unknowable aloneness: τῆς ὑπεραρρήτου καὶ ὑπεραγνώστου μονιμότητος.[70] The prefix, 'hyper', which is indicated in every negation, is ultimately a linguistic device which provides the key to the central dialectic in Dionysian thought: it indicates something positive, but it is an affirmation which can no longer be thought. Eriugena will follow Dionysius closely in this respect. The familiar direct juxtaposition of concepts in the Dionysian *corpus* has the same intention: God is mind beyond mind and word beyond speech;[71] nameless and many-named, eloquent and taciturn; always at rest and always on the move and never at rest and never on the move. The gospel itself is described as vast and small, wide-ranging and restricted; while we ourselves must lack sight and knowledge in order to see and know the divine darkness which is 'το ἀπρόσιτον φῶς'.[72]

Perhaps the most crucial paradox in Dionysian thought concerns the incarnation, which he describes as the most obvious fact of all theology, yet it 'cannot be enclosed in words nor grasped by any mind not even by the leaders among the front ranks of the angels'.[73] One very enigmatic remark concerning the incarnation in the *Corpus Areopagiticum* has long been the source of discussion: that even after the incarnation of the *Logos*, 'what is spoken remains unsaid and what is known unknown'.[74]

[68] *C. H.* IV, 1 (177D).

[69] On the transcendence of God as 'being beyond being', see F. O'Rourke, *op. cit.* pp. 76-84.

[70] See *D. N.* II, 4 (640D-641A).

[71] *D. N.* I, 1 (588B).

[72] 1Tim. 6:16. *D. N.* I, 6 (596A); *M. Th.* I, 3 (1000C); *Ep.* IX, 3 (1109D); *M. Th.* II (1025A) and *Ep.* V (1073A).

[73] *D. N.* II, 9 (648A).

[74] *Ep.* III (1069B): λεγόμενον ἄρρητον μένει, καὶ νοούμενον ἄγνωστον.

Theology Abandoned: From *Logos* To Unity

For Dionysius, negative theology does not stop at the simple level of negation or of super-affirmation: its fullest expression can be reached only when the mind leaves all intellectual pursuits behind and enters into *agnōsia,* the experience of unknowing knowing beyond all affirmations and negations: 'darkness and light, error and truth – it is none of these. It is beyond assertion and denial.'[75] The *katharsis* which is embraced at the final stage of theology has three levels: detachment, unknowing and union, and to explain this final ascent, Dionysius uses a scriptural illustration which had already been employed by Philo of Alexandria and Gregory of Nyssa much in the same context: the journey of Moses up the dark mountain of the *deus absconditus.* Moses first purifies himself and having separated himself from the unpurified, moves upwards towards the highest ascent, and finally enters alone into the darkness of unknowing through which he is eventually united to the unknown.[76] The treatise on the *Mystical Theology,* condensed as it is, will be remarkably familiar to readers of Gregory of Nyssa, for many of the Cappadocian Father's themes appear in this Dionysian work. The theologies of affirmation, symbolism and negation had remained on the level of intellection; the final stage in the Dionysian journey towards unveiled mystery is mystical theology, which involves a surpassing of the intellect in effecting a shift from knowledge to experience.[77]

The process of *aphairesis,* which had already entered into Christian thought through the writings of Clement of Alexandria, is expanded and developed by Dionysius in a most Plotinian fashion, for it is a concept which was not stressed by the later Neoplatonists. Abstraction involves the removal of all things starting from the lowest and working up to the highest;[78] it is detachment from

---

[75] *M. Th.* V (1048A-B) and *D. N.* II, 4 (641A).
[76] *M. Th.* I, 3 (1000C-1001A). The liturgical facet of the unifying experience of the *Mystical Theology* is brought out by A. Louth, *op. cit.* p. 101.
[77] *D. N.* II, 9 (648B).
[78] *M. Th.* II (1025B) and III (1033C).

everything, even the most holy things which are akin to the divine (divine lights, celestial voices and words).[79] When the soul has become free from all and released from all, it is then in a worthy state to enter into the divine darkness and to be raised into union with the divine: 'by an undivided and absolute abandonment of yourself and everything, shedding all and freed from all, you will be lifted up to the ray of divine shadow, which is above everything that is'.[80] However, in his exegesis of the Exodus text, Dionysius explains that in order to be raised unknowingly into union with God, Moses first of all sees the place where God is, not God himself who is invisible. When he finally breaks from all that is seen by silencing all intellectual pursuits and becomes an 'eyeless mind' (no longer a knowing subject), he enters fully into the darkness, there to be completely united with the transcendent Unknown (no longer a known object): 'being neither oneself nor someone else, one is supremely united by a completely unknowing inactivity of all knowledge, and knows beyond the mind by knowing nothing'.[81] It is, explains Dionysius in very Nyssean (and indeed Plotinian) terms, through 'not seeing', and 'not knowing' that one truly sees and truly knows.[82] *Logos* ascending into unity moves from the eloquence of many words, to fewer words and finally to no words at all: 'the more it climbs, the more language falters, and when it has passed up and beyond the ascent, it will turn silent completely, since it will finally be at one with him who is indescribable.'[83]

---

[79] Like Plotinus, Dionysius uses the image of the sculptor chipping away at a statue in order to bring forth its inner beauty to illustrate the kind of purification involved in *aphairesis*, see *Enn.* I 6, 9, 6; see *M. Th.* II (1025A-B).

[80] *M. Th.* I, 1 (997B-1000A); trans. p. 135. See also *C. H.* III, 3 (165D) and *E. H.* III, 5 (401A-B). According to J. Vanneste's interpretation, the kind of purification advocated by Dionysius is primarily intellectual and not moral; he concludes that the practice of *aphairesis* is not a Christian one; see *Le mystère de Dieu*, p. 230.

[81] *M. Th.* I, 3 (1001A); trans. p. 137.

[82] *M. Th.* II (1025A); trans. p. 138: 'I pray we could come to this darkness so far above light! If only we lacked sight and knowledge so as to see, so as to know, unseeing and unknowing, that which lies beyond all vision and knowledge'.

[83] *M. Th.* III (1033B); trans. p. 139.

The movement of the blinded soul throwing itself (*epiballein*) relentlessly against the rays of the divine darkness into *agnōsia*,[84] is literally a movement of *ekstasis*, and corresponds to the loving *ekstasis* of God in his bountiful procession into all things.[85] It is also the key to the crucial moment in the mystical experience of Dionysius, for it spans the boundary between knowing and unknowing, between intellection and union. This casting of oneself is by nature 'sudden' (*exaiphnēs*), the same word used by Plotinus to express the nature of *ekstasis*.[86] It is a projection of oneself, not into 'the immensity of Christ', as Clement of Alexandria put it, but into the darkness which God has made his hiding place.[87]

Although Dionysius speaks of God as darkness in terms of the final moment of mystical ascent, he is, properly speaking, 'unapproachable light', that excess of light which so blinds the eye that the gazer cannot see it.[88] The metaphor of darkness is, once again, a Christian one, and Dionysius exploits it fully, for it would appear to be the best way to express the idea that no senses are operative in the unity which lies at the summit of the apophatic journey.[89] The soul is in the same place with God, it does not know him intellectually; thus, Dionysius protects the inviolate unknowability of the divine nature. In symbolic terms, light becomes the medium in which things are hidden, contrary to the experience in the phys-

---

[84] *M. Th.* I, 1.

[85] See *C. H.* I, 1 (120B): every good gift descends from the father of lights and every outpouring is reciprocated by a reversion into union with the father.

[86] See *Ep.* III (1069B): The word 'sudden' was also used by Plato, *Ep.* VII (341C-D), Philo, *Mig. Abr.* VII, 1 (441) and Plotinus, VI 7, 36 (15-21).

[87] Dionysius refers to the darkness where God hides in *Ep.* V (1073A) and *M. Th.* I, 3 (1000C); see Ps. 17:11 and Ex. 20:21.

[88] 1Tim. 6:16; *Ep.* V (1073A).

[89] V. Lossky has pointed out that darkness and *agnōsia* have a double reference for Dionysius: objective and subjective: they refer to the eternally unknowable nature of God himself and also to the soul's inability to know God, see *In the Image and Likeness of God*, pp. 31-43; this view contrasts with the judgement of J. Vanneste, that darkness in Dionysius is devoid of mystical content; see *Le mystère de Dieu*, p. 222.

ical world: all things which can be known are those things which have been lit up through manifestation. The knowledge and light of beings (distinction) prevents the darkness (unity) of God being 'seen': 'darkness disappears in light, the more so as there is more light. Knowledge makes unknowing disappear, the more so as there is more knowledge'.[90] On the descent into manifestation, the *katabasis*, it is indeed quite legitimate to speak of the manifestation of God in terms of light; the contrary movement, the *anabasis*, must always refer to the divine itself as 'unapproachable light' which can never be attained to. Union for Dionysius is not the cosy intimacy of a private conversation with God: all emotion, sensing and intellection have long since been abandoned; to have made the return journey back to one's source is precisely to be unknowing in the same place with God. The Dionysian understanding of the final experience of the soul is one of unity with divine darkness, it is not an experience of the light of God which is unapproachable. In this sense, the soul is eternally at one remove from the unknowable God, for his light can never be seen.

Although the foregoing discussion of the methods of theology in Dionysius follows his own outline and progression, it should now be clear that even this division and conceptualization must be transcended. The two ways of theological analysis come together dialectically in pointing towards the unknown quality of the divine nature, and finally disappear in the darkness of unapproachable light.

Before I turn to some concluding remarks, I would like to note that a full understanding of Dionysian thought will necessitate a reading of the *Celestial Hierarchy* and the *Ecclesiastical Hierarchy*. The question of the relationship of these works to the *Divine Names* and the *Mystical Theology* has been regarded as problematic. However, the Dionysian understanding of final unity attained through transcending all sensible and intelligible images and symbols, is related to the notion of hierarchy with which a substantial portion of his work is concerned. Hierarchy, as the orderly arrange-

---

[90] *Ep.* I (1065A); see also *M. Th.* II (1025B).

ment of all things, at once delineates the distance between cause and caused, yet it is also the means whereby the mind can move upwards and back to its source. Mystical theology is the culmination of that journey; it is not an alternative way to God which can bypass either hierarchy or indeed Scripture, and it does not function as a tool for the deconstruction of the concept of hierarchy.

Dionysius: Patristic or Neoplatonic?

We can interpret the Areopagite's *apophasis* as a very definite strengthening of the negative theology of the Cappadocian Father, Gregory of Nyssa, through the use made of Proclean principles. However, there are many themes in the *Corpus Areopagiticum* which differ notably from the Nyssean form of *apophasis*. In Gregory, the unknowing soul knows itself as a mirror of the unknowable God; in Dionysius, only the angels are mirrors of divine goodness, although the orderly arrangement of all things as semblances of the divine, causes members of hierarchies to mirror the glow of divine light.[91] Absent too from Dionysian thought is the great Nyssean theme of 'eternal discovery': in Dionysian darkness the soul does not discover anything at all about God. Dionysius does not take up the Cappadocian thematic which had been a part of philosophical and theological discussion since Justin Martyr, namely, the 'ungeneracy' of God, and he does not use the Christian, and indeed Plotinian catchphrase: we know only *that* God is not *what* he is (although this is implicit in his thought). The Dionysian distinction focuses not upon *hyparxis* and *ousia*, but on *henōsis* and *diakresis* (unity and distinction). Gregory of Nyssa's influence on Dionysius is reflected most in the Areopagite's understanding of divine darkness, the focus on presence rather than intellection, and the idea that true knowing comes about through unknowing. The idea that words pertain only to the manifestation of the divine nature is, as we

---

[91] *C. H.* III, 2 (165A) and *D. N.* VI, 22 (724B).

saw, a very important concept in Gregory's thought and Dionysius adopts it readily.

Apart from the obvious Nyssean themes which can be
detected in the Dionysian works, there are also faint echoes of
the earlier Christian Alexandrian and Plotinian traditions which
somehow survive in spite of the strong Proclean influence. As I
mentioned in chapter six above, the later Neoplatonists were not
particularly concerned with the method of *aphairesis*, a theme
which had entered into the Christian tradition through Clement
of Alexandria. The great Plotinian exhortation, *aphele panta*, is,
however, taken up by Dionysius with enthusiasm.[92] Another
very Plotinian sentiment to be found in the Dionysian *corpus* is
that the divine is present to all things even though all things may
not be present to it.[93] Dionysius also echoes the Plotinian sentiment that by not seeing, one sees most of all.[94] Although these
echoes are faint, they raise the question of a direct Plotinian
influence on the Areopagite. Of course, Dionysius may well
have been open to an indirect influence of Plotinus through Gregory of Nyssa.

To conclude, I would suggest that there is little in Dionysius
which cannot be found already in his Christian and Neoplatonic
predecessors. His genius, daring and originality can be said to lie
in his comprehensive synthesis of Christian and Neoplatonic
apophasis and his relentless pursuit of the transcendent which
led him ultimately to deny even trinity and unity. As a result, the
writings of this most elusive champion of the apophatic way present the strongest account of negative theology thus far encountered in Christian thought. Few later Christian writers of the
medieval period take negation so seriously or apply it in such a
radical fashion. And yet, despite their strong Neoplatonic
themes, the works of Dionysius slowly but surely permeated the
Scholasticism of the Latin West. In perpetrating one of the

---

[92] See the closing remark of *Enn.* V 3, 17.

[93] *D. N.* III, 1 (680B) and *E. H.* III, 3 (400A); see also *Enn.* V 5, 12.

[94] *Enn.* V 5, 7, 29-30.

greatest forgeries in early medieval times, Dionysius undoubtedly spared himself the indignity of condemnation and ensured
the survival of a method of theological analysis, without which
the Scholasticism of the West would have been greatly impover-
ished.

CHAPTER ELEVEN

JOHN SCOTTUS ERIUGENA: A NEGATIVE ONTOLOGY

A most fortunate moment in philosophical history, not only in
terms of the intellectual development of Western scholarship, but
also for the development of *apophasis*, took place when the
Byzantine Emperor, Michael II, sent the celebrated manuscript of
the works of Dionysius the Areopagite as a gift to Louis the Pious
of France.[1] Hilduin made the first translation, around 830-835.
Eriugena's translation, done at the request of Charles the Bald,
heralded the entry of this enigmatic Irishman into the pages of
intellectual history.[2] Eriugena's translation, although deficient in
places, ensured that the principles of negative theology embodied
in the writings of the Areopagite would become part of the heritage of Western Scholasticism.[3]

Eriugena's work, therefore, is an important landmark in the history of Western philosophy, for he was the first Western thinker to
have taken such a comprehensive account of Greek Christian
sources. The most important of these for an understanding of the
negative theology of Eriugena, are Gregory of Nyssa and the

---

[1] This manuscript is still extant: *ms. Paris B. N. gr. 437.*

[2] Of Eriugena's life we know very little, and the few details we do possess are
largely unsubstantiated, such as William of Malmesbury's account of his death (*a
pueris quos docebat grafiis perfossus*); whether this story is to be understood literally or symbolically is still a disputed question; see M. Cappuyns, *Jean Scot
Érigène: sa vie, son oeuvre, sa pensée*, p. 252.

[3] Robert Grosseteste, who complied an edition of the Dionysian works criticizes
Eriugena's translation on a number of occasions without actually naming him: he
notes that Eriugena uses *invisibilis* for ἀνόμματος and *mundus* for κόσμος, see
U, Gamba, ed. *Il commento di Roberto Grossatesta al 'De mystica theologia' del
Pseudo-Dionigi Areopagita* (Milan, 1942), p. 35 (11-12) and p. 48 (30-31). On
Eriugena's translation and use of the *Corpus Areopagiticum*, see R. Roques, 'Tra-
duction ou interprétation'.

Pseudo-Dionysius. In his main work, the *Periphyseon*, we see the convergence of a number of different adaptations of Neoplatonic systems and ideas: the Plotinian/Porphyrian form of Neoplatonism present in the writings of Augustine, Eriugena's most important Latin authority; the more obviously Plotinian form of Neoplatonism found in Gregory of Nyssa; the Dionysian adaptation of Proclean Neoplatonism, and finally the re-interpretation of Dionysius by Maximus the Confessor.[4] It is a testimony to the genius of Eriugena that his philosophical system united Greek East and Latin West at a time in intellectual history when learning had reached a low point.[5]

However, Eriugena's diverse sources do not always fit comfortably together. There is a general underlying tension in his thought, not only between Christian and Neoplatonic principles or between *recta ratio* and authority, but also a more specific tension which can be described as the Pseudo-Dionysius versus Augustine ('sanctissimus diuinusque theologus'[6]). This latter tension is especially evident with regard to the thematic of negative theology, although even in his earliest work, *De praedestinatione*, Eriugena was aware of the importance of negative theology.[7] The *apophasis* he encountered in both Gregory of Nyssa and the Pseudo-Dionysius undoubtedly strengthened the kind of negative theology he would have found in the writings of Augustine. The systematic method of affirmation and negation in the *Corpus Areopagiticum* gave a very definite focus to the negative theology and ontology present in the writings of Gregory of Nyssa.

---

[4] On Eriugena's Platonism see W. Beierwaltes, 'Marginalen zu Eriugenas "Platonismus"' and 'Eriugena's Platonism'.

[5] On the intellectual background of the ninth century, see D. Moran, *The Philosophy of John Scottus Eriugena*, ch. 1 and M. L. W. Laistner, *Thought and Letters in Western Europe*.

[6] 803B; unless otherwise noted, all references are to the *Periphyseon*; quotations from the *Periphyseon* I, II, III are taken from the edition by I. P. Sheldon-Williams, and *Periphyseon* IV and V from *Patrologia Latina*, 122.

[7] Quomodo enim signa sensibilia, id est corporibus adhaerentia, remotam illam omni sensu corporeo naturam ad liquidum significare possent, quae uix purgatissima mente attingitur omnem transcendens intellectum? IX, 1 (390B), ed. G. Madec. See B. McGinn, 'Negative Theology in John the Scot', pp. 232-233.

As a Christian philosopher, Eriugena always attempts to steer a middle course in philosophical analysis, a mid-position between *auctoritas* and *recta ratio;* it is *recta ratio* which is his guideline as he seeks clarification of the truth of the divine essence.[8] For Eriugena, as for Dionysius before him, Scripture presents itself as an intelligible world consisting of four levels: *praktikē, physikē, ethikē* and finally, *theologikē,* which is concerned with the highest part of truth for it is the supreme contemplation of the divine nature.[9] Although Scripture itself is the ultimate guide to truth, reason is the tool whereby the correct interpretation is determined.[10] Thus, the basic method of Dionysius becomes the guiding principle of Eriugena's philosophical analysis.

Apophasis and *Kataphasis*

Book I of the *Periphyseon* gives the initial impression that it will explain the first division of nature: *creat et non creatur* (that which creates but which is not created). In fact, this book turns out to be an elaboration and explanation of the inapplicability of the ten categories to the divine essence. However, this apparent digression on Eriugena's part turns out, in fact, to be no such thing, for he uses the categories as a methodical means of testing the workings of kataphatic and apophatic theology.[11] According to Eriugena, definition is concerned solely with created effects, with coming into being, and he describes this process in a very Plotinian way: form is the measurement imposed on unformed matter

---

[8] 441A, 509A and 511Bff: Vera enim auctoritas rectae rationi non obsistit neque recta ratio uerae auctoritati. Ambo siquidem ex uno fonte, diuina uidelicet sapientia, manare dubium non est.

[9] 599B and *Homily on the Prologue of John*, XIII, 291B-C; for a more detailed discussion of the role of Scripture in Eriugena's writings see R. Roques, 'L'écriture et son traitement chez Jean Scot Érigène'.

[10] Reason probes scriptural texts in order to come to a correct interpretation of the allegories and transferred meanings contained in them, see 509A, 511B, 513A-B and 1010B-C.

[11] 463A.

which places it within the realm of limitation and, therefore, definability.[12] Definition, then, pertains to the 'whatness' of a thing and its focus is finitude.[13] Therefore, what the human intellect can know about created things stems from the fact that these things are differentiated: they possess quantity, quality, relations, have a condition, are in place and time, and so on. In other words, we are able to define things and come to a knowledge of them through the *circumstantiae*, the accidents and attributes which differentiate them and surround their hidden essences.[14] Like Gregory of Nyssa, Eriugena argues that the *essentiae* of things cannot be known without the clothing of accidents.[15]

Can we then use the ten categories to come to an understanding of the nature which creates but is not itself created? It would be rather surprising, to say the least, if Eriugena had answered this question in the affirmative. Since the categories do not properly pertain to the divine essence – we do not perceive God's quality, quantity and so on – it follows that we cannot know the divine essence at all; unclothed as it is by attribute (in Dionysian terms, unveiled without symbol), it remains inaccessible to the human mind. This approach, then, is not a superfluous exercise, for the dialectic operative between the terms created and uncreated, provides a starting point for the two theologies: the one pertains to affirmations (*creat*), and the other to negations (*non creatur*).

In his analysis of the five modes of being and non-being found in the first few pages of the *Periphyseon*, Eriugena elaborates the Neoplatonic principle that every order of nature can be said to be since it is known by the orders above it, and it can be said not to be since it cannot be known by the orders below it.[16] Thus Eriugena finds the grounding metaphysical principle for denying that

---

[12] 590A-B.
[13] 591B-C, 483C, 590A-B and 484Aff.
[14] 443B-C; 487A-B; 586C-D, and 587A.
[15] 487A.
[16] 444C: Hac item ratione omnis ordo rationalis et intellectualis creaturae esse dicitur et non esse. Est enim quantum a superioribus uel a se ipso cognoscitur, non est autem quantum ab inferioribus se comprehendi non sinit.

reason or intellect can understand the divine essence: that which has the capacity to define something must be greater than that something: 'maius enim est quod diffinit quam quod diffinitur.'[17] The human mind can define only that which is below it in the hierarchical order of creation; hence, it cannot define God. However, according to Eriugena's theory of the unknowability of *essentia*, it is because the essences of things are hidden in the divine essence (in the Primordial Causes), that we can know about things only the specific accidents which surround their unknowable essences. Therefore, the mind cannot know the essences of things below it; it can know only that they exist through the application of the ten categories. We cannot say *what ousia* is, only *that* it is.[18] Since all things participate in the divine essence – there can be no being outside of God – all things are ultimately unknowable. However, the fact that creation *is* in a sense the 'attribute' of God, it enables the human intellect to come to the knowledge *that* the divine essence exists. Therefore, although the ten categories provide the enquirer with the rational tools for defining things as they exist, they do not apply to the divine essence: both it and its extension in all things remains inaccessible to the human intellect. The intellect can, therefore, come to some knowledge of essences clothed with accidents – veiled in symbol, as Dionysius would say – and yet this is simply the knowledge that they exist, not what they are in their essential being.

Therefore, *apophasis* and *kataphasis* in the *Periphyseon* are not simply highly-schematized theological devices whereby we are enabled to speak, or not speak, of the divine essence; rather, these two ways are to be understood in terms of Eriugena's basic metaphysical analysis of divine, indeed all reality. It is via the process of dialectic that Eriugena explains how the two theologies are grounded in an ontological understanding. For Eriugena, like Dionysius before him, the Neoplatonic theme of *exitus* and

---

[17] 485B and 766B; Eriugena disagrees with Augustine on this point; see *De lib. arb.* II, 12.

[18] 487A-B: OYCIAN per se ipsam diffinire et dicere quid sit nemo potest; ... OYCIA itaque nullo modo diffinitur quid est sed diffinitur quia est.

reditus, by which God is understood as *principium* and *finis*, underpins the four divisions of nature and is the means whereby they can be reduced, first to two categories and then, ultimately to one.[19] Although Eriugena insists that we think of the divine essence as *archē* and *telos* as the result of our deficient understanding; our 'double contemplation' of it refers only to the human level, for in itself the divine nature is unity.[20] It is, then, the metaphysical concepts of *processio* and *reversio* which ground the two theologies, much in the same way that 'unions' and 'distinctions' had grounded theology in Dionysius. In the *exitus* of all things from the initial darkness of God, created effects are lit up in the manifestation of being; in the *reditus* we find the converse movement: all things which had become clearly visible in their differentiation, in their being, return again to the darkness of the divine essence.[21] Creation, then, in its vast cosmic cycle, becomes the instance of God's self-manifestation before it returns again to itself.[22] This *occulti manifestatio,* the manifestation of the hiddenness of God's own being, is a theme which Eriugena would have encountered in his reading of the works of Dionysius especially, but it is a theme also present in Gregory of Nyssa.

The whole focus of Eriugena's thought can be stated in terms of the Dionysian problematic of how the divine essence, incomprehensible in itself, can be comprehended and spoken of in its manifestation in creation: how God is understood to be both transcendent and immanent, similar and different, hidden and revealed.

---

[19] The four divisions of *natura* are: *creat et non creatur, creatur et creat, creatur et non creat, nec creat nec creatur,* see 442A.

[20] 527B-528A, 549B, 640C-D, 927B-928D and 1010A; for an expostion of the double aspect of contemplation, see W. Beierwaltes, '*Duplex Theoria.* Zu einer Denkform Eriugenas', in *Begriff und Metapher,* pp. 39-64.

[21] In his exegesis of Gen. 1:1-2, Eriugena describes creation as a process of manifestation, that is of light, see 551Aff.

[22] For a general introduction to the notion of creation as divine theophany, see J. Trouillard, 'Érigène et la theophanie créatrice', W. Beierwaltes, '*Negati Affirmatio*: Welt als Metapher', and S. Gersh, 'Omnipresence in Eriugena'.

nothing is more hidden than it, nothing more present, difficult as to where it is, more difficult as to where it is not, an ineffable light ever present to the intellectual eyes of all and known to no intellect as to what it is, diffused through all things to infinity, is made both all things in all things and nothing in nothing.[23]

Although Eriugena's language sometimes conveys what has been called 'pantheistic overtones', he is always careful to assert that it is the notion of *participatio* which is the key to understanding how the divine essence is in all things. Thus, we find him developing the Augustinian, Nyssean, and ultimately Platonic notion that God alone is true being. It follows that all things which come from this Being, will do so by means of a sharing in it.[24] God alone is true being because he alone sustains and holds all things in being. Eriugena explains this notion using a favourite simile of Maximus: just as air filled with light appears to be nothing but light, so God, when joined to a creature, seems to be nothing but God.[25] Being and other attributes, then, are predicated of the divine essence because from it created effects receive the capacity to subsist.[26] Everything that exists, exists not in itself but through participation in that which truly exists: the divine essence.

Divine theophany (expressed in kataphatic terms) is the only way the incomprehensible essence of God can be comprehended and spoken of; even then it is a partial comprehension only.[27] Eriugena's theory that creation has a sacramental value as a sign of

---

[23] 668C: ... qua nihil secretius nihil praesentius, difficile ubi sit, difficilius ubi non sit, lux ineffabilis omnibus intellectualibus oculis semper praesens et a nullo intellectu cognoscitur quid sit, per omnia difussa in infinitum et fit in omnibus omnia et in nullo nullam.

[24] 516C, 518B, 523D and 528B.

[25] 450A: Sicut enim aer a sole illuminatus nihil aliud uidetur esse nisi lux, non quia sui naturam perdat sed quia lux in eo praeualeat ut idipsum luci esse aestimetur, sic humana natura deo adiuncta deus per omnia dicitur esse, non quod desinat esse natura sed quod diuinitatis participationem accipiat ut solus in ea deus esse uideatur; see *Ambigua* XCI (1073D).

[26] 454A and 589A; on the idea of participation see 630Aff.

[27] Eriugena follows Pseudo-Dionysius, *Ep.* I (1065A) in the notion that if we think we understand God, that is not God but a created manifestation of him: 920C; see also 446C-D; 448B-C, 539C; 633A; 681A, 865D-866A.

the divine essence again reflects his Dionysian inheritance: while kataphatic theology contains at least some vestige of truth, the statements of apophatic theology are more properly true since they pertain to the supreme transcendence of the divine.[28] Eriugena has no hesitation in following his great apophatic mentor in asserting that God is both the maker of all things and he is made in all things: 'deus itaque omnia est et omnia deus';[29] although he is careful to stress the fact that to speak of God 'being made' in all things is to be understood as metaphorical speech. The implications involved in the truth that the divine essence is in all things and that it surpasses all things, must be clarified; again this is a basic Dionysian problematic. *Divisio* and *resolutio* can be best understood as an attempt of the intellect to impose some degree of comprehensibility upon the incomprehensible divine essence in terms of the familiar Neoplatonic spatial metaphor of *processio* and *reversio*.

Speaking The Ineffable

The task of language, which endeavours to describe a reality both transcendent and immanent, admits of two sets of problems. In terms of the *Periphyseon*, the first problem is centered upon Eriugena's scepticism regarding the inadequacy of language as it attempts to describe the excellence of the ineffable, incomprehensible and unnameable divine essence. The second, and perhaps more complex problem, concerns his belief, following Gregory of Nyssa and Dionysius, that theological language is not totally divorced from its objective ground.[30] Throughout the *Periphyseon* we find Eriugena seeking to balance these two apparently contradictory positions. Problems of speech about God are necessarily expressions of metaphysical problems; speech about God is sim-

[28] 539C, 633A and 865D-866A.
[29] 650C-D.
[30] For more detailed discussion see W. Beierwaltes, 'Sprache und Sache. Reflexion zu Eriugenas Einschätzung von Leistung und Funktion der Sprache'.

ply a human expression of the manifestation of divine reality. Eriugena never lets the reader forget this point.

If God's essence is unknowable, then there cannot be any true speech about it – for one cannot in general speak about that which one does not know; as Eriugena says: the *innuatur* of language cannot signify the divine nature.[31] Yet there can be some speech about the divine nature since, metaphorically speaking, its effects, its creative activity and self-manifestation do have quantity, quality, are in place and time and so on. The term 'metaphorically' is stressed here because it is in this sense that all things can be predicated of God as cause. True contemplation, as Dionysius had proclaimed, will establish that God is none of the things predicated of him through metonymy.

Where Augustine had been reluctant to face the problem of resolving the apparent conflict between 'effable' and 'ineffable', Eriugena, following Gregory of Nyssa and Dionysius, did not fear to tread. In, true apophatic style, Eriugena asserts that although we cannot truly speak of the divine essence, nevertheless, we are permitted to do so by that essence itself:[32] we can utter the unutterable, name the unnameable, and 'comprehend' that which passes all understanding.[33] Eriugena gives a threefold reason why we must be able to speak of the divine essence: for the instruction of simple minds, for the refutation of heresies, and so that we might be able to praise and bless it.[34] In Plotinus's words, there must be some speech about it because pure negation does not indicate it; the 'sheer dread of holding to nothingness', forces one back to the realm of concept and language.[35] However, it is not simply human inadequacy which necessitates the utterance of the unutterable, for creation itself, as the manifestation of God, makes it possible to speak of the divine essence in terms of its effects. So, if one is not going to keep silent about

[31] 522C; see also 455D, 460C and *De praed.* 390B.
[32] 509B, 518B-D and 528C-D.
[33] 512C and 619C.
[34] 509B, 518C and 614C.
[35] VI 7, 38, 9-10 and VI 9, 3, 4-6.

the divine essence in 'true orthodox fashion', then the best way
to approach an understanding of it is via the two main branches
of theology.[36]
Since kataphatic statements rest on the fundamental logic of
God's casual activity, it is the immanence of the divine essence
which establishes their validity as theology. Kataphatic theology
is permitted to predicate of the divine essence all the things that
are; it does not say that it is those things, but that they take their
being from it.[37] However, the names and terms applied to God
through affirmations are predicted in a transferred sense only, a
metaphorical sense: *a creatura ad creatorem.*[38] Even the names
and terms used in Scripture – which uses words understood by
the finite intelligence – must be understood in this way.[39] One
further interesting point occurs in Eriugena's discussion of the
names used in Scripture and that is that they all signify the
divine essence itself which is simple and immutable. Following
Augustine, Gregory and Dionysius, Eriugena argues that willing,
loving, desiring, and other such terms as can be adapted for the
human intellect, do not represent separate things in God, but
together point to his ineffable essence.[40] Affirmative statements,
however, do attain some measure of validity in terms of speaking the truth about the divine essence for they clothe its naked-
ness in terms accessible to the human mind.[41] In this way,
kataphatic theology represents not the truth about the divine
essence, but a trace of the truth: that which the human mind can
think about it.

---

[36] 458A: Vna quidem, id est ΑΠΟΦΑΤΙΚΗ, diuinam essentiam seu substantiam
esse aliquid eorum quae sunt, id est quae dici aut intelligi possunt, negati altera
uero, ΚΑΤΑΦΑΤΙΚΗ, omnia quae sunt de ea praedicat et ideo affirmatiua dicitur – non ut confirmet aliquid esse eorum quae sunt, sed omnia quae ab ea sunt de
ea posse praedicari suadeat.
[37] 458B.
[38] 458C, 453B, 460C 512C and 516C.
[39] 404B, 453B, 458C, 460C, 463B, 508D, 511C-512C, 518C, 592C-D and 757D.
[40] 518B-C.
[41] 461C: Nudam siquidem omnique propria significatione relictam diuinam
essentiam talibus uocabulis uestit.

Apophasis and Super-Affirmation

The successive moment of apophatic theology in affirming God's absolute transcendence, must, therefore, deny that the divine essence is any of the things that are, for these things can be differentiated, defined and understood.[42] Negative statements are not metaphorically but literally predicated, and as such have more power to signify the ineffable essence as it is in itself.[43] Apophatic statements do not say that the divine essence is not, for example, truth, beauty or goodness: they say that it cannot be understood properly as truth, beauty or goodness. Thus, the affirmations which had clothed the divine essence in comprehensible terms, are stripped away, leaving it once more naked.[44] It is because negative statements do not completely deny the truth of positive statements that the two ways of theology are not opposed when applied to God; they are rather, an 'ineffable harmony', for the conflict remains at the verbal level and not at the level of inner meaning. 'Haec enim omnia pulchra ineffabilique armonia in unam concordiam colligit atque componit.'[45]

Although Eriugena does not advocate a systematic method of negation, moving from the lowest to the highest as Dionysius had done, he follows his lead in denying even the highest terms of all, terms which had traditionally been applied to God without question. The reason Eriugena gives is as follows: to each of the terms we can attribute to the divine essence, such as being, good, beauty, truth, and so on, belongs an opposite term: non-being, evil, ugliness, falsity.[46] All opposition necessarily belongs to the realm of differentiation, that is, to created nature, for there can be no opposition in the divine essence, not simply because the categories do not apply to it, but because things in discord cannot be eternal.[47]

---

[42] 458A.
[43] 510B-C, 522B, 684D, 686D, 758D and 771C.
[44] 461A-D.
[45] 517C.
[46] See 458Cff.
[47] 459B: Nam ea quae a se ipsis discrepant aeterna esse non possunt. Si enim aeterna essent a se inuicem non discreparent.

The affirmative way of theology says that God is good, while the negative way says that God is not good; such methods of speech do not pertain to the unity of the divine essence which is beyond all affirmations and negations.[48] Although Eriugena stresses God's transcendence over against his immanence, in preferring negation to affirmation, he too, like Dionysius, understands that the negation of all created attributes implies a *super*-affirmation: '*hyperphatic*' theology, in which both theologies are ultimately transcended.[49] The divine nature can be called 'essence', since it is the cause of essence, but properly speaking it is 'not essence' for essence stands in opposition to non-being. It is, therefore, '*superessentialis*', 'more than essence'.[50] In the same way, God is said to be 'goodness', 'not goodness' and 'more than goodness'. This reasoning is applied to all the divine names in the *Periphyseon*, and Eriugena follows Dionysius closely when he includes the term *deus*, for the divine essence is, properly speaking, *plus quam deus*.[51] Even the affirmation of trinity (which is a 'trace' of the truth) must be transcended, for the differentiated names of the trinity denote relationship rather than nature.[52] Here we find an echo of the old debate between Eunomius and the Cappadocians, a theme which had been absent in the Pseudo-Dionysius. Strictly speaking, although all terms are ruled out, it would appear that the divine essence can be signified by these '*plus quam*' terms.[53]

However, here we come up against the original difficulty which had troubled Augustine, for if these terms are said *proprie* of the divine essence, then it is not, after all, ineffable, a problem which did not arise for Dionysius. It is in his solution to this problem that

---

[48] 461B-D.

[49] 459C-460B.

[50] 459Dff.

[51] 459D-460A: Deus dicitur sed non proprie deus est. Visioni enim caecitas opponitur et uidenti non uidens. Igitur ΥΠΕΡΘΕΟΣ, id est plus quam deus. ΘΕΟΣ enim uidens interpretatur.

[52] 456D and 614C. See also 457C: Non enim potes negare talia nomina, id est patrem et filium, relatiua esse, non substantia.

[53] 460C-D.

we find Eriugena advancing a most interesting theory with regard to language, one which he would have encountered in his reading of Gregory of Nyssa.[54] He differentiates between the outward sense of a word and the inner meaning by which the object is signified by that outward form. Since the '*plus quam*' terms lack the negative particle, they cannot be included in apophatic statements, but neither can we include them in kataphatic statements, for that would not do justice to the inner meaning of such attributions. In outward form the construction of the statement, '*plus quam bonitas*', is positive, but its meaning conveys the sense of the negative, for it does not indicate the nature of 'more than good'.[55] Since we have gleaned no precise knowledge of what 'more than good' means, such statements cannot be regarded as definitions; they do not say what the divine essence is, only what it is not – a theme which is laden with distinct echoes of Philo, Plotinus, Gregory of Nyssa and Augustine, among others. According to Eriugena, '*plus quam*' statements do no more than point to the existence of the divine essence, they do not define its nature. We can, therefore, know that God is, his *quia est*, but not what he is, his *quid est*:[56] '... superat enim omne quod est et quod non est et nullo modo diffiniri potest quid sit'.[57]

According to Eriugena, even in the attempt to divest the symbol of its outward form in moving beyond the symbolic manifestation of God in creation, we do not appreciate its immediate intelligible content, except insofar as it is a symbol of God's manifestation. Thus, in the surpassing of created effects we are left simply with the knowledge *that* God is and that the divine essence exists as the cause of goodness, beauty and being in the created world. At this point it would seem that despite all Eriugena's attempts to work

[54] 461Aff.

[55] 462B-D: Nam quae dicit: Superessentialis est, non quod est dicit sed quid non est; dicit enim essentiam non esse sed plus quam essentiam, quid autem illud est quod plus quam essentia est non exprimit. Dicit enim deum non esse aliquod eorum quae sunt sed plus quam ea quae sunt esse, illud autem esse quid sit nullo modo diffinit.

[56] 522B, 634B, 779C, 919C and 1010D.

[57] 572D; see also 487B and 585B.

out a systematic method of speaking about God, what he is saying
is that effects simply point to causes and the cause of any given
thing cannot itself be that thing.[58] Like Plotinus and Dionysius,
Eriugena affirms that the cause of beauty, goodness, truth, and
being cannot itself be any of those things: it must be 'more than'
beauty, goodness, truth, and being. God is, properly speaking, *nihil*
(no thing), because he is supremely transcendent. Therefore, to say
that the cause of all is *nihil* is simply to say that it is '*plus quam
essentia*'.[59]

In the *Periphyseon*, the divine essence, even when described as
the reconciliation of all opposition in the '*hyperphatic*' way,
remains unknowable. Although Eriugena appears to have found a
satisfactory way of reconciling the two ways of theology, of
enabling us to *speak* about the transcendent-immanent in appropriate terms, the '*plus quam*' way asserts most strongly that language
must always be regarded as inadequate in the face of that which is
essentially unknowable in its 'inaccessible light'; nevertheless it
remains a pointer in the direction of God. The very fact that '*plus
quam*' statements do not define and limit the divine essence,
means that they do not yield positive knowledge and yet they provide the imagination with enough to think, at least partially, the
unthinkable.

Language, then, is an expression of metaphysical reality, for the
visible world contains the symbols which point to the divine; created effects, as the corporeal expression of the incorporeal, are
reflected in the symbolic statements of kataphatic theology.[60]
Although apophatic statements speak the truth about the divine
essence as it is in itself, '*plus quam*' statements are still rooted in

[58] 482A, 589B and 622A.

[59] 634Bff and 680D: Ineffabilem et incomprehensibilem diuinae bonitas inacces-
sibilemque claritatem omnibus intellectibus sine humanis sine angelicis incogni-
tam – superessentialis est enim et supernaturalis. On the notion of *nihil* and *super-
essentia* see D. Duclow, 'Divine Nothingness and Self-Creation in John Scottus
Eriugena'.

[60] See 551C-D and 633B-C. The role of language in the *Periphyseon* is discussed
in the following articles by W. Beierwaltes, 'Sprache und Sache', and '*Negati
affirmatio*: Welt als Metapher'.

symbolic manifestation and do no more than stretch both thought and word, as far as they can be stretched, in the direction of God. Words which attempt to convey the nature of the divine essence in comprehensible form lie at a third remove from the reality they seek to express: language is the verbal expression of the corporeal manifestation of the incorporeal. Its authenticity derives from the fact that creation is in some sense part of the divine. An interesting parallel between language and divine creation is to be found in Eriugena's account of creation as the Father 'speaking' the reasons for all things thought in the *Verbum*.[61] The exteriorization of inner thought in the *processio* of all things points to a reversal in the *resolutio* – that is, movement away from speech to thought. Eriugena echoes a most Augustinian sentiment when he notes that the trinity is contemplated at a deeper and truer level than it can be expressed in speech, and is understood more deeply than it is contemplated and it *is* deeper and truer than it is understood, for it passes all understanding.[62] Language can never escape fully from its metaphorical moorings even when the symbol has been abandoned as far as it is possible to do so; neither can thought.

Just as the human mind divides divine reality in the attempt to understand God under the aspects of *principium* and *finis*, language reflects this duality of thought. It is thus that the famous dialectical statements of the *Periphyseon* can be understood correctly: the absolute unity of the divine essence ultimately resolves all distinction and opposition into 'a beautiful and ineffable harmony'.[63] Although Eriugena had very painstakingly worked out the '*plus quam*' method of theological speech, the dialectical bent of his mind turns again and again, not to affirmation, negation and super-affirmation, but to the double truth of the unity of the divine essence. In his dialectical expression of the 'dual' nature of God,

[61] 642B and 441A.

[62] 614B-C: Sed haec altius ac uerius cogitantur quam sermone proferuntur et altius ac uerius intelliguntur quam cogitantur, altius autem ac uerius sunt quam intelliguntur; omnem siquidem intellectum superant; see *De trin.* V, 3 (4), VII, 4 (7) and *De civ. Dei.* X, 13.

[63] 517C.

Eriugena confronts the reader with the full force of the inexplicable nature of God as the reconciliation of all opposites: God is the 'infinitas omnium infinitatum', 'oppositorum oppositio', 'contrariorum contrarietas'.[64] On the verbal level we will always find a tension between the notion of transcendence and immanence:

> For everything that is understood and sensed is nothing else but the apparition of what is not apparent, the manifestation of the hidden, the affirmation of the negated, the comprehension of the incomprehensible, the utterance of the unutterable, the access to the inaccessible, the understanding of the unintelligible, the body of the bodiless, the essence of the superessential, the form of the formless...[65]

God is 'mensura omnium sine mensura et numerus sine numero et pondus .... sine pondere'; he is the unformed form of all things, and that which contains all things without being contained.[66] This kind of understanding of the divine essence, which Eriugena develops more fully than Dionysius had done, reflects the metaphysical duality of *natura*.

Ignorantia and Divine Darkness

It is Eriugena's original discussion of the five modes of being and non-being in the first few pages of the *Periphyseon* that gives focus to the idea that not knowing is true knowing; he argues to this theory as follows. Human nature cannot know itself because its essence resides in the divine essence which is unknowable; it can know its own *quia est,* but not its *quid est.*[67]

[64] 517B-C, 515A and 453A-B.

[65] 633A-B: Omne enim quod intelligitur et sentitur nihil aliud est nisi non apparentis apparitio, occulti manifestatio, negati affirmatio, incomprehensibilis comprehensio, (ineffabilis fatus, inaccessibilis accessus), inintelligibilis intellectus, incorporalis corpus, superessentialis essentia, informis forma...; see also 678C and 680D-681A.

[66] 669B; see also 590B and 633B. The phrase 'unformed form' (599D-600B; 546D-547A and 525A) also occurs in Plotinus: VI 7, 33, 4; VI 7, 17, 35-36 and V 5, 6, 4-5 and in Augustine: *De trin.* V, 1 (2) and *Conf.* XIII, 6 .

[67] 768A-B, 770B, 443C and 771B; see B. McGinn, 'The Negative Element in the Anthropology of John the Scot'.

God alone is capable of defining human nature.[68] Thus far, Eriugena seems to hold a fairly reasonable position, and one which owes a debt to Gregory of Nyssa, but what about the idea that God cannot know his own essence? Surely this would appear to be taking negative theology too far in that it appears to contradict the traditional notion of God's omniscience? The doctrine that God cannot know himself is not original to Eriugena for it comes from the Neoplatonic, and specifically Plotinian criticism of Aristotle's self-thinking thought. According to Plotinus, if the One could think even self-thought, that idea would introduce duality into his nature, for the One would become both subject and object; since it is absolutely one, it cannot have thought.[69] In the same way Eriugena argues that if God could understand himself, he would become an object, a 'what', and he could then define himself. Since Eriugena has already established that God is not a 'what', (he possesses none of the attributes necessary for definition), it follows that he is unlimited, undefinable, and infinite.[70] If God could define himself, he would then be infinite and undefinable only to creatures and not to himself. The divine essence, as the uncreated, has none to define him, not even himself.[71]

At this point it would seem that Eriugena has taken *apophasis* to its utmost limits, he has reached an impasse: God cannot know himself, the human intellect cannot know God (except for the fact that he exists), or itself, neither can it know the created essences of the things of creation. The ultimate resolution to this problem is to be found in negation itself: just as we understand the divine essence more truly when we deny all things of it, so too God's ignorance of himself is an understanding that he is none of the things of creation. *Divina ignorantia* thus becomes an 'ineffable

[68] 770B and 768B: Possumus ergo hominem definire sic: homo est notio quaedam intellectualis in mente diuina aeternaliter facta.

[69] *Enn.* III 8, 9, 15.

[70] 589B-C, 590C, 470C-474C, 482C-483C and 586B-C.

[71] 587B-C, 586Bff and 589B: Quomodo igitur diuina natura se ipsam potest intelligere quid sit cum nihil sit?

wisdom', and it is wisdom precisely because God knows that he is 'more than' all things.[72]

In the same way, human ignorance of the divine essence is really true wisdom which comes from the realization that God is not to be understood in terms of the things that exist; we know the divine essence better when we know what it is not.[73] This Dionysian, and indeed Augustinian sentiment, becomes the key to a fuller understanding of *apophasis* in the *Periphyseon*, much as it had done in the *Mystical Theology* of Dionysius. We know God truly when we know that he is not one of created things; in this way our knowledge becomes true wisdom.[74] In this respect, Eriugena finds both Augustine and Dionysius in agreement.[75]

Thus, knowing that God is more than all things is the knowing which is above both knowing and unknowing; it is knowledge *quia est*, for knowledge *quid est* is absolutely ruled out. There is, then, according to Eriugena some positive content in this kind of knowing, but since it is 'unknowing knowing' it can no longer be described from a creaturely point of view. In the end, Eriugena does not, indeed he can not explain further, for the process whereby unknowing is transformed into knowing remains, in the tradition of all the great masters of *apophasis*, an ineffable mystery.[76] It would seem, then, that *recta ratio* has not fully refined speech and knowledge out of existence; but it would also appear that philosophical analysis can go no further, for the concept of unknowability does not have much credibility in any metaphysical analysis and the positive content of such knowing is not recogniz-

[72] 593C-D: Ipsius enim ignorantia ineffabilis est intelligentia; see 590B-D, 594A, 596D and 598A. See also 596D where Eriugena appears to make a distinction between God's *cognoscere* and his *intelligere*.

[73] 597D and 510B-C.

[74] 597D-598A, 686D and 771C.

[75] 597D: Nam quod sancti patres, Augustinum dico et Dionysium, de deo uerissime pronuntiant – Augustinus quidem 'qui melius (inquit) nesciendo scitur', Dionysius autem 'cuius ignorantia uera est sapientia' – non solum de intellectibus qui eum pie studioseque quaerunt uerum etiam de se ipso intelligendum opinor.

[76] 976C.

able as knowing according to the normal epistemological categories operative at the level of the knowing subject.

It is clear, then, that Eriugena does not diverge significantly from his Dionysian source in asserting the impossibility of attaining to a knowledge of the divine essence; he does differ notably from the Areopagite in that he appears to give little place to the Dionysian ascent into the realm of mystical theology. This difference is most apparent in Eriugena's exposition of the dark/cloud metaphor. He does not (except for one fleeting mention in Book V[77]) make use of the great Dionysian exegesis of the cloud of Sinai as expressive of the ultimate ontological and epistemological condition of the restored soul. Instead, we find him focusing upon the clouds of the New Testament: the clouds of the Ascension and Transfiguration, but more especially the cloud of heaven upon which the Son of Man will come (Matt. 26:64) and the clouds into which those who have died with Christ will be taken up to meet with the Lord in the air (1Thess. 4:17).[78] It is this eschatological dimension of Eriugena's thought which puts it at one remove from the more immediate spiritual and epistemological significance of 'cloud' to be found in Gregory of Nyssa and in Dionysius.[79]

In the *Periphyseon*, clouds symbolize the means of experiencing theophany; because God is invisible in himself, he can be seen only in cloud: 'Deus enim omnino nulli creaturae visibilis per seipsum est, sed in nubibus theoriae videtur'.[80] The ascent into the 'cloud of contemplation' is explained by Eriugena as the highest theophany, the vision of God 'face to face',[81] wherein each will 'see' God according to capacity.[82] It is this aspect of Eriugena's

[77] 999A; he does refer once in the *Commentary on the Gospel of John* to vision via the cloud: I xxv (302B).
[78] 998Aff and 945D-946A. At this point I note that Eriugena also uses cloud symbolism in a privative sense: the cloud of fleshy thoughts and the cloud of error and faithlessness of the anti-christ, see 683C and 996A-B.
[79] In fact, Eriugena repeats Ambrose's most un-apophatic description of cloud: the cloud of light which moistens the mind with the dew of faith and is sent by the word; see 1000A-B.
[80] 905C; see also 945C-D.
[81] 926 C-D; see also *Commentary on the Gospel of John*, I xxv (302A-B).
[82] 876B and 945C-D.

thought – which carries with it something of the sense of vision – that sets him apart from the Dionysian portrayal of the blinded soul throwing itself against the ray of divine darkness. In the *Periphyseon,* the eyes of the intellect are open, even though they do not see the hidden essence of the divine nature.

Eriugena follows Gregory of Nyssa in the idea that the quest for God is endless: God is found (as that) in theophany, but is not found as to what he is in himself.[83] Even in the final *resolutio,* neither human nor angel behold the divine essence unveiled, but through theophany.[84] The Seraphim cover their feet and their faces before the splendour of God, a sign of the limitation of their vision.[85] However, paradoxically, Eriugena's explanation of final theophany hinges on the great Platonic, and indeed biblical, theme of light: the divine essence is itself light, 'inaccessible light', which blinds the eye as the eye of the sun-gazer is blinded; it is thus that it is called darkness.[86] Here we find the notion of negation and deprivation linked to the positive idea of plenitude. Yet, in the last analysis, the soul is still left without knowledge or sight of the divine essence upon which it has returned to gaze. Even the final theophany of the righteous (the vision of God 'face to face') is a manifestation of God.[87] Eriugena argues quite consistently that the essence of God cannot be seen: 'Non ergo ipsum deum per se ipsum uidebimus, quia neque angeli uident (hoc enim omni creaturae impossibile est)'.[88] Although Eriugena stresses the cosmic nature of the process of *reditus,* there is one passage in the *Periphyseon* where he comes very close to the Dionysian explication

---

[83] 919C: ... semper quaerit, mirabilique pacto quadammodo inuenit, quod quaerit, et non inuenit, quia inuenire non potest. Inuenit autem per theophanias, per naturae uero diuinae per seipsam contemplationem non inuenit.

[84] 447Bff; 557B; 773C; 905C; 920A, and 926C.

[85] Is. 6: 1; see 668A-C and 614D-615A.

[86] 551C; 557B; 634B; 681B-C; 920A-B; 1010C; 1015C, and 1020D.

[87] Eriugena's understanding of final theophany as the 'vision' of God 'face to face' betrays an Augustinian theme, see J. J. O'Meara, 'Eriugena's Use of Augustine in his Teaching on the Return of the Soul and the Vision of God'; see also D. Carabine, 'Eriugena's Use of the Symbolism of Light, Cloud and Darkness in the *Periphyseon*', in *Eriugena East and West.*

[88] 448C.

of mystical theology. None can draw near to God unless the sensible and intelligible realms are abandoned. Then, through the unknowing of created nature, one can be united, as far as that is possible, to that nature of which there can be no reasoning, understanding nor word.[89] However, this text is singular in the *Periphyseon*; for the most part, the restoration to unity is described as a collective process, in terms of different classes of beings. I can find very little evidence to support the view that Eriugena did follow Dionysius up the cloud-wreathed mountain into the darkness of mystical theology.[90]

The negative theology to be found in the *Periphyseon* constitutes a broadening out of the frontiers of Dionysian negative theology, as we find Eriugena elaborating ideas he encountered in his reading of the Eastern Fathers, especially those of Gregory of Nyssa. Yet, there remains one vital and striking difference between the negative theology of Dionysius and that of Eriugena: in the latter gone is the lonely soul who struggles relentlessly in the purification both of itself and of its God-concepts, in the hope of attaining to unity with God. Instead, we find Eriugena centre his attention upon a more cosmic kind of *resolutio* which does not depend on individual purification except at the highest level of the deified. The individual ascent of the soul through the *via negativa,* as presented by Pseudo-Dionysius, would appear to loose its sharp edge in the *Periphyseon;* even so Eriugena did not escape the condemnations to which *apophasis* leaves itself open by the very nature of its less categorical statements concerning the divine.

It is extremely difficult to assess the influence of Eriugena on the development of *apophasis* in the Latin West, for it was Diony-

---

[89] 510C: ... ad quem nemo potest accedere nisi prius corroborato mentis itinere sensus omnes deserat et intellectuales operationes et sensibilia et omne quod est et quod non est et ad unitatem (ut possibile est) inscius restituatur ipsius qui est super omnem essentiam et intelligentiam, cuius neque ratio est neque intelligentia neque dicitur neque intelligitur neque nomen eius est neque uerbum.

[90] On the nature of return in Eriugena see S. Gersh, 'The Structure of the Return in Eriugena's *Periphyseon*'. A. M. Haas argues that Eriugena did take note of the mystical ascent of the soul, see his article in *Eriugena Redivivus*.

sius himself who appears to have exerted the stronger influence. In the tenth and eleventh centuries, the *Periphyseon* was generally seen as a dialectical exercise on the categories and the more speculative elements of Eriugena's thought were to a large extent ignored.[91] Although the twelfth century saw an awakening of interest in Eriugena, the successive condemnations associated with the *Periphyseon* ensured that its influence was marginal after 1225.[92] However, there are unmistakable Eriugenian traces in the writings of Meister Eckhart and Nicholas of Cusa. Whatever the extent of his influence upon medieval thought, Eriugena confronted the same problematic as did Plotinus, Gregory of Nyssa, Pseudo-Dionysius (and later Meister Eckhart and Nicholas of Cusa). What is shared by these thinkers is a basic scepticism regarding the inadequacy of language and the possibility of knowing that which is essentially ineffable and unknowable.

---

[91] See D. Moran, *The Philosophy of John Scottus Eriugena*, pp. 65-67 and pp. 271-281.

[92] See É. Jeauneau, 'Le Renouveau érigénien du XIIe siecle', in *Eriugena Redivivus*. Recent research has suggested that the influence of Eriugena can be seen in some of the less *a priori* scholars of the medieval period, such as Robert Grosseteste; see J. J. McEvoy, 'Ioannes Scottus Eriugena and Robert Grosseteste: An Ambiguous Influence', in *Eriugena Redivivus*.

EPILOGUE

The first time I saw a Kingfisher, a minute flash of brilliant blue as it swooped into the river to catch a fish, I was enthralled. I wanted to find out more about this little bird and searched through many books. I was disappointed, for none of the artists' reproductions fully caught its magnificent colour, Kingfisher Blue. We have named our colour after the bird, for no other words can describe its unique iridescence. In a similar fashion, followers of the *via negativa* have affirmed that we cannot adequately describe the divine nature, except in such terms as 'bright darkness', ineffable word', 'silent music'. Moses Maimonides has the following to say:

> In the contemplation of his essence, our comprehension and knowledge prove insufficient; in the examination of his works ... our knowledge proves to be in ignorance, and in the endeavour to extol him in words, all our efforts in speech are more weakness and failure.[1]

Here Maimonides encapsulates the essential principles of the *via negativa*, sentiments shared by many of the authors examined in this volume. However, the fact that God is ineffable, unnameable and unknowable, is not the whole story, for negative theology is not simply a theory of negative language. It can, of course, remain at the intellectual level, even up to the point of the *negatio negationis*, but it can also be a springboard into the search for unity with the transcendent. The kind of negative theology to be found in Plotinus, Proclus, Gregory of Nyssa and the Pseudo-Dionysius does not stop at pure negation, but reaches further and further towards the boundary of the unknowable transcendent. The journey's end for these lovers of wisdom is ultimately an unspeakable unity with the unknowable God.

---

[1] Moses Maimonides, *The Guide for the Perplexed*, trans. M. Friedländer, 2nd ed. rev. (New York, 1956), p. 83.

The general aim of *apophasis*, that is, freeing the idea of God from rational, conceptual representation and its successive embodiment in language, is an extremely difficult task for we do not have anything with which to replace language. The very fact that negative theology does not always remain on the level of philosophical/theological discourse leaves it vulnerable to misinterpretation. Many advocates of the negative way have advised that we become aware of the dangers involved in the expression of the divine nature. Nicholas of Cusa remarked that the works of Eriugena and Eckhart should never have been given to 'the weak-eyed ones' who would misunderstand them.[2] The dialectical method favoured by advocates of the negative way necessitates a transcending of its own tension and opposition. Any philosophical system which seeks to examine the relationship between the finite and the infinite, whether or not the method used is expressed in terms of negative theology, finds that it is a difficult task to which words do not easily lend themselves.

The application of the two theologies, both positive and negative, has a metaphysical foundation which is most clearly demonstrated in the Plotinian assertion that the One is all things and no thing.[3] The Christian expression of this truth is the affirmation of the transcendence and immanence of God. Therefore, all theological speech stresses one or other aspect of this truth and must be understood as an expression of the human understanding of divine reality. On the verbal level there will always be a tension underlying the intellect's understanding of the dialectic operative between the idea of transcendence and immanence.

In the end, it would seem that the negative theology raises more questions than it can answer, at least in philosophical terms. The familiar tension of the dialectical method of analysis and resolution, as it applies to *apophasis*, is a process which may, in the last analysis, lead into the realm of unity with the unknown, an area not open to general exploration. Ultimately, therefore, philosophi-

---

[2] *Apologia doctae ignorantiae*, ed. R. Klibansky, vol. 1 (Leipzig, 1932), pp. 29-30.

[3] Enn. V 2, 2, 26-28; see also Enn. V 2, 1, 1-2.

cal analysis can deal with negative theology only up to a certain point: after that, it too, like one who has not been ' There', as Plotinus would put it, eventually becomes bewildered. From an apophatic viewpoint, the only way to cross the distance that is seen to exist between the soul and the One, between the soul and God, is the breakdown and negation of all the normal epistemological categories of subject and object, which are, of course, the basis for all cognition. If as philosophers today, we are left bereft of our tools of rational analysis, in that we are no longer on solid ground with a sure footing in a familiar method of philosophy, either we must admit that a metaphysics which involves negative theology is nonsense, or else take up the challenge to rethink the role of philosophical analysis, keeping in mind that philosophy, as the love of wisdom, can sometimes lead into the presence of the Unknowable.

BIBLIOGRAPHY I

Primary Texts

Armstrong, A. H., *Plotinus*, 7 vols. Loeb Classical Library (Cambridge Massachusetts/London, 1978-1988).

Saint Augustine, *Aurelii Augustini Opera*, Corpus Christianorum, Series Latina (Turnhout, 1962-). Individual volume numbers are given in the footnotes.

Beaujeu, J., *Apulée* (Paris, 1973).

Brisson, L. et al., *Porphyre. La vie de Plotin*, vol. II (Paris, 1992).

Burnet, J., *Platonis Opera*, 6 vols. (Oxford, 1899-1913).

Cohn, L. and Wendland, P., *Philonis Alexandrinis Opera Quae Supersunt*, 6 vols (Berlin, 1886-1915).

Colson, F. H. and Whitaker, G. H., *Philo*, Loeb Classical Library, 10 vols. 2 suppl. vols. ed. R. Marcus (London, 1930-1953).

Corderius, B., *Patrologiae Graecae*, vol. III (Paris, 1857), reprint (Turnhout, 1977).

Cousin, V., *Procli Commentarius in Platonis Parmenidem*, Opera Inedita III, reprint (Hildesheim/New York, 1980).

Des Places, É., *Numénius. Fragments* (Paris, 1973).

De Vogel, C. J., *Greek Philosophy*, 3 vols. (Leiden, 1950/1960/1964).

Diels, H., *Die Fragmente der Vorsokratiker*, 3 vols. revised W. Kranz (Berlin, 1951-1952).

Diels, H., *Doxographi Graeci*, 3rd ed. (Berlin, 1958).

Diogenes Laertius, *Lives of the Eminent Philosophers*, vol. I, Loeb Classical Library (1925).

Dodds, E. R., *The Elements of Theology*, 2nd ed. (Oxford, 1963).

Floss, H. J., *Patrologia Latinae*, vol. 122 (1865), *Periphyseon*, Books IV and V.

Hadot, P., *Porphyre et Victorinus*, vol. 2 (Paris, 1968).

Helm, R., *Apuleius III. Apologia* (Leipzig, 1963).

Henry, P. and Schwyzer, H.-R., *Plotini Opera*, 3 vols. (Paris/Brussels/Leiden, 1951/1959/1973).

Hobein, H., *Maximi Tyrii. Philosophumena* (Leipzig, 1910).

Jaeger, W. ed., *Gregorii Nysseni Opera* (Leiden, 1952-). Individual volume numbers are given in the footnotes.

Jeanneau, É., *Homélie sur le Prologue de Jean*, Sources Chrétiennes, 151 (Paris, 1969).

Jeauneau, É., *Commentaire sur l'Évangelie de Jean*, Sources Chréti-ennes, 180 (Paris, 1972).

Klibansky, R. and Labowsky C., *Procli Commentarium in Parmenidem*, Plato Latinus, vol. III, reprint (Nendeln/Liechenstein, 1973).

Koetschau, P., *Origenes Werke*, vol. 2 (Leipzig, 1899).

Louis, P., *Albinus. Epitome* (Paris, 1945).

Madec, G., *De divina praedestinatione liber*, Corpus Christianorum, Continuatio Mediaevalis, 50 (Turnhout, 1978).

Nock, A. D. and Festugière, A.-J., *Corpus Hermeticum*, 4 vols. (Paris, 1972).

Roques, R., *La hiérarchie céleste*, Sources Chrétiennes, 58 (Paris, 1970).

Rousseau, A. and Doutreleau, L., *Irenaeus. Adversus haereses* (Paris, 1979).

Saffrey, H. D. and Westerink, L. G., *Proclus. Théologie Planonicienne*, 5 vols. (Paris, 1968/74/78/81/87).

Schula, B. R. *Corpus Dionysiacum I: Pseudo-Dionysius Areopagita. De divinis nominibus*, Patristische Texte und Studien, 33 (Berlin, 1991).

Scott, W., *Hermetica*, vol. I (Oxford, 1924).

Sheldon-Williams, I. P., *Periphyseon*, Scriptores Latini Hiberniae (The Dublin Institute for Advanced Studies, 1968, 1972, 1981), *Periphyseon*, Books I-III.

Tarán, L., *Speusippus of Athens* (Leiden, 1981).

Thesleff, H., *The Pythagorean Texts of the Hellenistic Period* (Abo, 1965).

Thomas, P., *Apuleius. De Philosophia Libri* (Leipzig, 1921).

Wendland, P., *Hippolytus. Refutatio omnium haeresium* (Leipzig, 1916).

BIBLIOGRAPHY II

General Works on Negative Theology, Plato and the Middle Platonists

Adam, J., *The Vitality of Platonism and Other Essays* (Cambridge, 1911).

Adkins, A. W. H., 'Greek Religions', in *Historica Religionum. Handbook for the History of Religions*, eds. C. J. Bleekar and G. Widengran (Leiden, 1969), p. 377ff.

Armstrong, A. H., 'Negative Theology, Myth and Incarnation', in *Neoplatonism and Christian Thought*, ed. D. J. O'Meara (Albany, 1982), pp. 213-222.

Armstrong, A. H., 'The Escape of the One', in *Plotinian and Christian Studies*, Variorum Reprints, vol. I (London, 1979), no. XXIII.

Armstrong, A. H., 'The Gods in Plato, Plotinus and Epicurus', *Classical Quarterly*, 32 (1938), pp. 190-196.

Armstrong, A. H., *The Architecture of the Intelligible Universe in the Philosophy of Plotinus* (Cambridge, 1940).

Armstrong, A. H., 'The Hidden and the Open in Hellenic Thought', in *Hellenic and Christian Studies,* Variorum Reprints, vol. II (London, 1990), no. V.

Armstrong, A. H., 'On Not Knowing Too Much About God', Variorum Reprints II, no. XV.

Armstrong, A. H., *An Introduction To Ancient Philosophy*, 2nd ed. reprint (London, 1984).

Armstrong, A. H., 'The Background of the Doctrine that Intelligibles are not Outside the Intellect', in *Les sources de Plotin*, Entretiens Hardt, vol. 5 (Vandoeuvres-Geneva, 1960), pp. 391-425.

Armstrong, A. H., 'Apophatic-Kataphatic Tensions in Religious Thought from the Third to the Sixth Century AD.', in *From Augustine to Eriugena*. Essays on Neoplatonism and Christianity in Honour of John O'Meara, eds. F. X. Martin and J. A. Richmond, (Washington, 1991), pp. 12-21.

Baltes, M., 'Numenios von Apamea und der platonische *Timaios*', *Vigiliae Christianae*, 29 (1975), pp. 241-270.

Baxter, T., *The Cratylus, Plato's Critique of Naming*, Philosophia Antiqua Series, 58 (Leiden/New York, 1992).

Beierwaltes, W., 'Negati Affirmatio: Welt als Metapher', in *Jean Scot Érigène et l'histoire de la philosophie*, ed R. Roques (Paris, 1977), pp. 263-275.

Betz, H. D., *Plutarch's Theological Writings and Early Christian Literature* (Leiden, 1975).

Bianchi, U. ed., *Le Origini dello gnosticismo*, Papers of the Messina Colloquium, 1966 (Leiden, 1970).

Boyancé, P., 'Fulvius Nobilitor et le Dieu ineffable', *Revue de Philologie*, 29 (1955), pp. 172-192.

Brumbaugh, R. S., *Plato on the One: The Hypothesis in the 'Parmenides'* (Yale University Press, 1961).

Burkert, W., *Lore and Science in Ancient Pythagoreanism* (Camb. Mass., 1972).

Burnet, J., *Greek Philosophy I. Thales to Plato* (London, 1920).

Carabine, D., 'Apophasis East and West', *Recherches de Théologie ancienne et médiévale*, 55 (1988), pp. 5-29.

Chadwick, H., *Origen. Contra Celsum* (Cambridge, 1953).

Cherniss, H., *The Riddle of the Early Academy* (Berkeley, 1945).

Cornford, F. M., *Plato and Parmenides* (London, 1939).

Curd, P. K., 'Parmenidean Monism', *Phronesis*, 36 (1991), pp. 241-264.

Daly, C. B., 'The Knowableness of God', *Philosophical Studies*, 11 (1959), pp. 90-137.

Daniélou, J., *Gospel Message and Hellenistic Culture*, trans. J. A. Baker (London, 1973).

Delatte, A., *Études sur la littérature pythagoricienne* (Geneva, 1974).

Des Places, É. 'Le Platonisme moyen au IIe siècle ap. J.-C.: Numénius et Atticus', *Koinonia*, 8 (1984), pp. 7-15.

Des Places, É., 'Numénius et la Bible', *Études platoniciennes. 1929-1979* (Leiden, 1981), pp. 310-315.

Des Places, É., 'Du dieu jaloux au nom incommunicable', in *Études platoniciennes 1929-1979* (Leiden, 1981), pp. 305-309.

Des Places, É, *La religion grecque: dieux, cultes, rites et sentiment religieux dans la Grèce antique* (Paris, 1969).

De Vogel, C. J., *Pythagoras and Early Pythagoreanism* (Assen, 1966).

De Vogel, C. J., 'A la recherche des étapes prècis entre Platon et le néoplatonisme', *Mnemosyne*, series IV, 7 (1954), pp. 111-122.

De Vogel, C. J., 'Problems Concerning Later Platonism I', *Mnemosyne*, series IV, 2 (1949), pp. 197-216; pp. 299-318.

De Vogel, C. J., 'Der sog. Mittelplatonismus, Überwiegend eine Philosophie der Diesseigkeit?', in *Platonismus und christentum*, Festschrift for H. Dörrie, eds. H.-D. Blume and F. Mann (Münster, 1983), pp. 277-302.

De Vogel, C. J., *Greek Philosophy*, 3 vols. (Leiden, 1950-1964).

Dillon, J., *The Middle Platonists* (London, 1977).

Dillon, J. and Long, A. A. eds. *The Question of 'Eclecticism'. Studies in Later Greek Philosophy* (University of California Press, 1988).

Dodds, E. R., 'The *Parmenides* of Plato and the Origin of the Neoplatonic "One"', *Classical Quarterly*, 22 (1928), pp. 129-142.

Dodds, E. R., *The Greeks and The Irrational* (Los Angeles, 1951).

Dodds, E. R., *Pagan and Christian in an Age of Anxiety* (Cambridge, 1965).

Dodds, E. R., 'Numenius and Ammonius', in *Les Sources de Plotin*, Entretiens Hardt, vol. 5, pp. 3-61.

Dörrie, H., *Platonica Minora* (Munich, 1976).

Dörrie, H., 'Der Platoniker Eudorus von Alexandreia', in *Platonica Minora*, pp. 297-309.

Dörrie, H., 'Zum Ursprung der Neuplatonischen Hypostasenlehre', in *Platonica Minora*, pp. 286-296.

Dörrie, H., 'Die Platonische Theologie des Kelsos', in *Platonica Minora*, pp. 229-262.

Dörrie, H., Die Frage nach dem Transzendenten im Mittelplatonismus', in *Les sources de Plotin*, Entretiens Hardt, vol. 5, pp. 191-241.

Eliade, M., *Myth and Reality* (London, 1964).

Eliade, M., *The Sacred and the Profane*, trans. W. R. Trask (New York/London, 1959).

Festugière, A.-J., *Le Dieu inconnu et la gnose. La revelation d'Hermès Trismégiste*, vol. 4 (Paris, 1954).

Festugière, A.-J., *Contemplation et vie contemplative selon Platon* (Paris, 1967).

Findlay, J. N., Plato. *The Written and Unwritten Doctrines* (London, 1974).

Findlay, J. N., *Ascent to the Absolute* (London, 1970).

Finley, M. I., *The Legacy of Greece* (Oxford, 1981).

Foerster, W., *Gnosis. A Selection of Gnostic Texts*, 2 vols. trans. R. McL. Wilson (Oxford, 1972).

Frede, M., *Essays in Ancient Philosophy* (Minneapolis, 1987).

Freeman, K., *Ancilla to the Pre-Socratic Philosophers* (Oxford, 1948).

Friedländer, P., *Plato. An Introduction*, trans. H. Meyerhoff (New York, 1958).

Gersh, S., *Middle Platonism and Neoplatonism. The Latin Tradition*, vol. 1 (Indiana, 1986).

Grant, R. M., *Gnosticism. An Anthology* (London, 1961).

Grant, R. M., 'Gnostic Origins and the Basilideans of Irenaeus', *Vigiliae Christianae*, 13 (1959), pp. 121-125.

Grant, F. C., *Hellenistic Religions* (New York, 1953).

Guérard, C., 'La théologie négative dans l'apophatisme grec', *Revue des sciences philosophiques et théologiques*, 68 (1984), pp. 183-200.

Guthrie, K. S., *Numenius of Apamea The Father of Neoplatonism* (London, 1917).

Guthrie, W. K. C., *The Greeks and their Gods* (London, 1950).

Hadot, P., 'Apophatisme et théologie négative', in *Exercices Spirituels et Philosophie Antique* (Paris, 1981), pp. 185-193.

Heiser, J., 'Plotinus and the *Apeiron* of Plato's *Parmenides*', *Thomist*, 55 (1991), pp. 53-81.

Hochstaffl, J., *Negative Theologie. Ein Versuch zur Vermittlung des patristischen Begriffs* (Munich, 1976).

Hofmann, R. J., *Celsus. On the True Doctrine* (Oxford, 1987).

Jaeger, W., *The Theology of the Early Greek Philosophers* (Oxford, 1947).

Jaeger, W., *Paideia: Die Formung des Griechischen Menschen*, vol. I (Berlin/Leipzig, 1934).

Jonas, H., *The Gnostic Religion*, 2nd ed. (Boston, 1963).

Jones, R. M., 'The Ideas as the Thoughts of God', *Classical Philology*, 21 (1926), pp. 317-326.

Journet, C., *Connaissance et inconnaissance de Dieu* (Paris, 1969).

Journet, C., *The Dark Knowledge of God*, trans. J. F. Anderson (London, 1948).

Jufresa, M., 'Basilides. A Path to Plotinus', *Vigiliae Christianae*, 35 (1981), pp. 1-15.

Kenney, J. P., *Mystical Monotheism. A Study in Ancient Platonic Theology* (Brown University Press, 1991).

Kirk, G. S. and Raven, J. E., *The Presocratic Philosophers*, reprint (Cambridge, 1971).

Kleve, K., 'Albinus on God and the One', *Symbolae Osloenses*, 47 (1972), pp. 66-69.

Krämer, H. J., *Der Ursprung der Geistmetaphysik* (Amsterdam, 1967).

Lee, P., 'Language about God and the Theory of Analogy', *New Scholasticism*, 58 (1984), pp. 40-66.

Loenen, J. H., 'Albinus' Metaphysics. An Attempt at Rehabilitation', *Mnemosyne*, series IV, 9 (1956), pp. 296-319 and 10 (1957), pp. 35-56.

Lossky, V., *In the Image and Likeness of God* (London/Oxford, 1974).

Lossky, V., *The Vision of God*, trans. A. Moorhouse (New York, 1983).

Lossky, V., *Théologie négative et connaissance de Dieu chez Maître Eckhart* (Paris, 1973).

Louth, A., *The Origins of the Christian Mystical Tradition From Plato to Denys* (Oxford, 1981).

Luce, J. V., *An Introduction to Greek Philosophy* (London, 1992).

Marion, J.-L., *Dieu sans l'être* (Paris, 1982).

Melling, D. J., *Understanding Plato*, reprint (Oxford, 1992).

Menn, S., 'Aristotle and Plato on God as *nous* and as the Good', *Review of Metaphysics*, 45 (1991/2), pp. 543-573.

Merlan, P., *From Platonism to Neoplatonism* (The Hague, 1953).

Merlan, P., 'Neues Licht auf Parmenides', in *Philip Merlan. Kleine Philosophische Schriften*, ed. F. Merlan (New York/Hildesheim, 1976), pp. 8-17.

Merlan, P., 'The Old Academy', in *The Cambridge History of Later Greek and Early Medieval Philosophy*, ed. A. H. Armstrong (Cambridge, 1967), pp. 14-38.

Meyendorff, J., *Byzantine Theology: Historical Trends and Doctrinal Themes* (London/Oxford, 1975).

Moreschini, C., 'La Posizione di Apuleio e della scuola di Gaio nell' ambito del medioplatonismo', reprinted in German translation in *Der Mittelplatonismus*, ed. C. Zintzen (Darmstadt, 1981), pp. 219-274.

Mortley, R., 'Apuleius and Platonic Philosophy', *American Journal of Philology*, 93 (1972), pp. 584-590.

Mortley, R., 'Fundamentals of the *Via Negativa*', *American Journal of Philology*, 103 (1982), pp. 429-439.

Mortley, R. and Dockrill, D. W., eds. *The Via Negativa, Prudentia*, supplementary vol. I (Auckland, 1981).

Mortley, R., *From Word to Silence I. The Rise and Fall of Logos* (Bonn, 1986).

Nicolas, J.-H., *Dieu connu comme inconnu. Essai d'une critique de la connaissance théologique* (Paris, 1966).

Nilsson, M. P., *A History of Greek Religion*, trans. F. J. Felden (Oxford, 1925).

Nock, A. D., *Conversion* (Oxford, 1933).

Nock, A. D., 'The Exegesis of *Timaeus* 28C', *Vigiliae Christianae*, 15 (1962), pp. 79-86.

Norden. E., *Agnostos Theos. Untersuchungen zur Formengeschichte Religiöser Rede* (Leipzig/Berlin, 1913).

Novotny, F., *The Posthumous Life of Plato* (The Hague, 1975).

O' Brien, D., 'Le non-être dans la philosophie grecque: Parménide, Platon, Plotin', in *Études sur le "Sophiste" de Platon*, ed. M. Narcy (Naples, 1991), pp. 317-364.

O'Meara, D. J., *Pythagoras Revived* (Oxford, 1989).

Peters, F. E., *Greek Philosophical Terms. A Historical Lexicon* (New York/London, 1967).

Philip, J. A., *Pythagoras and Early Pythagoreanism* (Toronto, 1966).

Pieper, J., *The Silence of Saint Thomas*, trans. D. O'Connor (London, 1957).

Puech, H.-Ch., 'Numénius d'Apamée et les théologies orientales au second siècle', in *Annuaire de l'Institut de philologie et d'histoire orientale, Mélanges Bidez*, vol. 2 (Brussels, 1934), pp. 745-778.

Rahner, K., '*Theos* in the New Testament', in *Theological Investigations*, vol. 1, trans. C. Ernst (London/Baltimore, 1961), pp. 79-94.

Reedy, J., trans. *The Platonic Doctrines of Albinus* (Grand Rapids, 1991).

Regen, F., *Apuleius Philosophus Platonicus* (Berlin/New York, 1971).

Rich, A., 'The Platonic Ideas as the Thoughts of God', *Mnemosyne*, series IV, 7 (1954), pp. 123-133.

Rist, J. M., 'The Neoplatonic One and Plato's *Parmenides*', *Transactions and Proceedings of the American Philological Association*, 93 (1962), pp. 389-401.

Rist, J. M., 'Neopythagoreanism and Plato's Second Letter', *Phronesis*, 10 (1965), pp. 78-81.

Rist, J. M., 'The Immanence and Transcendence of the Platonic Form', *Philologus*, 108 (1964), pp. 217-232.

Rosemann, P. W., 'Penser l'Autre: théologie négative et "postmodernité"', *Revue philosophique de Louvain*, 91 (1993), pp. 296-310.

Saward, J., 'Towards an Apophatic Anthropology', *Irish Theological Quarterly*, 41 (1974), pp. 222-234.

Sherrard, P., *Greek East and Latin West: A Study in the Christian Tradition* (Oxford, 1959).

Soury, G., *Aperçus de philosophie religieuse chez Maxime de Tyre* (Paris, 1942).

Tarán, L., *Speusippus of Athens* (Leiden, 1981).

Tarrant, H., 'Middle Platonism and the Seventh Epistle', *Phronesis*, 28 (1983), pp. 75-103.

Theiler, W., *Die Vorbereitung des Neuplatonismus* (Berlin, 1930).

Thesleff, H., *Introduction to the Pythagorean Writings of the Hellenistic Period* (Abo, 1961).

Tomasic, T., 'Negative Theology and Subjectivity', *International Philosophical Quarterly*, 9 (1969), pp. 406-430.

Totok, W., *Handbuch der Geschichte der Philosophie*. vol. I (Frankfurt, 1964).

Van Steenberghen, F., *Hidden God: How do we Know that God Exists?* trans. T. Crowley (Louvain, 1966).

Vlastos, G., *Socrates Ironist and Moral Philosopher* (Cambridge University Press, 1991).

Voegelin, E., *Israel and Revelation, Order and History*, vol. 1. (Louisiana State University Press, 1956).

Voegelin, E., *Plato and Aristotle, Order and History*, vol. 3 (Louisiana State University Press, 1957).

Wallis, R. T., 'The Spiritual Importance of Not Knowing', in *Classical Mediterranean Spirituality*, World Spirituality, 15, ed. A. H. Armstrong (New York, 1985).

Walsh, P. G., 'Apuleius and Plutarch', in *Neoplatonism and Early Christian Thought*, eds. H. J. Blumenthal and R. A. Markus (London, 1981), pp. 20-32.

Walshe, M. O' C., trans. *Meister Eckhart. Sermons and Treatises*, 3 vols. (London, 1979-1987).

Ware, K. T., 'God Hidden and Revealed: The Apophatic Way and the Essence-Energies Distinction', *Eastern Churches Review*, 7 (1975), pp. 125-136.

Waszink, J.-H., 'Porphyrios und Numenios', in *Porphyre*, Entretiens Hardt, vol. 12 (Vandoeuvres-Genève, 1966), pp. 33-83.

Wheelwright, P. ed., *The Pre-Socratics* (New York, 1966).

Whittaker, J., *Studies in Platonism and Patristic Thought*, Variorum Reprints (London, 1984).

Whittaker, J., 'Basilides on the Ineffability of God', *Harvard Theological Review*, 62 (1969), pp. 363-371.

Wilmet, R., 'Platonic Forms and the Possibility of Language', *Revue de philosophie ancienne*, 8 (1990), pp. 97-118.

Wolfson, H. A., 'The Knowability and Describability of God in Plato and Aristotle', *Harvard Studies in Classical Philology*, 56/57 (1947), pp. 233-249.

Wolfson, H. A., 'Negative Attributes in the Church Fathers and the Gnostic Basilides', in *Studies in the History of Philosophy and Religion*, eds. I. Twersky and G. H. Williams, vol. 1 (Harvard University Press, 1973), pp. 131-142.

Wolfson, H. A., 'Albinus and Plotinus on Divine Attributes', in *Studies in the History of Philosophy and Religion*, pp. 115-130.

Yannaras, C., *De l'absence et de l'inconnaissance de Dieu*, trans. J. Touraille (Paris, 1971).

Young, F. M., 'The God of the Greeks and the Nature of Religious Language', in *Early Christian Literature and the Classical Intellectual Tradition. Essays in Honorem R. M. Grant*, ed. W. R. Schoedel and R. L. Wilken, Théologie Historique, 54 (Paris, 1979), pp. 45-74.

Zintzen, C., ed. *Der Mittelplatonismus* (Darmstadt, 1981).

BIBLIOGRAPHY III

The Neoplatonists

Armstrong, A. H., *The Architecture of the Intelligible Universe in the Philosophy of Plotinus* (Cambridge, 1940).

Armstrong, A. H., 'Plotinus', in *The Cambridge History of Later Greek and Early Medieval Philosophy*, ed. A. H. Armstrong (Cambridge, 1967), pp. 195-263.

Armstrong, A. H., 'The Background of the Doctrine that Intelligibles are Not Outside the Intellect', in *Les sources de Plotin*, Entretiens Hardt, vol. 5 (Vandoeuvres-Genève, 1960), pp. 391-425.

Armstrong, A. H., 'Plotinus's Doctrine of the Infinite and its Significance for Christian Thought', in *Plotinian and Christian Studies*, Variorum Reprints, vol. I (London, 1979), no. V.

Armstrong, A. H., 'The Apprehension of Divinity in the Self and Cosmos in Plotinus', Variorum Reprints I, no. XVIII.

Armstrong, A. H., 'The Escape of the One. An Investigation of Some Possibilities of Apophatic Theology Imperfectly Realized in the West', Variorum Reprints I, no. XXIII.

Armstrong, A. H., 'Negative Theology', Variorum Reprints I, no. XXIV.

Armstrong, A. H., 'Negative Theology, Myth and Incarnation', in *Neoplatonism and Christian Thought*, ed. D. J. O'Meara (Albany, 1982), pp. 213-222.

Armstrong, A. H., *Hellenistic and Christian Studies*, Variorum Reprints II (London, 1990).

Armstrong, A. H., 'The Negative Theology of *Nous* in Later Neoplatonism', Variorum Reprints II, no. III.

Armstrong, A. H., 'Apophatic-Kataphatic Tensions in Religious Thought from the Third to the Sixth Century A.D.', in *From Augustine to Eriugena*. Essays on Neoplatonism and Christianity in Honour of John O'Meara, eds. F. X. Martin and J. A. Richmond (Washington, 1991), pp. 12-21.

Armstrong, A. H., 'Platonic Mirrors', *Eranos Yearbook,* vol. 55 (Frankfurt-am-Main, 1988), pp. 147-181.

Arnou, R., *Le désir de Dieu dans la philosophie de Plotin*, 2nd ed. (Rome, 1967).

Atherton, J. P., 'The "One" and the Trinitarian "APXH"', in *The Significance of Neoplatonism*, ed. R. Baine Harris (New York, 1976), 173-185.

Aubenque, P., 'Plotin et le dépassement de l'ontologie grecque classique', in *Le néoplatonisme*, International Colloquium of the CNRS, 1969, eds. P. M. Schul and P. Hadot (Paris, 1971), pp. 101-108.

Bales, E. F. A., 'A Heideggerean Interpretation of Negative Theology in Plotinus', *Thomist*, 47 (1983), pp. 197-208.

Beierwaltes, W., *Identität und Differenz* (Frankfurt, 1980).

Beierwaltes, W., *Denken des Einen* (Frankfurt, 1985).

Beierwaltes, W., 'Andersheit. Zur neuplatonischen Struktur einer Problemgeschichte', in *Le néoplatonisme*, eds. P. M. Schul and P. Hadot, pp. 365-372.

Beierwaltes W., 'Plotins philosophische Mystik', in *Grundfragen Christlicher Mystik*, eds. M. Schmidt and D. R. Bauer (Stuttgart-Bad-Cannstatt, 1987), pp. 39-49.

Beierwaltes, W., *Proklos. Grundzüge seiner Metaphysik* (Frankfurt, 1965).

Beierwaltes, W., 'L'Un et l'Ame. Marginalien zu Jean Trouillards Proklos-Interpretation', in *Néoplatonisme*, Mélanges offerts à Jean Trouillard, (1981), pp. 77-89.

Bos, E. P. and Meijer, P. A., *On Proclus and his Influence in Medieval Philosophy*, Philosophia Antiqua, 53 (Leiden, 1992).

Bréhier, E., 'L'idée du néant et le problème de l'origine radicale dans le néoplatonisme grec', *Études de philosophie antique* (1955), pp. 248-283.

Bréhier, E., *La philosophie de Plotin* (Paris, 1961).

Brons, B., *Gott und die Seienden. Untersuchungen zum Verhältnis von neuplatonischer Metaphysik und christlicher Tradition bei Dionysius Areopagita* (Göttinen, 1976).

Charles-Saget, A., *L'architecture du divin: mathématique et philosophie chez Plotin et Proclus* (Paris, 1982).

Combès, J. *Études néoplatoniciennes* (Grenoble, 1989).

Corrigan, K., 'Amelius, Plotinus and Porphyry on Being, Intellect and the One. A Reappraisal', in *Aufstieg und Niedergang der Römischen Welt* II, eds. W. Haase and H. Temporini, vol. 36, 2, pp. 975-993.

Deck, J. N., *Nature, Contemplation and the One* (Toronto, 1967).

Des Places, É., 'La théologie négative du Pseudo-Denys, ses antécédents platoniciens et son influence au seuil du moyen-age', in *Studia Patristica*, 17 (1982), pp. 81-92.

De Vogel, C. J., 'On the Neoplatonic Character of Platonism and the Platonic Character of Neoplatonism', *Mind*, 62 (1953), pp. 43-64.

Dillon, J., *The Enneads*, abridged (S. MacKenna's translation), introduction and notes (Harmondsworth, 1991).

Dillon, J., 'Philosophy and Theology in Proclus', in *From Augustine to Eriugena*, eds. F. X. Martin and J. A. Richmond (Washington, 1991), pp. 66-76.

Dodds, E. R., 'The *Parmenides* of Plato and the Origin of the Neoplatonic One', *Classical Quarterly*, 22 (1928), pp. 129-142.

Dodds, E. R., 'Numenius and Ammonius', in *Les sources de Plotin*, Entretiens Hardt, vol. 5, pp. 3-61.

Dodds, E. R., 'Theurgy and Its Relationship to Neoplatonism', *Journal of Roman Studies*, 37 (1947), pp. 55-69.

Dörrie, H., 'Plotin. Philosoph und Theologe', in *Platonica Minora* (Munich, 1976), pp. 361-374.

Dörrie, H., et al., *Porphyre*, Entretiens Hardt, vol. 12 (Vandoeuvres-Genève, 1966).

Edwards, M. J., 'Middle Platonism on the Beautiful and the Good', *Mnemosyne*, 44 (1991), pp. 161-167.

Festugière, A.-J., 'Proclus et la réligion traditionelle', *Études de philosophie grecque* (Paris, 1971), pp. 571-584).

Gersh, S., *KINHΣIΣ AKINHTOΣ. A Study of Spiritual Motion in the Philosophy of Proclus* (Leiden, 1973).

Guérard, C., 'La théologie négative dans l'apophatisme grec', *Revue des sciences philosophiques et théologiques*, 68 (1984), pp. 183-200.

Guthrie, K. S., trans. *The Life of Proclus or Concerning Happiness, by Marinus of Samaria*, reprint (Grand Rapids, 1986).

Haase, W. and Temporini, eds. H., *Aufstieg und Niedergang der Römischen Welt* II, vol. 36, 1 and 2 (Berlin/New York, 1987).

Hadot, P., *Plotin ou la simplicité du regard*, 2nd ed. (Paris, 1973).

Hadot, P., 'Fragments d'un commentaire de Porphyre sur le *Parmémide*', *Revue des études grecques*, 74 (1961), pp. 410-438.

Hadot, P., 'La métaphysique de Porphyre', in *Porphyre*, Entretiens Hardt, vol. 12, pp. 125-163.

Hadot, P., *Porphyre et Victorinus*, 2 vols. (Paris, 1968).

Hadot, P., 'Structure et thèmes du Traité 38 (VI 7) de Plotin', in *Aufstieg und Niedergang der Römischen Welt* II, eds. W. Haase and H. Temporini, vol. 36, 1, pp. 624-676.

Hedwig, K., 'Negatio negationis', *Archiv für Begriffsgeschichte*, 24 (1980), pp. 7-33.

Heiser, J., 'Plotinus and the *Apeiron* of Plato's *Parmenides*', *Thomist*, 55 (1991), pp. 53-81.

Heiser, J., *Logos and Language in the Philosophy of Plotinus*, Studies in the History of Philosophy, vol. 15 (New York, 1991).

Jufresa, M., 'Basilides. A Path to Plotinus', *Vigiliae Christianae*, 35 (1981), pp. 1-15.

Katz, J., *Plotinus' Search for the Good* (New York, 1950).

Leroux, G., *Plotin. Traité sur la liberté et la volonté de l'Un (Ennéade VI 8, 39)* (Paris, 1990).

Lloyd, A. C., 'The Later Neoplatonists', in *The Cambridge History of Later Greek and Early Medieval Philosophy*, ed. A. H. Armstrong, pp. 272-325.

Lloyd, A. C., *The Anatomy of Neoplatonism* (Oxford, 1990).

MacKenna, S., *Plotinus. The Enneads*, 4th ed. revised by B. S. Page (London, 1969).

Merlan, P., *Monopsychism, Mysticism, Metaconsciousness* (The Hague, 1963).

Merlan, P., *From Platonism to Neoplatonism* (The Hague, 1953).

Moreau, J., 'Plotin et la tradition hellénique', *Revue internationale de philosophie*, 92 (1970), pp. 171-180.

Morrow, G. R. and Dillon, J., trans. *Proclus' Commentary on Plato's Parmenides* (Princeton University Press, 1987).

Mortley, R., *From Word to Silence II. The Way of Negation Christian and Greek* (Bonn, 1986).

Nock, A. D., *Conversion* (Oxford, 1933).

O'Meara, D. J., *Structures hiérarchiques dans la pensée de Plotin* (Leiden, 1975).

O'Meara, D. J., 'Being in Numenius and Plotinus', *Phronesis*, 21 (1976), pp. 120-129.

Pépin, J. and Saffrey, H. D., *Proclus. Lecteur et interprète des anciens* (Paris, 1987).

Rist, J. M., *Plotinus. The Road to Reality* (Cambridge, 1967).

Rist, J. M., *Eros and Psyche* (Toronto, 1964).

Rist, J. M., 'Monism: Plotinus and some Predecessors', *Harvard Studies in Classical Philology*, 69 (1965), pp. 329-344.

Rist, J. M., 'The Neoplatonic One and Plato's *Parmenides*', *Transactions and Proceedings of the American Philological Association*, 93 (1962), pp. 389-401.

Rist, J. M., 'The One of Plotinus and the God of Aristotle', *Review of Metaphysics*, 27 (1973), pp. 75-87.

Rist, J. M., 'The Problem of "Otherness" in the *Enneads*', in *Le néoplatonisme*, eds. P. M. Schul and P. Hadot, pp. 78-87.

Rist, J. M., 'Mysticism and Transcendence in Later Neoplatonism', *Hermes*, 92 (1964), pp. 213-225.

Rist, J. M., '*Theos* and the One in some Texts of Plotinus', *Medieval Studies*, 24 (1962), pp. 169-180.

Rist, J. M., 'Back to the Mysticism of Plotinus. Some More Specifics', *Journal of the History of Philosophy*, 27 (1989), pp. 83-97.

Rosán, L. J., *The Philosophy of Proclus. The Final Phase of Ancient Thought* (New York, 1949).

Saffrey, H.-D., *Recherches sur Néoplatonisme après Plotin* (Paris, 1990).

Schul, P. M. and Hadot, P. eds. *Le néoplatonisme*, International Colloquium of the CNRS, 1969 (Paris, 1971).

Schwyzer, H.-R., '"Bewusst" und "Unbewusst" bei Plotin', in *Les sources de Plotin*, Entretiens Hardt, vol. 5, pp. 341-390.

Sedley, D., 'The End of the Academy', *Phronesis*, 26 (1981), pp. 67-73.

Sleeman, J. H. and Pollet, G., *Lexicon Plotinianum* (Louvain, 1980).

Smith, A., *Porphyry's Place in the Neoplatonic Tradition* (The Hague, 1974).

Smith, A., 'Reason and Experience in Plotinus', in *At The Heart of The Real*, ed. F. O'Rourke (Blackrock, Co. Dublin, 1992), pp. 21-30.

Theiler, W., 'Plotin zwischen Platon und Stoa', in *Les sources de Plotin*, Entretiens Hardt, vol. 5, pp. 65-86.

Trouillard, J., 'L' âme du *Timée* et l'Un du *Parménide* dans la perspective néoplatonicienne', *Revue internationale de philosophie*, 92 (1970), pp. 236-251.

Trouillard, J., 'Raison et mystique chez Plotin', *Revue des études augustiniennes*, 20 (1974), pp. 3-14.

Trouillard, J., 'Le *Parménide* de Platon et son interprétation néoplatonicienne', *Revue de théologie et de philosophie*, 23 (1973), pp. 83-100.

Trouillard, J., *La purification Plotinienne* (Paris, 1955).

Trouillard, J, *La procession Plotinienne* (Paris, 1955).

Trouillard, J., 'Valeur critique de la mystique plotinienne', *Revue philosophique de Louvain*, 59 (1961), pp. 431-444.

Trouillard, J., *L'Un et l'Ame selon Proclos* (Paris, 1972).

Trouillard, J., 'L'activité onomastique selon Proclus', in *De Jamblique à Proclus*, Entretiens Hardt, vol. 21 (Vandoeuvres-Genève,1974).

Wallis, R. T., 'Scepticism and Neoplatonism', in *Aufstieg und Niedergang der Römischen Welt* II, eds. W. Haase and H. Temporini, 36, 2, pp. 911-954.

Whittaker, T., *The Neoplatonists*, reprint (Hildesheim, 1961).

Wolfson, H. A., 'Albinus and Plotinus on Divine Attributes', in *Studies in the History of Philosophy and Religion*, vol. 1, ed I. Twersky and G. H. Williams (Harvard University Press, 1973), pp. 115-130.

BIBLIOGRAPHY IV

Philo and The Christian Fathers

Armstrong, A. H., 'The Escape of the One', in *Plotinian and Christian Studies*, Variorum Reprints, vol. I (London, 1979), no. XXIII.

Armstrong, A. H., 'Pagan and Christian Traditionalism in the First Three Centuries A.D.', in *Hellenic and Christian Studies*, Variorum Reprints, vol. II (London, 1990), no. IX.

Armstrong, A. H., 'The Plotinian Doctrine of *Nous* in Patristic Theology', *Vigiliae Christianae*, 8 (1954), pp. 234-238.

Armstrong, A. H., 'The Self-Definition of Christianity in Relation to Later Platonism', Variorum Reprints II, no. VIII.

Arnou, R., 'Platonisme des Pères', *Dictionnaire de Théologie Catholique*, 12 (Paris, 1935), 2258-2392.

Baarda, T. et al. eds. *Knowledge of God in the Graeco-Roman World* (Leiden, 1988).

Baër, D., 'Incompréhensibilité de Dieu et théologie négative chez Philon d'Alexandrie', *Présence Orthodoxe*, 8 (1969), pp. 38-46.

Balthasar, H. von, *Presence et.pensée. Essai sur la philosphie religieuse de Grégoire de Nysse* (Paris, 1942).

Barnard, L. W., *Justin Martyr His Life and Thought* (Cambridge, 1967).

Bauer, J. B. ed., *Encyclopedia of Biblical Theology* (London, 1970).

Bigg, C., *The Christian Platonists of Alexandria*, reprint (Oxford, 1968).

Billings, T. H., *The Platonism of Philo Judaeus*, reprint (London/New York, 1979).

Blowers, P. M., 'Maximus the Confessor, Gregory of Nyssa and the Concept of "Perpetual Progress"', *Vigiliae Christianae*, 46 (1992), pp. 151-171.

Boyancé, P., 'Études Philoniennes', *Revue des études grecques*, 76 (1973), pp. 64-110.

Bréhier, E., *Les idées philosophiques et religieuses de Philon d'Alexandrie*, 3rd ed. (Paris, 1950).

Brightman, R. S., 'Apophatic Theology and Divine Infinity in St Gregory of Nyssa', *Greek Orthodox Theological Review*, 18 (1973), pp. 97-114.

Carabine, D., 'Gregory of Nyssa on the Incomprehensibility of God', in *The Relationship Between Neoplatonism and Christianity*, eds. T. Finan and V. Twomey (Blackrock, Co. Dublin, 1992), pp. 79-99.

Chadwick, H., *Early Christian Thought in the Classical Tradition* (Oxford, 1966).

Chadwick, H., *Origen Contra Celsum* (Cambridge, 1953).

Chadwick, H., 'Philo and the Beginning of Christian Thought', in *The Cambridge History of Later Greek and Early Medieval Philosophy*, ed. A. H. Armstrong (Cambridge, 1967), pp. 133-157.

Cleveland-Coxe, A., *Fathers of the Second Century*, The Ante-Nicene Fathers Series, vol. II, reprint (Michigan, 1975).

Courcelle, P., 'Grégoire de Nysse lecteur de Porphyre', *Revue des études grecques*, 80 (1967), pp. 402-406.

Crouzel, H., 'Grégoire de Nysse est-il fondateur de la théologie mystique?' *Revue d'Ascétique et de mystique*, 33 (1957), pp. 189-202.

Daniélou, J., *Philon d'Alexandrie* (Paris, 1958).

Daniélou, J., *Platonisme et théologie mystique* (Paris, 1944).

Daniélou, J., *Gospel Message and Hellenistic Culture*, trans. J. A. Baker (London, 1973).

Daniélou, J., 'L' Incompréhensibilité de Dieu d'après S. Jean Chrysostome', *Recherches de sciences religieuses*, 37 (1950), pp. 176-194.

Daniélou, J., 'Grégoire de Nysse et le néo-Platonisme de l'école d'Athènes', *Revue des études grecques*, 80 (1967), pp. 395-401.

Daniélou, J. and Musurillo, H., *From Glory to Glory. Texts From Gregory of Nyssa's Mystical Writings* (London, 1961).

Daniélou, J., 'Eunome l'Arien et l'exégèse néo-platonicienne du *Cratyle*', *Revue des études grecques*, 49 (1956), pp. 412-432.

Des Places, É, 'La tradition patristique de Platon', in *Études platoniciennes 1929-1979* (Leiden, 1981), pp. 249-258.

Dillon, J., 'Philo', in *The Middle Platonists* (London, 1977), pp. 139-183.

Dillon, J., 'Origen and Plotinus. The Platonic Influence on Early Christianity', in *The Relationship Between Neoplatonism and Christianity*, eds. T. Finan and V. Twomey, pp. 7-26.

Dodd, C. H., 'Hellenistic Judaism: Philo of Alexandria', in *The Interpretation of the Fourth Gospel* (Cambridge, 1953), pp. 54-73.

Drummond, J., Philo Judaeus, vol. 2 (London, 1888).

Duclow, D. F., 'Gregory of Nyssa and Nicholas of Cusa: Infinity, Anthropology and the *Via Negativa*', *Downside Review*, 92 (1974), pp. 102-108.

Edgar Bruns, J., '*Philo Christianus*. The Debris of a Legend', *Harvard Theological Review*, 66 (1973), pp. 141-145.

Edwards, M. J., 'Atticizing Moses? Numenius, the Fathers and the Jews', *Vigiliae Christianae*, 44 (1990), pp. 64-75.

Epstein, I., 'Jewish Philosophy', in *Judaism: A Historical Presentation* (Harmondsworth, 1959), pp. 195-222.

Falls, T. B., *Saint Justin Martyr*, The Fathers of the Church Series, 6, reprint (Washington, 1984).

Festugière, A.-J., 'Philon', in *Le Dieu cosmique, La révélation d'Hermès Trismégiste*, vol. 2 (Paris, 1949), chs. 15, 16, 17.

Finan, T. and Twomey, V. eds. *The Relationship Between Neoplatonism and Christianity*, (Blackrock, Co. Dublin, 1992),

Fraser, P. M., 'Alexandrian Scholarship', in *Ptolemaic Alexandria* (Oxford, 1972), pp. 447-479.

Fraser, P. M., 'Currents of Alexandrian Philosophy', in *Ptolemaic Alexandria*, pp. 480-494.

Goodenough, E. R., *By Light, Light. The Mystic Gospel of Hellenistic Judaism*, reprint (Amsterdam, 1969).

Goodenough, E. R., *An Introduction to Philo Judaeus* (New Haven, 1940).

Goodenough, E. R., 'A Neo-Pythagorean Source in Philo Judaeus', *Yale Classical Studies*, 3 (1932), pp. 115-164.

Goodenough, E. R., *The Theology of Justin Martyr* (Amsterdam, 1968).

Graef, H., *Saint Gregory of Nyssa. The Lord's Prayer. The Beatitudes*, Ancient Christian Writers Series, 18 (London, 1954).

Grant, R. M., *The Early Christian Doctrine of God* (Charlottesville, 1966).

Guérard, C., 'La théologie négative dans l' apophaticisme grec', *Revue des sciences philosophiques et théologiques*, 68 (1984), pp. 183-200.

Hadot, P., 'Apophatisme et théologie négative', in *Exercices Spirituels et Philosophie Antique* (Paris, 1981), pp. 185-193.

Heinemann, I., 'Philo als Vater der mittelalterlichen Philosophie?', *Theologische Zeitschrift*, 6 (1950), pp. 99-116.

Hochstaffl, J., *Negative Theologie. Ein Versuch zur Vermittlung des patristischen Begriffs* (Munich, 1976).

Horn, G., 'Le "miroir", la "nuée", deux manières de voir Dieu d'après S. Grégoire de Nysse', *Revue d'Ascétique et de mystique*, 8 (1927), pp. 113-131.

Ivánka, E. v., *Plato christianus* (Einsiedeln, 1964).

Kadloubovsky, E. and Palmer, G. E. H., *Early Fathers from the Philokalia*, 8th ed. (London, 1981).

Kelly, J. N. D., *Early Christian Doctrine*, 4th ed. (London, 1968).

Lampe, G. W. H., *A Patristic Greek Lexicon* (Oxford, 1978).

Lilla, S. R. C., *Clement of Alexandria* (Oxford, 1971).

Lot-Borodine, M., 'La doctrine de la deification dans l'église grecque', *Revue d'histoire des religions*, 105 (1932), pp. 5-43.

Lossky, V., *Essai sur la théologie mystique de l'Église d'Orient*, reprint (Paris, 1990).

Lossky, V., *In the Image and Likeness of God* (London/Oxford, 1975).
Louth, A., *The Origins of the Christian Mystical Tradition* (Oxford, 1981).
Malherbe, A. J and Ferguson, E., *Gregory of Nyssa. The Life of Moses*, Classics of Western Spirituality Series (New York, 1978).
McKenzie, J. L., *Dictionary of the Bible* (London/Dublin, 1972).
Meijering, E. P., *Orthodoxy and Platonism in Athanasius* (Leiden, 1968).
Mendelson, A., 'A Reappraisal of Wolfson's Method', *Studia Philonica*, 3 (1974-75), pp. 11-26.
Merki, H., Ὁμοίωσις Θεῷ. Von der platonische Angleichung an Gott zur Gottähnlichkeit bei Gregor von Nyssa (Freiburg, 1952).
Mortley, R., *Connaissance réligieuse et herméneutique chez Clément d'Alexandrie* (Leiden, 1973).
Mortley, R., *From Word to Silence II. The Way of Negation Christian and Greek* (Bonn, 1986).
Mühlenberg, E., *Die Unendlichkeit Gottes bei Gregor von Nyssa* (Göttingen, 1966).
Nikiprowetzky, V., *Le commentaire de l'Écriture chez Philon d'Alexandrie* (Leiden, 1977).
O'Meara, D. J., ed. *Neoplatonism and Christian Thought, Studies in Neoplatonism Ancient and Modern*, vol. 3 (Albany, 1982).
Osborn, E. F., *Justin Martyr* (Tübingen, 1973).
Osborn, E. F., 'Empiricism and Transcendence', *Prudentia*, 8 (1976), pp. 115-122.
Palmer, D. W., 'Atheism, Apologetic and Negative Theology in the Greek Apologists of the Second Century', *Vigiliae Christianae*, 37 (1983), pp. 234-259.
Pelikan, J., *The Christian Tradition I: The Emergence of the Catholic Tradition* (Chicago, 1971).
Pépin, J., 'Linguistique et théologie dans la tradition platonicienne', *Languages*, 65 (1982), pp. 91-116.
Pépin, J., *De la philosophie ancienne à la théologie patristique*, Variorum Reprints (London, 1986).
Prestige, G. L., *God in Patristic Thought* (London, 1952).
Price, R. M., 'Hellenization and *Logos* Doctrine in Justin Martyr', *Vigiliae Christianae*, 42 (1988), pp. 18-23.
Puech, H.-Ch., 'La ténèbre mystique chez le Pseudo-Denys l'Aréopagite et dans la tradition patristique', *Études carmélitaines*, 23 (1938), pp. 33-53.
Quasten, J., *Patrology*, 3 vols. (Maryland, 1966).
Rist, J. M., 'Basil's "Neoplatonism": Its Background and Nature', in *Platonism and its Christian Heritage*, Variorum Reprints (London, 1985), no. XII.

Rist, J. M., 'Origen', in *Eros and Psyche* (Toronto, 1964), pp. 195-212.

Roth, C. P., 'Platonic and Pauline Elements in the Ascent of the Soul in Gregory of Nyssa's Dialogue on the Soul and Resurrection', *Vigiliae Christianae*, 46 (1992), pp. 20-30.

Runia, D. T., *Philo of Alexandria and the Timaeus of Plato* (Amsterdam, 1981).

Sandmel, S., *Philo of Alexandria: An Introduction* (Oxford/New York, 1979).

Sandmel, S., *The First Christian Century in Judaism and Christianity* (New York/Oxford, 1969).

Sandmel, S., *Judaism and Christian Beginnings* (New York/Oxford, 1978).

Sherrard, P., *Greek East and Latin West* (Oxford, 1959).

Simon, M., 'Éléments gnostiques chez Philon', in *Le Origini dello Gnosticismo*, ed. U. Bianchi (Leiden, 1970), pp. 359-376.

Stevenson, J. ed., *A New Eusebius* (London, 1957).

Theiler, W., 'Philo von Alexandreia und der hellenisierte *Timaeus*', in *Der Mittelplatonismus*, ed. C. Zintzen (Darmstadt, 1981), pp. 52-63.

Theiler, W., 'Philon von Alexandria und der Beginn des Kaiserzeitlichen Platonismus', in *Parousia*, Festgabe for J. Hirschberger (Frankfurt, 1965), pp. 199-218.

Tomasic, T., 'Negative Theology and Subjectivity', *Philosophical Quarterly*, 9 (1969), pp. 406-430.

Vanderlinden, E., 'Les divers modes de connaissance de Dieu selon Philon d' Alexandrie', in *Mélanges de sciences réligieuses*, 4 (1947), pp. 285-304.

Völker, W., *Gregor von Nyssa als Mystiker* (Wiesbaden, 1955).

Whittaker, J., *Studies in Platonism and Patristic Thought*, Variorum Reprints (London, 1984).

Wiles, M., *The Making of Christian Doctrine* (Cambridge, 1967).

Williams, R. D., 'The Logic of Arianism', *Journal of Theological Studies*, 34 (1983), pp. 56-81.

Winden, J. C. M., 'The World of Ideas in Philo of Alexandria: An Interpretation of *De opificio mundi* 24-25', *Vigiliae Christianae*, 37 (1983), pp. 209-217.

Winston, D., *Logos and Mystical Theology in Philo of Alexandria* (Cincinnati, 1985).

Witt, R. E., 'The Hellenism of Clement of Alexandria', *Classical Quarterly*, 25 (1931), pp. 195-204.

Wolfson, H. A., *Philo. Foundations of Religious Philosophy in Judaism, Christianity and Islam*, 2 vols. (Cambridge, 1948).

Wolfson, H. A., 'Greek Philosophy in Philo and the Church Fathers', in *Studies in the History of Philosophy and Religion*, vol. 1, eds. I.

Twersky, and G. H. Williams, (Harvard University Press, 1973), pp. 71-97.

Wolfson, H. A., 'Albinus and Plotinus on Divine Attributes', in *Studies in the History of Philosophy and Religion*, pp. 115-130.

BIBLIOGRAPHY V

Augustine, Pseudo-Dionysius and Eriugena

Allard, G.-H., *Jean Scot Écrivan* (Montréal/Paris, 1986).

Barnard, Ch.-A., 'Les formes de la théologie chez Denys l'Aréopagite', *Gregorianum*, 59 (1978), pp. 39-69.

Barnard, Ch.-A., 'La doctrine mystique de Denys l'Aréopagite', *Gregorianum*, 68 (1987), pp. 523-566.

Beierwaltes, W., '*Negati Affirmatio*: Welt als Metapher', in *Jean Scot Érigène et l'histoire de la philosophie*, ed. R. Roques (Paris, 1977), pp. 263-275.

Beierwaltes, W., 'Sprache und Sache: Reflexionen zu Eriugenas Einschätzung von Leistung und Funktion der Sprache', *Zeitschrift für philosophische Forschung*, 38 (1984), pp. 525-543.

Beierwaltes, W., 'Marginalien zu Eriugenas "Platonismus"', in *Platonismus und Christentum*, eds. H.-D. Blume and F. Mann, pp. 64-74.

Beierwaltes, W., 'Cusanus and Eriugena', *Dionysius*, 13 (1989), pp. 115-152.

Beierwaltes, W., 'Eriugenas Faszination', in *From Augustine to Eriugena. Essays on Neoplatonism and Christianity in Honour of J. J. O'Meara*, eds. F. X. Martin and J. A. Richmond (Washington, 1991), pp. 22-41.

Beierwaltes, W., 'Eriugena's Platonism', *Hermathena*, 149 (1990), pp. 53-72.

Beierwaltes, W., *Platonismus und Idealismus* (Frankfurt, 1972).

Beierwaltes, W. ed., *Platonismus in der Philosophie des Mittelalters* (Darmstadt, 1969).

Beierwaltes, W., ed. *Eriugena: Studien zu Seinen Quellen* (Heidelberg, 1980).

Beierwaltes, W., ed. *Eriugena Redivivus* (Heidelberg, 1987).

Beierwaltes, W., ed. *Begriff und Metapher. Sprachform des Denkens bei Eriugena* (Heidelberg, 1990).

Bett, H. A., *John Scotus Eriugena. A Study in Medieval Philosophy* (Cambridge, 1925).

Bettenson, H., *The City of God*, reprint (Harmondsworth, 1977).

Blume, H.-D. and Mann, F. eds. *Platonismus und Christentum*, (Münster, 1983),

Brennan, M., *A Guide to Eriugenian Studies 1930-1987* (Paris, 1990).

Breton, S., 'Language spatial, langage métaphysique dans le Néo-Platonisme Érigénien', in *Jean Scot Érigène et l'histoire de la philosophie*, ed. R. Roques, pp. 357-386.

Brons, B., *Gott und die Seienden. Untersuchungen zum Verhältnis von neuplatonischer Metaphysik und christlicher Tradition bei Dionysius Areopagita* (Göttinen, 1976).

Brown, P., *Augustine of Hippo. A Biography* (London, 1967).

Cappuyns, M., *Jean Scot Érigène: sa vie, son oeuvre, sa pensée* (Louvain/Paris, 1933).

Carabine, D., '*Apophasis* and Metaphysics in the *Periphyseon* of John Scottus Eriugena', *Philosophical Studies*, 32 (1988-90), pp. 63-82.

Carabine, D., 'Eriugena's Use of the Symbolism of Light, Cloud and Darkness in the *Periphyseon*', in *Eriugena East and West*, eds. B. McGinn and W. Otten (Notre Dame University Press, 1994) pp. 141-152.

Carabine, D., 'Negative Theology in the Thought of Saint Augustine', *Recherches de Théologie ancienne et médiévale*, 59 (1992), pp. 5-22.

Cayré, F., *La contemplation augustinienne* (Paris, 1954).

Clark, S., *From Athens to Jerusalem. The Love of Wisdom and the Love of God* (Oxford, 1984).

Cleveland Coxe, A., *Expositions on the Book of Psalms*, The Nicene and Post-Nicene Fathers Series, 8, reprint (Michigan, 1974).

Contreni, J. J., *Carolingian Learning, Masters and Manuscripts*, Variorum Reprints (London, 1992).

Courcelle, P., *Recherches sur les Confessions de saint Augustin* (Paris, 1950).

Courcelle, P., 'La première expérience augustinienne de l'extase', in *Augustinus Magister I* (Paris, 1954).

Crouse, R. D., 'Augustinian Platonism in Early Medieval Thought', in *Augustine. From Rhetor to Theologian*, ed. J. McWilliam, et al. (Ontario, 1992), pp. 109-120.

Des Places, É., 'La théologie négative de Pseudo-Denys, ses antécédents platoniciens et son influence au seuil de Moyen-Age', *Studia Patristica*, 17 (1982), pp. 81-92.

Douglas, J. W., 'The Negative Theology of Dionysius the Areopagite', *Downside Review*, 81 (1963), pp. 115-124.

Duclow, D., 'Pseudo-Dionysius, John Scottus Eriugena, Nicholas of Cusa: An Approach to the Hermeneutic of the Divine Names', *International Philosophical Quarterly*, 12 (1972), p. 206-278.

Duclow, D., 'Nature as Speech and Book in John Scottus Eriugena', *Medievalia*, 3 (1977), pp. 131-140.

Duclow, D., 'Dialectic and Christology in Eriugena's *Periphyseon*', *Dionysius*, 4 (1980), pp. 99-118.

Duclow, D., 'Divine Nothingness and Self-Creation in John Scottus Eriugena, *Journal of Religion*, 57 (1977), pp. 109-123.

Finan, T. and Twomey, V. eds. *The Relationship Between Neoplatonism and Christianity* (Blackrock, Co. Dublin, 1992).

Gardner, A., *Studies in John the Scot (Eriugena) A Philosopher of the Dark Ages* (London, 1900).

Gersh, S., *From Iamblichus to Eriugena* (Leiden, 1978).

Gersh, S., 'The Structure of the Return in Eriugena's *Periphyseon*', in *Begriff und Metapher*, ed. W. Beierwaltes, pp. 108-125.

Gersh, S., 'Omnipresence in Eriugena', in *Eriugena*, ed. W. Beierwaltes, pp. 55-74.

Gersh, S., '*Per se Ipsum*. The Problem of Immediate and Mediate Causation in Eriugena and his Neoplonic Predecessors', in *Jean Scot Érigène*, ed. R. Roques, pp. 367-376.

Gilson, É., *History of Philosophy in the Middle Ages* (New York, 1955).

Hathaway, R. F., *Hierarchy and the Definition of Order in the Letters of Pseudo-Dionysius*, (The Hague, 1969).

Heiser, J., 'Saint Augustine and Negative Theology', *The New Scholasticism*, 53 (1989), pp. 66-80.

Herren, M. W. ed., *The Sacred Nectar of the Greeks. A Study of Greek in the West in the Early Middle Ages* (London, 1988).

Horn G., 'Amour et extase d'après Denys l'Aréopagite', *Revue d'Ascétique et de mystique*, 6 (1925), pp. 278-289.

Jones, J. D., *Pseudo-Dionysius Areopagite. The Divine Names and Mystical Theology* (Milwaukee, 1980).

Jones, J. D., 'The Character of the Negative (Mystical) Theology for Pseudo-Dionysius Areopagite', *Proceedings of the American Catholic Philosophical Association*, 51 (1977), pp. 66-74.

Kirwan, C., *Augustine* (London, 1991).

Koch, J., 'Augustinischer und Dionysischer Neuplatonismus und das Mittelalter', in *Platonismus in der Philosophie des Mittelalters*, ed. W. Beierwaltes, pp. 317-342.

Laistner, M. L. W., *Thought and Letters in Western Europe AD, 500-900* (London, 1957).

Lees, R. A., *The Negative Language of the Dionysian School of Mystical Theology. An Approach to The Cloud of Unknowing*, Analecta Cartusiana, 107 (1983).

Lilla, S., 'The Notion of Infinitude in Ps.-Dionysius Areopagita', *Journal of Theological Studies*, 31 (1980), pp. 93-103.

Lossky, V., *Essai sur la théologie mystique de l'Église d'Orient*, reprint (Paris, 1990).

Lossky, V., 'La théologie négative dans la doctrine de Denys l'Aréopagite', *Revue des sciences philosophiques et théologiques*, 28 (1939), pp. 204-221.

Lossky, V., 'Les éléments de "Théologie négative" dans la pensée de saint Augustin, in *Augustinus Magister I* (Paris, 1954), pp. 575-581.

Lossky, V., *The Vision of God*, trans. A. Moorhouse (London, 1973).

Lossky, V., 'La notion des "analogies" chez Denys le Pseudo-Aréopagite', *Archives d'histoire doctrinale et littéraire de Moyen-Age*, 5 (1930), pp. 279-309.

Louth, A., *Denys the Areopagite*, Outstanding Christian Thinkers Series (London, 1989).

Louth, A., *The Origins of the Christian Mystical Tradition From Plato to Denys* (Oxford, 1981).

Luibheid, C. and Rorem, P., *Dionysius the Areopagite. The Complete Works*, The Classics of Western Spirituality Series (London, 1987).

Madec, G., 'L'Augustinisme de Jean Scot dans le *De praedestinatione*', in *Jean Scot Érigène*, ed. R. Roques, pp. 183-190.

Mandouze, A., *Saint Augustin, l'aventure de la raison et de la grâce* (Paris, 1968).

Martin, F. X. and Richmond, J. A., eds. *From Augustine to Eriugena. Essays on Neoplatonism and Christianity in Honour of John O'Meara* (Washington, 1991).

McEvoy, J. J., 'Neoplatonism and Christianity. Influence, Syncretism or Discernment?', in *The Relationship Between Neoplatonism and Christianity*, eds. T. Finan and V. Twomey, pp. 155-170.

McGinn, B., 'Negative Theology in John the Scot', *Studia Patristica*, 13 (1975), pp. 232-238.

McGinn, B., 'The Negative Element in the Anthropology of John the Scot', in *Jean Scot Érigène*, ed. R. Roques, pp. 315-325.

McKenna, S., *The Trinity*, The Fathers of the Church Series, 45, reprint (Washington, 1970).

Meagher, R., *An Introduction to the Philosophy of Saint Augustine* (New York, 1978).

Meyendorff, J., 'Notes sur l'influence Dionysienne en Orient', *Studia Patristica*, 2 (1957), pp. 547-552.

Moran, D., *The Philosophy of John Scottus Eriugena* (Oxford, 1989).

Mortley, R., *From Word to Silence II: The Way of Negation Christian and Greek* (Bonn, 1986).

O' Daly, G., 'Dionysius Areopagita', in *Theologische Realenzyklopäidie*, VIII (1981), 772-780.

O' Meara, D. J., 'The Problem of Speaking about God in John Scottus Eriugena', in *Carolingian Essays*, ed. R. Blumenthal (Washington, 1983), pp. 151-167.

O'Meara, J. J., *Eriugena* (Cork, 1969).

O'Meara, J. J., *Eriugena* (Cambridge, 1988).

O'Meara, J. J., 'Eriugena's Use of Augustine in his Teaching on the Return of the Soul and the Vision of God', in *Jean Scot Érigène*, ed. R. Roques, pp. 191-200.

O'Meara, J. J., *The Young Augustine*, reprint (New York, 1980).

O'Meara, J. and Bieler, L., eds. *The Mind of Eriugena* (Dublin, 1973).

O'Rourke, F., *Pseudo-Dionysius and the Metaphysics of Aquinas* (Leiden, 1992).

Pelikan, J., *The Growth of Medieval Theology (600-1300), The Christian Tradition*, vol. 3 (Chicago, 1978).

Price, B. B., *Medieval Thought. An Introduction* (Oxford, 1992).

Puech, H.-Ch., 'La ténèbre mystique chez le Pseudo-Denys l'Aréopagite et dans la tradition patristique', *Études carmélitaines*, 23 (1938), pp. 33-53.

Robertson, D. W., *On Christian Doctrine* (Indianapolis, 1977).

Rolt, C. E., *Dionysius the Areopagite on the Divine Names and the Mystical Theology* (London/ New York, 1920).

Roques, R., *L'Univers Dionysien* (Paris, 1954).

Roques, R., 'Symbolisme et théologie négative chez le Pseudo-Denys', *Bulletin de l'Association Guillaume Budé*, (1957), pp. 97-112.

Roques, R., 'Significations et conditions de la contemplation Dionysienne', *Bulletin de littérature ecclésiastique*, 52 (1951), pp. 44-56.

Roques, R., 'Note sur la notion de *theologia* chez le Pseudo-Denys 'l'Aréopagite', *Revue d'Ascétique et de mystique*, 25 (1949), pp. 200-212.

Roques, R., 'A propos des sources du Pseudo-Denys', *Revue d'Histoire ecclésiastique*, 56 (1961), pp. 449-464.

Roques, R., 'Traduction ou interprétation. Brèves remarques sur Jean Scot traducteur de Denys', in *The Mind of Eriugena*, eds. J. O'Meara and L. Bieler, pp. 59-77.

Roques, R., 'Contemplation, extase et ténèbre selon le Ps.-Denys', in *Dictionaire de Spiritualité* (Paris, 1952), cols. 1885-1911.

Roques, R. ed., *Jean Scot Érigène et l'histoire de la philosophie* (Paris, 1977).

Roques, R., 'Remarques sur la signification de Jean Scot', *Divinitas*, 11 (1967), pp. 245-329.

Roques, R., 'L'Écriture et son traitement chez Jean Scot Érigène', *Annuaire de l'École pratiques des Hautes Études*, 77 (1969), 304-315.

Roques, R., 'Théophanie et nature chez Jean Scot Érigène', *Annuaire* (1965), pp. 156-161 and (1966), pp. 162-167.

Rorem, P., *Biblical and Liturgical Symbols within the Pseudo-Dionysian Synthesis* (Toronto, 1984).

Rorem, P., 'The Place of the *Mystical Theology* in the Pseudo-Dionysian Corpus', *Dionysius*, 4 (1980), pp. 87-97.

Rutledge, Dom D., *Cosmic Theology. The Ecclesiastical Hierarchy of Pseudo-Denys: An Introduction* (London, 1964).

Saffrey, H.-D., 'New Objective Links Between the Pseudo-Dionysius and Proclus', in *Neoplatonism and Christian Thought*, ed. D. J. O'Meara (Albany, 1982), pp. 64-74.

Sheldon-Williams, I. P., 'The Greek Christian Platonist Tradition from The Cappadocians to Maximus and Eriugena', in *The Cambridge History of Later Greek and Early Medieval Philosophy*, ed. A. H. Armstrong (Cambridge, 1967), pp. 421-505.

Sheldon-Williams, I. P., 'Eriugena's Greek Sources', in *The Mind of Eriugena*, eds. J. O'Meara and L. Bieler, pp. 1-15.

Sheldon-Williams, I. P., The *Ecclesiastical Hierarchy* of Pseudo-Dionysius', *Downside Review*, 82 (1964), pp. 293-302.

Sheldon-Williams, I. P., 'Eriugena's Interpretation of the Pseudo-Dionysius', *Studia Patristica*, 12 (1971), pp. 151-154.

Sheldon-Williams, I. P., trans. *Periphyseon*, rev. J. J. O'Meara (Montréal, 1987).

Spearitt, P., 'The Soul's Participation in God according to Pseudo-Dionysius', *Downside Review*, 88 (1970), pp. 378-392.

Spearritt, P., *A Philosophical Enquiry into Dionysian Mysticism* (Bössingen, 1975).

Stead, C., *Substance and Illusion in the Christian Fathers*, Variorum Reprints (London, 1985).

Stock, B., 'The Philosophical Anthropology of Johannes Scottus Eriugena', *Studia Medievali*, 8 (1967), pp. 1-57.

Stock, B., '*Intelligo Me Esse*: Eriugena's *Cogito*', in *Jean Scot Érigène*, ed. R. Roques, pp. 327-335.

Theresia Benedicta, Sr. (Edith Stein), 'Ways to Know God: The *Symbolic Theology* of Dionysius the Areopagite and its Factual Presuppositions', *Thomist*, 9 (1946), pp. 379-420.

Théry, G., 'Scot Érigène: Introducteur de Denys', *New Scholasticism*, 7 (1933), pp. 91-108.

Tomasic, T., 'Negative Theology and Subjectivity. An Approach to the Tradition of the Pseudo-Dionysius', *International Philosophical Quarterly*, 9 (1969), pp. 406-430.

Trouillard, J., 'Érigène et la théophanie créatrice', in *The Mind of Eriugena*, eds. J. O'Meara and L. Bieler, pp. 98-113.

Van Bavel, T. J., *Christians in the World Today* (New York, 1980).

Vanneste, J., *Le mystère de Dieu. Essai sur la structure rationelle de la doctrine mystique du Pseudo-Denys l'Aréopagite* (Paris, 1959).

Vanneste, J., 'La théologie mystique du Pseudo-Denys l'Aréopagite', *Studia Patristica*, 5 (1962), pp. 401-415.

Vanneste, J., 'La doctrine des trois voies dans la *Théologie Mystique* du Pseudo-Denys l'Aréopagite', *Studia Patristica*, 8 (1966), pp. 462-467.

Völker, W., *Kontemplation und Ekstase bei Pseudo-Dionysius Areopagita* (Wiesbaden, 1958).

NAME INDEX – MODERN

Armstrong, A. H., ix, 8, 14-15, 42, 75, 76-77, 78, 103, 114, 115, 142, 143n, 149-150, 152, 198.

Barnard, L. W., 227n, 228n.
Beatrice, P. F., 259n.
Beierwaltes, W., 147, 182-183.
Bigg, C., 220n.
Bréhier, E., 194n.

Carabine, D., 232n.
Chadwick, H., 220-221, 230n.
Cherniss, H., 39.
Courcelle, P., 236.

Daniélou, J., 84n, 236, 253-254.
Des Places, E., 96n.
De Vogel, C. J., 96n.
Dillon, J., 35, 42, 55, 73, 96n, 156n, 157.
Dodds, E. R., 10, 22, 49, 52, 100, 110, 148, 193n.
Dörrie, H., 83.
Drummond, J., 221n.
Duclow, D., 239n.

Festugière, A.-J., 52, 81, 97, 218.
Fraser, P. M., 194.

Gersh, S., 35.
Goodenough, E. R., 194-195, 223n, 227n, 228n.
Guthrie, K. S., 94, 101.

Haas, A. M., 321n.
Hadot, P., 156-157.
Hathaway, R. F., 280n.
Heiser, J., 261n, 265n.

Jaeger, W., 15.
Jufresa, M., 86, 88.
Jung, K, 4, 104.

Kleve, K., 81-82.
Koch, H., 279.
Krämer, H. J., 81.

Lilla, S. R. C., 232n.
Lloyd, A. C., 157.
Loenen, J. H., 74n.
Lossky, V., 253-254, 261n, 272n, 281, 289, 296n.
Louis, P., 71, 72, 81.

MacKenna, S., 123, 130.
McEvoy, J., 322n.
Merlan, P., 43, 44, 72n, 141.
Mortley, R., ix, 6n, 32n, 37n, 43n, 56n, 78n, 79-80, 86n, 89n, 155n, 182, 207, 231n, 234n, 235, 240n, 257n, 263n, 270n, 276.

Norden, E., 52.

Otto, R., 199.

Puech, H.-Ch., 52, 93, 96, 281.

Rist, J. M., 48, 49, 103, 126, 137, 157, 236.
Runia, D. T., 26, 196, 205, 208n.

Schelling, F. W., 44.
Stiglmayr, J., 279.

Tarán, L., 41n, 42, 43n.

SUBJECT INDEX